# THE
# DIRECTOR'S
# CUT

# THE DIRECTOR'S CUT

## Picturing Hollywood in the 21st Century

*Conversations with 21 Filmmakers*

EDITED BY

Stephan Littger

Foreword by Dan Kleinman

**continuum**

NEW YORK • LONDON

2006

The Continuum International Publishing Group Inc
80 Maiden Lane, New York, NY 10038

The Continuum International Publishing Group Ltd
The Tower Building, 11 York Road, London SE1 7NX

www.continuumbooks.com

Printed in the United States of America

Library of Congress Cataloging-in-Publication Data

*"It all comes of liking honey so much."*
*Winnie-the-Pooh*

# CONTENTS

# FOREWORD

In Columbia University's film school, where I teach, we bring in a guest filmmaker almost every week to show a film and then have a question-and-answer session with students. The book you have in your hand is like a year's worth of those sessions, minus the screenings (which an enterprising reader could supply from the local video store).

Having led a couple of hundred of these post-screening discussions, I feel that I can recognize a good interviewer, and Stephan Littger is one. He knows the secret, which is to follow the subject's lead. He listens carefully, guides the conversation with skill and preparation, and doesn't try to compete with his subject. Always, he follows the advice Tim Story gives for talking to actors: Don't say too much.

Who are these people, and what do they have in common? Each one is an active director of Hollywood studio pictures, as distinct from independent films—though most have directed those, too, at the beginning of their careers, and a few still do. The whole question of how to tell an independent film from a studio film has become hopelessly complicated, but what matters here is that these directors are successful enough to have made films with large budgets.

To give someone tens of millions of dollars to direct a movie is an enormous act of faith, because the director is the one person on a film, other than the star, whom it is nearly impossible to fire once shooting has begun. These interviews tell us what it takes to earn that faith.

Not surprisingly, the most common credential for directing a high-budget film is to have already directed a lower-budget film. The exceptions are people who have worked on several feature films in another capacity—for example, acting (Sydney Pollack), cinematography (Andrew Davis), or visual effects (Andrew Adamson)—and have demonstrated a feeling for story and an understanding of the demands of feature filmmaking.

This raises the question, how does one get to direct a lower-budget film? And one answer is clear from these interviews: write it yourself. Almost every director in this book wrote his or her first feature film, even directors who have not written thereafter. Writing the first film is probably the second most prevalent trend in these interviews—the first being a certain personal quality, which I will discuss later.

A director, no matter how talented, is nothing without a script. For a director without a track record, the easiest way to obtain a script is to write one. That's one reason why, at Columbia, we require every director to study screenwriting. Writing a screenplay gives a director something that he or she owns and controls, something to rally support for, to call in favors for, to *make happen*.

With slight variations, the story of several of the younger directors in this book goes something like this: gets a camera while in grade school or junior high, makes films with friends and neighbors, goes to film school, struggles in low-paying jobs while writing screenplays, puts together a low-budget film that gets attention, gets offers to do bigger-budget films. Often, there is a detour to study acting. Often there is a helpful mentor who responds to the young director's drive and talent. Often, the budding director spends several years watching and learning from the films of the best directors, quite apart from any school.

The first film course in any American university was offered at Columbia in 1916. The first film school was started in 1929 at the University of Southern California. But prior to the mid-1960s, film schools were few in number and quite insignificant in the industry. The 60s was the decade when the ambition of undergraduates ceased to be writing the Great American Novel and became, instead, making the Great American Film. In 1966, for the first time, a studio hired a film student (Francis Ford Coppola) to direct a feature film (*You're a Big Boy Now*). For forty years, the number of film schools, courses, and students has steadily increased, and the growth continues to this day.

Regarding film school, I agree with the observations in two of these interviews. The first is by Bryan Singer: "In the old industry, you used to be able to come to Hollywood and you'd get a job working on the lot at the studio. But now it's a different world, and to know the business—unless you're raised into a family that's in it—film school is one of the few ways to actually get saturated in filmmaking and also build those partnerships early on that will serve you later." The second is by Tim Story: "What I love about film school is that there is a community. There are so many people I met there that have helped me with my career. . . . It is great to be part of that community, if you can afford it. If you can't afford it, then take the money you might have used on school and go shoot a movie."

As the cost of high-quality video goes down, and tuition rises, there may come a time when film school won't be the easy choice. However, it's great to be free to experiment and make mistakes, to learn all areas of filmmaking, and to find what you are best at. It's much easier to do these things in a school setting, and probably always will be.

*   *   *

These pages are full of insights into how to work as a director. Everyone will have different favorites. My own list would include Sydney Pollack's brilliant explanation of "the first thing you ask as a director." Also Stephen Sommers on a writer's discipline: "You have to approach writing like it's ditch-digging." And James Mangold on working with actors. But every director here has something penetrating to say about craft, usually about the aspect of filmmaking in which he or she is most successful.

A few paragraphs earlier, I mentioned a "certain personal quality" which permeates these interviews—which, in fact, can be felt in every one of them. That quality is a combination of drive, focus, and a willingness to take risks. These are people who, once they have determined what they want to do, pursue the goal with enormous energy and are not deterred by obstacles.

Nothing illustrates this better than the story Mira Nair (my Columbia colleague) tells about how she persuaded her father to send her away to a better school than the one in her small village in India. But see also Wolfgang Peterson's story of learning theater by watching rehearsals of a play every day for months, to the point that when an actor became ill, young Wolfgang was able to step in. And consider Tim Story, when the director of photography on his first film pulled out, going into a camera store and saying, "Teach me how to shoot this movie."

When you read about miraculous strokes of luck, such as Martin Ritt asking Richard Donner to be his assistant, you may be sure that a great deal of work preceded the "miracle" and followed it. Several of these directors describe periods of struggle in which they seemed to get nowhere for as long as seven years before success came. All of them use words such as "obsession" and "tenacity" to describe the qualities a director needs.

There is some debate in these pages about whether, if you keep at it long enough, talent and tenacity will always lead to success. I side with those who say no, talent and tenacity cannot guarantee success, though they make an enormous difference. If your heart is set on directing in Hollywood, I think you will need a bit of luck, too.

But, as Branch Rickey, the legendary baseball executive used to say, "Luck is the residue of design." Or, as an old college professor of mine said, "Chance favors the prepared mind." Or, as the last word, there is Bryan Singer to Stephan Littger, in the pages of this book: "You're a young filmmaker; just keep pushing through, anything can happen."

—Dan Kleinman, Dean of Columbia Film School

# WELCOME TO
## *THE DIRECTOR'S CUT*

There is probably no art form more interested in the life of ordinary human beings than filmmaking. And there is no other art form more closely associated with glamour and stardom than filmmaking. This can seem odd but turns out to really just be two sides of the same coin: exploring the whole spectrum of human existence, filmmaking is all about people!

As we observe the characters on screen, we can empathize and project our inmost hopes and dreams into their world. We start to identify and can suddenly touch emotions that the realities of everyday life do usually not allow us to experience in such depth . . . eventually, it's the theater lights that throw us back into the familiar universe of our regular lives. This is the fun little game we all play once in a while and call "the movies"—this is its illusion; this is its magic. If the movie was bad and a waste of time, we may get a little upset but quickly forget about it. If it was good, we are entertained but also get on rather quickly with our lives. And if it was one of those handful of great movies, something about it will actually stick with us—it might be just an atmosphere or an idea we have absorbed, but it becomes *ours* and from then on, it is part of who we are wherever we go.

The people featured in this book have at one point in their lives decided that watching great movies alone would no longer be enough: they decided to live and breathe the magic and the possibilities of an entire life invested in making movies. This courageous choice to continuously throw themselves into a fictional universe of their own making has made their lives extraordinary— for us; for them, too!

There are several perspectives from which we can try to illuminate the lives and the work of filmmakers and there are many fascinating lessons to learn from them, if that is our goal. There are, in fact, hundreds of successful filmmakers around and one might be tempted to just pick a few at random and hope that their narrative genius would suffice to fill the pages of an entire book. Another approach would be to follow the example of the directors themselves and actually tell a captivating story. I believe we should be able to expect that from a book, and so that is what you will find in this one: while the directors tell us their stories by tracing the significant moments of their creative journeys, this book tells the story of those directors in Hollywood: their "Director's Cut" for us!

But that story has many acts and there is no use in pretending that it could be nicely told in a linear way that obeys the chapter structure of a book. Hollywood in the 21st century is too complex and multilayered a universe for that—and the diversity of its filmmakers has probably never been greater in its hundred-year history. As the content of diversity pretty much defies any definition, I hope that all these conversations taken together will leave you with a vivid notion of what could be its substance.

One perspective from which we could picture Hollywood involves looking at the filmmakers' various backgrounds and origins—socially and culturally; also their gender. Even though directors have no defined ladder to climb, Hollywood itself is a strongly hierarchical system whose top positions have in many respects remained the domain of middle-class white males. Yet at the same time, Hollywood could never be the same without those who have entered the system nevertheless and given concrete shape to its very structure. In this book, you will find an exciting cross section of that structural landscape, offering a situational snapshot of today's Hollywood reality that I promise will be as colorful as the movies that are being produced there. While several filmmakers have agreed for the first time to participate in a collection of this kind, many of those you find in here have only arrived on the lot over the course of the last five to ten years. They have brought along new approaches as part of an ongoing process that allows Hollywood to playfully interact with quickly changing realities while staying in touch with an audience that is literally as broad as the movie-going public around the globe.

To many, the Hollywood "Dream Factory" is the very incorporation of the American Dream. And yet, one group of directors that has always been vital to its capacity for self-innovation is foreign filmmakers. Despite frequently clichéd criticisms of Hollywood style and output, the attraction it exerts on filmmakers everywhere in the world has never diminished. Eight of the 21 directors in this book are originally from outside the United States; four from Europe. I think that ratio is rather close to what we can actually find in reality.

A second and entirely different approach to picturing Hollywood diversity is the concept of "genre," which many regard as a direct product of Hollywood's Dream *Factory* aspect—sometimes critically so. Only a book that includes makers of basically any genre—including those who deliberately set out to ignore existing conventions—can aspire to present the industry somewhat appropriately. The table of contents therefore features directors you would typically not expect to see on the same list—at some, you might even turn up your own nose occasionally. But finding out what sets these directors apart and what ambitions they actually do have in common is part of our exciting quest of grasping the larger Hollywood picture. As the directors' background experiences and self-understanding invariably inform the kinds of films they want to make, the genres they work in are organically linked to the person they are and can therefore reveal a lot about them. Established genre structures help to provide a foundation to their ambitious endeavor to find genuine forms of expression that successfully translate their sense of truth to the audiences they hope to seduce and entertain.

And as the director's personality continues to evolve with every step of the way, so do audience expectations for the way genre constructs filmic reality. Genre must never be quite what we expect it to be. Otherwise it will overcome itself by turning into the tired and mediocre shadow of its own conventions. The filmmaker has to surprise the audience by giving them a taste his own point of view that feeds the structure of the film while offering something they haven't seen before. He takes them along on a ride and trusts that they will be able to connect with the humanity of the world they are presented with. In this sense, a film is a director's offer of friendship to an entire audience. If they enjoy the film, they will accept and give the recognition that, for most filmmakers, is the greatest reward imaginable. But if the spectators feel let down and sense insincerity, cliché, or the wanton desire to manipulate, they will quickly turn down the offer and let him fall flat on his face.

Truthfulness and the ability to be in direct touch with his subjective universe suddenly becomes much more than a filmmaker's ethical commitment: it becomes an aesthetic prerequisite and the very source of his ability to create something that is real and powerful enough for taking entire audiences on that emotional journey they are hoping for . . . It is the same sincerity that also provides an immediate foundation to these conversations, turning them into charismatic and often humorous testimonies of genuine insight into the directors' hearts and minds. I believe that the artist with something to say speaks like an amateur, never like a professional. Consequently, popular directors generally don't like overanalyzing their work and rarely use big words to describe it, knowing that such interpretive zeal would do nothing to elucidate the realities of the craft—rather, it would obscure them. And as you read through these conversations, you will gradually develop a sense of the sheer human richness that Hollywood has to offer via the lived realities of its filmmakers. The range of genres they feel naturally at ease with is an intimate witness to that richness.

And there is yet a third angle of picturing Hollywood's gathered diversity about which we usually learn relatively little: the directors' professional backgrounds. This is equally the particular angle I have chosen for the chapters of *The Director's Cut*. After having mainly selected the filmmakers on the grounds of the above two aspects ("origin" and "genre"), I initially wasn't sure how I could present their journeys in the most instructive way. None of the categories seemed comprehensive or original enough to grant the sort of insight I was looking for. Soon, however, the great variety of these directors' different interests and specializations *prior to* filmmaking struck me as being a greatly inclusive and potent expression of how their personalities and talents are inextricably linked in their work. While firmly incorporating the particular background and perspectives from which they have entered filmmaking, the professional angle additionally illustrates particular inclinations and skills that continue to inform—and often inspire—the individual manner and understanding with which these directors approach their craft.

When looking at the table of directors, you will quickly find that their past usually makes a lot of sense given the films they are making now. And while the division of directors into Part I and Part II of this book has been determined by that professional history, it is simultaneously a division along largely generational lines. Mostly those born during the 60s and 70s started to aspire to a director's life in their teens or even earlier. Many went to film school straight from high school. Others of that generation didn't go either because they couldn't afford it or because they hoped to make it without, showing that even a director's film school history can teach us quite a bit about his background or personality; or both.

Most filmmakers that I have spoken to and who were born before the 60s initially had no concrete desire to eventually own a Hollywood director's chair: their early career choices were mostly taken with other priorities in mind—usually also in film or a profession related to it, whether it be inside or outside the Hollywood system. As some younger directors also feature in Part I, this generalization is not true in every single case, but the tendency is clearly there for you to trace.

Some filmmakers in this volume express their opinions about whether this development has had any consequences on the kinds of movies that studios choose to produce today. But as part of the privileged viewpoint from which you can follow these discussions, it is ultimately you, the reader, who naturally has the last word on drawing any conclusions, reinforcing my belief that the conversational approach is particularly well suited to tracing the multifaceted Hollywood universe: none of these directors has all the answers, nor would they ever pretend that they do. They are not defending any theses, nor do they have to prove anything by trying to convert us to a particular worldview. In fact, they could care less about what we think.

What they bring to the conversations is their real experience of making movies, filled with the astonishing practical wisdom that comes from actually doing it. Reacting to my questions, they simply apply their personality: a form of thinking aloud. Very often, their replies are nothing but questions in disguise, whose real scope is to open the space of discussion even further so that new and richer ideas can enter: into their heads, my head, and yours, the reader, toward whom our journey together is indirectly addressed. It is between my questions and their tentative answers that a genuinely new space can evolve, revealing the only reality we can intuitively grasp: that which we re-create in ourselves.

In that sense, these conversations have much in common with the constructive process of filmmaking itself: the story told can only spring to life via the attentive and curious mind of an outside observer. And it is this inherently open, freely floating structure of the conversational space which instead of forcing readers into passivity requires their active involvement in order for the structure to hold and meaning to emerge. In fact, the reader's task becomes much like the filmmaker's task of taking on reality and making it his own through such transformative processes as empathy, identification, and interpretation. Suddenly, the very form of dialogue becomes integral to what I am trying to achieve in this book: understanding the creative journey out of the very people into whom those directors have developed over the years. Accepting their invitation for a comprehensive exploration of their lives vicariously becomes an invitation for a comprehensive exploration of your own lives, offering a wondrous space of discovery in which the adventurous reader will find an inexhaustible wealth of wisdom that is both raw and sincere. Quite substantially I, the interviewer, am just there to reflect the directors' own perspectives and deflect them into directions that will integrate and help us understand the significant moments of their lives, their craft: their person.

And if you read this book as what it sets out to achieve, you might actually be able to find some answers that allow you to strengthen your intuition of what it means to think and *live creatively*; like a filmmaker—

So in a way, this book is a "How To" guide without ever pretending to answer the question "how to?"—as that would destroy the very truths we are trying to get at. For some reason, we are frequently led to believe that it is possible find answers by studying facts instead of the individuals and the context in which they have taken place. But the featured filmmakers' individual life events cannot sensibly be examined or compared without soon losing touch with the very continuity out of which they have grown—their "artistic essence," if there is such a thing. If we don't make an attempt to reinstate the events into their lived context, they will become empty and meaningless facts that no longer harbor the exciting potential for insight they once had.

It is not because filmmakers were trying to follow some common factual advice on "what to do" or "how to be," or "how to write a screenplay" that their paths frequently resemble each other and have eventually crossed in Hollywood. No piece of knowledge can ever turn into wisdom unless it gets taken apart and reassembled by the person that is seeking answers. Appropriate answers are something we can only attempt to construct for ourselves via a relentless personal effort of a lifetime. No film school, no teacher, no dissertation, and no book can ever achieve that for us. So we can humbly give up our childish desire for definite answers by replacing it with a genuine interest in the humanity we share with those we respect and value.

And this is what these conversations can offer but never guarantee: a comprehensive and fun resource for the kind of knowledge you are seeking—what you will make of it is of course up to you and your personal motivations for reading this book. If you are a film student or an aspiring filmmaker, you will intuitively read it in quite a different light than if you are a film critic or a person who simply enjoys watching great movies.

Because of the directors' own differences, it would have probably been unwise to go about every conversation in the same manner. While their basic architecture and general direction originates in my desire to understand these filmmakers' journeys and working styles out of their inner motivations, the concrete conversational course naturally varied according to the perspectives from which each one approaches his craft—and our conversation. The resulting flexibility was also crucial in avoiding getting lost in petty details or irrelevant memories of facts which contribute little or nothing to understanding the individuals or their journeys any better.

To avoid having facts and figures I had read up on imposing my own perspective over theirs, I simply let everyone introduce themselves: let *them* have the first words on their upbringing, their family, atmospheres, and early fascinations. This relatively free opening allowed them to start out at their own pace and gave me time to attune myself to their mindsets of the day. We, the listeners, are granted an initial glimpse of the directors' memories and can empathize with the associations they most readily identify with—also their gestures, rhythms, tones of speech, etc. As it is obviously impossible to reproduce all of those on the printed page, I have left their style of speech as raw as possible: expressions, hyphens, interruptions, and even some peculiar uses of language or punctuation can reflect the uncensored spontaneity of the spoken word and provide us, I believe, with a fuller picture of the person we are dealing with.

Starting out, I was quickly struck by how the reality of the directors' upbringing becomes completely alive in them once they enter it. Listening to their opening words, I regularly got the impression that very early in their lives, they had been given the great gift of perspective by being raised within a world of contrasting realities: a slightly alienated world that for one reason or another put them into a position of an outside observer, encouraging a self-conscious awareness of themselves, others, and the environment they were raised in. Finding themselves in a universe of relative groundlessness, they had to construct their own grounds, values, and realities that from now on were no longer somebody else's, but *their own*. Knowingly or not, their family environment thus provided a fertile soil out of which the creative self-formation of those young individuals could take place.

The unfolding stories of these directors are great examples of how, if only we trust in their humanity, children will eventually find meaningful strategies of their own to deal with the many challenges and anxieties on the way, making them take real pride in who they are and what they plan to do in their lives.

And it is evident that today, still, the directors in this book take their younger selves seriously. They don't make any attempts to inhibit or patronize their reality from back then. Instead of cutting themselves off from those bits in their past that might be unresolved or can seem immature or pathetic at times, they fluidly understand their lives as one continuous journey whose emotional continuity serves them as a vigorous source of inspiration. The ability to confidently move back and forth in personal space and time equips them with the creative means to invent alternative filmic worls that remain truthful despite the highly artificial circumstances under which they came to be. While habits might have changed, it is this same old child who instinctively understands the world as his own and can playfully move or get lost in it outside the hostile gaze of convention—a world full of curiosity and wonder that is waiting to be explored in the concrete human context of the cinematic universe they create.

Today, it is the "adult" in them that has learned to give shape and direction to that process of self-expression. It ensures that all production departments are working together, creating a coherent and transparent version of this mental picture—however blurred it might initially be. Though filmmakers know the general direction they are headed, they do not necessarily know in advance what concrete solutions are best. They therefore make sure to surround themselves with professionals they are eager to work with—both on the human and the creative level—in order for their ideas to concretize step by step.

Many directors describe early difficulties in delegating responsibilities due to their instinctual desire to be in control of their film's every aspect. But they quickly learned that only by opening up to suggestions and not pretending to know everything ahead of time will they be able to generate something that is greater than what they originally anticipated. In fact, their increasing capacities to collaborate—and to create an atmosphere conducive to new ideas, which have not purely grown out of their own egos—have been a central ingredient in their pursuit of becoming better directors. This includes a tolerance toward different, often contradictory points of view, which they can take in and balance against each other. Eventually, they can identify which solutions are best suited for the kind of story they want to tell.

The concrete process that they go through in order to achieve that delicate balance, or "controlled freedom" as Barry Levinson calls it, varies greatly from one director to another. It can teach us so much about the intricacies of the filmmaker's profession, the concrete circumstances in which they work today, and the ways they bridge that gap between their personalities and the structures that they attempt to make their own.

Whatever the approach, it is only by learning to trust and actually take pleasure in the fragile nature of their intuitions that directors can hope to capture their sense of truth on film and not let the doubts and complexities of the filmmaking process overwhelm them.

The directors discuss extensively the creative strategies they use to guide them through the labyrinth that the process can be at times. What does a story need to attract their attention? In which ways do they translate their ideas onto the screenplay? What kind of person are they on set? How do they find their shots? Why do test screenings help them find their movie? Who are their closest collaborators? In what ways has filmmaking changed them as a person? These are but a few topics that each lay open alternative layers of the filmmaking realities that every director has found a very personal approach to.

The director's capacity to get completely absorbed in the process without however losing the sense of direction is quite clearly an ability in itself and demands a personal constitution that is cut out for that kind of exertion; *father*, *puppeteer*, *manager*, and *conductor* are some of the colorations used by directors in this book to describe their role. While working at full steam and almost simultaneously on all levels of their personal abilities, they throw themselves entirely into the world of their creation, knowing that the final result can only ever be as engaging as the degree to which they invest their own being in it. And to filmmakers, few things can be more exciting than extending the field of inquiry by channeling their personal curiosity into the world of the characters they portray. They become like the eyes of a camera, which can only ever be fully present by seeing something other than itself. Everything outside the scope of the lens becomes irrelevant. Instead of turning their attention inward, it is the directors' central medium—the film set—onto which they can project the inherent possibilities and truths of the story universe that they ultimately hope to communicate to the audience.

Suddenly, any story becomes possible as long there is a unifying mind to vouch for it, allowing us access to the fantabulous universes of *The Chronicles of Narnia* or *X-Men* as readily as the tragicomic Wall Street absurdities of *American Psycho* or that of a panic-stricken World War II German submarine crew. Sure, some we feel closer to than others. But movies that are well made can miraculously take us places by presenting us with the people that inhabit them. Good directors have to therefore be able to make use of their actors as adeptly as painters make use of a canvas. And as we are introduced to the world of the filmmakers via the characters they create, they have found an enticing means of expressing their personal universe they were anxious to share with us.

By their very constitution and the strange combination of their energies and talents, most filmmakers would have probably become rather imbalanced—if not unhappy—people if they hadn't found film. In fact, none of those I have spoken with has actually ever consciously chosen to be a director—it much rather feels like a profession that has chosen them. Quite often, they can still remember the exact situation in which they realized they wanted to make films in life—many directors will talk about that revelatory moment which, to them, has lost nothing of its piercing magic.

It is little surprising that many describe their work as therapeutic. Several were diagnosed with some kind of attention or behavioral disorder when growing up. But instead of turning the potentially self-destructive powers of their "symptoms" quietly against themselves, filmmaking has offered them a platform to productively apply these externally to the world of their creation, giving them a precious point of attack to a better understanding of themselves and the human interaction they are trying to show. The symptoms from once turn out to be little more than those residues of human behavior that the status quo of their early environment simply couldn't accommodate.

It is even part of the filmmaker's job to detect and to take an active interest in any such aspect of his personality that might shed light on the motives behind human conduct in general. In fact, his ambition is to find stories that can externalize feelings and tensions that might have previously only existed in the precarious and unpronounced reality of his own body—and, if he is lucky, that of his audience. It can help to explain this peculiar impression great movies can give us at times: that somehow they were only made for us personally. If that happens, the filmmaker has lived up to his ambition as eager scientist of the human condition by having shown something in a way that nobody has before him.

But there is an inherent danger in the filmmaker's obligation of uncompromising honesty: it renders him perpetually vulnerable. Directors constantly have to be willing to run into the open daggers of public scrutiny, never having any guarantee that their last success will in any way shelter from future criticism or ridicule—it is rather the opposite: the greater the success in the past, the greater is the potential to fall violently in the future. But many directors thrive on that fear, which simultaneously has the positive effect of preventing them from becoming decadent or complacent in respect to their craft. Even though it can at times be difficult to stay close to one's sanity in a culture that elevates celebrities into superhuman spheres, experienced directors know that complacency would be the surest recipe for failure on the next project. Only by staying in immediate touch with the realities of their grounded selves will they be able to take the audience by the hand and show them a world they can relate to. We are back at truthfulness and the capable directors' ability to put their own perspective *into* perspective. By having learned to not take themselves too seriously—even to frequently laugh at themselves—filmmakers can self-ironically give expression to their own whimsical tastes by translating those into a universally intelligible cinematic language.

And if directors succeed in being genuine parents to their productions, their innumerable decisions during the process will culminate in the unique atmosphere of the story universe: let's call it a filmmaker's "style." Not only the directors themselves, but entire audiences will be able to recognize that style by the distinctive yet never fully describable "something" that literally every frame of the movie is imbued with. Long before the credits roll, people will know who made it: who *directed* it—proving that he has done his job properly by having pulled the strings during the entire creative period. As a director who is in control, he has learned to embrace and overcome obstacles on the way by turning them into challenges that he could align to his own tastes and modes of perception.

And directors had to learn to do just that in their regular lives. All of the 21 in this book have taught themselves strategies to navigate through the completely different circumstances they encountered, but which eventually allowed them to get their break. Whatever the nature of the struggles they faced, they understood how to make them their own and to use them to their own advantage. Contrary to certain preconceptions that might exist, it is never because somebody's parents were a bit wealthier or another's parents were themselves artists that a director eventually succeeds. Understanding that it is not what happens *to* us, but how we handle it, which eventually defines our potential as a person is maybe the most eloquent lesson to draw from the totality of these conversations.

If his film is the complex imprint of the filmmaker's personality, this book presents you with something similar, only by very different means. Maybe I could compare these interviews—a bit crudely, I admit—to the negative image of the motion pictures the directors make. While on film they get to voice their reality via the world of others, in these conversations, they have to say it themselves. Even though directors get to invest their entire being in their movies, they are used to express it via things that are *not them*—actors, set design, sound, etc.—letting the movie speak for itself. In this book, they for once switch roles. What constitutes their style on film now suddenly translates into their charisma as human beings.

And I believe that there is a central seductive theme in every filmmaker's life that makes it possible for him to naturally extend his charisma onto film. It is that undefined concreteness that silently hovers above every conversation and gives the director's remarks the unique coloration that makes them unmistakably his. Now we are, of course, back at "style" and its entanglement with the director's very being.

There are certain sections and phrases throughout the conversations that seem to be particularly adequate in tracing that connection. I have called the most expressive one of them "The Director's Cut." You can find them on the fact sheet that precedes every conversation, and also on "The Director's Cut: *Uncut*" page. Reading them will give you a powerful impression of what directing essentially means to these filmmakers and allows them to do every single day of their lives. I am sure that you will quickly spot your own favorites among them.

The interviews in this book have taken place over a two-year period. None of them has been published before in its full length. I started this project as a student in Oxford and finished it as a filmmaker in America. During the majority of these interviews I was going through the production stages of my own short film. I can often still trace these as they helped me give a particular thematic focus to my one or two hours with the directors—a focus that was necessary because of the amount of time that urged me to sensibly concentrate on selected aspects, rather than trying the impossible task of covering "everything" but without achieving anything So while I was, for example, working on my script, I would be deeply entrenched in the various processes involved in constructing and writing a story for film. Or while test screening, I was wondering about the director's own take and experience on editing, re-editing, and how to incorporate audience reactions in a useful way. I realized that going through all these incredibly exciting and multilayered realities—and facing these questions—while actually making a movie myself, gave me an opportunity to integrate fundamental filmmaking dimensions whose existence I would otherwise not even have known about. It allowed me to overcome the gap between the inside and the outside of a world whose thrilling complexity I wish everybody could be familiar with. I additionally made a point of centering the conversations around aspects which I felt to be particular strengths in the directors' works.

I really hope that you will be able to pick up some of the enthusiasm and the spirit in which these conversations took place—also the chemistry that made it a true pleasure and a privilege to be able to speak to these special individuals.

And as the conclusion of this book also marks the beginning of a new chapter in my own life, it is reassuring to know that the inspiring words of these Hollywood filmmakers will be available to reveal some of their precious insight anytime we choose to revisit them in the future.

I am convinced that the power of their own words will at times even surprise the directors when reading them here for the first time. Many aspects of their work that they discuss with me, they have never consciously thought about before—they didn't have to! Being an integral part of the person they are, they instinctively got it right. If they first had to consult some sophisticated trains of thought before applying ideas to their craft, they would undoubtedly have failed. All they could accomplish would merely be the uninspired copy of something other than themselves. No, directors can in the long run succeed only to the degree to which their intuition gets it right. The best ideas and intentions are absolutely worthless if the audience doesn't enjoy the movie: it's *the one and only* thing that counts at the end of the day—for us; for them, too!

Stephan Littger
April 2006, New York

# ACKNOWLEDGMENTS

This book's genesis is all about trust. There would not be a *Director's Cut* without the extraordinary amounts of information and support I have received from all those wonderful people that have contributed to making this book happen—directors' assistants, publicist, managers, and of course the directors.

When I approached the directors' assistants, not only were they receptive to my requests, but they also found time in the directors' busy schedules to discuss it with them and eventually set something up—wherever in the world that happened to be.

Now, I was not a famous journalist, nor had any of the directors seen my own film at the time. Brett Ratner says that people are at the top because they "return calls." With the directors in this book, this has certainly proven to be true. They liked the idea of this project and simply decided to trust me that it would eventually be a success. I certainly did not want to disappoint them.

So here is my infinite thanks to the directors and especially their assistants, truly helping me wherever they possibly could; also the publicists and managers on so many occasions. I also thank my editor David Barker, who endured my extensive suggestions on this book's format and trusted that I would eventually deliver on my promises.

# DIRECTOR'S CUT: UNCUT

**Alejandro González Iñárritu:** "I felt that making films was an infinite, unlimited resource of being alive that I could also share with other people."

**Andrew Adamson:** "I liked my new job a lot—it seemed to satisfy both, a sort of intellectual and a creative need."

**Andrew Davis:** "I felt that I wanted to be part of images and have a voice about how the world could be."

**Barry Levinson:** "It was captivating how much effect you can have with the cutting of images, sound, and some kind of dialogue."

**Brett Ratner:** "'Dean, my whole life I dreamed of being a director. If you don't let me in, I'm going to be living on my mom's couch for the rest of my life.'"

**Bryan Singer:** "It's the same principle I apply to everything I do . . . it's a project and I am very obsessed with that project going well and being done to the best of my abilities."

**Chris Weitz:** "Paul and I had always spent a lot of time together as kids and shared the same sense of humor. . . . So we sort of decided to try and turn that into a screenplay"

**David Fincher:** "I just thought, 'This is fantastic, what a great gig: you get to build stuff and blow it up and hang out with Catherine Ross and travel around.'"

**James Mangold:** "One of the things that movies gave me was an incredible sense of connection to the world."

**Marc Forster:** "Growing up, my foundations were pretty much in my imagination and the little world I created in my games."

**Mark Waters:** "It is that thing when you're watching something and you're just taken by surprise by an inspired moment—in either art or just in life."

**Mary Harron:** "I don't think I was really a painter or a sculptor, even though I liked those things a lot. . . . The first time I walked into a film editing room I was like, 'This is where I want to be and this is what I want to do for the rest of my life.' "

**Michel Gondry:** "I saw how I could use my desire to invent things, create imaginary universes and the craft of making things—also the connection with music—all that at once."

**Mira Nair:** "Cinema gives me the umbrella to inhabit even completely different worlds so fully that I can hope to find the truth in them."

**Peter Segal:** "That was part of the whole magic of movies for me: Touching what was real and what was imaginary and crafted when wondering on the back lot."

**Richard Donner:** "Struggling to be an actor, I saw the other side of it and it was magical."

**Stephen Frears:** "If you ask me what I think I do, I can see that I can bring things to life."

**Stephen Sommers:** "I think if you have talent, you're willing to work your ass off, and you never give up, then success is inevitable."

**Sydney Pollack:** "Being one person isn't really enough for me . . . making films is a way of vicariously becoming all these other people and seeing the world through their eyes."

**Tim Story:** "There is definitely an obsession on my part to just capture human emotion. I think there is nothing like capturing human nature on screen and watching it."

**Wolfgang Petersen:** "When reading books or going to the movies as a teenager in post-war Germany, it was just a wonderful thing to get completely lost in stories, disappearing into different worlds—"

# PART I—HOLLYWOOD CALLING

## Section One: Entering from Outside Hollywood

# Donner, Richard

**DIRECTOR'S CUT:**
"Struggling to be an actor, I saw the other side of it and it was magical."

**BORN:**
1930, New York

**BACKGROUND:**
American
Television Director

**FILMS (selection):**

The Omen—1976
Superman—1978
The Goonies—1985
Lethal Weapon—1987
Lethal Weapon 2—1989
Lethal Weapon 3—1992
Maverick—1994
Conspiracy Theory—1997
Lethal Weapon 4—1998
16 Blocks—2006
Sam and George—2007

**MAIN GENRES:**
Mystery, Thriller, Action, Adventure, Drama, Fantasy, Comedy

RICHARD DONNER: I grew up in a relatively lower to middle class family in New York. I can say I grew up wanting to do anything until I really had the opportunity to do some acting; that was really it. One thing that preceded that is—and I was very young—my grandfather had a motion picture theater in New York, and my mother had five siblings. And when the sisters would get together, they would pick the kids and put them in the back row of the movie theater where they had a protective babysitting area. And I remember myself vividly as a kid watching movies. I don't know whether I was in awe of it or what, but I can say I remember seeing movies—little things stuck in my mind.

I was an infant—really, really young. They say these things can be an incredibly important part of your memory; certainly true for me.

My father's intentions were that I work for him and take over his company eventually. It was a very small, handmade furniture company. He took over responsibilities from his father, but I had no intention whatsoever to do that. I just knew it wasn't going to happen. So I started to try the acting class then.

SL: Thinking about that time you wanted to become an actor—what fascinated you so much about it?

RD: Life in general. I was a very outgoing kid, and it was an opportunity where you just wanted to be in front of the public and have people appreciate you. It was fascinating. I don't think I ever analyzed it too much, but it was this desire that enabled you to stand out in a crowd. Was it the fulfillment as a great actor to stand on a stage? That was part of it. But one of the major parts of it was: "Well, if I am good at this, I'll have recognition." *I think if actors are honest, it's one of the major parts of their careers: enjoyment of recognition of their success and their careers.*

SL: In which ways would you say that you are still very much the same person that you were as a teenager?

RD: I don't think that's possible to say. The road process is so extreme that I would be surprised to think anybody would assume that their likes, their dislikes, their appreciations of life in any way stagnated over all those years. I mean my life has been extraordinary. It has been a phenomenal road process.

SL: But are there no fascinations or wonders that you had back then and that still motivate you today?

RD: Only my curiosity. I was always a curious person. That's about it. My life changed so radically over these years and I am aware of the enormous enrichment I got out of this process. Being in this business and being relatively successful opens up doors that you never thought possible.

SL: What motivated you to change your name from Schwartzberg to Donner early in your career?

RD: You know, that's interesting because it adds to the process what we just talked about. I was doing a show in New York and the producer came to me and said, "What name are you going to use?" And I said, "I beg your pardon?" He said, "I don't think that's a great name for you. If you are going to be an actor, I think we should change your name now." He was really *telling* me to change it. I don't know whether it was too Jewish for him or what. I guess I really didn't stand up for myself at that point in my life. I was just so thrilled to have the job. That was when I was 19 or 20, doing my first TV show. Then I fell in love with the name and stayed with it—"thunder" in German: a pretty good name, don't you think?

SL: How old were you when you started acting?

RD: That was right after high school. I was going to school at night and the only reason I was going to school was to make my father happy. My first job as an actor was in a little theater. I gradually had the opportunity to try out more for a few little playhouses and playgroups. I also then got a part-time job at a production company, where they asked me to paint sets, and where I got to work in editing as an assistant.

SL: Did you ever think that you might be doing stage acting or was it clear that it would be in film?

RD: In New York, it was stage and life television. In those days they were pretty much the same. I never ever thought I would be in an airplane and go to California. That was the farthest thing to my mind. That was a dream you didn't even dare to dream.

SL: But it was in the back of your head somehow?

RD: It was too good to dream. No one around me in New York that was on a comparable income level had those opportunities—any success that you were going to have in the area that you were born and grew up in would have been great. But the idea that you would be successful and you'd end up in California: the farthest thing to my mind.

SL: So how did that transformation from actor to director happen? In particular, is it something that came rather natural to you or did you have to make some choices that you weren't immediately sure about?

RD: I got a great opportunity for a very small part—something like two lines—on a television show with a wonderful director called Martin Ritt. Through a ridiculously insecure argument on my part—I opened my mouth when I shouldn't have—it looked like I was going to get fired. The best I remember is that I hesitated to do what I should have done as an actor, and when he came down he addressed me and asked, "Why are you not making the move when you are supposed to make the move?" and I said, "I thought maybe I shouldn't." He asked me why I didn't tell him in time and I could only admit that I had no idea. I became apologetic.

However, instead of firing me, he said, "You're so independent, you ought to be a director." I guess that just intuitively he thought that here was somebody that was maybe a little unique and with a rather large ego; I don't know.

When I replied, "Easier said than done", he suddenly asked me to be his assistant on his next show. So I went: "What?", but he was serious. I ended up working for him and, after that, half a dozen really great TV directors. But in those days, TV directors were directors out of theater. They handled the set pretty much the way they would handle a theater stage.

SL: How did you actually get your first director's appointment?

RD: For the summer, I had been laid off the show I had been working on. I met quite a talented documentary and commercial writer, director, and cameraman called George Blake. He was nominated for an Oscar when he was 20 or so for one of his documentaries. Through some friends, I learned that he was looking for an assistant to kind of drive him around and take care of him, while he was recuperating from a heart attack he had at the age of 34, but was still running a company. So I applied for the job and became his assistant.

And that was a great learning experience. As I just mentioned, in the days that I had been in life television as an actor, I had learned that the actors had to adjust to the cameras around them. I had learned they were no reverses, really, because in a reverse you could see the other camera. Therefore the actors had to be arranged relative to the blocking of the cameras, not vice versa.

When I went to work with George as his assistant on the set of the first proper film shoot I had ever been on, I saw just the opposite was happening: *The cameras were set up relative to the actors. That was magic: I couldn't figure out how they were going to show the other side of the set without showing the camera.*

And then as time progressed, I realized that there was a new love in my life: I was madly in love with film.

SL: So the magic involved in being able to freely move the actors while making those cameras disappear helped you realize your love of film?

RD: It was that the actors were more important than the camera. And here was the kid that was trying and struggling to be an actor, and now I saw the other side of it and it was magical. So I stayed with George for three or four years during the mid-50s. I really became a student of what film was and what you could do with it. It allowed me to develop a pretty good gut feeling for the whole filmmaking process.

And then after a period, George gave me the opportunity to direct my first commercial. And to tell you the truth, I was up all night, totally scared stiff—

SL: Did you feel well prepared or was it him that convinced you that you could do it?

RD: He was convinced and that convinced me; not that I could—but that I would do it. And the moment I got on that stage, I knew that this was what I was going to do; everything just came so naturally to me. I loved it. I ended up directing a lot of commercials and little industrial films that had greater length.

Then a horrible thing happened: at the age of 38, George had another heart attack and died. It blew me away. With his death came a major decision in my life: that it was time to move on. I founded my own little production company for commercials and with which we did very well.

There was this producer Martin Ransahoff who had a production company in New York named Filmways. He offered me a decent amount for my company and the opportunity to go to California and direct commercials and whatever he had for his company—to kind of run their branch over there. I said goodbye to everybody and jumped on a plane. I was thrilled. And again, it was probably the best move I could have done. It was pretty obvious.

SL: So when first in LA, you continued directing commercials?

RD: That's correct. This, by the way, reminds me of an advice I would give to young directors: just do anything you can just to be doing it. Because I was doing a commercial at Desilu Studios: the commercial involved Lucille Ball, her husband Desi Arnez, and several actors from their TV show "I Love Lucy." So I was asked to do this commercial with all of them. And while I was shooting it with this really bizarre group of people, one of the men standing there and who was a friend of one of the producers came over to me and said, "If you can work with this crazy bunch, what do you think of working with Steve McQueen." And I said, "Oh my God, of course." So he said, "I am the producer of his show, I watched the way you work, and I would like to give you the opportunity to direct one of the films."

I had known Steve a little, because I met him in New York years earlier, where we kind of studied acting together. Then later we also did a bit of motorcycling. And Ed Adamson, that was the producer's name, invited me out to the set and wanted to talk about that job. So we went out there. Ed introduced me to Steve as the director of the next show. Of course Steve recognized me and said, "Oh that's nice, it's good to have you—" and he walked away. That night my phone rang and it was Ed, "Dick, we have a little bit of a problem. Steve doesn't want you to direct, because he feels you're an actor, not a director." And I said, "Look, I appreciate what you did for me—nothing I can say: it was a wonderful opportunity. Thank you and I'd like to follow up with you in the future." And he said, "No, no, no, you don't understand! I'm the producer of the show and you are going to direct it."

So, against Steve's better judgment, I was hired as the director. And I prepared the show as well as I could. On the first day of shooting I went out to the set of this western, which by the way are one of the most difficult things in the world to shoot. So while Steve wasn't there yet, I went over to the camera crew and I started to discuss my first shot with them—they were very cooperative. Finally, Steve showed up and he with his grubby voice, he went, "What are you doing?" I said, "Well, we are setting up a shot here." He said, "I wouldn't do it that way. I'm at gunfire, I would never put my back to the bar," or whatever—and so I asked him, "What *would* you do then?" "Don't ask me, you're the director, you do it!" and he went off to his trailer. "Oh shit," I thought. The camera people said, "Look, I don't know if he will like this, but we will help you to get another setup." So we got a different setup and he came out, was very reluctant about it, but he did that shot. Then I went to do the next setup, and he again gave me the same terrible hard time.

At one point, I saw Adamson the producer driving up the location, because he had heard of some difficulties. "Are there any problems?" he asked. "Yes, Mister Adamson, I'm sorry." So he asked me to continue and see what we could accomplish before lunch. So I got another couple of setups then, but we were way behind. Steve just wasn't cooperative.

So he, Mr. Adamson, said to the crew, "Since Friday you had a rough week, let's take the rest of the day off." He drove me back to the studio and I went, "Mr. Adamson, if you are going to fire me, I understand." "No, I am not firing you. It's gonna be tough, none of the things are easy, but stick with it." And he simply gave me a lot of incentive, he was wonderful.

So I went home and the lady I was living with was over and we were really, "Oh this is just a terrible week—it's never going to work out." So by Sunday afternoon, I decided it would be best for everybody if I quit the show. I called Steve and I said, "Steve, I have to quit the show. Obviously you are not happy with me; Adamson was really good to me and I don't want to hurt anybody." Steve only went, "I don't understand! Nobody quits my show. Where are you, where do you live? Be at my house at a quarter to seven tonight." So I drove over, waited outside his apartment and at exactly quarter to seven, I rang the doorbell. A whole bunch of guys—some of them from the pictures, some I knew from motorcycling—was sitting around drinking wine and having a good time. Then at ten o'clock that night, I went to Steve and said, "We got to talk—we got to iron this out." And he just went, "No, we're gonna talk tomorrow.' So I told him I had to go home to bed—and he said, "No no no, you can't drive." As I didn't know what to do, I fell fast asleep. At six thirty in the morning, Steve woke me up and said, "Let's get up, get your shower! We got to get going!" So in his one-seat racing Jaguar, we drove to the studio over Mulholland Drive, breaking every speed limit there was, never saying a word. Once we arrived, all he said was, "Shoot the movie, pal." And that was it. He came out on the set, we did two days of work in one, made up for my lost time, and I was hired to do five or six more McQueen shows. It was an incredible experience.

SL: What caused his sudden change of attitude and did you draw any lessons from that experience?

RD: To this day, I will never know what it was. But it was definitely that he was challenging me from the beginning, and when he realized that it had gotten out of hand, he just decided to stop that process—the only thing I can come up with. I mean I used to ask him, "What was it?" and he would just go, "Are you looking for an argument, or what?" and I'd just, "No, no!" And we moved on and became extraordinarily close friends for a lot of years.

*You know I'm a firm believer that there is luck out there for everybody. But some people don't see the luck at all, and other people see it as bad luck, others at good luck.* I always kind of felt good luck is out there and I want to handle it that way. I think the power of positive, affirmative thinking is what life is all about. And that started my career.

SL: You then worked for television for about ten years before making your first big-screen movie. For you, what were the new elements to directing motion pictures compared to television?

RD: It is a really good question and I have a really personal answer to that: I was so fortunate in directing television that I never thought of pushing myself to make the next step into motion pictures. I was thrilled to be doing what I was doing. I knew I was doing it right and I was doing it well, because my career was going well. But in those days, you would do anything between nine to twelve pages of dialogue a day. Sometimes you weren't allowed the fourth wall on set, so you had to stage it totally differently. And when I drove home at night, I would think that what I had done was right—it worked for television and I loved it.

But I used to think—not that it would actually happen, but, "What *would* happen if what I had staged, shot, and worked today, was not television but a feature?" I wanted to know. Sitting around the house with my girlfriend, I would have another drink and think about it a tremendous amount of time, "What would I have done differently?" I would restage it in my mind, and it really fascinated me. To learn how the work would be affected by it—the fourth wall would become an important wall, I would have more time to rehearse the actors, more time to spend with dialogue: more time with just everything. I came to the conclusion that if I had had the opportunity, I would have done those twelve pages probably in four days. Then, all of a sudden, it all felt right as a movie.

SL: Suddenly, your work felt more like that of a director than that of a technician or craftsman applying certain formulas?

RD: Yes. You know, in the end what I was doing, was not wrong but right—but for television. But then, quite honestly, when I had the opportunity to do my first picture, I wasn't really ready for it. I did a picture called the *X-15* with Charlie Bronson and Mary Tyler Moore—I did an average job. I wasn't truly ready or I was scared. It was much bigger than what I was prepared for: And that's what put me back in television. I didn't go back reluctantly, because television had been good to me.

SL: Were you artistically disappointed by your own failure to fully live up to your own ambitions?

RD: Quite honestly, I didn't really have the proper expectations formed. I wish I had had, but I didn't. They loved it that I went back, so that I realized that TV was my niche right there; so I stayed with it and it went well.

My next picture developed from a TV series I was doing with Sammy Davis and Peter Lawford: "Wild Wild West." And we three really hit it off. They liked my work and together they were quite crazy. One day, Sammy Davis took me aside, "Would you like to do a movie with us? Just come up with an idea and we can get it made." I was thrilled with that possibility. We hired a writer called Michael Pertwee and we came up with this crazy story called *Salt and Pepper*, which we shot in London. It was my first movie of such proportions and it was a major opportunity.

I did the film, but I realized I was not having a very constructive or good time with Sammy or Peter. There was a lot of drug and alcohol use in those days and it was terribly undisciplined. I had lots of fights. There were a lot of ethnic and religious jokes I didn't feel were appropriate at the time, and they largely disagreed with me. Then there was a lot of them wanting to change the script, finishing when the day was half over, or simply not showing up at all. Anyway, I finished shooting it and Sammy had me fired before the film went into editing. In those days, I didn't have much of a leg to stand on to fight.

The editor that eventually did it—he at least knew the direction I was going with this movie. So the picture turned out not bad and became a huge success. United Artists decided to do a sequel, directed by Jerry Lewis. In fact, I felt pretty much used by them, and so I returned to television [*chuckling*]—

SL: Your safe haven—

RD: This time I went back I was angry. I was upset at the way I was treated and the lack of discipline in that world. But my career then was really successful in television. It is certainly true that there was also some attitude—an Old Guard—concerning television directors wanting to enter motion pictures. That certainly didn't make it easier; but really I have never experienced it directly: I heard about it, also read it here and there.

SL: At the time, did you feel in any way that you stagnated in a sense because you had failed a second time trying to get recognition in the motion picture world?

RD: I felt I had a second shot at it and I was badly mistreated. I was disappointed, felt it was unfair, but figured that that's the business. Listen: you let this business get you, it will kill you—I was never going to allow that.

SL: That seems very wise for the young director you were at the time—

RD: Well, I had seen too much around of the horrors that were really out there and what happened to people. *I learned that early in my life that I was never going to be emotionally affected by this business: I would live in it, I would have a good life, it really made me relevant: no way was I going to let it kill me.*

SL: So you had to wait another couple of years, to finally have you breakthrough with *The Omen*—

RD: That's right. I was happy doing television, when I got to read a script called *The Antichrist*. It had been turned down by every studio in town and Warner Brothers thought they would have to let go of the project. When I read it, it had a lot of flaws—like obvious things of a cheap horror movie that you had to get rid of—but I immediately fell in love with the story. I wanted to take it towards some kind of mysterious thriller. At Warner Brothers, they called me and announced that it had just been dropped, but know what? I had just sold it to 20th Century Fox after showing the script to a man there. In fact, it was the head of Fox who has become a great friend of mine: Alan Ladd. Alan also stood up for me when at Fox, a man called Mace Neufeld, who took executive producer credits for *The Omen*, told them to go with a different, better director he had in mind. Alan told him simply, "He brought it to me, he'll direct—or I won't do it." To this day, people like Alan are very rare in the industry.

So I did *The Omen*; never went back into television after that. But the road towards finishing it wasn't always easy. We were making the picture for almost nothing—we had a two million budget—and I was afraid to disappoint people, especially after all the trust that Alan had put into me. In fact, it was panic all the way through.

But then, after the first industry screening, it became obvious that *The Omen* would become my big break. The phone didn't stop ringing. I mean it was crazy.

SL: On both *The Omen* and your movie directly after that, *Superman*, you weren't afraid of making drastic changes to the original scripts you were presented with; in fact, it seems that only by making those changes could you make the project truly yours.

RD: *On The Omen, there were antichrists and cloven hoofs literally written into the script and we had to get rid of that. You simply can't do a thing so obvious and assume people will buy into that and like it.* Things happening in the movie had to look circumstantial. And that's also what convinced the actors Gregory Peck and Lee Remick every time they had any doubts about the story. I just told them, "Think of it as a spree of bad luck to the point were you are driven insane and could kill a child." It was that ambiguity that made it so exciting to watch, but also the most difficult thing to do. So yeah, only by doing it that way I think we could make this work.—It both, fascinated and horrified people.

On *Superman*, I just told them that we would have to start all over or it couldn't be done—at least I couldn't do it. The producers, the Salkinds, had already attached a director to the project for over a year. But it wasn't really going anywhere. As the Salkinds weren't very responsive to my suggestions, we went to Warner Brothers; we more and more became responsible to them: We told ourselves that we could do it without the Salkinds. Warner Brothers back then was very supportive so that we could go ahead and do the things we wanted to.

See, the original script they approached me with had something like 500 pages and lacked any sense of truthfulness. I mean, apart from its length there were so many things wrong with that script that I wouldn't even know where to start. It really meant starting from scratch when I got on it. Only by making it real—the characters, the story—could we manage to keep it alive.

So with *Superman*, when I had a bad relationship with the producers, I was able to make the movie without them. It bothered me, because I am a pretty harmonious person: I love good relationships, I love a good crew and I love it when all around me have a great time. And on that movie, it made it rough. But by that time I was able to handle it because I was my own person—I was in control by then.

SL: On *Superman II*, you had again a difficult experience finishing the movie—

RD: *I never made it to editing* Superman II—*they fired me before I could finish the movie and removed my credit as a director.* The producers were simply giving me such a hard time, being very counterproductive in so many ways. Maybe half of what you see of the final product is mine.

SL: Tell me clashes that developed with the producers for *Superman II*.

RD They were I think unprepared to make such a large movie. I think in hindsight they regretted the relationship. I saw them afterwards and kind of went up to them for a drink. But I always have that thing in the back of my mind that I could have done more with that picture if only they had allowed me. And it's too bad.

But those were the circumstances and it goes right back to what I was saying earlier: you got to learn to live with what you have and make it work. That's exactly what I had to do on this picture.

SL: Talking about your creative aspect of your work, what elements are you concretely looking for in a good script?

RD: You know, it's a much simpler question for me than what one would think. I am looking for entertainment. I am looking for something that I read and I can't put it down because I see it as I read it. And when that happens, then I want to make that movie in self-defense, because I don't want anybody to make that movie but myself: I have seen it already and I know how it should be done. I simply love to be entertained in a film. If you can incorporate messages under the guise of entertainment, I love that also.

SL: What's entertainment in a movie?

RD: Spellbound the audience: you have brought them into your world and you have created an environment that is totally different from what they expected. Then you take them down a whole new road. I remember when I did *The Omen*, I used to love to go to the theater, sit in the front row, and knowing when something really frightening was about to happen, I loved to turn around and watch the audience. It was like taking them down a road they have never been on. That's entertainment, you know?

I mean, we are illusionists and the idea of how do you create illusive illusions of laughter, or fear, or humor—that's the game, and I just love to do that.

SL: How would you describe the style you have as a person when you are on set?

RD: I have no style. I am a very open and happy person on set. I love with a passion what I am doing. The set is the light bulb time in my life. I love to be on that set. I like everybody on that set to feel that they are part of it. I want their cooperation and their input. I want to enjoy coming to work; to feel that we are a homogenous and we all care about what we're doing. And if they have a thought, I want to hear it. And I will listen to everybody on the crew, and if I don't use something, I thank them and usually tell them why. But at the same time, if I do use it, I tell everybody, "You know what? George just came up with this great idea, it works very well for the picture and we're going to do it, guys, so give George a hand!" It's just a nice feeling for everybody.

At the same time, I like a tremendous amount of discipline on set. I like that we enjoy each other, we're all thrilled to be there—if we're not, we are going to figure out why. In fact, I cast my crew sometimes, like one would an actor. *If you have one bad apple—one unhappy person—even though he may be the right person for his job, maybe I will go for somebody that is not quite as good as he is, but who is going to make that journey—that marriage of all of us—a happy one for everybody. Very important! If that's a style, that's my style.*

SL: How do you deal with situations where you sense conflict arising between you and your cast or crew?

RD: For the absolutely most part of my career, I had wonderful experiences with my cast and crew. I have had several jobs in life and I can empathize with people around me—and with the actors. I have been an actor myself and I know how it is to put yourself out there: you are in an extremely vulnerable position. So I try to treat my actors in the nicest and most gentle manner so they feel comfortable to experiment.

Everyone in the cast will bring their very own, subjective points of view and ideas to the set. As a director, it is my job to combine those perspectives and give a clear sense of direction to it all. If as a director you don't know where you are going, your picture will lack that common thread and will have as many subjective points of views as your movie has characters. You have to find ways of making the actor perform what you want him to do. Hopefully he will understand. If he can't bend, or doesn't want to do it your way, then things become more tricky. It can start to contaminate the whole filmmaking process. You can begin an argument and get nowhere, or you can be clever about it and find ways to somehow put your words into their mouths—then letting them say it back at you so they think it's really them who wanted it. Really, it's about learning to communicate properly with your actors that will make it work out in the end.

I can give you an example of when Gene [Hackman] got on *Superman* for the role of Lex Luther. I met him at his publicist's office right when I got hired to do the job. He was nice, but I wasn't sure of how eager he was to do my film. So I didn't want to say too much to upset him. I said, "You know Gene, everybody knows that Lex Luther is bald and it would be awkward to have you wear a skullcap the whole time. Would you consider shaving your head?" He just replied, "No skullcaps for me, and I won't shave my head." Then he also had that mustache, and I went. "But the mustache you will get rid off?" "The mustache stays!" he said. I was like: "Oh shit, what now?"

I was not only faced with a Lex Luther that wasn't bald, but also one that had facial hair. So I went home and thought of a way to make his hair look very different each time, so that we could make it look like a wig. But for the mustache I didn't know.

So on the first day of shooting—I hadn't seen Gene yet—I called down the make-up guy and asked him, "Does Hackman still have his mustache?" "Oh yes!" he said. So I told him, "Make me the best mustache you have ever done. I want it to look absolutely real."

So with my nice fake new mustache, I went in a little later to meet Gene in his make-up room for the first time. They were just doing different styles for his hair to see what it would look like. So I said, "So that's all worked out—there is only this one scene at the end where you will have to wear a skullcap." He was really nice to me and also fine with that one shot at the end. Then I said to him, "But you know, that mustache, it's really got to go." "No, no, the mustache is not going."

Now it was time to play my game, "Know what? I'll take mine off if you get rid of yours." He went like, "Oh, yeah?" and I said, "Yeah, really." "OK, alright then." I told the head of make-up, "Stuart, take Mr. Hackman's mustache off." Stuart started to shake and I told him, "Take it off now!" So he shaved it all off, then Gene looked at me and said, "Now you, pal!" I looked at him and started to peel off the edge of my mustache. I saw how his entire body was suddenly pounding. I just thought, "Shit, he's going to beat the shit out of me." But instead, he looked, then smiled at me and started to laugh: "You got me, pal. I owe you one." And that's how we hit it off. We became great friends on and off the set.

So that's an example of how as a director, I could have either started an argument with him—and we would have hated each other—or set the fundament for a wonderful collaborative, constructive experience together.

SL: In your experience, what has significantly changed over the last 40 years you've been making films in Hollywood—both creatively and technically?

RD: Well . . . you're into dangerous territories here [*laughing*]. Let me think . . .

You know, when I came into this business, there were obviously a group of people who sat around and said: "Boy, is this business changing!" And you'd hear all these upstarts coming in, with new styles and changing the ways things were done. And it's the same thing today. *There is a wonderful new, exciting group of filmmakers coming to life, and I look at them with great respect and admiration.*

So I have to say that I don't think the business has changed at all. I think, it's gone through its normal gradual changes, just as anything else has. Sure, it's now run more by corporate structures and by people that are more concerned with the money than the projects. Maybe there is a little too much—not "maybe": there is too much analyzing and researching, rather than going by your balls, and seeing in advance, and going by your instincts. That's what you're being paid to do. But as I say, that's what the business is. That's what's happening to us.

SL: Have these changes around you had any effect on you personally and the way you go about directing a movie?

RD: It has evolved. It's a constant process of evolution. And you got to go with it or get out of it—and I tried to go with it. At the same time going with, I know it's still me: I make movies my way, and if I can't do that anymore and I will come to a point where I can't make people happy anymore, then it's time for me to move on. But right now, it's been pretty damn good to me and I have very few complaints.

SL: You mentioned young directors and the respect you have for their ways—is there anything in particular that springs to your mind?

RD: What it is now: I look at so much of the films made today, and I see much more what feels like music videos on the screen, rather than motion pictures—but it's the style: the audiences love it, and there are moments in which I love good music videos myself. But when they are incorporated in motion picture visuals, I don't enjoy it.

SL: Any examples?

RD: I would hate to say it because that's putting down other people's works—just different styles of filmmaking. I love a sense of visuals, and if I can't see it or have no chance to absorb it, I am bothered by it. And a lot of films are so stylized now—the cutting and so on—that it overpowers the picture.

I am also not a great lover of much modern, abstract art. But I know I love art when I see a story. I have to see the story in something. I love the visuals I find in a lot of the older films; and I love the visuals in my films. I sit back home to enjoy them. And if that's taken away and somebody says I can't do it like that anymore, then I have to move on.

SL: Back in the 60s, people often said that once you had job inside the studio's gates, the system carried you up the hierarchy and took care of you. Today, this has changed. In your perception, how can a young filmmaker attract attention and gain the respect of the industry?

RD: Look, if somebody has a great story, I believe that that story is going to get made. I really believe that! How is it going to get made? Perseverance, pride, direction, using every will and whim of the individual to get in the door to get somebody to read it. I daresay, I don't know of any great film that has lain around for that many years and never got made. I think they get made.

If you want to be a filmmaker, be a filmmaker. Don't talk about it, but go out there and just do it: that's what it's all about. The wise sage has spoken . . .

SL: How much should a director be willing to compromise in order to get his/her material made?

RD: I think we're a life of compromises. I mean, there is nothing wrong with compromises. Sometimes we have to compromise to come to the right conclusion. Compromising isn't losing, but a value; just another step to open a door and make something happen—as long as you have the intelligence to know you are compromising. Then suddenly you are really kind of in control of the compromises. Only when you compromise at such desperation that you give up your values, that to me is horrible—

SL: But a young filmmaker doesn't always have the choice—

RD: When you are a director you make a lot of compromises and it is your job that you got to know when. Sometimes you compromise because it is a top moment with an actor, and to keep that actor going—and with it your film— you got to make a compromise. You know in your heart that you did it for the good of the film. You are going to get something out of that compromise that is not going to hurt you or your film. It's just a bad moment that you are trying to get around of. We live our comprises and we simply have to be aware of them.

SL: When you are at the point of embarking on a new project, which inner processes are you going through that make you decide in favor of one project over another?

RD: When you start on a new project, you're starting a new moment in your life—it's going to be a least a year. It's got to be able to become a great passion: you know it's the whole ride. It's a *year* of your life at a minimum. And what is that year? Is it going to be a year that you look back on and love? And we all make mistakes. I won't go through the pictures I shouldn't have done, because there were friends where I compromised in a way I shouldn't have. But it happens. I don't think it's the end of the world. It's part of the job and you can't be destroyed by it.

SL: But what is some center of enthusiasm that drives you every time you embark on a new project—something that connects you, your work, and that which you hope to get out of the entire experience?

RD: I am trying to think: there is definitely something that is re-occurring every time I start something new but I don't know what the hell it is. . . . *You know, every time I start a project, life becomes something like this wonderful new woman in my life; I am going off on another adventure—it's something wonderful and it I'm going to be able to go live that fantasy of what that movie is.* You know you are really living fantasies when you make motion pictures—you're in another world. Although, I know some people who live in those worlds and don't get out of them when they are not filming . . . that's not me. But I love that whimsical, crazy moment accentuating my life where we're off on another bold adventure, "Where the hell is it gonna take me?" I have *no* idea whatsoever, but I know I am so looking forward to it!

SL: Would you be able to put into words how making films has transformed and shaped you over the years—and possibly how that can be seen reflected in your works?

RD: You know what? It's so simple as that; I am aware of that, and it has been brought to my attention by a lot by my friends and critics I am passionate about the experience of a motion picture: coming out of a theater and feeling good. So, I firmly believe that the terrible situation our world is in—our country especially—that there is so much bad news and depression, that if you want to be depressed, you can do it for free by watching the news or picking up a paper and read it. For me, if you are going to go to a movie, I want them to feel good, I want them to feel as if they escaped for a little while from whatever it is they have been tied to in their personal lives; that for 90 minutes or two hours they really come out feeling entertained. A friend of mine, Jack Haley, made a movie called *That's Entertainment*: I love this. That's what we're talking about.

SL: Is there any kind or type of project you haven't done or dared yet for whatever reason and that would challenge you to do in the future?

RD: Well, *I would have loved to do the new* Superman, *but somehow I guess the people at Warner Brothers didn't think highly enough of me as a filmmaker.* I think I would have found a way to keep the tradition pure.

But there is something else I would like to do: A western I have been wanting to do for as long as I can remember. However, I always had a hard time finding a writer who could get a handle on that piece. Just recently, I got a wonderful writer called Brian Helgeland. He got the academy award for *LA Confidential*. So he has written my script and I hope to be able to do it right after *16 Blocks*.

You know, doing westerns for television: I loved them. But in my mind, there has always been that unique perspective of what a western could be—it will be quite different. But it's character-driven. I'm a great lover of character films. For me, if you don't have a strong character, you don't have a film. If you don't care about the people you see, you might as well not see the movie.

SL: Let's do a fun question at the end: if you were to compare your mind and the way it works to any object or machine in the material world, what would that be?

RD: Do you know what a Model T car is?

SL: No—

RD: It was a car, built in the 30s by Henry Ford. It made automobiles available to the entire world. They were made for the public, making it accessible to them in price, value, and appreciation. It changed the world because it made relocations possible and made people realize that there was a world out there that they could be a lot happier about than they already knew possible. So if anything—I have never thought about this before—I think I'd compare myself, not to Henry Ford, but to the Model T car.

SL: What did it look like?

RD: It was a beautiful piece of artwork!

# Frears, Stephen

**DIRECTOR'S CUT:**
"If you ask me what I think I do, I can say that I bring things to life."

**BORN:**
1941, Leicester, UK

**BACKGROUND:**
British Television Director

**FILMS (selection):**
My Beautiful Launderette—1985
Dangerous Liaisons—1988
The Grifters—1989
High Fidelity—2000
Dirty Pretty Things—2002
Mrs. Henderson Presents—2005

**MAIN GENRES:**
Comedy, Drama, Romance, Thriller

STEPHEN FREARS: I grew up in Leicester, a town full of small business people. My father was the eccentric member of my family. He had worked in the family firm as a chartered accountant, which must have driven him insane—but it can't have been very long because then war broke out. So my father was away, my brothers were sent away, and I grew up really with my mother. When my father came back from the war, he went off to London to study medicine.

We were brought up in a large house, but where there was no heating. In England in winter it was very difficult, so most of the rooms remained closed. So I grew up sitting in the little kitchen with my mother, really. For middle class English people, life was very difficult. And then slowly after the war, things got better. In one sense, I have a really conventional middle class background, but it was much more complicated than that . . .

SL: Did you feel subject to any expectations by your parents?

SF: No. Well, *I think my mother was very ambitious for us. My memory of my childhood is of not fulfilling my mother's expectations. The expectation was that I think we would end up in prison rather than becoming successful middle class people, which we all became.* I always assumed that I was meant to be a lawyer or a something like that: something straightforward and respectable.

When I was in my twenties, I discovered that in fact my mother was Jewish. But my memory of my childhood was going to the Church of England every Sunday. So my mother was living with a sort of secret that was kept from me. And I had quite a complicated relationship with her. When I was eight, I was sent away to boarding school.

SL: Did you have the chance to see any films at boarding school?

SF: I saw a lot of films at my boarding school. There wasn't anything else— there was no other entertainment. They used to show a film every Saturday, and then they'd show it again on Sunday as a way of keeping order, really. It was just as a way of entertaining the children. So I saw a film and then I saw it again the following day. So I know a lot of films of that period very, very well—quite inappropriately well. Occasionally, I see something on television nowadays and realize that it was one of the films I saw. And certain films I remember very vividly. *A Night in the Opera*, and the Marx Brothers and David Lean's films.

As part of the class system, first we went to this thing called a preparatory school and that was preparing you for the public school. That's where the ruling classes went or where the middle class children went. Then I went to Cambridge.

SL: When graduating from school with Cambridge as your next destination, what did you hope to achieve in your life?

SF: I was probably very confused . . . what happened in my teens in the late 50s, I spent a year at home before I went to Cambridge. I had just moved to a wonderful town called Nottingham and I had gotten to know a group of actors. It was also a great time of the beginning of great changes in British society. 1959 was a wonderful year for me. I would go to the local theater a lot and started to want to work with the theater.

And then I went to Cambridge later that year. In Cambridge, the theater was very vigorous. From the very beginning, I would go and see plays with people performing I had known all my life. *I think theater was seen as a tremendous opportunity for very, very quick advancement and to a more interesting life.*

SL: Being at Cambridge, you had already reached the pinnacle of academia— but that wasn't what you wanted?

SF: By saying pinnacle you are being very conventional. I've gone where "people like me" went. I had sort of "fulfilled my destiny" of a bright, young middle class boy. I read law at Cambridge. I don't know why I read law: it was very, very boring. So my interest in the theater grew—in a very complicated way. When I got my degree, I quickly abandoned the law.

SL: In order to work with theater?

SF: That's what I thought I was interested in. Of course it was the time of, you know some of the European films: so it was a very good cinema and important at the time. I spent a lot of time to see films and talk about films but it never really crossed my mind that a) I could make films, and b) that anyone could make films—that it was something "you did": a job. It simply was outside my experience.

SL: So film wasn't on your radar when you left university?

FR: No, no, no, not at all. You know, there were people that were interested in film; sort of intellectuals: people who subsequently become critics. So there was a lot of interest in films, but in a particular area—not very much interest in practical filmmaking.

And I wasn't brought up to be an artist. I was brought up in a more bourgeois way. The notion of art, or being an artist, wasn't something you would consider in a serious way, except for the theater: theater was the only outlet that I had any experience of.

SL: How did you gain access?

SF: I met an actor I got on with very well and he knew the man who was about to run the Royal Court. And he recommended me: Patronage and privilege— you know the usual way. It wasn't very difficult. I'd just stumble my way there and it didn't take very long. When I got to the court, two things happened:

First, working with very brilliant, the most brilliant young people in Britain at the time who were working at the court, *I found that I was absolutely emotionally out of my depth—that I was in many ways very, very immature.*

And then I met Karel [Reisz] through Lindsay [Anderson, also a director]—I was like an apprentice to her. And Karel was a much more tender, more mature, and more sort of civilized young man. He was more that family man with rounded values because of the story of his own life. He said: "Come to work on my film," and I went to work with him as his assistant and I have no idea why [laughs]—although he said to my ex-wife that I was a very good assistant. So I ended up having a sort of goal and apprenticeship; apprentice to two or three brilliant men.

SL: Did you feel comfortable with the role of an assistant to a creative person?

SF: It's difficult. There is a structure in the industry—it's an administrative job, but I wasn't bothered by it. I was really an apprentice and Karel took me into his family as part of the apprenticeship. And that was my good fortune. So it wasn't creative but, of course, you are allowed to be within two inches of the person who was. I was like the little boy allowed to ask questions and he'd explain it for me.

SL: He became a father figure for you?

SF: Yes he became a father figure. He was a wonderful man. After being with Karel for several films, I went to work with Albert Finney who directed a film . . . well, Albert had to be taught how to direct a film in a sense and, of course, I was at the lessons end [laughs]. But really, Albert somehow allowed me to be his eyes and I was full of ideas. And then after that I started to direct.

SL: Did you have a smooth start?

SF: Yes. Well, you know, it's very difficult and it didn't seem very smooth at the time. Friends of mine, Michael Apted and Mike Newell, when they came down to Cambridge, the TV companies used to come looking for bright young people. I would get on their shortlist and then I got rejected and they got accepted. There was a structure then and they were supposed to come out as directors. I would just go from day to day. It was quite frightening.

But by the time I started directing, I was familiar with the world where films were made and I decided to make a short film. *I found a very good story and was able to raise money through a combination of good fortune and influence and knowing people and privilege.* When you look back you think: well I was very, very privileged. It is hard to deny. You know, I was allowed to go places where other people had no access to.

And in a way it all goes back to my family. In school, I remember in '49 or '50, boys were asked by the teacher what the parents were going to vote. And everyone said their families were going to vote conservative, except my for my brother and I who said our family were going to vote Labour—cause we were the children of what with a better word you'd call "intellectuals." From then on, we were regarded as slum children—as very, very deprived people and ridiculous and pathetic and smeared at by the other children. So on the one hand, there was the other children thinking that we were poor and disgusting and shouldn't really be at their school and on the other hand I could see that I was extremely privileged. So somewhere in there, there was confusion.

SL: So you felt that you had access to a privileged world, but as an outsider or observer, rather than as a member of it?

SF: And also being Jewish and not being told. It's very peculiar and complicated this notion of the outsider. While being privileged, emotionally I was an outsider.

Maybe class gave me confidence. And then, if you work with the court, you work with very good writers. Simply to have gotten that far, they must have had good judgment. So almost without thinking about it, you had access to a certain level of taste—the court was a writers' theater.

So I found a short story that was layered and complex and metaphoric and very well written. It was called "The Day" and I made a film called *The Burning* about South Africa. I was 26 then. It must have had qualities of intelligence and sensibility—you know, whatever it is that stirs your imagination.

SL: How concerned were you about people's reactions to your film at the time?

SF: I don't think I saw beyond that. At that time, all I was concerned about was earning a living because where I was working wasn't structured. You know, when these people went into the television companies, they were paid and there was this sort of industrial life ahead of them. But I was in fact like a sort of student, really. Although I attached myself to people, which I can see now was what I was doing, I was very, very anxious. I lacked a sense of structure and actually I am happier the way I have been freelance all my life—quite large parts of it I have spent within institutions against which I have been rebelling.

SL: So how was your film received?

SF: Rather well. I started getting employed mainly in television. There was a man who ran children's TV in one of the companies. He was sort of crazy about films and he started employing a number of very good directors—people who have gone on to be successful directors. I started to work on a weekly basis—you know, like a proper job.

I did that for about one year. The following year I met a man called Neville Smith. We were both out of work. I said: "Oh, we should write a film."

It turned out that without my knowing, he was a much more complicated, tortured fellow—he was a sort of genius and a brilliant writer. So we started to write what turned out to be *Gumshoe*: My first film and a wonderful piece of writing. It was really quite inappropriately dazzling for what I was asking to do: *I simply stumbled on a very, very good writer—maybe that's being unkind to myself, but it wasn't calculated; I didn't know what I was doing.*

SL: So you had an instinct for talent and good writing?

SF: That's really what kept me going all these years [laughs]. Neville was the working class brat—his mother was a cleaner: Catholic, two years older than me, and he started writing, understanding absolutely what I wanted. It was as if he was writing the inside of my head. It was so easy for me to understand and enjoy and delight in what he was writing. And in a way what he was writing was a very modern film. He'd write with a pen, he'd bring the pages out like a child, and I would type them out. I was just amazed; as if something that I had never articulated before, something I had never thought about was suddenly there on paper. When I read it, I thought that it was absolutely my dreams. . . . He was really writing a sort of pastiche; a portrait of himself.

SL: Over the years, you have often switched between directing for TV and for cinema; how does the medium change the ways you work?

SF: I don't have too much of an opinion about the different platforms I use for my films. You know, for me, making films is like therapy, really. I know that in TV, there will be less pressure—fewer people pointing guns at me.

And I do operate from fear, really. So when I am asked to make a film, I make a sort of internal calculation: In a sort of silent way, I think: "Would anybody want to see this?" or I simply go: "Can I imagine myself to going to the cinema and see it." So when I made *Dirty Pretty Things*, I actually could imagine. When I made a film about the English Prime Minister, I simply couldn't imagine people walking to the cinema and paying their money.

When I was asked to make *Liaisons Dangereuses*, I thought it was absolutely wonderful: "That is how I wish to spend the rest of my life: Seeing films like this." And that was the film I made. So the whole time you are guarding yourself against terrible things happening; against failure and humiliation.

Because I did so much work in TV, I know that one of the ways to protect yourself is to make TV; at the end of the day, they have to fill their screen, so somebody has to film it. So in an elementary way, with a movie it is a different ambition. How do I get the money to make the film? How do I get everyone to see it?

SL: Do you have an opinion for which medium you have done your best work?

SF: When you ask the film critic David Thomson, he'd say for television in the 70s. But I feel there is no need for me to think about that. I prefer not making any judgments about it. I think TV has turned out to suit me very, very well.

Over the last fifteen years, I have really been learning about the audience, and the need to make things accessible; the need to open up, to let your curiosity and your experience guide you and let go to a point where you don't want to control it all in advance. It's such an overwhelming, such a frightening experience. You can't deal with that at the moment you are shooting. So most of the time when I'm teaching, I'm trying to calm people's fears. I know I have been very, very frightened. I realized quite late that I was so frightened.

SL: Are you aware of telling stories differently depending on whether you make them in America or in Europe?

SF: Yes, because you spend more money over there—it's as simple as that—Money defines many things about how to tell a story. I tend to read a script and then I think: "Look, I can make the script in Europe or in the States."

Frequently, I have made films "over there" [USA] because it was safer. *At any point, what you are trying to do is to protect your films in a hostile world, because the world is unbelievably hostile and unnerving. And a lot of films need all the protection they can get.*

When you make American studio films, you have this huge machine behind you and you start from a different position. It is a very, very powerful economic machine and if you can get it behind you, you never stop, really.

My recent film about the Prime Minister is about domestic British politics and there is no reason why anybody else in the world should be interested in it. So I won't make it over there, I'll make it here—a little bit finer maybe.

*Snapper* I made for British TV, because I didn't want to put it out for competition. Also, people wouldn't get angry with me for wasting their money in the cinema. That's why I made it for TV: to protect it. And in a sense, I have minimized the chances for failure. The fact that it ended up in cinema is a nice end to the story. *Snapper* was about modest people and as a result, we made it for very little money and very quickly.

*My Beautiful Launderette* was the same: we looked rather stupid afterwards because we had been so cautious. But it meant that the film could be made without any pressure. I didn't have to cast anybody famous and we didn't have to make any concessions to anybody. The way we did it just seemed to be the right way to make it. I don't mean that morally—it's just that I don't really know any other way.

If a friend said to me: "We'll give you the money but you gotta cast famous people," I simply wouldn't know how to make that film.

SL: Does a big studio production alter your influence on cast or various creative processes in significant ways from smaller productions?

SF: A critic once said: "Frears doesn't like working with stars." No, that's complete nonsense! I am not saying that I am anti the American system. I'm in love with my actors and I love stars. It's just that it seems to me you have to get the circumstances right for each film. I cast instinctively. You know, you start playing the game they tell you to—you try to find what game they are in. When I made *Grifters* after *Liaisons*, it was clear that this film was going to be made—and they clearly approved of me.

But it was as if Hollywood was decided which actors I could have. I saw an early cut of a film called *Moonstruck* and I thought: 'Oh, would like to cast Cher', but then *Moonstruck* became a huge hit so I knew I wouldn't get her. And it was as if they were deciding "We'll give you this person, and this person, you can't have that person but you can have this person, then I know this person is on *this* list, you can have one of these . . ." and since I ended up with very good actors I have no complaints, but it was as though it wasn't entirely my decision.

I remember that I was going to make it with one cast and he dropped out. The financers said: "Look we want *your* film"—it was a wonderful thing to say.

So I was always casting, but in concertation with other people. But nevertheless, I had the strong sense that it wasn't my decision; that I was told by the town. So it wasn't the producer, it was really the agents, and the industry . . . a rather complicated process, not maliciously, though. A very interesting process.

SL: Could you put into words what a story needs to fully grab your attention and makes you want to shoot it?

SF: It is rather abstract, rather inexpressible. It's like falling in love—it's much more helpless, much more impotent than that. Often you read something and it's wonderful and then it stops halfway through and I say to myself: "I wonder if this will ever be finished." Somebody who writes a good first act or a good first two acts and you think: "I wonder whether he can get the third act right"—and always I am trying to delay the decision. Earlier this year, I was thinking that maybe I'll never find something I'll like again. And then of course a day later, two wonderful scripts, absolutely great.

I'm not sure about personal criteria that I could be objective about. Afterwards I think "well, it was funny, it was romantic, it had a good story, had this and had that . . . ," and then you fall in love. I was also making films and afterwards people say something to me or I go: "Oh *that*'s what I was thinking about," and you discover. You think about yourself, things about life and other people . . .

It's very childlike, you know? I can remember reading the *Snapper*: I couldn't wait to see what was on the next page. It was so funny and so touching, the story was so magnificent: you just wanted to know what would happen next. It is simple and really complicated.

It always seemed to me that my great contribution to *My Beautiful Launderette* was that I recognized it and said we should make it *now*! And that is what it needed: that someone to say something as simple as that. And then, of course, afterwards you think: why has no one made this film before—it's so obvious.

SL: You said earlier that making films is like therapy to you. Can you see ways in which making films has changed and shaped you over the years?

SF: I couldn't tell you how it has changed me because it has been my life—I can't be objective about it. *I suppose if you'd got me up against the wall [chuckles]—I hate to say this, but I suppose I have become more of an artist than I ever imagined.* I wasn't brought up to be any kind of artist. That really surprised me.

SL: Why don't you like the idea of having become an artist?

SF: Because the way it is so rather self-important. Matisse was an artist; and also because you make films in an industrial situation. Whatever you are working on, you are still in a sort of industrial environment.

So it's very hard to bring myself to use the word, while in fact it exactly describes me. I don't really understand why you are interviewing me, because I don't set myself out as one of those people. So, I feel like a man fighting in retreat. But I can see that I have led a much more artistic life than I would have expected and that I have been allowed to behave in a way that nobody . . . that my mother used to try to stop me from [*chuckles*].

SL: You also reject the cliché of an artist?

SF: Well it is a cliché and it isn't. Look at all the successful directors in Britain: Ken Loach is the son of a doctor, I think we are all the sons of doctor, we are all middle class. Mike Newell went to Manchester, Ken went to Oxford, I went to Cambridge. Everybody! Sam Mendes and Stephen Daldry were intelligent enough to more or less make the transition into film. So they came in their own way from positions of high privilege.

We are all really the products of a combination of very traditional elements: we're all children of the welfare state, we're all . . . it's just a particular way of thinking. It's very, very narrow and you see it in the product: a sort of English eccentricity and the class system. Occasionally, people like Lynn Ramsey or Nick Rode, they are sort of freaks, they come from somewhere else.

And film schools don't produce people like us. The most brilliant student I have ever had is the daughter of a multi-millionaire. It explains much about England and how class-ridden it is. And the most successful directors are middle class.

SL: So resonating with a broad audience is closely linked to being middle class?

SF: Other classes wouldn't be accepted. I don't know where Danny [Boyle] comes from and maybe he has absorbed middle class values. He came out of television, but most came out of the theater. When we talk about film schools in England, I know perfectly well where directors come from.

SL: Do you see any similar phenomenon in the States?

SF: I don't know—I do see it in Tarantino, though. Tarantino is a good middle class boy—different generation but with absolutely the same background. In the end, he is more interested in Godard than anything else, really.

SL: Does that mean that you would recommend a young person to spend several years exploring the real world, rather than going to film school? In how far can filmmaking be taught, anyway?

SF: *You know, filmmaking can't be taught, it can only be learned.* You can talk to people who say: "Well this is what I would do," and you discuss values and emphases like that. What film schools offer is an opportunity to make films. And if you take advantage of that opportunity, you learn slowly how to make them. Then it's up to you. When I went to Cambridge, the theater there gave you the opportunity—whether you took it or not was up to you. People were very interested in putting on plays and they needed directors. So in however complicated and outsider-ly a way, I took advantage of what I was offered.

And at film school it's like that. Somebody saying: "Look in the next year you can make, say, four films."

SL: What would you recommend a young director with a script he wants to do?

SF: Well the illusions are so powerful that surround the whole thing. A young person now will want to go to Hollywood. I didn't. So I would just say: concentrate on making a good film. It's much easier to make a first one nowadays but much harder to make a second [laughs].

Films you can make very cheaply nowadays. I think making a good film is all that matters. If you make a good film people will come to you. Whether you get noticed or not—that's sort of down to God. In my experience, I remember when I was thinking about casting Glenn Close, I said to the producer: "What happens if I cast her?" He said: "Well, you'll get a very, very good opening weekend." "Then what happens?" "Then it's up to whether the film is good or not." Well, the film opened in America in three cinemas, so it would never have a very good opening weekend. On the other hand, I think we made a good film.

You know, the film did well because it was Glenn's work as an actress that was really good. What I mean is that we implicitly rejected those values and we simply concentrated on Glenn being good in the film. So my advice to somebody would be: simply concentrate on the film and you'll be all right. People can tell when things are good.

SL: What attributes make, in your experience, a good director?

SF: If you think like that I suspect there is a problem. I just read a script and now I want to make it. It's very, very simple, it's not complicated at all. I may say: "This doesn't work towards the end," or: "It runs out of steam"—that this sort of impulse, the inspiration lessens . . . it's funny, because I never remotely analyze that.

If you ask me what I think I do, I can see that I can bring things to life. If you asked me what I worry about at night, it would be that, that the ability to bring things to life has gone. That today the work will be dead—that's what I lie awake panicking about. They are my nightmares, that you can't bring it to life.

Like some screenplays, some films have life in them and some don't. If you can't bring things to life, I don't know what you do. But of course in bringing things to life, they have their own lives, though not your life [chuckles]. So you have to know how to deal with others. I think that's what I think. And when things come to life, you are probably all right. That is what I think matters. But that, in turn, involves a whole series of judgments which you hope you should prepare yourself for.

*I don't know where that quality comes from. I don't know why I can do that. Quite often I believe in God.*

Of course, I can also see a certain ambition and things like that. And I can see fear, which plays an enormous part in it. I know I am not an idiot, so I understand about certain people's desire to create a sort of alternative life in their heads. I don't like to think too much about these things, because you are afraid in thinking you will destroy your intuition.

SL: You fear analysis will destroy it?

SF: Yes, yes, I can see that. *The best times is where it comes just out of the air; just comes from nowhere. I can see that when you talk to David Fincher, it is to do with the structure of the shots and so on—mine it's just the life itself.*

SL: So you're making a living out of making films now seems like the natural choice to you?

SF: Well it chose me. That is why I say sometimes I believe in God because I don't know that I played much part in it. Afterwards you think: "Oh I can think that this profession really suits me," but I don't know that I knew that. And how lucky I am that there was a profession that suited me.

SL: What would Stephen Frears be in a conventional life?

SF: . . . I'm trying to think. He would be much unhappier; probably dead. Or maybe he could have created his own life in another domain. It's all come as a big surprise.

SL: Would you be able to put into words what making films has given you?

SF: *It has given me a life. Yes, it has given me the most extraordinary life—incredible—I never thought I'd have the life I live.* You know after the war it was very, very constricted—horizons were so limited. It took me a long time to sort of lift my eyes up. I think I drove many people mad on the way—you know you were supposed to keep your head down. It's as if my life only began when I met Karel.

# Petersen, Wolfgang

**DIRECTOR'S CUT:**
"When reading books or going to the movies as a teenager in postwar Germany, it was just a wonderful thing to get completely lost in stories—disappearing into different worlds."

**BORN:**
1941, Emden, Germany

**BACKGROUND:**
German Television Director

**FILMS (selection):**
Das Boot—1981
The NeverEnding Story—1984
In the Line of Fire—1993
Outbreak—1995
Air Force One—1997
The Perfect Storm—2000
Troy—2004
Poseidon—2006

**MAIN GENRES:**
Drama, Adventure, Action, Thriller

WOLFGANG PETERSEN: I was born in a small Northern German town in 1941, before moving to Hamburg in 1950—so my upbringing and early adulthood was really there. My parents were both business people, my father being a ship broker at the Hamburg port, my mother being a housewife at first. They had nothing to do with the film industry or any other sort of creative work. *So for my parents, it came a little bit as a surprise when at the age of twelve I told them that I wanted to become a film director.* I felt that way very early on. If you ask me why that was so, I can only tell you that sometimes there are these kinds of things that just happen—it's an obsession. I don't know why. I mean the only explanation I have is that around the ages of nine to eleven, I was finding myself more and more drawn to the movies; especially American movies. Not so much German movies, because though the movie industry was quite successful there in the 50s, the movies were superficial, and creatively not so exciting.

I was right away hooked to American stuff that came over to Germany in the 50s; also the older films that during the Hitler days had never been shown. So I saw all these—from *King Kong*, to *Gone With The Wind*, to all those big classics from the 30s and 40s. I loved westerns, too. John Ford was my big hero. So I started to not only see these movies and sit in the movie theaters all the time, but also to study them. I tried to get books about how films were being made. I was absolutely fascinated by that world and I asked my parents to buy me an 8mm film camera. Because it was a very expensive thing to own, I told them they shouldn't buy any toys for me anymore, as it was more important for me to have that camera.

They were a little bit amused of course, and said: "OK, that's just an idea"—so they bought me that camera and I started to make my early films. When I was fourteen, fifteen, sixteen, I had done quite a few films with my friends. I was really quite consequent about it, really following my dream in a way.

SL: Is there any one film that sticks out as leaving a particular impression on you?

WP: One film I really remember was the western *High Noon* that I saw as a boy—but I liked all of the Fred Zinnemann films. I also loved Gary Cooper, who I thought was a wonderful movie actor and star. I was so impressed of his character in the film. I thought it was a great portrayal of a man who's not the youngest man any more and on his way out to leave this dangerous profession as sheriff. He gets challenged one more time by the people he put in jail. He is afraid, but he goes anyway. The courage this man showed, while we could at the same time feel his intense fear—I just loved that. But there are many other films—you know all the westerns you can think of: all the John Ford westerns—I saw basically everything you could get hold of. *I think that was my first important film school really: learning, dreaming, loving film.*

SL: So when you finished high school, you were still as hooked and fascinated by the world of movies?

WP: Oh yes. I thought about what to do now. I was nineteen and I said to myself: "What can I do now to make movies?" You know my parents—my whole family—had no idea of what to do.

SL: Did you get to show your short films to others?

WP: Well I showed them to my parents. Film school didn't exist in Germany at that time—so there was no way to do that. I remember myself often standing outside the very big film studios in Hamburg. Another one was out in a little town called Bendesdorf. Very longingly and mesmerized, I peaked inside. But of course, I could never get in there; there was no way to do it.

But then I was kind of lucky, because a friend of my mother's knew an actor. He was an actor at *Das Junge Theater* in Hamburg—an independent, very well respected theater. I said that maybe instead of just waiting for what's never going to happen at this point when I was 19, I might just as well spend a little time there and sit and watch. So the actor brought me in there and that's what I did. I watched their rehearsal and that kind of stuff. Out of that came a situation, when an actor all of a sudden got sick three or four days before the opening of a show. I quickly said "I can step in and you guys can still rehearse. I have been sitting hear for weeks now and I know every word." They were very surprised and also moved that this nineteen-year-old kid, sitting all the time in the dark, suddenly comes out of that darkness onto the bright stage.

SL: Before you were just watching—

WP: Just silently watching, never talking to anybody. The actor told me, "if you sort of silently tiptoe into the room, you can just sit there in the dark and watch us—it's no big deal." You know, at that time, I didn't really know what to do with myself—I was bored. Using that opportunity just to watch and see how theater works—my God you're nineteen and you don't know anything. But I watched the director and it was very fascinating.

I then played the part—and then I did it again and again because the actor was very sick—and everybody was so moved and impressed. I was probably pretty awful; probably terribly overacting. But they were very moved. Especially the director; I never forget his name: he was a Czechoslovakian with long black hair. A typical artist called Wasca Hoffmann. Afterwards, *he asked me, "You've been sitting here for weeks now and you know every word: what do you want to do with your life?" I said, "I don't know, I am just fascinated by all this. I want to make movies or theater."*

So he asked me to be his assistant in his next play. He said: "You're good. You've got an obsession here, I love that and you can be my assistant." I said: "WHAT? Yeah, of course, I would love to do it." There was a vacancy there, because his assistant was about to leave. On his next play, I became his first AD so to speak.

And I liked it a lot. I was really, really enjoying it. Obviously I was pretty good, and obviously people felt that there was a determination, an obsession, and a love for everything that they were doing. So the owner and director of the theater saw me of course all the time. He asked me to stay with the theater as a permanent assistant and I liked that. So I was starting a career at the theater. I signed on for a year; then another year. In the end, I stayed for five years.

SL: What happened to your dream of directing?

WP: Well, I directed already a year later. I started with children plays. But then also I did O'Neill: *A Moon for the Misbegotten* and *Children have Wings*. Also, I was starting to act, taking acting lessons. Suddenly I understood more about acting. It was a wonderful time. But at some point—I was 24 or 25—I went, "I have to stop this because I want to make movies."

SL: You always had this in the back of your head?

WP: *I must tell you that at some point when I took acting lessons, vanity kicked in and I thought, "I may become an actor."* But then I was really watching myself a little bit thinking about it and saying, "To be honest, I think I'm not very good as an actor." So I abandoned that dream that I had for a while and I said, "I think that is all BS. Other actors are much better and that's not really what you want. Come back to what you always wanted and that's making movies." So I decided that's the right thing to do.

In '66 and when I was 25, Germany's first film school opened in Berlin: Deutsche Film-und Fernseh-Akademie. I was really happy that I had a place now, where I could be with films and learn film. So I started to make films there. Short films and of course I had good connections with the actors from the theater that I worked with for all my first films. I knew about acting and I knew how to work with them. I think the short films were quite good and quite interesting.

SL: Do you feel film school was crucial for developing both the technical and artistic skills you needed as director?

WP: Probably it was important. I mean that's always hard to tell. But I loved the time at film school. There was no professional pressure really, or that I had to earn money. I got support from my parents, so that I could live quite OK in Berlin. It was just great to be independent, and to not be tied up with any professional or family obligations.

It was a typical student life and the time of the '68 student revolution in Germany and everywhere in the world. The Film Academy was one of the centers of it, next to Freie Universität Berlin. As we all know, these were exciting times. So it was also a political process. You were still so young, and you could do everything you wanted having a movie camera in your hands.

But then it wasn't for that long. I mean it's three years and then its over. At the end, I was 29 and we had to make our exam film. I made a 95-minute black and white film called *Ich werde dich töten, Wolf* (*I will kill you, Wolf*). We had not much money to shoot it—I had like ten thousand Deutsch Mark, which wasn't much at the time, either. For the amount, you could normally only do like a ten- or fifteen-minute film. But I thought: "I have just done a couple of those shorter films, I really would like to do a film that has the breath of a long film, like at least an hour." I knew that it would help me much more to get the attention of people later on, as it would already have the pacing of a long movie. So actually I wrote a script that was not really ten to fifteen minutes, but much longer. We spent that money allotted to the film in a week, and I went to the film school's director, "I'm sorry, I just totally miscalculated everything, I'm in big trouble."

SL: Though really you did calculate things ahead of time?

WP: Yes, I did. I told myself, "I really have to do something here. Maybe it all works out for the best in the end." So he asked me to see the dailies and what we had done so far. He liked it and said, "Boy, that would be a shame to stop all that. It looks like really good material—" "Yeah that's the problem, I don't know what to do," I replied. So he went like, "What the hell. Let's say we pay for what you need now to finish the film. And then maybe somebody will buy the film—like television—and then we might get out of it OK."

I thought it was very generous. But I also think he smelled something there; that it could be good. But it was also very risky for them. It wound up costing about fifty thousand Deutsch Mark. For a standard feature length film, that was very cheap. But for a student film it was very expensive. But it paid off: the NDR (Northern German public broadcasting station) bought my long film for seventy thousand I think. So while the school even made some profit, I had my long film.

On top of it, the NDR then hired me right away to do a first, really major production. There was some event-television going on at the time. It was called *Tatort* and for television, those were quite high-budgeted films. It was quite cool to get that offer, coming right from film school. So my whole thing paid off. I'm not saying that necessarily I wanted to do television at that time, but it just happened like that. I was a little bit nervous about having to wait again after film school—and here I had the opportunity to at least do something with film. Even if it's television, it's still film. So I did it.

I was very lucky with the cast I selected. An actor called Klaus Schwarzkopf as the Commissar was very good. *Blackshot*, the first out of a series of six *Tatorts* I signed on for, was very successful.

SL: You did not write the script to that episode?

WP: No, but I was very, very involved. Herbert Lichtenfeld was the writer. We were sitting together in his house for weeks and weeks, working on the scripts. I mean it was his scripts and I am not credited as a writer, but I was very involved in the scriptwriting process. So that's how it all started

SL: How confident were you about storytelling in the beginning and how would you say you learned it?

WP: I don't know. I cannot say I learned it at film school. There I had a forum and it was being paid for. I had a camera and sound and people to do it. It was not so much that I discovered a whole new world there and that it taught me things.

I must really say that I think I learned it when I was between ten and eighteen. My first films school was when I saw all these movies; just by liking, loving, hating them—whatever it was. I think that went into my system. My whole obsession with films had probably to do with being entertained by these storytellers. Working at the theater was a continuation of the learning process: having to do with great plays, learning about the structure of storytelling as well as dialogue and characters there. I have got the feeling that film school was more about, "Now it's time to execute what I know and what I feel."

The learning process was more outside of school: European films at the time of the 60s were very influential. *As film students, we were also quite arrogant. The first generation of teachers soon left, because we were all in our own world—we didn't accept anything that they were trying to teach us.* We were saying, "We know what to do"—the thing about film school students quite obviously seems that they have the tendency to be quite self-confident about what they want to do.

Our heroes were not the teachers, but rather the Francois Truffauts or the Jean-Luc Godards, or the Fellinis, Antonionis, and Bergmans. We were looking at those.

So I had actually two important learning phases and influences in my early life—one was when I was very young in the 50s, and now in the 60s, when the European film really started to blossom; in England, in Poland, in Sweden, in Italy, in France of course. And it even started in Germany in the early second half of the 60s, with the first young German directors doing something completely different from what the 50s German cinema was.

SL: You just mentioned the two strands of influence. How did you and others perceive their mutual influence and cross-fertilization that was taking place—especially of American film on European film?

WP: I was a tremendous fan of François Truffaut. I just liked him a lot, as of course all of the French *Nouvelle Vague*. But I was already in love with American film so much. Now that higher level of *cinéastes* also discovered it. It's interesting, but I had a strong feeling that I knew already what they were doing. And they, too, just loved American film, really building a bridge to American cinema.

They sort of rediscovered for me the John Fords and the Howard Hawks and the Hitchcocks of this world—let's call him an American director for this moment. So there was no arrogance at all at the time towards American film.

SL: So what about your own plans and dreams at the time. Did you project yourself as a European director, or were you rather dreaming of a career in Hollywood?

WP: Well, for me it always goes back to the 50s. I did always have in mind that probably the center of filmmaking and the most exciting place to make movies is Hollywood. It was in the 50s like that, and even later on when I was surrounded by great European film. Also I think that American films were still there in my mind, because some of the European filmmakers were so much looking up to American film.

So in a way yes, I always had an instinctive feeling that maybe at one point that's something I would like to do: making films "over there." Not that I was actively seeking it. When I had big success in Europe, I even became increasingly reluctant to go. But then at one point I said "Why not! At some point it's too late and you're getting older, so why not give it a shot now?"

At the time, I did a lot of television. I had done like 25 films or so; sometimes three or four a year. I was working like a madman. But it was great: German television in the 70s turned out to be a fantastic place for young directors to do interesting, creative, and quite provocative films. We only had two channels then—so if you made interesting films, half of the nation could watch it. It was an exciting time. I had the luck to make films that somewhat left quite an impression on the television landscape. Films like *Smog* or *Reifezeugnis*, which was the last *Tatort* film I did. It featured Nastassja Kinski and might actually be the most popular film in the history of German television.

When they reviewed my films, *all the critics said that I was making movies for television. And that's how I felt, too.* I said, "At this point I really don't care anymore if it's for television, but they are movies." They were all like 90-minute or two-hour movies for television: the aesthetics of it and also the way I worked with the camera. The channel would call it like "Movie of the Week."

Then one day, the head of Bavaria studios offered me to direct this huge motion picture project they were planning to do. He knew I could handle it because he had seen me doing it in so many TV films I had done for him.

SL: That initiated your long journey towards America?

WP: *Das Boot* was the big turning point, really. As you know, it was a big success and won six academy award nominations. I was over in LA for the Oscars—then an American agent came and wanted to get me to Hollywood. I said no, because I had my next project in Germany already lined up: *The Never-Ending Story*, for which Warner Brothers became a partner. And even though we shot it in English, it was still a German production.

*I told myself that maybe I wouldn't have to go to Hollywood because now I could do really international films in Germany. Also, the idea that maybe we could do something similar to Hollywood in Europe was quite exciting to me.*

But then I felt that I was just lucky by having two wonderful international projects to work on. Germany did not have a great movie infrastructure and not many great scripts were around. So I increasingly got the feeling of not knowing whether I could really continue to work on the level of *Das Boot* and *The NeverEnding Story*.

Then, Fox came and asked me if I wanted to do *Enemy Mine*. Production had already started and then stopped because Fox didn't like what the director was doing. They had already shot in Iceland and sets were being built in Budapest.

They simply went, "Could you take over?" I said, "That's weird, taking over a story." I then read the script and met with the writer. I kind of liked the story. I suggested relocating the film to the Bavaria studios in Munich. After having shot my two previous films there, I was also really comfortable there. So I told them that if I could do it all in Germany, then I would consider doing it. As I told you, I liked the idea of bringing a big international American production there, as it was also good for the German film industry and European film. And they said, "Yes, we can do that." So we shot a complete American production with American actors in Munich and some of it in Lanzarote.

So I still found a way to do another big movie and an interesting story in Germany—even if it failed later on in the box office.

After that, I had the feeling that now it was really time for me to go, having done everything I could over there. I didn't see any interesting material for me out there in Germany or German stories that I wanted to do. At that point now, Hollywood was really asking me if I would come over to LA.

It started with an offer by Al Ruddy, the producer of the first *Godfather*. He had a project called *Alicia's Book*. I really liked that story. Kathleen Turner was a big star at the time and supposed to be the lead. I met her in New York. I liked her a lot and said to my wife, "You know what, maybe now it's the time to go and make a movie there." So we came over to LA in '87.

I was here, preparing the movie for months, working on the script with the writer, and meeting with Kathleen Turner whose belly was getting bigger and bigger: she was pregnant. The whole process was slowed down, but the studio wanted to wait for her. But you know how it is: having to wait like six or so months for her, somewhat the air went out of the project. *So the movie never happened; not a surprising thing in Hollywood. There are a lot of things that never happen here.*

In the meantime I was here—we had lived in Santa Monica for eight months now and we liked the life we had.

SL: Did people in Hollywood still remember you?

WP: Oh yeah, absolutely. Especially the reception of *Das Boot* was such a big success and quite something over here. I have to really tell you that it was admired by the people, the industry, and simply everybody. It was always like, "Oh, *Das Boot, Das Boot!*"

That's good about Hollywood: they never forget. If they fall in love with a film, you can ride on that for quite a while. And it was only like five years ago or so.

SL: So you never doubted that you could get your next project up and running?

WP: Well, yeah . . . I mean the two to three years from '87 to '89 were quite frustrating—a lot of doors opened, a lot of people invited me, projects were discussed; I started here and developed there and had to learn that you have to be patient. Let's put it that way: it's a lot of hot air over here; a lot of talk-talk.

SL: You had your company Radiant Productions that you had already founded in Germany. Did that help you?

WP: Not right away; a little bit later when I had to deal with the studio. First, the only thing that I had was a project called *The Plastic Nightmare*, later called *Shattered*. I bought the rights to the book already in Germany before making *Das Boot*. I loved that thriller and I always wanted to do it, but it never happened. I then wanted to do it here, because it was a story that took place in San Francisco.

So that became the film I eventually made. At first, I told myself that maybe I should produce it and direct something else, because I feared that I had lived with that project for too long now. So I thought that maybe it would be good to give it to another director and go with something fresh that I could get more excited about. But as nothing really worked and nothing was about to happen, I said, "Ok, that's it now; I'll do *Shattered* myself." And since I brought that project along and owned it, I wrote the screenplay myself here. Everybody liked it. It was not so difficult to set it up and get it going. This was the beginning of it all in 1990, becoming my first American project.

SL: How well was it received?

WP: Again, this one did not work at the box office—at least not here in the US. Still, Clint Eastwood would for example love the movie. He was instrumental also when I was interested in the script of *In the Line of Fire*. When he heard that I liked the script so much, he really wanted to meet me. He also loved *Das Boot*. After our meeting, it was a done deal that we wanted to do that movie together.

SL: You said somewhere that when you did *Enemy Mine*, you also discovered your taste for epics. What's your fascination with those great, bigger-than-life stories?

WP: There is an autobiography of mine out, where it says, "I love the great stories." It's just that I love to get lost in stories. It was always like that. When reading books or going to the movies as a teenager in postwar Germany, it was just a wonderful thing to get completely lost in stories, disappearing into different worlds. Germany after the war was a very dull zone. It was a world that wasn't much fun for a youngster to grow up in. Everybody was so serious and concentrated to put Germany back together. And there was such a feeling of guilt about the past. It was a kind of situation, where a young boy would love to dream of better worlds—let's put it that way. That's partly also why I like westerns so much: the endless landscapes of the American West, and the wonderful stories that take place there, with these bigger than life characters and heroes. You could find that with most of the American films really. You see, we were not allowed to think of any heroes—that stuff was behind us. You know we, or at least our parents, were mostly in the mea culpa world of "we are bad people"; we were ashamed.

SL: Do you feel that moving to America has altered or influenced your storytelling in any way?

WP: I really don't think it did; or maybe a bit. I am making films that are more for mainstream audiences. Of course, when you're here and you're learning more about how Hollywood works and what's important to an audience, you automatically get more familiar with what that audience wants. I mean to sit in a movie theater here in America and see how they react and what they love and what they don't like, of course that influenced me. But I think that in general, it hasn't changed much.

In fact, it is just the opposite: *I hope that a lot of my European roots, cultural background, and upbringing translate into the films I do here. So that it leads to a good marriage of what I learned as a kid from American and European films, and then my own life as a European.* What I've learned in school and wherever else is also very much part of my work here. It gives it the special Wolfgang Petersen feel to it, instead of simply being very typical American styled. I know I'm quite a bit under attack from Germany these days. But that's very typical: when you leave your country for Hollywood, they say: "Now he's lost soul and it's all very American." I think that's all complete bullshit. Simply look at my films or films of other European directors who work here: they bring their heritage and their upbringing all with them. And I think there is quite a good group of directors that have a very special style.

SL: Is there any tangible difference between being a European in Hollywood opposed to being an American. Do you maybe get offered different projects?

WP: I don't know. That might be. They like to call me "German-born Wolfgang Petersen." To tell you the truth: I think most of the executives and people of the studios don't think much about it anymore. German or not, I'm just the filmmaker Petersen.

So I doubt that they really say, "OK this is more a project that's good for Wolfgang because he's from Europe." I don't think so.

The difference is more for me when I say "I think I give something to it that might be a little different." I don't know though, if they really realize it. I do have my doubts there.

I surely don't find it more difficult for me to get certain things offered here—not at all.

I'm in a position right now where I would say that I'm getting a pretty good look at the top project in town. I don't think that there is a special group of projects reserved for me because I am from Europe.

SL: Apart from being European, what are three or so personal attributes of yours that allow you to make the films you do?

WP: I think "obsession" is a word that really works for me and was important. And I think in our conversation that came out quite clearly. It started for me when I was very young. Look at the way I actually started when I was twelve— there were American and Hollywood dreams that were definitely there. Now, I am at the end of that journey, as I don't think I will come back to Europe. Though the journey is not over, I am now here to stay in Hollywood. Obsession was definitely necessary to get me here, let's put it that way.

The other thing is: you have to care for people. My whole life, I think I can say I was very much a caring person, if I may say that about myself. I am not a cynical man and I like people. I think I always liked the way that for example François Truffaut portrayed people. That's why I am so in love with his work, because he cared for people: he loved people. And he had a tenderness about how he portrayed them. I am not saying that I can do it as well as he did, but it impressed me and I found a resonance there that I felt and heard also within myself. Caring, liking, loving, and being curious about people, giving them the attention they deserve are, I think, good attributes to have for a filmmaker. And I told you in the beginning how much I loved the portrayal of Gary Cooper in *High Noon*: the humanity of this man. Yes, it's a larger than life character— but still so human.

And another thing I think you got to have is courage. At some point, you have to step out of the darkness of that room as I did when I was nineteen, and just go onto the stage out there and bark your part. But it's a tough thing to do; it's not easy, especially when you have been sitting there for weeks and you don't know these people and you just go there and do it. But it was worth it, because I saw a chance there to do something and to get attention. You have to do it. *So at some points in your life you have to be bold and courageous to fight for the things that count for you.*

SL: When looking at the nature of your past projects, can you see anything that you can learn about yourself?

WP: I think it is definitely there. In the past, especially with *Troy* more recently, a lot of questions like that came up. Or you know journalists telling me that they feel more and more that one theme is coming over and over again in my movies. I have to say: "Yes, it's very true." It's not that I am doing that on purpose. It has maybe to do with my real love and passion for boxing. I love fighting. Again, it goes way back to my childhood, when I would just love boxing. I trained boxing as a young man—I just admire the drama of it. And the symbolic thing of two people fighting in a ring against each other—it's some kind of existential metaphor to me. In my movies, the fight between two people is very, very often at the center of the story. There is a film like *One of the Two of Us*, a German film, all the way to *In the Line of Fire* between Clint Eastwood and John Malkovitch. There is *The Perfect Storm*, where George Clooney fights in this case not a guy but a wave; or *Troy* and the standoff between Hector and Achilles. I always come back to that. Though one should not overanalyze, I think it has very much to do with the fact that deep inside, I have that feeling of two forces fighting each other in my own chest. That fight within you is a very human, existential thing. But you don't know: is it good against evil?

Whatever it is, it is the two sides of the same coin; the dark side in you fighting the light side. I've always had that feeling that when Achilles is fighting Hector, you don't know who to root for. That is the fantastic concept of Homer: of having two great warriors fighting and you root for both in a way, as both are part of yourself. So I think that's something that is reflected in a lot of my movies in that sense.

*You know, I wanted to make Batman versus Superman—a project that I thought was really an exciting concept. Not to do a single Batman or a single Superman, but to have both of these comic book heroes in the same movie, and to have them really fight it out.* They both stand for totally different things. Again, one stands more for the bright, light, and optimistic side of life, while the other is the dark side and character of it. Then at one point they would have to fight it out. I think that's kind of a theme that—more by instinct in the beginning, but later on, once you think about it, you go: "Yes it's true. It is obviously something that means a lot to me and that is very dramatic to me."

SL: What is it about directing that gives you the strength to carry on fighting?

WP: For me personally, directing a movie is my life. It became my life when I asked my parents for that camera at the age of twelve and telling them that I wanted to become a director. I was so serious about it. I knew that this is what I want to do and that it would be the fulfillment for my life. It was, and it still is.

I'll never forget when I was doing *Perfect Storm*, and my friend Steven Spielberg came to visit me on the set. At that point, he hadn't made any film in three years. He told me, "Oh my god, I envy you so much. Can I do a little bit of second-unit work for you, or anything? Because you're making a movie and I am not." And that was Steven Spielberg—he could be doing every year five movies if he wanted to. But he said, "I am stuck in development hell and I am stuck left and right." So I said, "You know, you're so right! Every morning when I step onto the soundstage here for another day of work on one of my movies, I am a happy man." It is the creation of something that is hopefully eventually seen by so many people around the world—it is a constant source of energy and such a joy-giving experience for me. It makes me feel like I am young, I am vital, and I am energized. The process of creating something is just such a wondrous, wonderful thing and I am thankful for every day that I can continue to do it.

# Harron, Mary

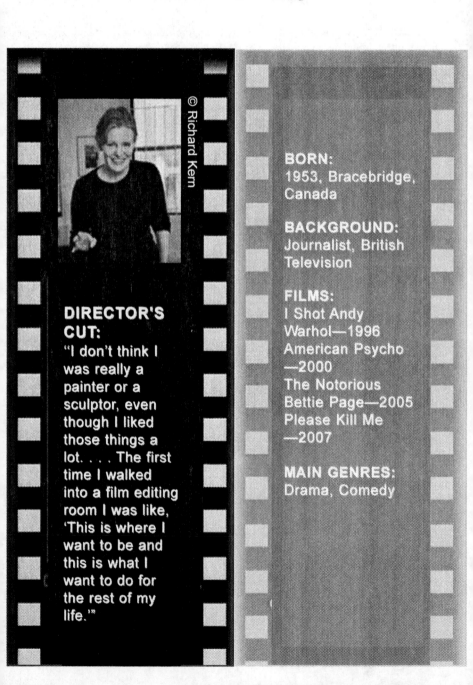

© Richard Kern

**DIRECTOR'S CUT:**
"I don't think I was really a painter or a sculptor, even though I liked those things a lot. . . . The first time I walked into a film editing room I was like, 'This is where I want to be and this is what I want to do for the rest of my life.'"

**BORN:**
1953, Bracebridge, Canada

**BACKGROUND:**
Journalist, British Television

**FILMS:**
I Shot Andy Warhol—1996
American Psycho —2000
The Notorious Bettie Page—2005
Please Kill Me —2007

**MAIN GENRES:**
Drama, Comedy

MARY HARRON: I was born in North Ontario but grew up in a lot of different places and atmospheres. Though mainly working as a comedian now, my father is an actor and used to travel a lot. During my childhood, I lived with my grandparents quite a fair amount of time. They lived in a classic small-town Canada village. And then we lived in New York in Greenwich Village for a while, because my father was on/off Broadway. We then moved from this little New York apartment to a big house in Beverly Hills because he signed a contract with Paramount. After a few years, we moved back to New York and my parents got divorced. Then my sister and I moved back in with my grandparents in that little town. That was all by the time I was seven!

My mother married again when I was eleven—that was the Hungarian writer Stephen Vicinczey who wrote *In Praise of Older Women*. We lived in Italy for a year where I didn't go to school, then we moved to London when I was thirteen. I spent the rest of my school days there.

My father being an actor, I guess my early memories of him taking me along to work left quite an impression. I have very vivid memories of all that. In that sense, I was probably lucky because the idea of working in film wasn't an unknown, unimaginable world to me.

Now I am taking my two daughters to the sets and I wonder how much they will remember . . .

SL: Did the set mesmerize you as a girl?

MH: I don't remember the set, but I remember being shown dailies. I remember there was a car driving up—I guess my dad was in the scene. And the scene was shown many times. Just the oddness of watching that scene over and over—you know as a child you go, "I am going to see a movie," but then you are watching the same thing happening over and over an over. And everyone's watching and everyone's very serious sitting in the dark—

SL: And you wondered what the point to all that might be—

MH: Yes exactly!

Also, I got taken to the theater from very early on. You know when I was like three or four, my father would take me to see those Shakespeare plays. So I guess that all left an impression on me somehow.

Then I remember walking all over the cities by myself. Today, kids are kind of supervised, but even when I was in Toronto at eleven or twelve, I went everywhere on my own. The same thing I did in London at fourteen or fifteen. I'd go to art galleries and to the National Film Theatre. I guess that was the biggest thing for me. We started getting the British Film Institute's magazine *Sight and Sound*—a really big thing for me. I would read about all the news I hadn't heard of. And I remember the pictures; the cover photos being very, very evocative. When I was about sixteen, I would enjoy going to the film festival and see some strange Yugoslavian film or something. I saw things like Fritz Lang's *M* or *Double Indemnity*. I read up everything about these movies.

I really read a lot as well. I thought when I'd grow up I'd be a writer. Then, when I was a teenager, I wanted to be an artist. At one point I was going to go to art school.

SL: Were you worried by the idea that sooner or later you'd have to make some sort of decision?

MH: Well, I thought I'd be a writer or a painter. *I surely didn't have any notion that I'd be a director—it never occurred to me that I would or could ever do that. I think that was so because there were no women directors. There was Leni Riefenstahl and that was about it.* I think the first film I ever saw by a woman director was *Swept Away* by Lina Wertmüller.

Then I had the idea that I would maybe write movies. But I can't remember when I got that one.

SL: Did you have any particular people that you looked up to while trying to find your way?

MH: I think I was honestly influenced by my parents because they were in artistic careers; my father also wrote. My stepfather was a novelist and a critic. So we had a lot of literary people in the house.

SL: Did that also stir you towards studying English at Oxford—

MH: I guess that happened in my lower sixth form. I had thought I would apply to art school. Then my English teacher said he thought I could get into Cambridge. I was very flattered that somebody thought I could do that. That kind of made a big change for me and I am still wondering that if I had gone to art school, I probably would have ended up in film as well, because I don't think I really was an artist.

SL: "Being an artist" is kind of a tricky notion anyway—

MH: I don't think I was really a painter or a sculptor, even though I liked those things a lot. So I think at art school, I might have ended up in film earlier. But you never know.

Oxford was a big challenge and I wanted to win that challenge.

SL: What effect did that university have on you?

MH: I was friends with a lot of different people and social groups and liked going to their parties. I had wide acquaintances. The first couple of terms I was involved with the theater people. And I did a lot of acting. And then that sort of stopped, because I never lost my Canadian accent and I never got cast for the big roles.

Then, a friend of mine at my college at St. Anne's was one of the feature review editors at a university magazine called *ISIS*. He said, "We need somebody to do the movie column" so I did that for a term. I went to that old picture theater. I just reviewed what was on that week. I really enjoyed writing about movies—it was a great start because everyone liked what I wrote. In my last year at university, I became the magazine's editor with Patrick Wintour who his now a foreign editor at the *Guardian*. So from my midpoint at Oxford, I was very much involved in journalism. My friends and I were suddenly all aspiring journalists. I was very set on that.

Also, I still had the idea of maybe ending up in Hollywood writing screenplays. *Certainly I liked the romantic idea of writers who somehow end up in the movies. I had some idea that the screenwriter's life was an artistic battle: that they are all tortured and terrible, leading invisible lives and have horrible times with the studios—I thought it kind of interesting to have that tragic experience.* It wasn't really necessarily that I wanted to suffer but I was interested in the life that those screenwriters had: people like Scott Fitzgerald had a terrible time—Dorothy Parker also had gone out to Hollywood.

SL: Looking at it now, to what degree was your interest guided by visual storytelling and directing?

MH: I didn't think about directing until a little bit later. It just hadn't occurred to me. Theater I could have considered. At one point I thought of directing a play, but then it seemed like too much to take on. I just didn't think I'd be good at it.

It was mainly the idea of being *involved* in movies. Writing seemed to be the one way I could get involved.

SL: Last day at Oxford: what happened?

MH: I think everyone had been applying and looking for jobs, but I wanted to go to Latin America. In my year before college I had gone and traveled all over Mexico for three months. I would just make a living somehow and travel around the world.

But then I just wasn't sure what to do and went back to Canada to stay with my sister for a few months: I had that post-college letdown where we were told that we had to face the real world now.

At that point, I was also interested in religious cults—I thought of writing maybe a book about that. So I'd look at some of the different cults that were around—things like "Children of God."

Then, a friend of mine invited me to New York for his 21st birthday party. I took a train down and had this weekend in New York: I was just completely in love with that city. At home, I put all my research stuff in garbage bags and went back down. And that was the big event in my life: moving to New York!

I had no idea what I would be doing there. I stayed with a friend for two nights. Then they found me this cheap hotel, the Martha Washington "for women only" and 35 dollars a week—they had these jobs that you would look at for room and board. I went to about five different interviews and I chose the craziest one: a movie company. This was 1975. The job was on Second Avenue in the East Village, which at this point was considered very rough. There were these abandoned buildings that they really took over. In turn for working, you got to share an apartment; food as well. They had all these people working for nothing on this terrible movie they were making. So I guess this was my first job in the movie business.

At that point, I had more of an English accent from growing up in England—this kind of classy talk. So they made me do this telephone stuff where you call people up and try to get things for free—and I was terrible at that. I hate the telephone anyway and I'm not that good on the phone with strangers. I hate asking for stuff.

After a few days of that, the cook had left: I offered to run the kitchen. Doing that during a few weeks, I was much, much happier. This was perfect for me, because I was able to run my own life: I did all the shopping.

SL: During that time, were you ever afraid of getting lost and not being able to live up to your own talents or expectations?

MH: Later on I did, but not at that point. I thought I was young and this is what life is supposed to be: to go and have adventures. *I guess I had a certain confidence that I would find my way. I was so young.*

There were later times in my life when I felt lost and didn't live up to my potential. My time in New York was really fantastic, though. After a month of running the kitchen, this young kid, Lesley Neill, came in. I thought he was very smart, cause all the people I was around with at the time seemed just crazy to me. To me, they were all just completely deluded and exploited. I didn't think that this movie was ever going to come out.

But I didn't really care, because I was in New York and able to live. And so Lesley came in and said, "These people are crazy!" and I said, "Yes, they really are!" I said I'm a writer, and he asked me to work for this magazine called *Punk* that a friend of his was starting.

He went on to talk about the CBGB off the Bowery—the first punk rock club in New York at a time when maybe ten people there had heard of punk rock. I had never been there. One night he took me and his friend and magazine editor to see the Ramones there and we met Lou Reed when we arrived. I interviewed the Ramones as the first person ever—and I also interviewed Lou Reed for what was to become the first issue of the first *Punk* magazine. That was me becoming part of the New York underground rock scene which really took my life over during the next year.

SL: How did that then eventually lead you towards film?

MH: You know, it was a long road. After a year or two in New York, I started to think about going to film school at NYU. The idea of making films had definitely taken over. I decided that if I was going to stay in New York, I would ask my father for help so I could go back to school. And that would have definitely led me into film.

But then I decided not to stay. I went to Paris for six months, which was a mistake, because I had nothing really going on there for me. I just taught English and I did some writing. When I was 26, I moved back to London. At that point I felt like, "Oh my god, what's happening to my life?" Because all the people I had been at Oxford with had careers now. People I was really envious about worked in TV and at the BBC, doing documentaries and stuff. That had become a very powerful attraction to me. But then it felt like, "Oh I'm so old now . . ." It's so funny: now I'm over 50 and I can't believe I thought I was old at 26.

When I was 27, I got a job writing reviews for the *Guardian*. It was a good job for a writer; lots of people were wanting to do that. But by the time I was in my late twenties, I was really miserable. I was so frustrated in London. I didn't like what I was doing. I knew I wasn't really a music writer and it was not the right job for me.

SL: Journalism wasn't right for you—

MH: You know I started to lose my real love. Even though I was still interested in some of the stories, *I felt I had lost my way. I felt I was meant to do something creative. I was like, "I know I have some kind of creativity." I didn't know what it was, but I felt I wasn't using it.*

Then I was very lucky. Somebody I had worked with was starting a Channel 4 music show called "Earsay." It was the first kind of pop-magazine show and they asked me to come in as a researcher on pilot.

Then after a few months of that, I got a job on the "South Bank" show as a researcher. It was shot on film. And the first time I walked into a film editing room—and I remember that very clearly—I was like, "This is where I want to be and this is what I want to do for the rest of my life." At that point I was 31.

SL: What was it about that editing room?

MH: I don't know—it was the combination of the dark room and the images on the screen.

SL: So when for the very first time did you think that not only you wanted to, but also that you could direct?

MH: I think when I was on that very first show "Earsay" doing some little stories and we would go out. Everyone'd say I had ideas of how to shoot things. And I started to think, "Maybe I can shoot this."

SL: So the decision to direct was more of a process that grew out of the kind of life you were living.

MH: Yeah I think it was more organic. The thing is: the move from journalism to documentary is not a difficult one in that you're telling stories. Many people do that, as it is more about content. You don't have to be a great visual person. It's not like saying, "Oh I want to edit a feature film."

But it is also about storytelling: I have to say that documentary was a very good training and it taught me a great deal. It is editing and it is narrative.

It's very close to journalism, where you're also supposed to be telling the real story, even though of course it is a select version. You're trying to get some truth and a portrait about a real situation: it is factual and reality based. From writing an article about for example Heavy Metal kids in Sheffield to doing a documentary about the same thing is not such a huge step—only that you have a camera instead of writing it out.

I certainly felt like I could do documentaries; but the idea of directing feature films: if that's something you would have said to me back then, I would have been amazed.

The step from documentary to feature film simply seemed much more remote. I had some notion that you have to know a lot about lenses and cameras and lighting. I guess a lot of people have that, while I just thought, "Well, I can't talk technically." And of course I worked with a lot of young men who were all very interested in technical aspects. You know how they do it, planning their shots. . . . So I thought I probably wouldn't be any good at that.

SL: Your first TV feature directing was in '89—

MH: I directed a lot of short films for "The Late Show" on BBC2. It was an influential show that I was on for several weeks. I could make it in any style I liked. So that was great, and I did some very stylized pieces—it was a really fantastic opportunity. Several film directors came out of that—Anand Tucker for example who did *Hilary and Jacky*.

SL: It was like a playground for you—

MH: And we worked incredibly long hours—70 hours a week, just like junior doctors. I remember finishing editing one show fifteen minutes before it went out on the air. That was very exciting and I got to try out a lot. I also started to become a lot more confident in myself as a director. I was 36 then.

From the time I was 30, I started also to write screenplays. The woman who ran the theater company on which we had done a documentary, Elizabeth LeCompte of the Wooster Group, said I should come and write a screenplay with her. This was a big thing for me—so exciting. I felt I was promoted from nothing to work with this brilliant woman. And also Willem Dafoe, who had recently done *Platoon*, was in the company. Suddenly there was also a connection to movies. [Steve] Buschemi was also there. For a couple of years, I spent all my money flying to New York to work on that screenplay.

And though it didn't happen in the end and I never got paid for it because we never got the rights, I learned a great amount and it was a great privilege to be working with Elizabeth. She had never written a screenplay either—so we just sort of plunged in and did it the way we sort of wanted to: it was about the last years of Jackson Pollock's life from the perspective of a young girl, who later became his lover and was in the car with him when he died.

After doing that, I was working on a documentary about Andy Warhol and I had this idea of doing a film about Valerie Solanas, the woman who shot him. I got completely fascinated by her, even before I started directing. This happened like a year before I went to the BBC to direct. I then already had this project in my mind.

SL: So that project became your first movie—

MH: I think I got the idea of *I Shot Andy Warhol* in 1987 and I didn't film until 1995.

SL: Why so much time in between?

MH: First I tried to interest people at the BBC. And then eventually it took me many years to persuade a producer-friend there and whom I always had in the back of my mind to put some money into the project. That didn't happen until '92. I got back to New York and knew that once I was there, I could get my project going, because I could do all the necessary research.

SL: New York seems to have been this crucial place for you to get inspired and the energy necessary to tackle new challenges—

MH: *To me, because that punk rock era was my happiest time, I always dreamed of going back to New York. The idea of being a filmmaker there was like heaven to me.*

SL: So the money you initially received from the BBC triggered the film's realization?

MH: I think that it was a very significant moment in terms of kick-starting it and getting it done. In order to get the money, I also found a production company that was interested in the idea. Though in the end they pulled out, I got to write a proposal after years of doing research on it. I basically wrote it in a night.

It outlined the territory the story would cover and why it was interesting— the significance of it. At that point, I thought it might be a sort of hybrid and have both, dramatic and documentary, archival elements in it. A lot of people at the BBC were doing drama-docs at the time. It took me a while to move towards having the confidence to do it completely as a drama. My friend at the BBC didn't think it could be a full-scale drama because he felt that I wouldn't be able to cast somebody as a convincing Andy Warhol. But once I immersed myself in the project, got somebody to do some research for me, and started writing on the script—from about '92 to '94—I realized it wouldn't work as a documentary. Nobody remembered that woman. There was no material, there was no footage. So while investigating it, the idea of doing it as a full-scale drama started to take place in my mind.

SL: How much money did the BBC contribute?

MH: The BBC offered a hundred thousand pounds.

SL: Had you budgeted it already?

MH: No. We did know, though, that it would cost much more than we had: I had to go find other money. Many people over the years thought that it was just a crazy idea, going, "Why on earth would you want to do this?" But I went to see a friend who was casting on a film called *Swoon*. I felt that they were going to raise all kinds of objections, but they just said, "No, it's a really good idea."

So at that point, I had the BBC and I had a production company that was going to oversee it and help me to find investors; in the end I found them: Christine Vachon and this company that Christine and Tom Kalin, the casting director, had.

Eventually, I started to show my material to my best friend in New York, who understood it so well and was very encouraging. He was a huge influence on me and I started writing the script with him.

SL: How did you sustain yourself?

MH: I had like seven thousand dollars research money but basically, I did all that stuff for nothing, financing my life by doing documentaries and journalism. When the script finally came together, we went to all these different movie companies.

Lili Taylor had signed on early on to play Valerie; just based on my proposal. I kept in touch with her while I was writing the script. Finally we staged a reading—with a lot of actors, many of whom I knew from the Wooster Group. A lot of producers came, among which there was woman from the so-called "American Playhouse"; it had done a TV series on PBS, but was also financing low budget movies. She saw the reading and found it really interesting. She persuaded her company to finance it for 1.7 million dollars.

SL: Was that a budget that you were expecting to have?

MH: I guess so. In the end it doesn't buy you very much. I didn't know what I was going to get. I would have made it with less if I had had to.

SL: So together with this new team you developed the project?

MH: They encouraged me to make it a drama, but they didn't really have so much input. I didn't think that drama-docs worked very well.

My state of mind at the time was, "Oh my god, I am going to actually direct a movie!" That seemed so amazing. I didn't know whether I was going to be a great director or not—it wasn't about that. And I knew I wasn't super technical. *But I think what always has carried me forward has been that I have something to say: stories to tell that are really worth telling, even if I am not the best director in the world. And I felt that being a woman filmmaker, I have a lot of material, or an attitude, or approach that has not necessarily been seen before.*

SL: The strength of your story gave you the confidence of not having to worry about whether you could be a director?

MH: I always felt the story would carry it, whatever I did with it. I put my faith in the story, more than in myself I think.

SL: Do you remember your thoughts when you first read the story of *American Psycho*?

MH: I read it several years before they asked me to work on it. When it came out, it was a big scandal; that's why I picked it up. People were so horrified by it. I thought it was very funny. Once I started reading the first twenty or so pages, I felt that it had been completely misjudged: this book had been completely misinterpreted—often funny, very satirical. And then of course later on, you hit these horrific passages of violence. I still kept going to the end and felt it was a very fascinating, experimenting novel.

I didn't think about it as a movie, until somebody called me up and asked whether I wanted to direct a movie based on it. That happened after my first film had come out at Sundance.

SL: When you started to think about writing the script, what was most clearly in your head—what did you start with?

MH: When I start on a project, I always have a kind of feeling and intuition about how I am going to do it very early on; also visually. For *American Psycho*, I had an immediate intuition that it was going to be a period thing: a film about the 80s as well as a social satire. The other thing that I have is that I just like ideas to come to me. I don't puzzle things out: I just let the things come as I read the material.

The other idea I had was that the chapters in the book were chapters about music and that I was going to take these chapters and turn them into monologues. Bateman would address his victims with these monologues before he was going to kill them. That gave me a kind of structure.

The beginnings and the endings of my films tend to not change. Everything else in the middle goes through a lot of alterations.

I think I trust very much my instincts. But then I rework and change the order and what's in it a lot—the script will vary a lot. But the basic concept, I tend to stay with it.

SL: Tell me how concretely you worked on the script?

MH: Genevieve and I went to Mexico for a few days and got a lot of work done there. We went through the book together and wrote out a list of the scenes and dialogues that we liked—we used Final Draft: that's a great program because they have that thing where they'll print out the scene list for you and that made my life much faster. I don't do cards unlike a lot of people, especially men, I know: my husband is a director. *Men* seem to like cards that they put on the wall. I just like a list. And I look at the list and I play with its order, the story structure, a great deal.

I don't like standing outside and analyze it, or even use my critic's part of the brain at all.

SL: Would you be afraid to lose your intuition by using your critic's part of the brain?

MH: Yeah. Don't try and analyze that and don't try, "Oh, that is what a screenplay should be or this is what you should do." I don't work that way.

You know people talk about the beats of a scene—I just don't ever do that. I didn't go to film school. Somebody said that I am probably lucky. I don't write the scenes out or sketch them either: I just write it. And if it doesn't work, I just rewrite it.

SL: You read none of the scriptwriting books?

MH: Oh no. Ew, no! When I first started, I bought some of them and I never read them.

SL: Do you read other people's scripts?

MH: I usually really hate other people's scripts. I like them when they are good; like David Lynch's scripts are amazing. I get sent a lot of bad Hollywood scripts by my agent.

SL: What questions then do you go through when narrating your story? What do you do in order to stay focused on the story you are telling?

MH: I really don't analyze it that way. *I just go, "This is the scene I am writing and is it good or isn't it? After that scene, what should the next scene be?"*

SL: But what do you wrap the audience's attention around?

MH: I don't know—I think there is no answer to what hooks an audience. A screenplay is either interesting or it isn't. Anyway, I just think of the specific story I am telling, not about general questions what a good screenplay should be.

SL: This might be a difficult principle to go by when trying to convince a producer who asks, "Why should we produce your movie?"

MH: But then it's like, "Why should you produce anything?" And either you can see that as your movie or you don't. I can tell them why I think that story is interesting, but why they should produce the movie, that's for them to say. And my dissertation of why they should produce it isn't going to make it a better or more successful movie.

SL: Do you try to sort out genre questions when writing your scripts?

MH: No, 'cause my movies cross genres I think.

SL: How important is the exchange and the communication of ideas with others during the creative process—maybe in a team or with friends?

MH: I prefer to write with somebody, because it's more fun. And even when I write things on my own, I would always show it to two interesting people. But you have to be careful who you show your material to, because it has to be somebody on your wavelength; otherwise you just get too much input. And when it goes to the movie companies later on, it will get loads of input anyway.

SL: How do you deal with that fragility of your ideas during the stage where you're trying to give them a form and structure? Initially, they just exist in your head and you might have a hard time to translate it onto the page—

MH: Yeah, and lots of times, people don't like my scripts. To me, I know exactly what they mean or what I am doing with them. A lot of the times, my scripts go round and round and people don't want to make them, until finally they hit the right place. That's happened with all three of my movies: very, very hard to sell.

To me it's very clear. Like on my first movie: *I got on the set and it was only halfway through shooting that my gaffer said to me, "I didn't know this was supposed to be funny." I was like, "You really didn't know?"* To me it was as clear as daylight. So obviously, my scripts don't necessarily communicate well.

SL: Why?

MH: You see I don't know. I think tone is a difficult thing to communicate in a script, and tone is a lot of what makes things work. But also, I am writing it in my head and for myself, so I know what I am doing with it. And I think that maybe I am not always putting everything down that I know is going to be in there.

SL: How important is it to you that your actors know what's going to be there?

MH: They have to know their character. They have to understand the tone of the film. And they have to understand who they are.

SL: But they don't have to understand your vision of the whole thing?

MH: I don't think so, because I don't think that's clear to anyone before they see the final thing. I am happy if they do. But you can tell if an actor is getting it; getting the tone right.

SL: Do you have a method of working with your actors?

MH: I think you have to work with different actors in different ways. A lot of directing actors is very simple. You have to have a good rapport with them and make them feel comfortable and confident that they can try things. Lili Taylor said that she felt I gave her a safety net that allowed her to go out there with her performance and try things; that I was understanding. Also, you have to be very clear—I mean emotionally concrete things and what the scene is about, "Now you're in this room, you're sitting in this chair, this is how you're feeling about this person, this is what you want to do."

SL: How much room do you leave in your scripts for an actor's character input on set?

MH: I think when I write a script and when I have lived with a story for that long, I have a pretty clear and detailed sense of what the character is like and of their development. And then sometimes an actor might surprise me and bring the scene into another place. I am open to that if I think it's right. Obviously, actors bring another element to it all. When I cast the actor, that person becomes superimposed onto my existing image of the character.

SL: You were told to cast Leonardo DiCaprio as you leading character in *American Psycho*. Your existing image wasn't flexible enough?

MH: The producers tried to everything to make me cast him. It doesn't matter how good an actor is: if they are not right for the part, they are not right for it. *Producers will always try and cast the wrong people. They are only thinking about the financing—and only you as the director are thinking about what the film needs. DiCaprio was too fragile and poetic, also young-looking. There was just something instinctual that felt completely wrong about him.* His gift is a poetic gift. He didn't seem like a tough young Wall Street guy. Also, I needed somebody who looked like everyone else and could blend in with the others, because so much of the film is about mistaken identities: you could never get six different Leonardo DiCaprios. Why would they all be boyish-looking? Film casting, unlike theater casting, really does rely a lot on what is in a person already: on their inner lives. Chris [Bale] had a certain mysteriousness and toughness that was just right for the character; and sense of humor, too.

He got the sense of humor so perfectly. That was a case where he and I were completely on the same page when we first met. He thought about it exactly in the same way I did which most of the actors hadn't. Us having the right rapport and him having the right inner qualities—and then of course he had absolutely the right physical quality.

But in terms of the sense of humor, a lot of people took *American Psycho* too earnestly, too literally, and they didn't see the comedy in it. They didn't feel that I was making fun of this character; that it was satire.

SL: So audience reactions were often disappointing. How much do you try to work with the audience in mind and anticipate their reaction when crafting your scenes?

MH: Everybody on the set does their job better than you as the director would. The designer designs better than I would, the cinematographer shoots better than I would, the actors act better. But my job is—and the director is the only person who can do this—to have the whole picture in the head. You're like the conductor of the orchestra. And the conductor is about tone and pacing and intensity; when to lighten up, when to go heavier, when to speed it up, when you're getting the right emotional quality—and that's the funny task you do.

I think it's about keeping the whole in your mind, rather than getting taken away by the details. It's a double thing: because when you're on set, you're very immersed in the details. It's like, "Take that lamp away, or that color is wrong, or can you do that line faster." You're in fact dealing with details all the time, constantly discussing with every department head: costume, make-up, hair, lighting. So I rely a lot on talented people around me. But while they are developing the details with the people whose job it is to create those, I have to keep the whole effect in my head.

SL: Are their any departments whose decisions you tend to get involved in more than in others?

MH: I get very involved, I think, in the production design—the design-concept of the film as well as the basic look and the broad patterns: I want to have this feel, I want to evoke this, but then they really make that work. *I still feel a certain weakness and less assurance when talking about the camera and lighting. At the same time, I think I can get a concept and overall look.* But I am still aware of a lack of knowledge.

SL: Do you edit while shooting?

MH: No, I don't have time. I only watch dailies. I have an editor who's working all the way through, comparing and assembling for you. And as soon as I stop shooting after a few days, they finish their assembly.

SL: What's your reaction when the editor first presents you with his cut?

MH: You know, usually you think, "Oh my God, it's terrible!" and then you have to go back to the editing room and find out what you have. Though that's not always true—you don't always think it's terrible—they show me what they put together and then I have to go back in and take everything apart and look at it again.

I think a lot in the editing. I still have that habit from working in documentary. So I tend to shoot a lot because I like to have a lot of options. I very much see the edit as a process. I enjoy it more than anything—it's my favorite stage. I can really focus the way I like to focus. I like the early script stage and I like the editing, because it's just you and the material. And if you have an editor you get on with, that's a really wonderful thing.

SL: So you have a core team for that?

MH: On each movie, I had a different editor; it's a good process and I liked everyone I worked with. I was going to work again with the editor of *American Psycho*, but he wasn't available. We definitely worked very well together.

SL: Do you test screen a lot?

MH: Yes, I test screen a lot.

SL: What about the first showing of *American Psycho*?

MH: Oh we had terrible test screenings. Like half the audience of *American Psycho* just hated it. The versions we showed were rough cuts—and I learned a lot from it. We had one disastrous screening, where people hated it so much. Then Andy the editor and I went back and really recut a lot and took a lot out. It was too long and ponderous.

I test screen even more than the movie company usually wants me to, because I really like to feel that the audience is focusing. And I like to feel when things are too long—I don't like to be boring. And I really like to feel what's working and what's not working.

SL: How many cuts of *American Psycho* did you go through?

MH: We probably screened three or four versions, and then we premiered at Sundance. Then Andy and I went into the editing room and took another few minutes out.

SL: Were you surprised, when first screening it, that people could perceive it so differently from you and the story you thought you'd be telling?

MH: Oh yeah—you think it is more ready than it is. What interests me is that people just didn't know what to make of it. They just didn't know what it was. Because it's a mix of genre, both horror and comedy, people didn't know how to deal with it.

But then you have to make a distinction between when people start reacting badly because it really is not working—because it's too long or too clumsy or too obscure. And then the other case is where you're very happy with the film and people reacting badly to it—maybe because it's challenging them—but I think it's fine and just say, "Well, that is how it's gonna be."

SL: So what form of criticism is most instructive to you?

MH: It's really feeling when they get bored. Feeling them lose concentration.

SL: How do you notice such a thing? Do you ask them, or observe their reactions?

MH: No, you feel it, you know? It's partly probably just some definite physical things that people start shifting around or moving: you feel restlessness and you feel when people are concentrating.

SL: The editor Walter Mirch has that theory in which he believes that you've got the audience once they are all blinking at the same moment—

MH: Oh, how interesting! I definitely feel that what people *say* is less reliable, because the questions they ask on these forms are also very often limiting the responses. And *people are also not always honest about their own responses and feelings. Sometimes they are embarrassed saying they enjoyed a picture.* You know, they feel they should like certain kinds of things more than others. *But what does not lie is their restlessness.*

And then when I sit there, I transform. A lot of times I got bored with my film and that bears the danger that I'm going to cut it down too much—'cause I go, "Oh this scene doesn't work, I'm so tired of it." And then I sit there with the audience, seeing it in a new way. So for all those reasons, an audience is essential.

SL: Does the audience feel when as a director you are not sincere—when they realize you want to manipulate them gratuitously?

MH: In some ways, I think you can manipulate more on film. I think most audiences don't also really care about who the director is. I think the audience would always sense if there is no purpose to something. The question of sincerity is really a difficult thing.

SL: Does the fact that you are a woman in a still male-dominated domain have any significance to you?

MH: Well it definitely was harder as I didn't feel I was entitled to direct and didn't grow up thinking I could do it. Definitely when I worked with the BBC, a lot of people were very patronizing. And in TV in Britain, I was with all these young men who seemed so much more confident than I was: they probably felt like they *were* directors, long before I felt like I was a director. I just didn't take it for granted at all. But in the end I know that I had this great advantage: I had all this material and an approach that hadn't really been taken before. Bringing that perspective was an important thing.

SL: Why do you think directing is still such a male universe?

MH: It's just rough. I have been directing for twenty years. I have done three movies and a lot of television. *I just did an HBO show in California. The DP refused to do a shot that I wanted and he would have never done that to a man. I had to call the producers in.* It was a reminder to me—I thought I had *so* moved beyond it, but it is amazing how badly people can treat you. You do have to be tough.

SL: Any advantages you had directing as a woman?

MH: Maybe just because there are fewer of us, it makes you stand out more. I felt like the advantage I had was in the stories I could tell and the approach I brought. And then also maybe thinking outside the box a bit: by being less technical, I maybe came to things from different angles. There is a lot where classic female ways of dealing with things make you a good director.

SL: When I watched *American Psycho* for the first time and I didn't know that you made it, I remember thinking that it felt like a woman might have actually directed it. I think it was that unusual, uncanny perspective of being satire about a male universe like Wall Street; also the sex scenes were filmed very differently—

MH: Definitely! a man would have done all those sex scenes very differently. I thought, "I have a great opportunity of exploring new territory"—and I feel this in everything I do now. I feel very fortunate. You know, all these different stories and perspectives that have not been told: a wonderful opportunity! But getting there was not easy—you have to be very determinate.

SL: Do you see things changing or will that happen automatically?

MH: I don't know whether things change or not. I go to speak at film schools a lot and I was invited to NYU recently. There were about half women and half men in the audience, but only the men were talking. Why don't the women talk? Why are they not more confident? So I told them, "Talk more!"

But then there are also different working environments for women: if you go to California, you're more likely to get an all male crew, though on the last movie I did, I had a lot of women as crew. Women face the assumption—

especially with more old-fashioned crews—that you are just not going to be good at what you are doing.

I have had a lot of women on the crew walking up to me and saying, "Oh it's so nice to have a woman director." Because it does follow a very traditional line: a woman is typically script supervisor, or costume and make-up, or assistants—very rarely are women in the camera crew. On my first movie, I had a female cinematographer, which made a huge difference.

SL: How did that make a difference to you?

MH: In the sense that to me, opening up is much easier if there are women in the crew. Otherwise you feel they are slightly waiting for you to fail. You simply don't feel that you necessarily have the support you would like. But if the crew doesn't like you, you just have to live with that.

SL: Could you express in more general terms how you think that directing might have influenced and changed you as a person?

MH: I think it made me a better person [laughs]. *I was just reading somebody's quote—maybe it was Marc Rothko—about how terrible it would be not having found the thing you're good at. And I felt like that until I was in my thirties: I had not found the thing I am good at. And once you find what your talent is, it releases something in you and settles you and allows you to maybe even stabilize.* I don't know, but finding that thing that I was meant do was the most important thing to me.

SL: "Meant to do?"

MH: Well; that was right for me. . . . Directing is a very odd thing; a very odd combination of talents. Maybe there are directors that are brilliant editors or cinematographers, but on the whole, I don't think directors have any one of these particular talents. Their talent is being the leader of the orchestra, the bandleader, and it's a funny talent.

# Nair, Mira

**DIRECTOR'S CUT:**
"It is not my nature to observe life only. I want to get into it."

**BORN:**
1957, Bhubaneshwar, India

**BACKGROUND:**
Documentary Filmmaker

**FILMS:**
Salaam Bombay!—1988
Mississippi Masala—1991
The Perez Family—1995
Kama Sutra: A Tale of Love—1996
Monsoon Wedding—2001
Vanity Fair—2004
The Namesake—2006
Gangsta M.D.—2007

**MAIN GENRES:**
Drama, Comedy, Romance

MIRA NAIR: Though my family is from the north, I grew up in a very small town called Bhubaneswar in a state in Eastern India—remote even by Indian standards. It was a state that was supposedly backward, but it also had two thousand great temples—we used to play hide-and-seek in these fantastically carved temples. But the most exciting thing was to watch the planes take off from the tiny local airport.

I studied the sitar for some years and also I read a lot. I had two older brothers with whom I'd often play cricket. So I was always the youngest and very much teased; not spoiled at all. Never getting an audience, I realized very young that I really had to earn people's attention for them to listen to me.

And I was very interested in people. *I'd go out running in the morning and would come back with the milkman because his story was more interesting than anything I had heard. I was very curious and I remained curious.*

And then as a teenager, my father got transferred and I came to this great capital city Delhi to study for two years. He didn't have much income, but as civil servant, you have a great status and administrative power.

So I tasted the fruits of being in an exciting big city. It was a really exciting and challenging time for me, both intellectually and culturally. I went to an Irish-Catholic convent school, where I did very well. So when I returned to my small village at the age of thirteen, it was impossible—I couldn't stand it.

My two brothers had been sent to prestigious boarding schools. I was expected to stay in the all-girls' convent, but I just didn't want to. So I conducted a campaign in the school: everything I did for months was gibberish—it didn't make any sense. I was trying to expose that the teachers were terrible. Because I used to do very well and they were lazy, they just would still give me straight As without obviously reading my work.

So after having conducted this gibberish campaign for a few months, I showed the work to my father. It was my evidence that I was not learning anything because the teachers were just ladies in waiting. So my parents had to accept the evidence.

I got admitted and sent to a very exclusive, privileged school in the mountains, two days away by train from those Catholic nuns who had run the school in Delhi when I was thirteen. It was a lot like in *The Sound of Music*: "up there in the mountains . . ."

The point I am a making is that you have to carve your life; you have to forge your own way. I think it was through books—I'm not sure—but whatever it was, when I was growing up in this tiny town, I knew that there was a huge world out there.

SL: And you were extroverted enough to find a way of expressing it your way. Was there anything or any person you looked up to and that inspired you at the time?

MN: The only standard then was these two years spent in the city of Old Delhi and going to an excellent school where I had those bright people around me.

But I topped them all in all and everything. I was really challenged and I thrived on that, I guess. So coming back to that little town where there was no challenge and nothing happened—I didn't even think of going to that prestigious school, but just of wanting to get out.

SL: So arriving at that new school . . .

MN: . . . was very difficult. It was all skirts and blouses and burgundy socks and Mary Jane shoes and blazers—and I was in country clothes until my uniform got ready. It was a very exclusive school and I was only a little country bumpkin. I suddenly felt very exposed in a school where I was the only girl wearing something of my own.

You know how that makes you feel. *In my little hometown, I was a sort of tomboy. I never knew about fashion at all until I came to America, in fact.*

SL: Were you at all surrounded by film at your boarding school?

MN: There was nothing. There used to be Hindi movies around, but I only saw a couple; the most popular ones. I would see *Dr. Zhivago* many times. The first film I watched was *Hatari!*

When I was fifteen, the theater became my catalyst. I would see this avant-garde theater that came to our towns and schools and it was mind-blowing and; so exciting: new forms of Shakespeare, sometimes in English, sometimes not in English.

When I went back to my little town in which supposedly nothing happened, I discovered that actually a lot happened. What used to come through that town were these traditional folk theater companies—just people with seemingly nothing that spun these wild, fantabulous mythological tales: like Greek myths but from our folks. It was just amazing how they created such a magical universe with so little. I was very inspired by that form which is called *Japlin*.

During my summer holidays, I got involved with a radical Bengali theater company which made political and protest plays about political apathy and so on.

SL: So suddenly you discovered theater, combining many facets of life that fascinated you?

MN: Yes, yes. And then I had to go to university, where I chose sociology. Theater wasn't being taught; though theater was basically all I did for the two years I was at the university in Delhi. I was part of a group and I was part of a college society; I played Cleopatra in *Anthony and Cleopatra*. I played all sorts—Joseph Shakan, Peter Brook—all these were the heroes then. We used to do amazing things.

But then, I was under the illusion that I was an academic. I had a scholarship to Cambridge in England because I was top of my school in India. But I turned that down because I had a chip in my shoulder about England.

So two years later, I applied to all the big universities in the United States. I had seen Harvard in *Love Story*. Though my family had a very good reputation, there was no question of being able to pay for undergraduate education here. So the place that gave me a full scholarship and credit for the year I had spent in Delhi was Harvard, where I arrived in '76. It was my first time outside India.

SL: What impact did that suddenly have on you?

MN: It was both a place that I looked at with very open eyes and a sense of wonder. You'd go to a coffee shop and stand in line next to a guy who had literally won the Nobel prize—and then you'd sit and have a conversation with him.

But it was equally a place that I wasn't daunted by. Loads of people around me were much more overwhelmed and dumbstruck about having reached Harvard. I didn't grow up with the myth of Harvard; I just got the full scholarship. In fact, I don't think my parents ever got a report card—it almost didn't matter.

*In my first year at Harvard, I studied a course called "Love" about the sociology of love. The opportunities, the facilities, the freedom with which the courses were taught: you'd never think like that in India.*

So Harvard was very interesting: incredibly privileged, and also about excess, like everything in America.

SL: How did your experience there eventually guide you towards film?

MN: At first, I took theater there. It was just extracurricular and interesting, but not taken seriously.

I came to New York City for a while and studied with a group on the Lower East Side that was mostly experimental theater. I just looked around and saw all the people I had worshipped. Then I went back to Harvard and took a course in photography. I made some interesting photographs and got very interested and into it. That got me into Harvard's very competitive film program. They only took ten people, some of whom majored in it.

SL: Theory or Production?

MN: Production

SL: Does it still exist?

MN: Yeah. I studied Ricky Leacock, who is the great legend of documentary filmmaking. I was twenty years old and for the first time, I was exposed to cinema as a serious art form and as a form of expression and communication, which could be studied.

SL: Was that surprising to you that film could be studied academically?

MN: Yes, very much so: the fact that film is serious. I mean I didn't know that. So here is what happened: I was disillusioned with the theater, I went into photography, which was really interesting. But it is not my nature to observe life only. I want to get into it.

SL: What disillusioned you about theater that you could find in film?

MN: First year, I was engaged in theater as an actress. I was intuitively happy performing—I loved it. But actors had no control—absolutely no control about what we were chosen to do or not chosen to do. I just knew that I would not be able to do that for my entire life.

SL: But you could have done theater directing?

MN: It didn't occur to me. But also I had a full scholarship for two more years and I had to return to university. I took these photographs, which these guys in the department loved. Otherwise I wouldn't have had a ticket to get into film, you know?

For me, documentary film—I never studied fiction film—was a way to engage with the world. You know politically, hopefully artistically, visually, and to be with people.

SL: How did they teach documentary?

MN: You'd have groups. Then you'd choose one subject and make a film on that as a collective crew. In you second year, you'd make your own documentary.

SL: Out of that emerged your first documentary in '79?

MN: I took a semester off and went back to India, near to my university in Delhi. It is a mostly Muslim community, where instead of wearing a veil I wore a camera. I was just trying my hand at filmmaking really. It was a pursuit that was very difficult, but it was something that I just couldn't let go of. To me, it became a passion and a disease, you know? Going through every single aspect of making this film—from shooting it myself, to doing the sound and cutting my own negative: it was just the whole deal.

SL: Did you consider any alternative options at the time?

MN: I didn't consider doing anything else. That was it. *I was blessed that I had found my vocation very young. There was no doubt—no doubt!*

SL: The film was financed by Harvard?

SL: A rich professor and very famous documentary filmmaker, Robert Gardner, gave me stock he had and also lend me a Bolex camera. And then I had worked as a waitress in New York saving some money towards the costs. . . .

In the end, it did cost quite a bit, but we managed.

SL: How was your first documentary received?

MN: Actually, it did really well. It even got a feature film release in New York, which was unheard of at the time. I would just send it to festivals and go with it there. I went everywhere I could go or was invited to. And then, it got invited to the prestigious places, like Film Four or Cinema Real. I then tried to sell it to television.

SL: When did you start to think about feature filmmaking?

MN: Feature filmmaking came into my head six or seven years later. I was getting exhausted not just by the struggle to make these documentary films and to raise money for them, but much more by the struggle to find audiences. I had a feeling that these films are not making any difference.

I would sell them to TV—but TV always feels like a void to me. Even though it reaches millions of people, I never know what those are really actively thinking about my work. So that was one frustration. Here the second thing: I knew that I wanted to make a film about the street kids in Bombay. I also knew that with that subject matter, I didn't want to make a hit-and-run film like documentaries are.

By that time I had made five documentaries, and I was really finding myself more and more interested in the narrative of a film, in the sense that I would create these stories in the editing room. Sometimes I would also wish for more control over a light that would fall there or something that's happening over here, or whatever: story itself. So that propelled me, alongside with wanting an audience, to think of *Salaam Bombay* as a feature film.

SL: Did you ever edit documentary as if something had happened that hadn't really?

MN: No, no—not in the documentary form. Because I came from *cinema verité*—literally the truth of life.

SL: You believed in that?

MN: Yeah: truth. I mean it is manipulated simply because you're there and all that, but it is not docu-drama: you don't stage something by asking somebody to walk through a certain door twice. I didn't. You're just there, hoping that what you're filming is interesting.

*I do think that the truth is really always more powerful and stranger than fiction—and that is what documentary has given me in my fictional work.* That I go for authenticity and inexplicable truth—but I create, I stage that. I guess what I'm most excited about is this kind of seamless meeting between documentary and fiction: drama that feels utterly real but is heightened. So that's what I think I have pretty much done in my work.

SL: In feature filmmaking, you can, for example, choose to make the audience side with the bad as well as the good guys. Ethically, people wouldn't accept that in a documentary. Do you feel you enjoy greater creative freedom in features?

MN: Of course. Any influence that one has had in life can in a very tangible way be channeled into feature filmmaking. What I enjoy in doing fiction is precisely that you can portray sometimes whimsical, but always complicated universes. It is such an eclectic mélange, mixing great edges with beauty.

SL: Did people like possible investors directly take you seriously when you announced an interest in feature filmmaking?

MN: People who had invested in me before soon took me seriously, because they knew that I was serious about films.

I went first and only to the people who had invested in my documentaries. That's how I started. Channel Four, the French, the Germans—anybody who had bought my films from television. Anybody. But it was of course still very difficult to raise the money.

SL: So it was European financed?

MN: And Indian. And then I wrote grant proposals.

SL: Did you have any particular audience in mind when you wrote the script?

MN: Actually, the audience was really street kids in India who were fed on a diet of hardcore Bollywood productions. Anytime they make enough money, the theater is where those kids go.

There was no model before that which allowed me to even imagine success with the audience in America. Spike Lee and I, we are good friends and we used to share the same editing room in New York to save money. He had just finished *She's Gotta Have It*, which became a big success.

So I had these examples of independent successes around me in New York, but I never thought that an Indian film—made in Hindi about street kids in Bombay—could even go down that route. Forget about it! I swear I didn't even think about it. I was just, "Eyes on the prize; I have to make this film." I was totally silenced by these kids, whom I had encountered and lived around while I was making documentaries.

SL: So you imagined you might have to go back to India to do your films?

MN: It's not that I had an agenda and went, "I better go back to India." In fact, it's not like that at all. First and most important is that the idea must totally possess and obsess you. It was about, "Here's the story I want to tell." I saw their lives face to face for months, and for me, that idea was the one.

It's better. There is a line in the *Bhagavad-Gita*: "Beware the fruits of action." Don't tangle your fruits of action before you fully make the action. So I went into *Salaam Bombay* with that simple attitude. I mean to raise the money and make it was a total life and death kind of experience.

But then what happened to the film was a fairytale. It literally won everything. It went to the Oscars; it sold in every country. It was just one of those things. *And* with the profits of that movie we created the Salaam Bombay Trust, a center which is now thriving and has changed the Indian government's policy on street kids. More than five thousand street kids go through our centers every year. So the film did a lot on many levels.

SL: So you advise to do the action, not to think about the consequences—

MN: Yes. I think there is a lot of contamination of action by ambition. It contaminates your brain, you know? Especially in this culture, where you can be instantly famous; the younger you are and the more nerve you have, you can be that much more famous.

*The point for me is that you can still do what you want to do. I mean* Salaam Bombay *is an example of how you can do what you want without thinking of it all—and then suddenly they want you. You knock them out so hard that they want it.*

SL: You have done how many feature films now?

MN: I think at least ten . . . ten, seven, or eight, I think . . .

SL: How do these stories come to you?

MN: There are different ways. For *Salaam Bombay*, it was just seeing on a daily basis the total flamboyance of the street kids in the face of having nothing. Day after day they would pirouette, they would dance, they would do all kinds of wild stuff—but they had nothing. That would just inspire me. Then one thing led to another . . .

   With *Mississippi Masala*, it started by me being a brown person as a student in Harvard, in between black and white. I wanted to make a film about the hierarchy of color and this line that separated us all. That thing led me to the expulsions of Asians in Uganda. Each film has a different kind of hook that gets me.

SL: So let's discuss the creative process you went through concretely in the case of *Mississippi Masala*.

MN: I read a very interesting non-fiction story about an Asian family expelled from Uganda. Uganda expelled most of its Indians in 1972. So that family came to England and suddenly their life had been turned upside down. Then I read a piece in an Indian newspaper here in New York, that you cannot find Americans anymore who own an older Mississippi motel. Indians have simply taken over those.

   I thought this was an extraordinary trick of history, where Indians that had only known Africa as home were being expelled and landed in Mississippi, which itself was where the civil rights movement was born. Now, here they were surrounded by African-Americans who had never known Africa as their home. Then I thought, "What if there was an interracial love story between an Indian girl and a black man?"

SL: You wrote the script with Sooni Taraporevala?

MN: Yes, and the way we worked is that we both would go on research. Anywhere I could find them, I interviewed people who were Ugandan-Asian exiles. Then, we both went to Mississippi in a car, living in these Indian motels. Just observing, talking to people, eating meals, writing notes—just doing social research and talking all the time about what the story could be. Then we developed the story. Sooni writes the screenplay and dialogue. And then I edited it with her, and we exchange it; a very intimate collaboration. So that's how I work.

SL: So the story was fictional, assembled out of the many reality pieces you gathered?

MN: Yes. We would mix it out of everything. On a certain simple level, the storyline is about "what is home" and the irony of it: Indians and Africans who had never seen their continent, all in love with each other.

And it's about that hierarchy of color that I have been talking about. It's also about people like me who lived in these countries—people who live in between worlds. And in this case, Harry Patel, the Indian protagonist, was twice removed: he was an Indian, but not from India but Africa, then thrown out and now living in America.

SL: Are you more of an analytical or rather intuitive when thinking about how to tell your story?

MN: I have to be everything—analytical and emotional. Everything has an intention in feature filmmaking.

SL: Which you are also conscious of all the time?

MN: Firstly, you have to be aware of what's your intention of every moment. And then you have to be aware of how and with what elements you express and propel that intention. That is where the plasticity and the enormous richness of the cinematic medium come in. It can be done in so many different ways. Of course, it is really a beautiful blend in the image that is almost unself-conscious: the sound, the performance of a particular frame—every single thing.

SL: So you script has to maintain a certain openness in order to allow for that emotional cinematic moment to happen?

MN: You have to plead for that moment—you have to create it while shooting and then of course, the editing is the third time you write something. Also, you can help to create those moments through the tricks of editing [*laughing mischievously*]—that's how it happens.

SL: What role does humor take in your storytelling?

MN: For me it's very vital. For me, the sound of laughter is the sweetest sound. *I think that emotion, or pain, or tears are only that much more enhanced and effective if it is preceded or followed by laughter. And that is pretty much the principle of life to me—and of cinema.*

SL: What's the meaning of laughter to you then?

MN: I'm not interested in taking myself so seriously. It's pretentious. And I just find it offsetting what could otherwise become pathos or sentimental.

I'll give you an example of *The Namesake*: The scene is the mother and the father saying farewell to each other at the airport. She doesn't know this of course, but he will die and it is the last time she's going to see him. I wanted to make it a really deep love story. They are 50-something years old. They are of the old world, where you don't touch or say "I love you": nothing. They just separate. He is in a line of people who are going to board the plane; she is standing at a distance. The camera is over her shoulder. You see him in the long line, just looking and having eyes for her. You don't see her, but you see her hand waving. And that's the moment. You could create it with violence and have it all going crazy. But here's what I did: he doesn't move the line—and the people behind are starting to get nervous. They are patting him in that American, let's-get-on-with-it style. He smiles and realizes, "Oh god, I am just lost in you." Then he moves on. And she turns around smiling, because he also made her smile—and leaves.

SL: You visualized that already when writing or it only emerged on the set with the actors?

MN: It is not scripted and there are no words. In the script, it was just written as a moment of farewell. I thought that *The Namesake* is about travel: it's got movement; it's got people who live between worlds again. We're always moving somewhere. So this movement is the visual metaphor of the film. That's why I also use airports a lot. I was trying to think of how to look at the interior of the airport, when I saw an amazing photograph by Garry Winogrand—I love to look at contemporary photography and it is a big fuel for me. So I saw his picture showing a long line of people. It's just an image and I wanted it to shoot it this way. So I constructed this frame. I wanted to put all the ideas I just talked about into one frame because I don't have time . . . but I wanted to do it authoritatively

SL: So in this case, laughter helped you to punctuate the meaning of your narrative?

MN: I like to achieve at least two or three things in one moment. So you're looking at these two people and you know they love each other. But it's not enough to just show that. Everybody shows that. I want to show that and make you laugh, while at the same time making you understand something about the nature of the story.

SL: The framing of the images is very important to you. How do you manage to stay in control of that?

MN: It's a long process, because I bring a lot to the table using preparational material: photographs, painting, fabric, advertisements, anything—and of course some movies, too. So I create a sort of visual binder, which I share with all heads of department. Of course, I discuss notably with my DP, with who I then travel to look at the locations. He and I spend at least two weeks, designing and breaking down the scenes in those locations. I don't storyboard, I just know the shots. Then I look through the camera and I look at the actors—the frame is vital for it, but I really look at the performance. And that's it really.

SL: In your recent films, you're not credited as a writer anymore—

MN: I struggle with myself. It's a tricky thing to talk about—I don't know whether I want to. With struggle I mean I have a lot to do with the writing of the script. But I also feel that directors get enough credit already. So there is no point in getting all the credit in every single way.

SL: But you're as much involved in the scriptwriting as before?

MN: Yeah. Well, it depends: in *Vanity Fair* not, because it was a novel. I am very involved, but more by giving briefs and editing the script.

SL: Is it as easy to identify with the script if you don't write it yourself?

MN: *Completely investing myself is the only way I know how to make and direct a film. I mean completely, so that I can truly capture the moment.* It's always full on. A script is of course vital, but if you don't capture the essence of what the moment is about, then what?

Obviously, as a director I have to know everything—everything has to make sense to me, so I can explain to everybody why we are doing it.

SL: Do you have to know that ahead of time or do these things become clear as you go along?

MN: I am very prepared. I usually don't have very much money and I have an expansive vision. I want to achieve a lot and my films are very dense. So it has to be hugely prepared in advance: number one. Number two: I am so prepared that I am calm at the moment of execution. I am not going to be frantic. And when you're not frantic and at that state of receptiveness, that's when inspiration truly blooms. Then you can see what an actor is doing, and what they are comfortable and not comfortable with. Or sounds that are supposed to happen at that time; or a location that suddenly is not available and a new location has to be immediately invented with the same resources.

SL: Sounds are already very much in your head when you shoot?

MN: Sound is very important to me. I am like a nut about sound. A lot of sound is done in the design later, but I often look and occulate my frames with objects that can give me the possibilities of those sounds later. The film I just did is a deeply atmospheric film, and the images are imbued with that. But while the objects and sounds are very important, in the end it is always about the people in my films.

SL: How do you work with your actors?

MN: It varies, depending on what kind of actors I work with. You know, in *Monsoon Wedding*, I worked largely with non-actors and mixed them with two legendary actors. We had a three-week workshop where we just trained like in the theater—from the morning to the night; everybody together, scene by scene. I would be available as much as possible. I like to create a safe place where we can all make fools of ourselves during that time. All the cobwebs and questions are answered before we're shooting. On *Monsoon Wedding*, we had 30 days to shoot a massive production. That was the experiment of it.

SL: Having non-actors was a choice and part of your experiment?

MN: Everything is a choice. I thought I would just cast the best actor. But sometimes the non-actor just felt absolutely right or real. I was very open. In all my films, I mix stars with non-actors or first-time actors.

I was never insecure about how to work with these actors, because I was myself an actor. And I love actors. Somehow that comes to me easily—because I know what I want from them and I make them feel safe, helping the best I can to make my idea come true.

Obviously, the kind of actor I am working with influences my approach. With a pro, it would be more like a reading. With the other actors it's important just to be available. With the street kids, it was a combination of physical work like yoga and all sorts of workshop kinds of techniques. On *The Namesake*, I did rehearsals with the actors on the set, so they could really understand what it felt like before the crew would come in. So I use very different techniques.

SL: Do you like to shoot a lot of material?

MN: No, I never had that luxury. I shoot maybe three to five takes of a given shot. But if I am not getting all I want, I just try to find another way to get what I want.

I have two editors that I work with; one at a time. Allyson Johnson who cut *The Namesake*, also edited *Monsoon Wedding* and *Vanity Fair*.

I am present at every moment of the editing process. I mean she does a lot of work, but I have to be there because of the shaping of the scene. There are so many ways to do that; it's not just about which takes you choose.

SL: How important are test screenings to you?

MN: I test screen a lot and they teach me a lot. By its nature, confusion obstructs clarity. When you're confused, my intent is obviously not clear to you and I am wasting your time. That is what I want to get rid of, so that all my intentions are really clear; and that I am clear with you about what you are feeling and thinking. *The worst is if I fail to move or engage the audience. If there's just something they are observing but not feeling, then I feel that I have failed.*

SL: But how do you filter audience reactions? They can be so diverse, often even contradictory.

MN: By intuition. You have to be fierce, though. You know the joke is, "I am very open, as long as it's me that has the last word." And that is true: I really listen to everything very, very attentively. But I have to know that in the end, I am listening to myself.

SL: And you have indeed managed to stay very independent—

MN: It suits my spirit—even when I only had myself in my bedroom [*laughing*]. Over the years, I learned to know where I am most happy. It's very important because filmmaking is one part of my life—a big part. But I am equally a homemaker, a very passionate gardener, and I run Maisha: the institute for East African and South Asian screenwriters and directors I have founded. I have lots of interests.

So you know, it has to be worth it for me. The choice to make a film is always made at the sacrifice of other choices: always! So I obviously have to evaluate the experience I will have. *Yesterday I was offered a very interesting film—fantastic idea and I liked it very much. I went there to tell them that I was going to do it. I met one of the two producers, and he was wonderful. And then the other guy came and he was such a disaster. So disharmonious, such an arrogant prick, that I thought to myself, "Would I want to be in this company for a year in my life?" No way!*

SL: Unless you were in a position where you could fire him?

MN: Yeah [*laughing*]—I would! But usually what happens is that I have my own ideas and I just bash them through. And as I produce my own films, I don't have to even deal with these people.

SL: Is it true that you were offered to direct *Harry Potter and the Goblet of Fire*?

MN: Sort of true. When I was asked to meet on it, I was already deep in preparation of *The Namesake*. And yet, everybody around me forced me to take it seriously. Like, "How can you not?" And that created a lot of tension: I felt like I had to take it seriously. Again, it was relative to my experience: I had just come back from England and I wasn't sure about going immediately back there. It was about quality of what was going to happen to my life at the moment. Harry Potter just wasn't worth it.

SL: Did the mere proportions of that production and its budget attract you or rather keep you away?

MN: Listen: what you're working on in these bigger budget films is the same act—it's the same thing. In fact, you work much harder on smaller budget films. I mean *Vanity Fair* was 24 million dollars, which is not exactly a small budget. But the act of making a film and saving money remains the same. Of course, *Harry Potter* would have been a learning experience with computer work and all, but frankly, it's not my cup of tea.

SL: When financing your films now, are people knocking at your door, or is it as much a hassle as it used to be?

MN: Oh no, I have no problem financing at all. It's never been fully simple because it depends on the subject—and my subject matter is never mainstream in an easy sense. I mean I have to work on it, but I have some very, very passionate budget supporters.

SL: How do you calculate your budget? Do you at all go by its market value and the potential size of the target audience?

MN: I go by what the film will actually cost to make. With a film like *The Namesake*, which is completely my own production, you make the most rigorous budget based on your vision. Then you go ahead with it. Lydia Pilcher, my producing partner, and Bart Walker, my agent, we create a plan and a budget. Then the three of us decide who we're going to approach for the finances. For *The Namesake*, it took me two months to raise nine and a half million dollars.

*Vanity Fair* is a very different example because it's a studio film. They evaluate and you also evaluate. It's all about money. They would never make a profit if it was a hundred million budget—if it is *Star Wars*, you can do that. But you cannot even think of a period drama for more than 20 or 25 million dollars. It wouldn't make economic sense.

SL: Does your own production company Mirabai Films finance any proportion of the budget?

MN: *I* don't have any money. No, no. It's financed through financiers. I use my own money to develop my work, so that nobody owns my brain and my idea while I'm formulating it. Once the idea is formulated and the script is written—I pay up to that moment—I finance the film and reimburse myself the money that it cost to develop it. That's how I work.

SL: You never worked your way up any kind of hierarchy, as has virtually no A-list director. Instead, becoming a first-time director seems to require a lot of cheekiness and unearned ego. Might such a system possibly make it easier for young men than for young woman directors to emerge?

MN: It depends where you are coming from. A lot of South Asian films are directed by women. There, you find examples of those that have not responded to a hierarchy—who have just believed in themselves and got it done. If you look here, it's almost per capita harder: you know women go through the system, and then they get subsumed by the system as opposed to believing in themselves and just going for it.

That is not the case in cultures I come from: we lead nations without a blink of an eye. It's uncanny, the kind of self-belief that lots of us have coming from our parts of the world: we really believe that we can do anything.

SL: So that's the kind of attitude you grew up with?

MN: And it's totally not uncommon. I always work for myself.

SL: Might it be that your minority role here in the States has helped you to beat the odds of the system and not being subsumed by it?

MN: That's possible. But I think that this culture gave me also a lot of power and strength: that everything is possible. At university you could study any and everything. It was not prescribed and strict the way it was when I grew up. *So I really felt that it was absolutely possible to graduate from college at the age of 21, write a script, raise money, and make my own movie.* I'm sure if had lived only in India, it would have taken me many years longer to get to know the machinations of how to make that movie happen. Twenty-five years ago in Harvard, there were seminars, there were other people. Everybody I knew had three jobs. We were waitresses at night, gallerists during the day, and then we would write proposals. You know living the dual life: getting your money, but living as an artist. Everything was about excellence. One didn't have that kind of rigorous life in India: it was much too comfortable, and there wasn't that kind of hunger that is under your bum all the time.

SL: Do you feel like an entrepreneur for your own cause?

MN: I mean people say I have a business head, but I don't think so. I just have a business head until the moment I have the money it takes to make my films. Then I am making my film. I don't sit around thinking I'm an entrepreneur.

What I have is the refusal to accept no for an answer. If somebody rejects me, I walk along to another person that will accept me. I believe in what I am doing and I find a way. And fortunately I made enough money and enough prestige for whomever, so that I now have a home where they believe in me.

SL: Are the hurdles a young filmmaker faces to finance his or her own film then really more rooted inside that person?

MN: Yeah. It depends on that situation, but they are not to accept it. You know I teach film at Columbia. There is one uncanny thing that happens: I recognize who is a filmmaker and who is not.

SL: In their work exclusively or also in the person?

MN: It's always in the work. You can't just look at the person's appearance or their intelligent talk. Sometimes it is slightly tragic when you see somebody paving the streets for years who's really not a filmmaker; maybe. It's hard to see that.

SL: Do you tell the people directly what you think?

MN: I sometimes do if I'm close enough to them and if they want to hear it. But I don't go around warranting my opinions [*laughing*].

SL: What if somebody is a filmmaker in your eyes and struggles after all?

MN: That also happens—that's the tragedy of it. There are a hundred reasons how it could happen. You know what it is? This filmmaking world is so obsessive, that it has to kind of almost choose you. And if you have the capacity to take on less creative jobs, then you're not cut out for it. Whereas if you can't handle those jobs and it's just not something that you would consider, then you can probably handle film.

I have friends like that, who are making maybe five crappy Hollywood films, so that they can put their money together for their own project. But after the seven or eight years it's taken them to make these crappy films, they ain't got the heat anymore, baby—they haven't go the fire in their bellies anymore. They changed, and they can't go back to sitting on an apple box instead of a trailer, you know?

So you decide what your life is. You cannot say, "I'm going to do that for a few years." *I always say to my students, "Do not consider anything you do as a stepping stone for something else." Be what you do as fully as possible, because you have no idea where it will take you.*

I made *Monsoon Wedding* out of making a documentary before that. I was very depressed and made a documentary on laughter and people who take laughing seriously. It's called *The Laughing Club of India*. It was shot on DV by me and friend of mine in a truck: for two weeks, finding eighteen people who take laughing seriously and making a portrait of their lives. I cut the film for six weeks. We invented a form that was very interesting and free-wheeling. It was a portrait of the city of Bombay through a montage of old songs, interspersed with those eighteen people that take laughing seriously. It was a wonderful film.

And that gave me the exact style—the monsoon, the structure, the montage: the stylistic genesis of *Monsoon Wedding* was from that documentary.

If I hadn't made that little film for no money and with nobody, I would not have made *Monsoon Wedding*, one of my most successful films in my life. I didn't have any idea what I was making the film for—I wasn't making it for a reward.

SL: Can you relate to anxieties—often of financial nature—that could harm your creative playfulness and hunger for cinematographic exploration?

MN: Oh yes, I can! I felt it a lot. These days, New York City and the overhead are substantial. Most of what I do now is non-profit. It's not that I have a lot of income. I am making a low budget film for one year and a half and I am running Maisha, a non-profit organization. That's what I am doing. So it is not exactly rolling in the dough.

SL: How did you manage and deal with your anxieties in your early filmmaking days?

MN: I dealt with my situation very carefully. You know: 138 dollars a month rent. Eating out for seven dollars a meal was considered special. Keep a very simply life. Work and live cheaply.

SL: Did you ever feel that those money issues ate up your time, which otherwise you could have invested somewhere else?

MN: Of course, and also the pressure of that. But it also very much had its positive sides creatively. You know I used to work as a waitress in an Indian restaurant. I could see the hierarchy of color there, with the illegal Mexicans in the basement skinning the chickens; and me.

Every experience—even that of being a waitress—has directly informed my professional documentaries: *So Far from India* was about an Indian who lived here. I wasn't afraid to take on these jobs. You can't be precious about these things—you just do it, because you have to. I didn't want to ask my family to endlessly support me. That's why I did it.

SL: If a young filmmaker has the alternative, should they rather take on an assistant job in the film industry or wait on tables to support themselves?

MN: I think it depends on whom you assist. If it is a generous director—a generous artist you admire who'd talk to you and who is accessible, showing you more than just how to pick up their laundry—then it would be great to be an assistant. Then you will see it first hand and you'll see the unglamorous world of its challenges; from start to finish of a project. Whether you are on a film set where you observe, or in the trenches of developing material with a director: the real world of film is important to witness if you want to make a film. That's what you will witness as an assistant. Don't make a career of it, though.

Always inform yourself about everything that you can inform yourself with. As a director, it is very important to know what each one of your team members does. Do not just be woolly about it.

SL: Would your advice to men be different from that you'd give to women—Asian or non-Asian?

MN: I don't think so. Obviously the focus of whatever they want to do will be different.

*The other piece of advice I would give is to never be afraid of who you are, but to turn your distinctiveness into your motivation.* The fact that I'm an Indian woman in New York City makes me the one who tells the story about the Indian immigrant in New York the best way. That's what I would say in my grant proposal 25 years ago, "I know something you can't know, because you're not me. So therefore give me money, so I can show you what I know." Rather than saying, "I'm going to make the best American movie, even though I am Indian."

SL: Do you feel that your decision to direct was in itself a strategy of coming to grips with your own identity and the complex person you had grown to be over the years?

MN: I think it's precisely because I know where my roots are that I can explore. And it's because I am secure about my identity that I like to explore the whole state of being between identities or between worlds. This is the theme of *The Namesake* and many other films I've made.

Yet the world is becoming so increasingly porous and fluid that people are increasingly settling and unsettling in other lands. And I am always very curious about that journey and the universality of it—it is a balancing act and a dilemma at the same time.

Cinema gives me the umbrella to inhabit even completely different worlds so fully that I can hope to find the truth in them. And then if I do, they become kind of universal stories about love or whatever the theme is. It can go from understanding the trashed world of *Hysterical Blindness* in New Jersey to inhabiting an upper class Indian landscape in *Monsoon Wedding*. For me it is about embracing the global quality of our lives—the way I actually live it personally. So that's what I like to do.

All these issues used to be my confusion, but now it's my energy, I suppose. Out of that energy, I create a world that I want to bring people into: to see, to hear, to feel, to laugh, to maybe weep. That's the real privilege of making cinema. It is absolutely extraordinary to move people in such a way. It's a very big privilege.

# Section Two: Emerging from Inside Hollywood

# Pollack, Sydney

**DIRECTOR'S CUT:**
"Being one person isn't really enough for me . . . making films is a way of vicariously becoming all these other people and seeing the world through their eyes."

**BORN:**
1934, Lafayette, Indiana

**BACKGROUND:**
Actor

**FILMS (selection):**
This Property is Condemned—1966
They Shoot Horses, Don't They—1969
Jeremiah Johnson—1972
The Way We Were—1973
Three Days of the Condor—1975
Tootsie—1982
Out of Africa—1985
The Firm—1993
Sabrina—1995
The Interpreter—2005

**MAIN GENRES:**
Drama, Romance, Thriller, Comedy

SYDNEY POLLACK: I was born and grew up in a small town in Indiana. At the time, the Midwest was something of an island between the two coasts. It was a relatively unsophisticated, uncultured area. It was a factory town area with a good University, Notre Dame. But it was not a strong area of cultural activity or interest; there was no stimulation in that respect. I can't recall having access to art of any kind. You know, primarily there were three big factories and that's what most people did to make a living. My father was a pharmacist and my mother was just a housewife.

SL: As a child, what did you think about adult life and what it would be like?

SP: Well I suppose initially, like almost all teenagers, I was not a particularly happy teenager and felt like I was weird or different or at least not like everybody else. *I assumed that when I grew up, I would understand both myself and the world better, and feel less of an outsider or less strange.* A part of that was growing up in an area where there was almost no Jewish population at all and I was Jewish. I was not religious at all. Neither my mother nor my father went to a synagogue or celebrated the holidays, though I had grandparents on both sides, who were quite religious. When I would see them I would get kind of imbued with this background. But I lived in an area, where you know, I think there were maybe five or six Jewish families in the town. I knew one or two. So it was very much a minority at a time when the country was still extremely divided in terms of minority groups, whether they were black, Jewish, or other. It was before the 60s. And I suppose that contributed somewhat to my feeling as something of an outsider if you will. I didn't feel like I belonged in a synagogue, but I also didn't feel like I belonged with everybody else, because there was so much consciousness of a kind of anti-Semitism there.

SL: Switching perspectives: where would you say that today you are still the very same person, with the same fascinations and interests, as you were back then?

SP: Well it's never changed. I mean in truth, I still feel very much a part of the kid that I was in South Bend, Indiana, which is where I grew up. I mean that part never changed. I have extremely clear and vivid memories. I still have a deep kind of attachment of my first girlfriends there and a sense of what it was like to be first coming into puberty in high school and all that—trying to play football and not being very good at it and then developing this kind of strange interest in theater and feeling terribly self-conscious about it. You know I wasn't playing football, and Indiana was a big football and basketball town because of Notre Dame. So being interested in acting wasn't a very popular thing for you socially. But I felt extremely at one with myself at that age. You know it's just that at my age now, having lived as long as I have, I have different insecurities—they are not the same—but still have loads of insecurities.

SL: How do you explain your interest in theater that gradually took over in you?

SP: There was a very, very, unusually strong-minded guy who ran the theater department in all of the school system of South Bend—about four big grade schools and four big high schools. And when I was maybe in the third, fourth, or fifth grade, he came round to our school and held kind of auditions for kids. He was going to do an original review and we all showed up. He gave us each something to do: it was a terrifying thing to get up in front of classmates and do this—I think I had to sing a song or something like that. But I can remember that it was also very exciting to do and I started little bits in plays directed by this guy called James Louis Cassidy. He was a very culturally literate guy for South Bend, Indiana, and he taught us a lot about classical theater and I continued to do that. I tried to play football as well so I wouldn't get beat up for being in the plays. But I did stay with the plays. In high school I started to do bigger and bigger plays—some of them well known, some of them original.

Then when it came time to get out of high school and figure out what was ahead, I had a talk with my father. He really couldn't afford to send me to college, but he wanted me to and I wanted to. I thought I'd go to Northwestern. But there was still a draft going on in 1952. What I said to my father was: you know if I wait a couple of years I'll get drafted and then I'll have the GI bill and then maybe I could go to college. I had saved up money from jobs. I had jobs all my life, delivering papers or driving lumber trucks—whatever worked. I talked him into letting me go to New York on my own and try to go to an acting school.

SL: You went to the New York Neighborhood Playhouse [NP]?

SP: I got accepted at the NP, which turned out to be an extraordinary school. At the time, I didn't realize it, nor did I have any ambitions towards becoming an actor for film, let alone becoming a director. I simply went there because an old friend of mine told me that this would be the place to go to learn acting in New York. The course was for two years—studying dance with Martha Graham and acting with Sanford Meisner. I also studied fencing and mime. Altogether, I was very, very fortunate to have had this opportunity to study with all those great teachers I encountered at the Playhouse.

Soon after I got out, I started to make a living by getting small acting parts around town, starting to make an OK living at it. Then, when I was nineteen, Sandy Meisner asked me to come back as a teacher. Sandy was really the most influential man in my life and the reason really why I accepted his offer was to be able to keep observing him at work.

Then I subsequently did get drafted, but by that time I was convinced that I wanted to try to have a life in the theater. I didn't ever think about film or television. I was at that time giving acting classes and that's what I came back and earned my living at. Then while I was in the army, I got married.

SL: What was it your learning experience at the NP and the impact it had on you?

SP: I learned first of all how to form a goal and how to decide what one is trying to do when one acts. *What it was all about, really, was trying to understand what truthful behavior was and what theatrical behavior was and how to find theatrical behavior that was filled with truth: behavior that was both interesting and unusual and theatrical but also rooted in the truth.* That was a lot more difficult than I had imagined. And that became, while I was unaware of it, the foundation for all the directing I did later on. I was only thinking of it in terms of an actor and teaching it. But without knowing it, I was really forming a very strong foundation for a technique as a director.

Everything I have ever done as a director—writing, production, casting, design, staging—the genesis, the seed of it has come from the work I did absorbing the principles and ideas of Meisner, trying to understand how to break down a scene and then a play in terms of goals and wishes and objectives—tasks that an actor sets for himself or herself, and how behavior is derived from attacking that task.

It's a truthfulness that is not a literal truth but theatricality and a choice that's executed with a kind of truth. And that can be applied to every aspect of directing, not just acting but to the writing of it, the photographing, the editing, and so on.

SL: So without your formation as an actor you wouldn't have had the competence to be a director.

SP: Well, I don't think I would have had the technique; I would have probably had an intuition, and sometimes that's more important. But the technique is a safety net for you—at least I have a systematized approach, which I can use when I sit down with a script and ask myself a series of questions: what is that about?

SL: What questions would you concretely ask yourself?

SP: The first thing you ask as a director is: what is this about? The answer to this can't be: the story of a film. You know, I have just done *The Interpreter*, which is a thriller. Now the idea of what it's about for me is not something that has to be visible to an audience. But it serves as a superstructure like the studs and the steel girders in a building that are not visible when the building is finished, but which really hold it up. So when I say to myself that this picture is about diplomacy versus violence; and this is a picture about one person that believes in the power of words and another person who's totally cynical and believes words are used to lie—like politicians and world leaders—and that action is the only thing that counts. That gives me some sort of structure around which to build a movie. That doesn't mean that I ever say those words, or that I ever let the audience know that's what it's about, but if you were to analyze it you'd see that that's what it's about. It's giving me a path to go down. And then I have to try to break down each scene from that sort of spine or armature that makes up the heart of the movie, like the trunk of the tree, when all the scenes are branches and then leaves, and so on; but they are all coming from this trunk. They are all springing from this central idea if you will. And it is the way an actor works on a part; but it also can be very, very productive for a director to work that way.

SL: You have treated an unusual amount of different genres. Does that come naturally to you, or does each genre require a qualitatively different attitude and approach?

SP: Each genre has certain demands, but that doesn't mean that the central concerns can't be similar. I mean I am the same man when I direct whatever it is: if I am doing a comedy like *Tootsie*, or a drama like *Out of Africa*, or a thriller like *Three Days of the Condor*, or a western *The Electric Horseman*, or *Jeremiah Johnson*, I am still the same man.

I am trying to observe certain rules of the genre but I'm also trying to explore what interests me primarily, which is always men and women and the central argument that separates them; the thing that keeps permanent committed relationships almost impossibly difficult. They happen, but they are always difficult. All love stories—the greatest love stories—have been about irreconcilable obstacles that can't be overcome. *Romeo and Juliet*, *Tristan and Isolde*, *Heloise and Abelard*, *Doctor Zhivago*, or *Brief Encounter*: the greatest love stories do not resolve themselves where the lovers walk into the sunset. They usually are couples that cannot get together and that's been true for all of the films that I've made. *It doesn't matter whether I am making a thriller or a comedy or whatever—I'm always doing love stories: they are all love stories.*

SL: In how far do you feel restricted by established genre rules?

SP: You don't have to follow all of them. *Jeremiah Johnson*, for example was a rather unusual western; I mean it was unusual enough that it was the first western ever to come to Cannes. It wasn't a guy in a black hat and a guy in a white that are shooting it out on horses, but it was a western nonetheless. It was almost a silent movie but again, the heart of it was a man and a woman and a child and the tragedy that happened to them. But I still had certain rules that I had to observe. There have to be certain tests of strengths when you're doing mythical, heroic characters. Those characters need a series of tests that they fail or pass. And they are tests of will and stamina and courage. And the characters become wise by the end in a certain way. So that that man was a baby in the landscape in the beginning that became a giant in the landscape by the end. That's rather traditional. In a comedy like *Tootsie*, which is based on a pattern of farce, where the confusion breeds more confusion until in the third act all of these confusions start to pay off and fight each other.

So you have a guy who's trying to hide the fact that he's pretending to be a woman, falling in love with a woman who doesn't know that he's a guy and is about to find out, while his best friend who's in love with *him* doesn't know that he's taken her part away, while the father of the girlfriend he's in love with doesn't know he's a man and falls in love with him; and another guy on the soap opera is proposing to him. So you have to start accelerating these confusions. It's like all they do. A farce is where everybody retires to the castle and they all sneak out on the balcony and sneak in each others' rooms and then somebody knocks on the door: you know that is a classical structure. But nevertheless, I'm trying to keep that comedy as real as possible. My way of working on *Tootsie* was to forget that it was a comedy. I mean nobody laughed on that set. Nobody laughed. We approached it like Chekhov because that made it funnier to me. I do not have the gift of sight gags or something like Blake Edwards had, who was really an extraordinarily imaginative director of a certain kind of movie—he was the best there was. That's simply not an area that I have any strong muscles in. Where I felt capable was the area of reality; what's the truth of this. How close to the truth can I get with this absolute ridiculous, outrageous situation?

SL: And the humor comes naturally out of that reality?

SP: The humor comes out of the fact that the situation itself is absurd. And the more truth it's played with the better it is. And that's a lesson I learned from watching "Candid Camera." *You know there's nothing funnier than "Candid Camera," because it's absolutely real people doing truthful things. So there you've got a rule.*

*Three Days of the Condor* is a thriller. A thriller dictates a certain kind of disciplined pace. You can't slow it down. You can do it a little, but a thriller requires you to define in a very difficult way the difference between mystery and confusion, which is very hard to do. You do not want to know the plot of a thriller in the beginning or it's ruined. But you have to gage what the audience will find appetizingly mysterious or annoyingly confusing. It's those differences that may something work or not work in that genre. Somebody can say, "Well this is just hopeless: I can't follow what the hell's going on here" or somebody can say, "Geez, I don't quite know what's happening, but I can't wait for the next development." That's a different thing.

SL: During which stages do you feel you are at your most creative? During preparation where the key ideas are born, or during principal photography when you can actually transform them, or the editing when you see everything coming together?

SP: Truthfully, they are equally creative. I think that there are many approaches to directing. But if I can divide them into two main approaches, there is an approach to movie-making where you know everything: you know every shot, every line of dialogue is locked, and the filming is really essentially a recording that you have already given birth to in the formative stage. There are many great directors that work that way and many great films made that way; and that is a way of working I can't do. I don't understand how to do it and always feel bad that I can't do it. Because no matter how hard I prepare—and I get a lot of things *solved* in the preparation work—it's maybe a third of it. When I start to shoot, I rewrite every single day that I am shooting and I'm constantly on the phone with writers. Or I'm writing and changing myself—actors get very upset with me; crews get very upset with me. And I come in every day with new stuff and give it to the actors or the scriptie or whatever. So it changes there.

Then I come into the editing process and say, "Oh wait a minute. You know, that scene and this scene and this scene are all too rhythmically similar. I've got to separate them now or I'm going to make a montage out of these three pieces," or whatever: so writing goes on. I mean the creative part for me doesn't finish until the end, and I wouldn't say there's one that is better than the other.

SL: Are all equally enjoyable?

SP: No—in all candor, I would say that I am not a director that enjoys directing. I find it full of too much anxiety to say it is enjoyable. I obviously enjoy having *made* a movie: I enjoy when it's over with. Then I'm glad I did it, I'm happy that I did it. But the process itself seems extremely difficult to me and I go through hell every time I make a movie.

SL: Tell me essential attributes or character traits that you feel a good director must have.

SP: Well I think the primary one is patience. You have to have patience.

Also, you have to be fluid inside your own personality in the sense that you have to be all of the characters. You can't take sides. You have to be the man and the woman and the crook and the bad guy and so on to make a really complex film that reflects life in some way; unless you're making a fable or a cartoon. But you need to be able to have the kind of imagination that allows you to be somebody else completely. And that's not always easy. *I think that's why people who work in the arts in general tend to be more liberal and less conservative because they are accustomed to seeing many sides of the question.* It's very unnatural to them to be, let's say, committed to only one point of view and everything else is evil and wrong.

Oh, and you have to have a lot of stamina as a director.

SL: Where has yours been coming from over the last 50 years?

SP: Well, because one life isn't really enough. I mean being one person isn't being enough for me. I am just one person at a time: I have one age, one family, one marriage, I have one relationship: I want more than that! And making films is two years out of my life and a way of living with a whole other group of people and *becoming* them in a way. You know I have to become Jeremiah Johnson: I learn what it's like to be a fur trapper or whatever I'm working on at the time. Or I can become both, the man and the woman: I can feel what is *that* like. I have to be her too—I mean, I have to find pleasure in seeing the world through her eyes; and that broadens my life enormously. I mean I am never going to be literally those people. So making films is a way of vicariously becoming all these other people and seeing the world through their eyes; and that's a very enriching experience. Of the nineteen films I've made, they are all different characters. And I had a big learning experience each time I made a film having to try on these arguments.

SL: Do you ever encounter conflict within yourself when working on a project between your director's perspective and your producer's perspective?

SP: Very rarely. The discipline it requires to be both is part of what drives you to be inventive. If there was no discipline and you could just do everything you wanted, I don't think the satisfaction would be so great. If you could just say, "you know what, I want to do this for the next five days in five different ways no matter what it costs." The fact that I have to finish today and that I don't have 10,000 people but only 400 or four that I have to make look like 10,000: that's a challenge that sometimes leads to the most creative of *all* your work; so I don't find the two things to be in conflict. Every once in a while, yes! Every once in a while I say I wish I had another million dollars because then I would shoot this way instead of this way. But most of the time it's a good thing. I prefer producing my own pictures to be honest.

SL: Looking at Hollywood today and the changes that happened over the last 30 or 40 years: which of these do you regret, and which do you feel are actually a good developments?

SP: *Well I think guys of my generation, we're somewhat sad by the industry's consolidation, which has narrowed the possible choices— there are a lot of movies that I have made that I wouldn't be able to make today;* I probably wouldn't be able to do *Jeremiah Johnson*; I don't know. The fact that the studios are all owned by multinational corporations has created a sort of blockbuster mentality where all the studio films are looking to be blockbuster movies. That is: movies enjoyed by everybody in the world, everywhere. Whereas the movies of the 70s—let's say that twenty-year period from the middle 60s to the middle 80s—was I think as great a period America has ever had: some of the greatest movies were made because the variety was limitless. Studios were still individual small houses; movies did not have to make 100 million dollars prior to *Jaws*. You know a movie would cost two or three million dollars and if it earned back ten million dollars that was hugely profitable—

SL: Any improvements?

SP: No, not necessarily. The penetration of movies is bigger. Everybody in the world has become movie conscious. Everybody knows about movies, everybody knows the grosses of movies, everybody knows the technicians in movies: it's a movie-literal world suddenly. I simply think that's kind of fun.

SL: You were one of the founding members of the Sundance Institute. With which ideals and goals in mind did you decide to join?

SP: This is something Redford talked about for years, and I had made a lot of films with him. The idea was always to find an alternative to the Hollywood system; to find a way to make special projects of special interest that maybe 20 million people didn't have to see; maybe a million people could see and it would be successful: the same I was saying before. All that time we were interested in what were the alternatives to getting accepted in this mainstream Hollywood world; where could one work more experimentally, more boldly, where could one break a few rules, where could one try specialized subjects dealing with minorities, and dealing with many of the subjects that were taboo in Hollywood movies; also find and nurture new talent. And it has been an enormous success story.

SL: So what would you recommend a filmmaker today that is starting out?

SP: Today it's a different world. If you're a young director today I'd say make a film. You can make a film for a thousand dollars now—less! With inexpensive good digital cameras and editing equipment on computers there isn't anything stopping you. Before all of this, there was a catch-22. You couldn't get a job until someone wanted to trust you with millions of dollars. Nobody would trust you with millions of dollars till they saw a movie that you had made. But you could never make a movie because no one would give you a first movie. This is not true anymore. You can come out of film school with a thesis movie—or you just go make a movie, without film school. *Borrow a thousand dollars from your parents and go make a movie.*

SL: By watching your films, what can we learn about the person Sydney Pollack?

SP: I don't know. I'd just say you have to take it from the films. I'm doing it, I'm inside: I don't think I could possibly be objective at the same time . . .

# Davis, Andrew

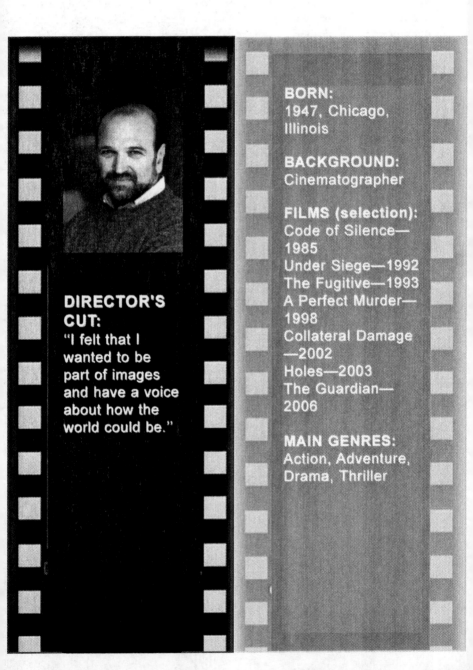

**DIRECTOR'S CUT:**
"I felt that I wanted to be part of images and have a voice about how the world could be."

**BORN:**
1947, Chicago, Illinois

**BACKGROUND:**
Cinematographer

**FILMS (selection):**
Code of Silence—1985
Under Siege—1992
The Fugitive—1993
A Perfect Murder—1998
Collateral Damage—2002
Holes—2003
The Guardian—2006

**MAIN GENRES:**
Action, Adventure, Drama, Thriller

ANDREW DAVIS: I feel very lucky to have had my parents because they are very creative and socially conscious people. They actually met in a Chicago theater in the 1930s, when my mother was only eighteen, my father 23. They were involved in socially conscious, progressive left-wing theater in a group called the Chicago Repertory Group, which had people like Studs Terkel as members. They performed Clifford Odets and stood on picket lines for strikes in unions, fighting fascism and depression going on. Those were very exciting times. My father went off to World War II, landed in Normandy. My mother was raising my older sister. When my father returned from the war, he did radio for a while to support the family, though he ultimately became a wholesale drug salesman—but he always kept his hand in the theater when he could, he really didn't like his work very much. Much later in his life, he got back into acting, performing in movies like *Risky Business* and *Thief*; also in my own productions such as *Stony Island*, *Code of Silence*, *The Package*, and *Holes*.

But I grew up around actors—people that were my parents' friends from youth, who'd come over and reminisce and tell stories and act out scenes from plays. So I was always comfortable around actors.

And at a very early age, I was interested in photography. I don't know why. I was a member of the South Chicago YMCA Photography Club. Funny thing is that years later, when shooting *The Fugitive*, that YMCA was two blocks away from where we were shooting one of Harrison's hideouts.

Then later on in grammar school, I found myself projecting movies to the classes—I was a projectionist. By the time I got to high school, my interest in photography had somewhat lessened, but I got very involved in music. I was mainly a guitar player and I had a band which performed Bob Dylan songs. *The vice-principal of my school said to me, "You know, the FBI used to investigate kids like you who sing subversive songs, you understand?"* I was very aware of the politics of the 60s on my life, because the civil rights movement was going on and the antiwar movement was beginning as Vietnam was just cranking up. I had always felt that I wanted to be a part of images and have a voice about alternative visions of how the world could be. So I became a journalism-major at the University of Illinois, studying from '64 to '68, which were very volatile times in America.

SL: So growing up, you developed a sense of the suggestive powers that images can have, first attracting you to photography, then also journalism. Did you ever think about using them in film?

AD: Films were not on the radar, really. I went to movies, but I didn't think about making them. At a very early age, I asked my mother, "What would you have done if you could have done anything in your life?" She told me, she would have been a photographer. So when I went to college, I studied journalism, but also did photography. I worked in a television station, I was in a band, and I did lighting for theater. Then, one of my classmates was a guy named Tom Holman. Tom is the creator of *THX* and I got a real technical background from him. I had a really wonderful experience at the University of Illinois in terms of being able to do all these things; and there I also started to watch movies extensively.

SL: So it was at university that you woke up to the world of cinema?

AD: I was pretty aware of the world outside cinema before. It was the height of the Vietnam War. I was involved in the civil rights movement: I went to Alabama, doing voter registration work to get blacks to vote for the first time; it was very dangerous to do that kind of work in those days.

Then, I got a job in college, working for a film unit—they didn't really have a film program at the university, but they had a film unit that made documentaries and training films as propaganda for the United States Information Agency. I remember working on a documentary for the USIA called *Spooks* about how wonderful Tai students were doing in the United States.

A Canadian named John Weir was part of the film unit. He taught me how to load a magazine and to be a filmmaker. So that was really very exciting.

I graduated with the ability to take pictures, load magazines, and shoot film; but I didn't know what to actually do now.

I remembered the first thing that my photography teacher Art Sinsabaugh—a very famous photographer—said to me, "Everything you need to learn about photography you can learn in six months. What's really important is what's in your heart and in your head."

SL: So you had interests that led you into two directions: you were very political, but at the same time had a keen interest in various artistic, especially visual ways of expressing yourself. Did you initially find it difficult to bring together both aspects?

AD: Well yes—first of all *I was very aware of how my father was sort of caught in a position of doing a job he didn't want to do.* And actually, I worked my way through college washing dishes, working in fraternity houses and in Chicago steel mills during the summer. In fact, I have not had a regular job since I was nineteen years old. I've been freelancing, allowing me to find freedom and to be able to travel and see the world. And that's where journalism and photography were very exciting to me.

So when I got out of school, I didn't know whether I was going to be a still photographer or whether to get involved in cinematography.

Shortly after my graduation in '68, the Democratic National Convention was in Chicago. And there is a movie called *Medium Cool*, directed by Haskell Wexler, who is one of the great cinematographer/directors—he won two or three Academy Awards. Haskell was a friend of my parents', and he allowed me to shoot with the second unit as an assistant cameraman. The Convention turned into this incredible riot, where the police were beating up all these kids. We were sort of a non-union, phantom 16-mm unit for all the riot footage. The story *Medium Cool* is woven around the footage and the riots.

Haskell's support became critical to me: having someone who was part of the Hollywood system, who was a maverick in his own right with had political and artistic connections, saying to me, "You know, you are doing OK kid; keep working hard and I'll try to give you some advice." That's how I became a protégé of his.

SL: So he was somebody " 'up there," but at the same somebody you could identify with and approach with your own concerns?

AD: Exactly: as a cinematographer. So he was the guy who I really could turn to and get advice from. So with *Medium Cool*, two months after graduation, I was working on my first feature film. I was way in the shadows, but I could observe, you know, and run around loading magazines.

And so I started becoming an assistant cameraman in Chicago. I did everything from commercials to industrial films. And I became an assistant to a guy named Frank Miller who really taught me how to have discipline and routines about being an assistant cameraman.

And shortly thereafter, I met director/producer Walt Topel, who had worked at one of the big advertisement agencies in Chicago. I would be ordering their equipment, and hiring the crews, and running around trying to do and to be everything I could in order to be as professional as possible. *Walt saw how attentive I was to details and how I was willing to bust my ass to learn to do a good job—I wasn't laid back at all. So he said, "Why don't we shoot this thing together?* I'll direct it and give you my point of view, you order the equipment and light it."

And he gave me an opportunity to shoot my first commercial with Duke Ellington at age 20 or 21. I not only got to light, but even shoot it, which was unheard of at the time.

So I started putting a reel together of pretty impressive commercials when I was young. And then I came to San Francisco just a year later and showed that to Haskell Wexler and director Hal Ashby: he did *Harold and Maude, Bound for Glory*, and *Shampoo*—a lot of wonderful films. Hal saw this reel and told me, "I want you to shoot second unit on *Harold and Maude*." So the commercial reel became my calling card as a cinematographer—sort of like the way MTV music videos and commercials are calling cards for young directors today.

It was the combination of, you know, the support I had from my parents and being comfortable in the world of actors, images, and politics, that enabled me to find my way. There was a real base of nuts and bolts through my commercial, industrial work, and also my political and artistic work. It was part of being formed in those volatile times in the 60s, where there were like-minded people, trying to make things that mattered politically and cinematically.

When I moved to California, Haskell was involved with George Lucas and Francis Coppola. Haskell at been a teacher of Lucas's at USC—they shared an interest in cars. And Coppola had a company called American Zoetrope, with which they were making a movie called the *Rain People*. Lucas was doing *THX-1138*, which was his first movie.

After doing commercials in San Francisco for about a year and half, I then moved to LA, and I was recommended by Haskell once again: I started working on these 300 thousand dollar feature films for a guy named Gene Corman: we usually had a 30-day schedule and it was like graduate school.

SL: At that time, did you feel that cinematography would remain your artistic home?

AD: Well, you know, my goals gradually developed. When I started, it was, "If I could only get a job"; then, "If I could only be an assistant cameraman"; then, "'If only a first assistant"; then, "If I could only be a cameraman," until I eventually asked myself, ". . . and if I shoot a feature?" But at the time, directing still wasn't on my horizon. I just wanted to be a cameraman—a Director of *Photography*.

Now here's what happened that changed everything: the unions in California were very, very corrupt and they would not allow young talent in, because they were threatening the jobs of the older members. I had shot about six non-union pictures that looked pretty good, and people wanted to hire me to do studio pictures, but they weren't allowed to. So I started a class-action lawsuit, which involved a lot of famous cameramen, like Caleb Deschanel, Allen Daviau, Tak Fujimoto, and others. We sued both the union and the studios, for illegally using a seniority system. It took a couple of years to settle, but we won in 1976.

And what this suit did, it opened up opportunities for all kinds of people in California who had been struggling to get into the union—not only cameramen, but also editors, electricians, and others. So a whole new generation got into the studio system.

While the legal battle was still going on, it was so frustrating trying to be a cameraman that I said, "To hell with it, I'll be a director instead." I had worked with a bunch of first-time directors and I was learning how to do it. I saw *American Graffiti* and I saw *Mean Streets*, and I said: "You know, I think I could do this: I could make a movie like that!"

So I decided to base a movie on the life of my brother, who was a young musician in Chicago. I met a writer and producer, Tamar Hoffs, who had a brother with a similar background: making music, blues and R&B. We wrote a script together called *Stony Island*, which became my first film as a director.

SL: Before that however, you already wrote a movie called *Paco*—was it a way of exploring new territory and see how it feels out there?

AD: Yeah, I cowrote a movie I shot in Columbia. Having these frustrations, I knew I wanted to make my own movie. The plan was to work on really small movies, so that when I would be doing my own film as a director, I'd know how it was done. So I wound up being the associate producer, the cowriter, and the DP.

You know, in order to be a good director, you have to know everybody's job: you have to know what to expect from them, what they should be doing to help you, and how you can reach out and use their talent. And so it was a great learning and also life experience—I told you that the reason why I wanted to be in the business in the first place was to travel the world and see things.

And then I came back from Columbia and said *Stony Island* is the movie I want to make, because I knew I could hire my brother for no money [*laughing*], and I could use his friends, and I knew Chicago like the back of my hand—so I could run around and steal shots.

It took a long time to put that movie together—'cause I had very little money, I was trying to be everything at the same time—also trying to put together tax shelters, raise money and learn all about business.

SL: Did you invest much of your own money?

AD: I invested my own money in the sense that I stopped working. I was on the phone all day, trying to figure out how to do this. It took about two or three years, and we raised 300 thousand dollars eventually.

When we made this movie, it was my calling card to say, "I'm a director." And it was very well received. It was kind of a loving story about a white kid growing up in a black neighborhood, making it as a musician. And it was based on a lot of real things and new talent that later became famous—it was a lovely movie. In America, I sold it to a small distributor—it got very good reviews. It didn't do well financially, because at the time, the black/white issue was very delicate. It was before hip-hop, before breakdancing, before rap. *Theater owners imagined that black kids would want to come see that movie in their theaters, so they went, "Ay ay ay, we don't want black kids coming into our neighborhood."* But the film got a lot of attention anyway. It was invited to the Deauville Festival and it won awards all over the world.

SL: Being a director now, what did directing allow you to do artistically that you didn't find as a cameraman?

AD: Well, I think the whole idea of getting involved in feature films is the understanding of script and story, also of editing. Working with actors is really important, too—communicating and understanding what they need to perform. You need to learn how to be incredibly organized and on top of all the details, but still not let that bog you down.

I think the most important thing for a director today—I mean it's very difficult; directors come from all walks of life: writing, producing, acting, art department, cinematography—but to me, it always felt that if you don't understand the camera, you will really get lost. It's like trying to conduct a symphony without the ability to play an instrument, because you know, we are in the *motion picture* industry. And movies that try to tell the story with pictures are the best movies.

So because I feel so comfortable visually with what's going on, my appreciation now is writing. And I am in great awe of guys and gals who have the ability to write exactly what they want to shoot.

SL: Do you write a lot?

AD: I do write, even though I am not credited for it. I am writing all the time on my movies, because I am creating ideas and images and rhythms and dialogue. So I feel like I get to write and shoot my movies anyway—and sometimes I am credited for it, sometimes I'm not.

I mean, as a good director you are always working closely with your writer. For example, you don't need to say it and then see—it's one or the other. Movies would be boring if you'd get the information twice. *When you are trying to tell a story, whatever you can see without saying it, the better—and use the words as the seasonings, the garlic and the flavorings of the character. But tell the story visually if you can.*

SL: What gave you the necessary confidence early on that you'd be able to tell a captivating story in a motion picture?

AD: Well, I think it's mainly an amalgam of watching film. When I was in college, every Sunday night I watched all the great European directors. Roger Ebert was the editor of our college newspaper, and I remember they'd have a Sunday night foreign film festival. We'd watch Fellini, Godard, Lelouche, Jan Troell, you know. And it was just eye opening to me to see what these guys were trying to change.

And now the language of cinema has changed. When you think about the beginnings: everything was very formal and staged and composed, and then years later, people said, "We want it shaky and out of focus and have some kind of honest energy to it." And then it became a phony energy, because it was like commercials, where they would make everything have a documentary feel when they were selling a perfume, you know?

So the style of cinema, the manipulation of images has accelerated tremendously. And now with digital effects, it's a whole new world—not necessarily a better one, but different.

SL: When you direct, can you now truly let go of the cinematography aspects—or is it even desirable to you as a director?

AD: Well as a director, you're able to create an environment where you guarantee it looking the way you want it to look. I mean, I'm involved to a certain degree, and then let the cinematographer do what they have to do. And if I look through the camera and something bothers me, then I'll whisper it to them and they'll adjust it.

But basically, it starts much earlier—from first hiring the cameramen, from picking the locations, from working with the art department, to checking out how the lighting is going to affect the set: everything. So I do stay very involved, but I try not to step on the feet of the camera people I am working with.

*In general, I think that the position I am in as a learned cinematographer is both a blessing and a curse in a way.* I won't allow the cameraman to be put in a position where he is going to do lousy work. At the same time, I may be more involved in some cases than they would like. But overall, I am very happy with the way most of my films look. I think there is a kind of consistency, there is a kind of reality and honest lighting to them, which is I think is exactly the style I want it to be.

Most of my films have been contemporary reality type films. *Holes* was a film that had three or four different time periods in it—it has mystery and magic in it—all that came out of such a wonderful novel. It was great fun for us to create those kinds of worlds. I think it has to do with casting, writing, the look of the film—and you gradually learn how in a good movie all of those components are working together towards one end.

SL: How much was the ability to let go and trust your crewmembers part of your creative learning process towards becoming a better director?

AD: You see, especially when starting out, you can easily be overwhelmed by all the aspects you have to be on top of on the set. And that's why going into directing from being a cameraman is a great place to come from: because you've been the captain of the set in many ways. You understand all the different departments' needs; you understand the rhythms and the priorities of the set. It makes it all a lot easier. It's like becoming the captain of a ship after having been the helmsman.

And as a captain, I have to be able to rely on my crew, but at the same time, if I don't like the way something looks, I will stop immediately—I'll fix it. For example, I know when it's good enough to say [*annoyed*], "We are not lighting anymore, let's go: I wanna shoot!" Whereas the cameraman would say, "No, I want ten more minutes." And I say, "You know what? We don't have ten more minutes and I can tell you that the part of the set that you don't like right now, I'm never gonna use, anyways."

SL: If you were to tell me a center of enthusiasm that motivates you and has given you a clear sense direction and satisfaction on the movies you have worked on, what would it be?

AD: I think it's the collaboration; it's closing your eyes and saying, "I'm gonna try to make this scene or act of a movie *feel* like this, because this is the best way to tell the story." And then you go about doing it, you work with people and you go out of your way to see if it's going to work. And then you go to dailies and go, "Oh my gosh, we pulled it off!" That's the fun, you know? Then *later you cut it together and you make an audience cry or laugh or scream, or get scared and you go, "See, it works!" and it's very rewarding. It is something that can be shared for many years all over the world. You feel like a puppeteer in some cases.*

SL: What kind of personality are you, the puppeteer, on set?

AD: I'm told by people, who've worked with other directors, that the sets we have are very relaxed. I am very respectful of people. I'm not a screamer, I'm not a tyrant, and I'm not one of these guys where they go, "Oh, he is such a perfectionist and crazy about such and such a detail." I mean, at the end of the day, I pretty much have the same momentum I had the first hour of the day. I'm very aware of what we have to do to get done with the day.

I really like collaborating. And I like the ability to let things evolve, so that actors and crewmembers have an opportunity to contribute to what has been preplanned. I like the opportunity to have a certain level of improvisation when you finally see it all come together for the first time—with the lighting and the costumes and the location and the actual words. Cause you know, the rehearsals are pretty different from what it will be in the end. I mean, you can get a lot out of rehearsal and I like doing that, but you need the ability to adjust to make it even that much better. And a lot of times you're fighting time, or the weather, or the sun, and you have to rush—and sometimes you do great work when you are rushing.

SL: We discussed your early inclination for expression yourself, both politically and visually. Today, are you aware of combining both elements into one larger motion picture?

AD: It's funny, because last night they had one of my films showing on television called *Chain Reaction* that I did with Keanu Reeves and Morgan Freeman. It didn't do that well. I walked in while my daughter was watching and thought, "What a very, very provocative movie it is!" It's about what would happen if somebody developed a true alternative form of energy, and how the world and the oil companies would be so threatened by it that they would have to shut it down. It's a provocative theme and idea. This is something that in general is important to me. You can make films on all kinds of levels, and I to want entertain people and let them have fun: that's great. But I think it's even better if they can come out of the theater and are a little smarter, or a little more connected to humanity or certain issues, or even their own feeling that they usually don't get by watching television, the news, or other kinds of movies. *If a movie allows you to discover a new perspective, then it's special.*

I think that basically what I set out to do, I have been able to achieve in most cases. I personally like films that are like an interesting stew and where it's not just one type of movie. Sometimes, there can be differences between yourself and the producer or studio about what's important to leave in or what should go. That can create grave problems of coherence and perspective. For example, a political tone that was important to me and that I wanted to keep, but the producers would say: "It's too leftist, we don't want to see all those victims of American bombings. We don't care about them." And I'd go, "No, no, we do care about them." Another example is from the TV version of *Collateral Damage* that I did recently. I had to take seventeen minutes out of the movie. I didn't care about the action sequences so much, but about the scenes with the political content.

SL: You founded your own company 1994. In what ways did it help you to make the movies you wanted to do?

AD: Well, it didn't. Basically, I did *Under Siege* and *The Fugitive* back to back, and both were very successful movies. So I was a hot property at the time. There were people who wanted to give money to make films and have the ability to be part of what I wanted to do. And I live in Santa Barbara, I always dreamed about having the ability to work and edit and mix up here—so we were able to put together this company. It just allows me to have what I would have at a studio, but up here—office stuff and development and assistance. Plus we have a THX dubbing/screening room here, which is pretty unique.

But now that everything is getting smaller with the digitization, you can do it in your garage almost.

SL: But did it any way help you to gain a certain creative and strategic freedom you wouldn't have had otherwise?

AD: Well, first of all, it's a quality of life issue. I'd rather live in Santa Barbara than in LA and I could raise my children here. I haven't yet found the time or energy really to do things for other people. Maybe one day I will just stop directing and instead produce for other filmmakers. It's one film at a time for me at the moment. I really don't know what the future holds—it depends. If I get to make movies that I care about and people still continue to give me money to do them, then I'll do it. If I'm forced to make movies I can't stand, then I won't do it. But before that happens, I think I'd wind up doing smaller and smaller movies that I really care about. I love the fact that documentaries are now finding their way—I think I could blend documentary in a dramatic story together and it would be really wonderful. It would be fun to be able to take chances—not follow formulas—and still be able to get your money back. Small interesting movies that allow you to do that would be terrific.

SL: But don't the current developments in Hollywood rather suggest the pendulum going into the opposite direction?

AD: It's going in two directions: on the one hand, they are making movies now for over 200 million dollars, the average Hollywood production already costing over 100 million. The other direction is where they want to make movies for nothing.

At the end of the day, the studio will pay everything that makes money. So I really believe that it's all up to you. It's between you and the audience and whether you can get it distributed and marketed properly.

SL: Looking at your films, there are certain key ideas that return: persecution, political injustice; also revenge and strong heroic characters. What do these recurring themes reveal about you as a person?

AD: I think there is the idea of going somewhere where you usually don't go, or seeing behind the scenes of how things really work. *Code of Silence* was my first commercial movie. It dealt with police corruption and a cover-up: the police make a mistake, kill the wrong kid, they put a gun on the floor and set up a kid for doing something he didn't do. At the same time this cop is being hung out dry, because he won't cover up the murder of an innocent kid. Well that's a contemporary story—today for sure, you know. *Above the Law* deals with the use of narcotics to fund secret government operations. *The Fugitive* deals with a drug company that's trying to manipulate the results of a test, to the point where they are willing to kill a doctor that is saying that the drug doesn't work. It's about corporate greed and power. The institutions, whether they be government or corporations, are willing to go to almost any lengths to protect their interests.

Some of the things I have dealt with in my early films have become standard kind of fare now, while at the time they came out, they were still sort of provocative. I mean the idea that government was using illegal drugs to fund covert operations when the president's wife was saying, "Just say no to drugs." And there is certainly some kind of journalistic exposé that I tried to achieve. It's a warning to people to look out and to question things and do your own research. Where does the money go, whose interests are at stake here?

SL: By suing the Cinematographers' Union you had a very personal experience with that—

AD: It's funny, because I was raised to be a supporter of unions. I believe that the unions I was raised with would have tried to get everybody in. But here was a union that was so protective, trying to keep out young people and certainly women or minorities. They became reactionary and made deals with the studios to keep jobs for their members only.

I think at this point, the films I am working on now, some have a real political base, some are based on classics which have great dramatic qualities to them. So I try to have a body of development of all kinds of films. At the same time, what I really like is black comedies: where people can have fun, but with a wink, hence revealing something they maybe didn't think about before.

SL: What do you think are general character traits essential to a successful director?

AD: Well, I think, number one is persistence. *You've got to really fight and you can't let the bastards let you down. You've got to keep struggling to get where you want to go: it's not going to be easy!*

You've got to be focused, which is sort of like persistence. I think you need to really have a mentor of some sort; find someone to look up to, learn from, to model from. And also find your own voice. When I did my first movie, I tried to do something that was very close to me and that I understood. It was a world that I had grown up in myself. I wasn't trying to take on something completely different. So whatever you do, especially for your first film, be very comfortable with that arena.

And I think that the ability to write and communicate is very important. I'd say: Whatever you can do to be on a set, to be with talented people, do it. If you have to bring coffee for people or whatever the most menial job is: be around and watch it happen. See how the interactions take place. Become and assistant to somebody who's doing it. The kids who work for me, who have been able to be on a movie from beginning to end, have learned a tremendous amount about the process and the frustrations and the successes and the joys in this.

I think the idea of going to film school and studying film courses is not the best thing to do. I mean, you can do that, but the technical parts are not that complicated. I'd work in the theater, I'd learn how to write, I'd understand history, literature, and politics—you know, I believe art history to be an important part of filmmaking—and having something to say, rather than saying, "Oh I want to make a film just like this guy made." It's about having some inner voice and personality, which has a sense of both contemporary history and classical history.

SL: Do you believe that Hollywood will eventually recognize talent?

AD: Not necessarily. I think there are great filmmakers who don't get recognized, while there are filmmakers within the studio system who are very mediocre. I think there are good films that don't get seen as much as they should, and films that are really stupid that make a lot of money. So it's not a fair world. But if you find a way . . . basically, your goal is to get maybe two or three hundred people to be in a theater and really enjoy your movie. The question is: can I make a movie that I can show it in front of some executives and they go, "Wow, that's really good!"? And that's what it comes down to.

SL: What's the greatest thing that making films has given you personally?

AD: I feel very, very, very lucky to have become what I guess many would perceive as a successful director, though sometimes I feel I'm not so successful. However, a lot of directors never know whether they are going to make another film after their last one.

I think, what it has given me is that I have had tremendous relationships with a lot of wonderfully talented people—from actors, writers, producers, and crew people. *So I have a lot of family—every movie is like a separate child, which means I've had eleven or twelve children now; and that's just for the ones I've directed . . .*

And in terms of my own personal life, my family has had a very rich and exciting life. We took our kids with us all the time—we've lived in Chicago five or six times, they were in schools in different places . . . I think it has made them more worldly.

I think that hopefully, some of the films that I have made entertained people and made them feel good and let them think about things they normally wouldn't have thought about. And I hope I get to keep doing that.

# Levinson, Barry

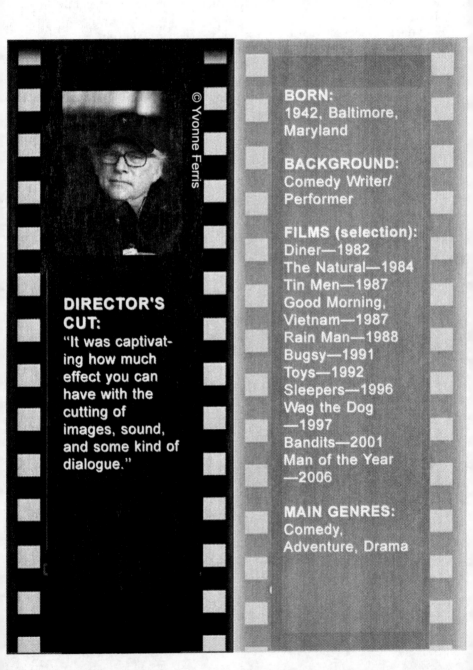

© Yvonne Ferris

**DIRECTOR'S CUT:**
"It was captivating how much effect you can have with the cutting of images, sound, and some kind of dialogue."

**BORN:**
1942, Baltimore, Maryland

**BACKGROUND:**
Comedy Writer/ Performer

**FILMS (selection):**
Diner—1982
The Natural—1984
Tin Men—1987
Good Morning, Vietnam—1987
Rain Man—1988
Bugsy—1991
Toys—1992
Sleepers—1996
Wag the Dog —1997
Bandits—2001
Man of the Year —2006

**MAIN GENRES:**
Comedy, Adventure, Drama

BARRY LEVINSON: Growing up in Baltimore, I basically spent my time doing nothing. I spent a great deal of time hanging around, you know: with friends and just this kind of avoidance-of-responsibility period of time. It was like: "School is school, but so what?" "Who cares if you get good grades? What's the difference?" "What kind of fun can I get into?"; that kind of attitude—

For me, Baltimore simply stands for where I come from—circumstances and people that I was around and influenced by, which is kind of a middle class, city/suburban background. If you watch the movies I've done about Baltimore, I think that they illustrate the atmosphere I grew up in very well—better even than I could explain it.

You know, those first eighteen years of your life are incredibly influential—maybe more so than any other period, I think. It is amazing that people can remember so many things and are so affected by events that took place in high school—it was only three years of our lives; that's all! And it seems like it was so much longer and so much more went on. Think about friendships and relationships with girls over that very short period of time: they may have only been two years long. Obviously I have been influenced by a number of things that have gone along, but high school was a very informative period for me; that shaped a lot of what I am—whether I like it or not.

SL: You enjoyed doing "nothing"—what was that?

BR: "Nothing" was like: going to a movie was great fun; playing ball was great fun; meeting after school was great—certainly all things that involved lack of responsibility were very high on the chart.

SL: Your parents encouraged your doing "nothing"?

BR: Yes and no. You know, how much do parents know about what you do with your free time; that's always the question . . . [chuckling].

SL: Any particular person you looked up to?

BR: I was not particularly impressed or impressionable to that regard. I think in hindsight, I was fascinated by film and television. I watched a lot; I was very influenced by it not just simply as a viewer, although at that time I don't think I would have known more than that. But in fact, it was extremely influential and I didn't realize it until much later. I mean, my friends liked going to the movies like I did, except that I was, as they say, not just the casual viewer.

But I never thought about doing that in my life because I never knew anyone that wrote or directed or acted or had anything to do with the business. So it would not be something you aspired to, because you wouldn't even know where to go.

SL: But somehow you watched these films with a different eye—

BR: I think so. I didn't realize it until many decades later, but when I was around twelve years old or so, I saw *Marty* on television. *Marty* was a Paddy Chayevsky play about this guy who was a butcher and would hang around with his guys, always trying to find dates and that sort of thing. Now, I don't remember much about it—so I don't have any real great recollection of seeing it, except that I loved the dialogue [*in Baltimore accent*]: "*What do you wanna do Marty?*" "*I don't know, what do you wanna do?*" *That stood out in my mind: it was like the greatest, most amazing piece of dialogue I had ever heard.* Now jump forward 30-something years—several years after doing *Diner*—and suddenly I go, "Oh, my god, *Diner* is in a sense completely about that kind of ordinary dialogue"; the dialogue that is so ordinary that you think you wouldn't write about it. This connection simply didn't occur to me before.

SL: And that is very much your upbringing in a nutshell: "Hanging out; doing nothing"—

BR: ". . . what do *you* wanna do?" That was like the essence of dialogue to me and that's basically what my first film is. And I wasn't even aware of the influence of *Marty*, except being so affected by it when I saw it. Those little connective things, they were all there. They are almost too subtle to pick up.

SL: Around the time you finished high school and had to decide where to go next, what did you imagine you life would be like?

BR: Avoidance. I mean the first thing I started to do in college was to take courses in radio and television. I only took them because I figured: "Well, how hard can they be? Radio I listen to; I watch television. That's all simple; that's what I'm doing." And so I thought: "Well, maybe I can get to be a disc jockey and just play rock 'n' roll." Though I didn't have a good enough voice to be a disc jockey, I still took the courses. I was fascinated by it and then one thing led to another: I ended up going to American University studying broadcast journalism. I met a professor, who was a program director of a television station. He took a liking to me and got me a job there. That's how I started making the transition which was the beginning of it all.

SL: Was there ever a time where you worried about your future?

BR: I mean I was young. I was only twenty and I was working in a television station—by then, I had found something. *Even though I didn't know where I would go to, I was in a world that I liked.* I wasn't like saying, "Well, I'm gonna take these steps and then that will lead to those steps that then will lead to this . . ." I didn't have any kind of planned view of the future—I was not blocking it out as much as I was wandering through things that were beginning to interest me.

And next thing I know, I am a floor director on working with hand puppets on kiddy shows. And then because I like that, I am suddenly coming up with skits for these puppets to do and things that they can play with. I am playing and performing with puppets, then I begin to discover things like, "Oh, look how music can be used, look how you can get laughs with this—." I am working with film and music, cutting music with picture and go: "Look what happens with the juxtaposition, look what happens if you're playing this kind or that kind of image; look what happens!" I was just captivated by it.

I didn't have anybody to teach me this, but since I was left alone in the building, I began to play with all the elements. Then I got a chance to do on-air promotions.

SL: And so suddenly doing "nothing" and avoidance turns into working late hours on something very concrete. Can you describe what it was about all these things that suddenly motivated you?

BL: First of all, I began to be fascinated by how music worked with images. It was captivating how much effect you can have with the cutting of images with sound and music and some kind of dialogue. Though I ended up doing a lot of on-air promotional work—baseball and things—I was doing them in ways that were unusual for the time. Later, I began to write dialogue more specifically.

In-between still taking classes and running back and forth, nothing mattered other than "leave me alone in the building and let me play with these things"— that's what I did all the time. After being also the floor director and assistant director on a news program, I ended up getting an opportunity to direct. I was immersed in all those elements, and things were happening rather quickly.

SL: What a great place that allowed you to do all these things.

BL: Well, they had this training program, and for 50 dollars a week, you worked 40 hours. But when left alone, I started wondering in the bowels of the building. Because it was a radio and television station, they had a massive music library. I would listen to music for hours and hours and try to imagine different kinds of visual scenarios by hooking stuff together. Then they had all of that newsreel footage and things that went way back to the beginnings of film.

SL: But at one point you decided you had to leave—

BL: Yeah, that's when I finally came west. I got to a position where I thought I didn't have anything else to do in television except get promoted. *Getting promoted, you would get further away from actually playing with those things and become much more of an executive, which did not appeal to me at all.* And so I ended up packing up going to California not knowing what to. Then by circumstance and accident really, I got involved in an acting school through a friend. I had no desire to be an actor, but I was interested—even fascinated—by the process of doing this. The people who ran it sort of all came from the same group of people that ran the Neighborhood Playhouse in New York—it was sort of mostly techniques based on Sandy Meisner.

SL: So arriving in California, you still didn't know what you'd wanted to do?

BL: I would look to all sides and just loved it.

SL: . . . and would discover comedy for yourself—

BL: That came directly out of the improvisational exercises that we did a lot in acting class in which I would have a tendency to drift towards stuff that was comedic. Though dramatic in its structure or its intent perhaps, I began to figure out how you can get laughs.

Sometimes, I would get teamed up with Craig Nelson for certain improv things and we used to get laughs together. One day we were sitting around and I said, "Maybe we should put some stuff together and maybe we can play some local gigs and earn some money," because neither one of us had a dime. We worked on some material, went to an audition and actually got a job doing comedy material. But Craig didn't want to be a comedian; I didn't want to be a comedian. He wanted to be an actor; I didn't know what I wanted to do. I didn't want to do it, but we were making some money—

SL: Not a bad premise for a comedy duo—

BL: Yeah [*chuckling*]. So we were just doing it and making some money. I wrote down some of the pieces that we had done and I said, "Maybe we can sell this stuff." I took it around to some places and we got soon hired as writers on a show.

It was a bizarre circumstance. I mean it's one of those fluke things: they were rehearsing with performers they had on the show. We didn't know any better and said, "You really should do this, because you'll get a better laugh." Now, they didn't know that we had performed this material before. And somehow the performers took offense to it and were all pissed off and weren't going to do it. You know, we were just kind of trying to explain because we had done it. And in explaining, we kind of did a piece of it and the producers said, "Well, why don't you do it?" We got some laughs and that's how we became writers/performers on the show. It's like one of these bad movies where one goes, "Well I'm not doing this" and then he ends up doing it . . . [*laughing*].

SL: What did you consider yourself to be at the time?

BL: Well, once I did that show, I considered myself a writer. I never considered myself a performer. If anyone would have asked me, I would have said, "Well, I'm a comedy writer." But I didn't want to be a comedy writer. Probably at that point, I wanted to write full stories—screenplays.

SL: And by meeting Mel Brooks you got to do both: write comedy as part of full-length screenplays—

BL: For three years, I was a writer with him on two movies. It was like the best education you can get because every day, you are meeting, you're having breakfast, you're hearing stories, you're talking about stuff, you're throwing ideas around, you're going back to the office, you're writing. Then you're at lunch together every day. Then after lunch, you write until about four in the afternoon and you're working with this guy who was this giant in comedy. And so not only was I there during the writing period, but also during the filming period. That was so great about it.

There were three of us and Mel. We were there during the writing, the casting, the filming, the cutting, the mixing—the whole process. I got a chance in a three-year period to see two movies being done: from inception to completion—see what it's like on a daily basis; how to make the scene work, what's wrong with the scene. How come the scene doesn't seem to be playing as well as it should? Why is that?

You're getting this kind of education and being paid at the same time. Mel was very open and allowed us access to everything—you know, *every part* of it! And because he was actually *in* the movies, we were like watching and you would say things like, "Well, Mel, if you came over here and bla . . ." and sometimes he would shout, "Terrible idea, terrible!" Or if he liked it, he would go ahead and do it.

So now my own mind begins to wonder: "Oh, what happens if you move the camera here? What happens if you take this kind of shot? What happens if you do this?" And all of a sudden, my brain is beginning to move into that mode of . . . directing.

SL: So the circumstances drew you towards that mode of thinking?

BL: Yeah. Well, it was everything and how the whole process worked. I was there and I had an investment in making those moments that were on the page funny—and if I could, I would help to improve them. In the final analysis, it was all Mel's baby, but he was inclusive enough that if you had an idea, he'd use the idea—or he would discard it and tell you why it's no good. So that became this incredible apprenticeship.

SL: Can you put into words what lessons in artistic creation you took with you by observing and closely collaborating with Mel?

BL: I don't know if it did in terms of personality. It's not like me observing, "Well, this is the way Mel does it and etc, etc," because it wouldn't apply to me. Because I mean there is only one Mel Brooks who can do and say when Mel Brooks can do and say; he is very much one of a kind in that regard.

What did apply to me is that you got to follow through with your ideas. And that's what I took away from it. *Mel was trying to basically preserve this thing that existed as of something that you wrote on paper, that you finally built the set and hired actors for and that you then wanted to make sure it's still funny: that you didn't lose the funny along the way*—or that the tempo or the camera angle or the colors or the costumes made it not funny. The big challenge was: how do you protect it from that one first moment when you laughed, all the way through until an audience saw it in the end? There are just so many things that can impact on the material until it suddenly isn't anymore what it was.

The director's job is to figure out how to do that: you have a little bit of water in the palm of your hand and you got to find a way to hold on to it—that kind of commitment, that kind of perseverance not to lose it to the machinery.

You know, another thing about directing is that you have to hire all these people and everybody's got different ideas. And there is a long list of strong-willed people involved. Now the big test is: let's not get a bunch of people that aren't strong-willed and then do whatever I want. No. It's how to bring all these strong-willed, talented people together and still preserve the initial inspiration. The question is how does everybody support it and make it even better if possible. And it's like glorious when it works: because *all* of these people came together and they even made it better—not: they all came together and it all got lost.

SL: What combination of character traits or values might be able to achieve or preserve or create these moments of cinematic magic?

BL: Well it's tough. It's a hard one to say. Because, you know, on one hand, you have to listen to all the people you brought together. You have to find a way to communicate what you want to all of these people. And the far side of it: you also have to have a certain degree of stubbornness, because if basically you can't stand up to the things that you want, you end up with something else of which you're not sure what it is. *And it's a very thin line between being stubborn and going off the cliff, and being stubborn and keeping everyone from keeping off the cliff. You can't really put it into words.*

I kind of would refer to it as "controlled freedom": that somehow you give everybody this complete freedom and at the end of the day, it's always controlled. But you want to be able to see what everybody can bring to the plate.

SL: In how far did your experience during those years help you find your own style of writing?

BL: I mean Mel was incredibly influential, even though the kind of comedy he did was not the comedy that I would ultimately do. Mel has his own kind of comedy. I could work on it, but if left to my own devices, I wouldn't write it.

That's why I began to think about writing outside of what he does—and that led to . . . *And Justice for All*, which was a dramatic comedy.

SL: You wrote six screenplays together with your partner, after which you started to write them by yourself. In what significant ways does that have an influence on your writing process?

BL: *If I write alone, I basically just write it from beginning to end. Period.* I have nothing more than that—I don't outline it, I don't do anything. Like *Diner*, I sat down and just wrote it. I generally write very fast when I write alone. There are scripts that took me three weeks.

If I work with a collaborator, I spend a lot of time. What happens is that not only do you have to find an idea that you can agree upon, but basically have to go through: "Should we do this should we do that? Well I don't know I don't see that. Maybe if we . . . ," you see? There's a lot of talk that's sort of peripheral to what you are going to write. It's a whole other way of working.

But, you see, I don't collaborate as a writer anymore since I did *Diner*. Anything I have written I have written myself. I mean I have of course worked with other writers on pieces that I did and I'd have an influence, but I don't consider myself the writer, nor would I take credit for it.

SL: Could your preference to writing alone be an indication that maybe while scripting, you were always already directing in your head?

BL: You know, when I was first writing, I wasn't aware that I wanted to direct. But in retrospect I was, because I remember the first film for which I wrote something with somebody else directing it. When the set looked completely different, I was sort of like completely confused by it—it suddenly seemed wrong. So therefore I realized that when I was writing, I was actually visualizing how the whole thing would work. But I wasn't consciously thinking of it that way. When I saw the set, it was for example too light while it should have been darker; or I was thinking that it was moodier and the furniture was in a different place from what I thought. It's then that I realized: "Oh, I actually have a very specific idea what it's supposed to be. Oh . . . !" [chuckling]—you know what I mean? Then I thought, "Well, it was like a naïve thought to have these ideas."

SL: So the visual idea for a scene is prior to the actual written words in the script?

BL: Yeah, because I was thinking of what it looked like. And when it didn't look like I pictured it, it wouldn't work the same. Because in terms of screenwriting, scenes don't just work anywhere: they only work in certain places. Say a scene that's supposed to be inside it shot outside: there might be too much air around if it's outside—it must be inside in a dark room with a big ceiling; and it doesn't work in a little tiny room either. That's the way I like hear it in accordance to what the environment is—

SL: So there is an attunement to the environment?

BL: Yeah. I remember saying to a director one time on a movie, "If I had known that the scene is gonna take place there, I would have written another scene," cause it wasn't what I thought it was.

SL: Did that upset you?

BL: No, because I didn't write that many things before I started to direct. In a sense, rather than being upset, I realized: "Well, you know something? I need to direct." Everybody has a different way of seeing something. My thing was: "I can't be upset. What I need to do is try to do it myself if I can."

SL: Or become bitter—

BL: Yeah [chuckling].

SL: Did you discover any new dimensions to your craft as director that you did not experience as a writer before?

BL: Because of the time I had spent with Mel Brooks and being there every day on a movie for three years, I think I was pretty well prepared. It is one thing if you write and somebody makes a movie of your script. It's another thing if you are there during the whole process and you see the ebb and flow of everything taking place. So by the time I got to direct, I was trying to simply now follow through on some of the things I wanted and felt were necessary to the piece that was in my head.

You see, not only had I now been involved in two movies, but I had also studied theater seven days a week for two years. So I felt pretty comfortable about how to approach or to resolve certain problems that might come up—and all the fears and anxieties that come with directing a scene.

SL: And of all the things you tried before, you found that directing suited you personality most—

BL: I think I enjoy it the most and I instantly felt pretty good about it. It's not to say that I wasn't surprised and had problems initially with various things on the set, where I went, "Well, wait a minute, this isn't right, this is whatever." But there are always going to be surprises when you direct.

SL: How did the fact that you had studied theater and done comedy yourself help you concretely with the actors and the ensemble performances you created?

BL: You have to learn to trust, especially when you do improvisations—and that's what my own experience doing improvs taught me and prepared me for. For me, the key to everything is how you cast your people. Improvisations don't just come out of the blue. You have to sort of have an instinctual ability to pick certain people that you know can be free enough to try certain things—and some can't.

*I tried to put together groups that I thought could play off one another—as I did in* Diner. *The way it works is that certain personalities, if you leave them close to what in fact they are, they will feed one another.*

SL: How flexible are you during this process?

BL: Well we are back to controlled freedom: on one hand, the actors are free to do certain things, however they are only free to do it within certain limitations. Because otherwise, if we push it too far over here, then we are off completely towards something that's not going to be relevant to the movie.

It's small things. There is for instance a scene in *Diner* when they are all driving and we are in the car with Mickey Rourke and Paul Reiser. Paul is talking about nuance. He is not comfortable with that word "nuance." And that in fact came out of a conversation where I had said to Paul, "If I am cutting from car to car, I just need a little moment here in the film—a little something." And in that conversation, the word nuance came and we started to talk about it for a couple of minutes. I then just put them in a car and we decided to go with it—just Paul talking about nuance. Mickey isn't paying much attention to him because as usual his friend is just rambling on about something. Suddenly we start to understand something about their relationship without ever talking about anything substantial.

SL: So there was this structural moment in the script, but it wasn't concretely written out yet?

BL: Yeah, it wasn't defined. I just felt that I needed to do something in that spot. And if it didn't work, it didn't work. If it did, it just filled the moment leading up to this accident—you know, it's a combination of things: You need to know when you can try certain things and when you can't. You have to know when there is some room for something to happen and when there isn't. You have to understand the structure and the rhythm you're working in; of the piece and where there is room to elaborate. You have to keep those elements in your head and then with it, you try to find certain unexpected moments that reveal something about a character. We all do it all the time—filling our conversation with nonsensical pieces of information that in fact make us understand the other person. Sometimes in a film, they are directly connective to a plot, and sometimes it's just basically giving us a little bit of a coloring of a character.

Producers sometimes don't necessarily see that. When I did *Diner*, an executive told me, "You know, you really have to learn about editing." And I said: "I'm sure I do. Do you have an example?" "Well that roast beef sandwich thing. He wants to have that sandwich; he's going to ask for it and 'cut': you get on with the story. He's not going to keep talking about it." I explained to him that this "going on about it" was the story. And it's been like that all my life, you know, "We can cut it here and you should cut some there"—but if you do that, you lose what you were really trying to bring across with that scene.

SL: Do you make a distinction between typecast actors that can handle that sort of freedom and actors that are taking on a role as somebody they are really not?

BL: Yes. And at certain times you are not going to get that from a certain actor in that he won't have this sense of freedom. So typecasting is very important. But then in certain roles, you have other requirements and different qualities are needed. But if you say, "Look, these are guys in there twenties blabla . . ." then I say, "Let me get a guy who is gonna be sort of like what I think their character is going to be" and not have somebody else play it—in a sense, I restrict it that way. You want somebody that makes the character evolve even beyond what you have on the page, if possible.

SL: So typecast actors help you to better tell your story?

BL: Well, if you use some of the Baltimore movies as an example, you have to believe that these people really know one another—that they know one another well enough so you don't have to mention, "Gosh, how long have we been friends?" That we as an audience just inherently believe this relationship. You know, in *Diner* we never talk about friendship, but we know that they are friends. We know that they can argue with one another; that they can get pissed off with one another. We know all of these elements. I have to create and establish that not through the dialogue talking about those things, but different things—even then it tells us about the characters and the relationships to one another.

SL: Have audience expectations relative to plot and characters changed over the last three decades?

BL: I think there are shifts that are taking place. It seems that movies are becoming much less about human beings and relationships on the whole; there are fewer movies that are dealing with lifelike characters and interactions. At this point in time, it is in a sense on the downside of the curve. We are in an age of sort of second and third generation movie reality. So it's not as much about anything that is connected to life, as it is to movies.

SL: So not about lived human reality, but filmic realities?

BL: Yeah, yeah. We have a time now where people are growing up so much on movies that they begin to write about scripts whose references is movies, not life.

SL: Have you developed something of a hunch of how your movies will do with the audience before they hit the theaters?

BL: Well, it keeps on taking me by surprise, because you never know. An important factor is that I don't work that much in genre, and so I don't have that security of saying, "OK, I don't know how big it's gonna be, but I'm in that genre, so therefore I will gross at least such and such." Also, if you work in a genre, people and critics writing about it already know because there is a reference to it—sometimes if you do movies that are outside of that, they don't know how to write about it because they are not on surefooted ground in a way. And sometimes those who make the trailers don't know how to make a trailer of it because they don't know what the hell it is.

Whereas if you are making a full action movie, they know how to make a trailer, because you just chop it up with all kinds of things: cars sailing through the air and crazy stunts that you blast with a lot of music and clangs and bags—they know how to sell that. But if you have a piece that is more complex, then it is a more difficult element to sell to an audience.

SL: How much of an influence can a particular climate and atmosphere in which a movie gets released in have on its performance?

BL: I think it's possible, but I don't know if you can take questions like the climate and whatever is in the air into account—I don't know how you can deal with that. You just say, "Look, this is the nature of the business and it continues to evolve." All I can do to protect myself is to make the movie that I believe in and hope that I can be successful with it. Period.

I don't believe that by putting your finger up to the wind you can figure out what the hell you should write or direct. I think your gut feeling is all you have and you basically just have to fight on. I mean you just do it.

*Of course you can go and be more calculating—and God knows there are people out there that are calculating in choosing their projects. I don't do this.* Look, I did a little movie called *The Everlasting Piece* about Northern Ireland in the 80s and it was a comedy. I just felt it was interesting. It was never really seen in the United States and never had a chance to be seen here. But I believed in it even though I never got too much money or attention for doing it.

If I wanted to be more in terms of protecting my career, thinking about what the right choices would be, then I would probably not make it. Like: "This could be rather dangerous" and then if it doesn't do well: "Oh, how am I going to be perceived?" If I did that, then I wouldn't have made most of the movies that I have made.

SL: Do you ever feel that there is a danger of losing your fresh approach and motivation that allow you to explore?

BL: Yeah I do, and I think that this stands in direct context to what I just said. If you are having a career about what you should do and what you perceive the right thing to make, then I think you will ultimately become stale because you are not really feeling with your own instincts and your passions. And when you go down that road, you will ultimately lose the fire to want to make certain things.

If you ask me what I would recommend to young filmmakers, then it would be to keep in mind: "Hey, what are you interested in? What story do you want to tell?" And if that's the story you want to tell, then tell *that* story.

*I basically only react to what motivates me and not to what I believe is expected of me. If I did that, I would just be repeating myself.* I keep changing all the time. If I was in search of box office, I couldn't have made *Rain Man*—back then people didn't even know what autism was. What would be the reason that that movie would do well? Four directors dropped out before me on that project, the last one being Sydney Pollack. I could only do it because I believed in it. When I went off to do *The Natural*, everybody was saying that the idea of a baseball movie would be basically suicide because baseball movies don't work. And not only hadn't there been a successful baseball movie in years, but on top of everything else, it was a fantasy movie. So it didn't even plug into that genre.

I don't think that any of my biggest successes could have been predicted in any way. *Good Morning, Vietnam* in retrospect looks like, "Oh that's a good idea—it's gonna be successful." No: the studio was panicked at a certain point in time. *There was this movie about Vietnam with a lot of humor in it and everybody thought, "How can you make anything with humor and Vietnam?"* We weren't making fun of the war, but still at the time, they were very, very nervous about that film.

SL: Now here's the chance for the pitch of your life—literally. What would be the plot outline for the film on Barry Levinson's life?

BL: That's a hard question [*laughing*]. Because I think you would be pitching a movie where people would say it's too improbable and it doesn't sound like it would be successful. Well, you might take a guy who sort of lacked motivation or any vision of what he thought he should do and then because of improbable circumstances ends up in a profession that he never imagined—and ultimately becomes a success at something that never occurred to him. It's called *Just Hanging Out.*

# Weitz, Chris

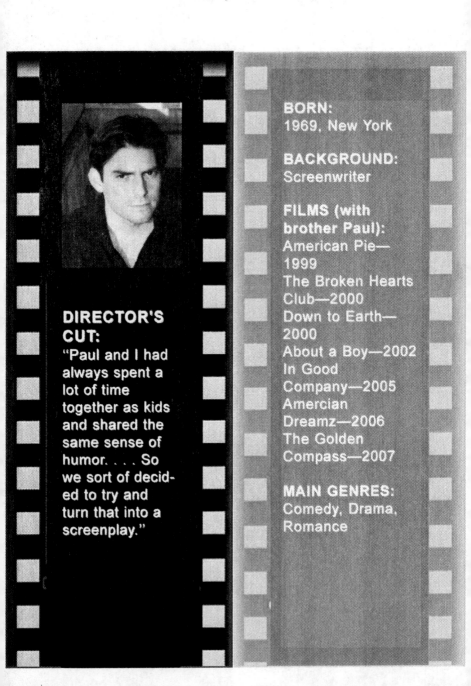

**DIRECTOR'S CUT:**
"Paul and I had always spent a lot of time together as kids and shared the same sense of humor. . . . So we sort of decided to try and turn that into a screenplay."

**BORN:**
1969, New York

**BACKGROUND:**
Screenwriter

**FILMS (with brother Paul):**
American Pie—1999
The Broken Hearts Club—2000
Down to Earth—2000
About a Boy—2002
In Good Company—2005
Amercian Dreamz—2006
The Golden Compass—2007

**MAIN GENRES:**
Comedy, Drama, Romance

CHRIS WEITZ: I was born in New York in 1969. My mother was a Hollywood movie actress raised in Los Angeles as the daughter of the movie producer and agent Paul Kohner. My grandmother was a Mexican film actress, Lupita Tovar. She was the star of Mexico's first talking picture. So on that side there was movie background.

My father was German-born. He moved to London when Hitler came to power. He had immigrated to the States in 1939, I think. Although he was very Anglophile, he sounded American.

My parents were what I suppose you could call society types, but both were very cultured. My father was a fashion designer, but he also wrote novels and biographies. He had been hired by the OSS as a spy during the war. You could say I grew up in this very European household, transplanted into New York City. We had fairly hierarchical European family structures, not American at all. So, in a way, I had a much more structured upbringing and existence than some of my peers.

First of all, my brother and me, we grew up in a big sort of generation gap to our father. So I grew up steeped into European culture, etiquette, and also artistic influence. You know, my father who hadn't really had the chance to do everything he wanted because of the war, encouraged my brother and me to become artists. This is not to say necessarily visual artists, but that we pursue our cultural leanings. So quite interestingly, my brother became a playwright and I became a journalist—if only by default.

When I was fourteen, I went to my father's own school in London and later took A-levels there. I ended up sort of stuck in London trying to be what was a freelance journalist—a difficult and miserable existence. It was a stupid choice in a way.

I was then also accepted to Yale at the same time I got into Cambridge. I had an English girlfriend at the time. That persuaded me to stay at Cambridge. I read English there between 1987 and 1990. Though I got dumped by my girlfriend in my first term and got kind of stuck there in the beginning, I started making really good friends and I enjoyed my time there.

*You know at Cambridge, nobody thinks in a really vocational manner—it is sort of a sense of being member of an A-league which is just going to inherit financial, political, and cultural power. So nobody really tells you, "You gotta get off your ass and get a job."* I didn't do any of that, until the very end. Then I was stuck and didn't know what I was going to do.

SL: How did you spend your time at Cambridge?

CW: Well, they had some very bad student drama. I was once a really bad production designer. I also performed in a lot of pretty bad productions and wrote a few articles for a bad paper. Other than that, I wasn't really much of a go-getter.

There wasn't anything like a film program or a film society per se. We had a good art cinema, but that was about it. The idea of a career in film wasn't really a consideration.

And then, after I graduated, I didn't really know what I was going to do with my life. So I was kind of desperately trying to get journalistic assignments. I also applied to the American state department for the American Foreign Service.

One part of me just wanted to stay in school for as long as humanly possible because I didn't know how to negotiate the real world.

SL: Something that happens to a lot of people—

CW: Oh yeah. I remember applying for an MLit at Cambridge for Renaissance Literature, and I was turned down. I think basically on the recommendation—or rather on the warning—of one of my directors of studies it said that I really wasn't cut out for it.

And then I studied Mandarin for a really brief time at the Chinese University of Hong Kong. But I realized pretty quickly that I had no idea what the hell I was doing there. So I left.

SL: Did you invent some vocations that you might cut yourself out for?

CW: Well, I mean I had a vague notion of becoming a diplomat. I thought that learning a bit of Mandarin would help. Really, I just liked the way Chinese characters looked—I was kind of fascinated with that. I still am. But it was much too difficult and too long a process for the sort of dilettante I was at that time.

Eventually, the only really positive vocational stuff I looked into was with the State department. And I got in. It was some very difficult exams and a really rigorous interview process in Washington, D.C. So I got in, but was going to have to wait for a posting. I thought that's what I would do. But in the meantime, my brother and I started writing together. We thought it might be fun to write screenplays—so that's what we did.

SL: So your brother had already been doing that for a while when you joined him?

CW: Well, he was working as a playwright. *I'm sure I wouldn't have ended up in film without my brother—and probably vice versa*; he was working very hard at writing, but you can't make a living as a playwright in New York; I mean, maybe four or five people can. So he was also working for this theater bookshop on Times Square, amongst all the loonies and transients. I think when we started together, we just had a bit of time on our hands and a growing sense of desperation.

We had always spent a lot of time together as kids and shared the same sense of humor and had fun. So we sort of decided to try and turn that into a screenplay. But I don't think we had a concrete notion of an eventual career in Hollywood or in the movies or anything like that. It is pretty bizarre to having ended up here from such sort of vague beginnings.

SL: But you felt encouraged by your parents to explore for a while?

CW: Well, there was a little of economic freedom, because we were still living off my folks until I was about 21. So they were generous enough to keep me going until then. I'm sure that they were starting to get worried that I was gonna be a deadbeat my whole life; I knew a lot about Renaissance poetry, but nothing about anything else.

SL: So how did you make the jump from writing?

CW: A writer called David Seltzer, who had written Richard Donner's film *The Omen*, also had a production company in New York that was funded by MGM. *MGM the studio in Hollywood, as I'm sure you know, is the most sort of downtrodden and reviled and laughed at,* because they fell from the highest heights to being incapable of making anything successful except for *James Bond.* So this guy David had a production deal with MGM—and an old friend of my brother's was his head of development. It was a very strange setup, because these were two sort of very New York and artistically inclined types.

They brought us into a meeting because they had seen my brother's plays. We pitched them this idea about a nonviolent Hindu detective basically. This was during the height of the buddy-cop genre era, around '92. So it was kind of a *fatigue* of the buddy-cop movie.

They convinced MGM to pay us to write it. Nothing ever came of it at all, but it got us in the door. It's weird: once you've sold a screenplay, you sort of reach a certain plateau that it's very difficult to get thrown out of.

SL: Did you have an agent?

CW: No, we sold it before we had an agent; but we had one pretty soon after. I mean we were going around for somebody to represent us, but frankly, nobody wanted us until we sold something—and then everybody did. Because what was the cost to them? They get a share of the deal and a shot at somebody who might make more money for them.

So it was a lot of writing spec scripts that nobody bought, doing little assignments, rewrites on other stuff that was never made. I mean there is a whole mini-industry of screenwriting in which you can never ever get anything propped to the screen but still make a living.

SL: So you would take a couple of days to rewrite stuff they assigned to you . . .

CW: . . . or weeks. It was movie rewriting. And then it was seven years before we wrote *Ants*—we got a chance to that with Jeffrey Katzenberg and animation people at DreamWorks. When we got that job, we ended up working for that film for two and a half years or so. Animation is a really lengthy process. And I'm sure the reason they hired us was that we were clearly willing to hang in there for that long a period of time.

SL: So while the concept was not yours, the story was?

CW: Well, as a matter of fact, neither the concept, nor the story was by us. Most of that general stuff was already in place: that there was going to be a film about ants which was going to be a parable of some kind, starring Woody Allen. Well maybe they never thought of it being a parable in that way—we were really the ones who wanted to make it about the individual and society and have some weird Marxist undertones to it. I think we sort of added that—and also a lot of the tone and most of the dialogue is our doing. In fact, almost all of the Woody Allen stuff. The reason why I say "almost" is that the storyboard artists get their hands on your dialogue and start fucking around with it. But normally, dialogue is recorded before animation, so that the lip synch can be done properly.

SL: So you got to spend a lot of time working with Woody Allen?

CW: I wish I could say that we had lengthy collaborations and meetings with him, but we really didn't. In animation, the lead actor will come in for four or five days and record.

SL: So he didn't have time to be picky or difficult about his part?

CW: I don't think he was. I imagined he would have been picky had it totally violated the sense of what he wanted to do. I mean, we really had been brought in to pretty much secure his participation. They already knew that they wanted him, but we had about six weeks to get a draft that he would be willing to do. And then he just came in and did it. I don't think he knew exactly what the process was before he signed up to do it.

It was very strange that Woody agreed to this project anyway. I think that Jeffrey Katzenberg is a very convincing and persuasive man that can get people to do interesting things that they might not otherwise have thought of doing.

SL: When working on the project, did you think of yourself as a professional writer now?

CW: I don't really know—I mean I still don't consider myself a writer in that sense. I shutter to think of myself as a writer. *I'm not sure that screenwriting is exactly writing per se. I always feel like it's sort of filling in the blanks,* or *just roughing out things for the actors and the director, too.*

SL: So you immediately visualize as you write?

CW: That's what happens. I mean I never had big ideas of being a director. It just became obvious that it would be better to screw up your own writing than have somebody else to do it.

I think that if you can, in movies you want to cut out as many middlemen as possible. So you want to be a director, in order for the stuff that you wrote in the script to be more clearly executed in the way that you thought it would be. I'm not sure I ever had any grand ideas or visions of being an *auteur* or anything like that.

SL: What do you consider yourself then? Your production credits say "Producer," at times when in reality you direct on these pictures as well.

CW: I don't know. The problem is that a lot of people that go on about being film directors are not necessarily people whose work I admire. You're faced with the fact that most American films are no good—actually most films are no good. That means that most directors are making films that are no good.

So why should I really want to be identified per se with those people? It's not about what I call myself. I am hopefully just pursuing things that are kind of entertaining to me, that I can make a living at and that I find satisfying. But if you told me like I'd never make another film for some reason, I believe that I could be happy. I really wouldn't give a crap about making more films; I'd rather sit and watch them.

SL: Did you analyze and read a lot of theory in order to learn how to write?

CW: No. I feel like I know as a sort of received idea what for example McKee has to say. And I think I remember reading, not one of Sid Fields main books, but one of his subsidiary ones. All of that seemed fairly obvious to me—all the stuff they had to say, I think maybe it's useful in clearing away some of the clutter in your mind. But I didn't really feel as though I needed any sort of film theory of how to go about.

Also, I never read any film theory, as it is really suspicious to me. It kind of seems to me that the people who went into film criticism and film theory were the people that didn't really hack it in literary criticism and preferred to enter this sort of a much smaller pond. I never felt as though it had much to contribute to my attitude to writing screenplays, although there are some people I really admire and who have worked in film studies. The head of the department in Wellesley, Janine Basinger, is one of them.

There are only a couple of things that you need in order to be able to write a screenplay. You need to look at how it is formatted—the dialogue of the middle of the page. And you need to have a sense of what you enjoy and care about. And the rest of it will come from experience. Eventually you learn, that you shouldn't really write gigantic crowd scenes of 10,000 people because there is an obvious practical barrier.

Concerning structure, I think by watching enough American movies, you get a sense that there is a beginning, middle, and an end: another way of putting the three-act structure. I mean that whole thing is fairly straightforward. It's obvious that it starts with the character who learns something by the end, and the moment of greatest turmoil will be somewhere towards the end because otherwise the movie would have already been over. I mean that seems kind of almost built in to the meaning of the term "story."

SL: But knowing how a story is structured is different from knowing how to write it.

CW: Right. *Of course there is a big difference parsing out between literary and practical criticism and actually writing a poem—so there is a big difference between being able to identify a three-act structure and being able to write it.*

I mean eventually, I think you just either develop a personal style or you don't. There are a lot of things that I used to do that I don't do anymore. For instance parentheticals in dialogue: I won't use them as much anymore, because I realize that actors have something to bring to it and want to have a say for themselves. I would write dialogue like, "Jack (convincingly) says: 'I love you.'" It's not possible to connote that kind of thing without an actor's participation. And I don't write direction into screenplay so much anymore; like "close up," or "wide shot," unless it is in very broad terms. Because I know that directors get annoyed and things always turn out differently.

SL: *American Pie*, your first director's job for both you and your brother, was your next major assignment after *Ants*. How did you make that jump?

CW: Well that's a really weird transition in my life. *I'm not sure how that happened. We didn't make any shorts; we never directed anything until we directed our first feature. The last thing I ever wanted to say was, "I want to direct a movie."* There are a lot of people who want to do that. And I always thought that I just wanted to shut up about it and maybe the chance would appear at some point. Rightly or wrongly, *Ants* was kind of a cult hit amongst executives; I mean they liked the screenplay a lot. As a result, people wanted to have us write things and rewrite things quite a bit.

There was an executive at Universal who wanted to work with us as writers for a while, but we were never available, rewriting here and there. They had this little movie that they couldn't find the right director for. They knew it was going to be quite inexpensive—about eleven million dollars—which was small by studio standards. And they thought, "What the hell, maybe we'll go with writers, instead of video or commercial directors."

I think because Paul and I, we had no notion of getting the job, we just went in the meeting like that. It was one of those moments where you just say what springs to mind, because you don't have anything to lose. And suddenly we found ourselves in a position to direct. I mean, we had been wanting to direct something—but only from that point of view of wanting to have as much to do in the making of a film as possible.

SL: Did you have any distinct directorial visual ideas going in?

CW: I think it does come from the story. In the case of *American Pie*, it was a fairly simple story. We didn't go into the meeting talking about how it's going to look except that it's going to be straightforward. I mean we had things that we wanted to stay clear of: anything that was very heightened and broad and zany. I suppose if there was any sort of literary style, it was more of a neo realist, kitchen-sink look; like the English films of the 1960s, or Truffaut, where the style is fairly unpretentious and matter of fact. And you feel from the way the movie is shot, that you're dealing with real people, not some sort of any literary, cultural films.

SL: But it sounds that you were fairly self-confident about the look of it?

CW: We have always been fans of American screwball comedies of the 30s and 40s—especially my brother. And we do have our little weird influences. I mean,

I am a big fan of Yasujiro Ozu, who makes these very quiet Japanese movies; also movies that enter in certain domestic scenes. I guess these are close to *American Pie* in a way, but we certainly didn't come out of the box, saying to the studio people that it's going to be like that. We just said: "One of the great things about this as far as art directing goes is that visually it is a fairly simple movie. You need to know the timing of jokes, and you needed to convey the sense that these people were real in some way; that they weren't stereotypes or caricatures." So we suggested a very simple style of shooting.

SL: And you were also confident that somehow you would make it through production, having no directing experience whatsoever?

CW: That's kind of fortunate for me: it is where that kind of Oxbridge arrogance comes in. It's like: "I'm sure if other people can do it, I can manage. So I'll just sort of wing it." Which is pretty much what happened. You know I couldn't tell you at the time we were gunning for the job what a schedule or a budget was. I wouldn't have known what kind of lens was telephoto and what kind was wide angle. But I will say to our credit that we were always willing to admit things that we don't know. And that helps us to learn a great deal. So we were willing to learn from our first AD and our cinematographer. I think they actually appreciate when you're upfront in that way.

SL: Where you ever afraid you could fall into teen comedy genre clichés when working on *American Pie*?

CW: Well, it's strange. *When we were making our first film, it wasn't really natural for us. I never had any affection for teen comedies. They always made me feel like, "Those kids should get a job and get a life."* So in other words, we weren't in love with the genre. So we didn't have to enshrine any of the standard things and cliché.

Also, I think Paul and I, we have a very good cliché meter inbuilt. I think especially for those genre pieces, the first thing we would do is to identify the clichés and avoid them as much as possible. I mean obviously you have archetypal characters, but it's a real fear of being bad that keeps us from doing things that might have ended up as cliché. And we were fortunate because we didn't have enough money to get big TV stars do it. We had these real unknowns, lending a real freshness to it. We really didn't know what we were doing in the sense of not knowing all the things that might have gone wrong, not knowing all the demographics that we were supposed to be addressing. We were just really, really lucky in being free enough to sort of make this film the way we wanted to. Part of that was that Universal at the time was *Meet Joe Black* and *Babe: Pig in the City*; both of which were huge productions that were going to end up not making any money.

We had a really great cast and a really good writer who stayed working with us. We honestly didn't know any better.

SL: How would you say that you and your brother's personalities translate into your filmmaking?

CW: *Well, I think that both my brother and I, we have a fairly heightened sense of the absurd. That's how we understand life in one way. I think that's why we ended up making comedies.* One approach to art—which is sort of a more high-art approach—is to identify and associate the various dark elements in life and the disappointments and pain. Instead, we've always found it easier to deal with the utterly absurd aspects of human behavior. So I think I have a pretty good sensibility in that regard. Personally, I have the tendency, which is somewhat inherited from my family, to be gloomy and brooding *slash* depressive. I think *About a Boy* was a movie about that. I was really drawn to both the Hugh Grant and the Nicholas Hoult character, because they dealt with depression.

I think a lot of people that make comedies are the class clown or naturally funny people. I'm definitely not like that. If anything, I'm very gloomy and dark.

SL: So how do gloominess and *American Pie* go together?

CW: Well it's really easy. It takes a lot of commitment to make a film. You have to be really driven to sort of spend the incredibly long hours and the focus and concentration that it requires on this massive industrial process. So a lot of doing comedy on film is really about covering all the bases, thinking things out very carefully and being very serious about what you're doing.

I've also always been really driven. Maybe not always in a good way, but driven to move on to the next thing in order to have new stimuli—because I didn't really want to stay still and think about life as it was. So my brother and I were constantly—at least from my point of view—taking on bigger challenges and biting off more than we can chew so that we work hard and get to this next level of accomplishment or whatever it may be. And probably part of that came from our immigrant background and from having fairly accomplished parents and grandparents. There was a real desire to move forward. More than anything else, the real difficulty has been to take things easy and to stop working.

SL: So your upbringing was vital?

CW: It's not exactly in the sense that everyone talks about how Asian families are very education-oriented. It was never beaten into my skull, but there was a sense of proving yourself. You concentrated and you worked hard.

And in comedy in general, it is not as fun as people imagine it is. I mean the film hopefully is. I worked with Mike Myers at one point on a film that eventually didn't get made. He works incredibly hard. He is incredibly driven—almost to a worrisome degree. It's a very sort of nerve-wracking business to go into.

SL: What are some major personal attributes that you feel you need to succeed as director?

CW: Persistence and sociability, actually. Because you're really dealing with a large crew of people and you have to be able to get the best out of them. And

I'd like to say also experience, even though I don't have enough of it. I think experience of films first of all, and experience of the process as well. It really helps knowing the way this business gets done.

*There are two words that really bother me when people talk about directors: "passion" and "vision." I think they are both sort of bullshit, because it takes a lot more than passion and vision to make a film.* It just takes *Sitzfleisch*—isn't that the German expression?—the ability to show stamina and to just stay on something.

Vision conveys the notion that there is this one image of the film that you have in your mind and that it is simply a question of executing it. It think the director is the guy that takes responsibility for coordinating all the various aspects of what goes into the film. The result is a tremendous amount of pressure, because people are asking you questions all day long. And if you can't handle that sort of responsibility, you really shouldn't get into it. And it tends to eat up your entire life. But if you're very good at marshalling the resources of all the various and hopefully talented people that are working for you, the end result can be pretty extraordinary. If you think about it, it is this tiny quintessence of two hours of celluloid. But in order to end up with those things, you have to make enormous sacrifices in terms of your personal life and certainly your time.

Hopefully there's sort of a central organizing principle in terms of what you have in mind in the end. If you want to call it vision that's fine, but I don't think it's as concrete as that. Unfortunately there are so many compromises on the way that it's not going to look precisely whatever you had in your mind in the beginning.

SL: In your mind, how has making films transformed you?

CW: Well, it gave focus to my dilettantism. And it gave me something to keep me off the streets, basically. I mean obviously it transformed my life. I've been able to make a living at it and meet a lot of people that I like and admire. It has moved me from New York to Los Angeles. It's changed my life from this sort of European-influenced, very kind of cosmopolitan life, to this weird, lotus-eating Los Angeles, Californian, existence. I was surely annoyed at first, but now I kind of like it, I think it's pretty amusing and fun.

SL: Are you escaping tradition?

CW: This; but there is the film industry, which is its own weird hierarchical structure. You have to subscribe to it to a certain degree in order to prosper as a studio filmmaker. Though it has given me a lot of freedom eventually, I sometimes just want to slowly fade it out of my life.

SL: Any ambitions for the future?

CW: The one thing I want to make is either an epic, or a kind of very ambitious film in terms of scale. I'd like to make a very visually resonant film. There are two directors I really, really admire and they are not funny at all. That's David

Lean and Akira Kurosawa. So it would be fun—actually not fun but miserable, but also worthwhile to me to make a big wide-screen epic.

SL: And finally not be miserable behind the camera anymore . . .

CW: . . . yeah. I mean I had fun learning more about the visual and technical aspects of filmmaking. It's going to the point where it's so hard to make a film that I am telling myself, "If I am going to drive myself nearly insane, I want to at least do it on a very big project." And I think, if I could do that, I could sort of step away and feel I wouldn't have anything to prove anymore. That's kind of where I see it going.

In a sense, I would like to make one last big effort at making a big significant—with a capital "S"—film and then see how I feel after that.

# Adamson, Andrew

**BORN:**
1966, Auckland, New Zealand

**BACKGROUND:**
Computer Graphics, Special Effects

**FILMS:**
Shrek I - 2001
Shrek II - 2004
The Chronicles of Narnia: The Lion, the Witch and the Wardrobe - 2005
The Chronicles of Narnia: Prince Caspian - 2007

**MAIN GENRES:**
Animation, Comedy, Adventure, Fantasy

**DIRECTOR'S CUT:**
"I liked my new job a lot—it seemed to satisfy both a sort of intellectual and a creative need."

ANDREW ADAMSON: I was raised in a very free atmosphere. The most formative part of my childhood was actually growing up in Papua, New Guinea, up on the equator. In was a relatively undeveloped, rural country, and consequently I grew up driving motorbikes and four-wheel drives in the bush at the age of thirteen. I had a very supportive family. I think both of my parents felt all of us could do whatever we wanted to do. Not in that running wild kind of way so much as that they would just support us in any of our choices.

SL: As very often with film directors, you were the youngest in your family?

AA: Actually, I have two older brothers and a younger sister. Because I was scribbling and drawing at an early age, my parents sort of decided from very early on that I was going to have some kind of artistic outlet. So they encouraged that with gifts of various art implements and supplies. You know, all through high school they really felt that it was just about creating opportunities. If I had wanted to be a brain surgeon or a gravedigger, they would have supported me.

SL: What did you spent your time doing apart from scribbling?

AA: It varied throughout my childhood. I did a lot of model-making and puppet-making. As I got older, I was more into motorcycles and cars. *For the longest time I thought I was going to be a mechanic, until I realized that I would always have to have dirty nails and go through an apprenticeship [laughing]—which is basically generally being the general dog's buddy, the errand boy. That wasn't too appealing.*

When I left high school, I was actually planning to get into architecture. It's similar in a lot of ways to computer animation and computer imagery because it's a combination of the aesthetic and the technical. It involves arts and science. By that stage in my life, I had realized that both were kind of interesting to me.

The only reason I didn't get involved in architecture was that I missed university enrollment. I messed myself up in a car accident and got hospitalized for a couple of months. That left me with a year on my hands to figure out what to do. That was around '84–'85.

I saw an advertisement for computer animation, which was a very new field at the time. It sounded interesting to me, also as I had grown up around computers since the age of nine.

My brothers and I had been writing games programs when I was fourteen. So very accidentally I got into it. I was young and gullible and willing to be paid nothing to be working loads of hours.

It was a company in Auckland looking for graphic artists. I rang the guy and said, "I don't have any sort of formal training, is it worth coming in?" And he said no. But then I rang back a little while later and said, "Look, I am actually really interested in what you are doing, can I just come in and see." And he said, "OK, fine. Bring your portfolio with you."

Partly because I hadn't gone to any of the schools, my portfolio was really different from everyone else's. Then he was having a problem with his computer that I could solve while I was there for the interview. So that's how I ended up getting the job.

SL: And the job consisted in what exactly?

AA: At that point, it was mainly doing station IDs for programming and sort of early effects for commercials.

SL: So pretty quickly you gave up on your idea of becoming an architect?

AA: I liked my new job a lot. Like architecture, it combines so many of the same kind of things. It seemed to satisfy both a sort of an intellectual need and a creative need. It's like so many things that you do by accident and than you find out you have an aptitude or a like for it. Then you just kind of keep going, then something else comes up, then you do that . . . and that keeps you going for a while. *I can't say I ever had a grand plan to my career. It has all been pretty accidental.*

SL: You hardly could have at age nineteen—

AA: Yeah, well I still don't know . . .

SL: . . . at twice that age.

AA: Exactly [*laughing*].

SL: So you found an outlet for your various talents—

AA: Absolutely. It was 50 percent design and 50 percent sort of execution. Execution was the very technically satisfying part—figuring out how to do things that hadn't been done before. And the design was the creatively satisfying part. TV3 was a new TV station that came on the air—believe it or not, at that point they only had two stations in New Zealand. So when the new station came on air, it was a big deal to design the opening graphics. And that was a very satisfying thing to be doing at that time.

I was working with all these briefs of how they wanted to appeal to what kind of audience and how they wanted to be new and tied to the mythology of New Zealand. All these kinds of things had to be folded into what basically was a flying logo—at that time of my life, I found that creatively very satisfying [*laughing*]. I don't know if I would now, but back then . . .

SL: Well it was high-tech in those days—

AA: That's the strange thing. You look at that stuff now and it has that lovely cheesy 80s appeal, but at the time it was a huge challenge.

SL: At what point and why did you go to America?

AA: In '91, I was recruited over here for PDI. Before that, I had worked for another New Zealand company called Video Images. I ended up sort of running their graphics division. I figured I kind of tapped out as far as I could go in New Zealand and planned to travel to Europe and work there. I started traveling up to Thailand and got as far as Turkey, where I ran out of money. I had to make a decision between going on to London and getting a job there or going back to New Zealand. The company there persuaded me to go back by offering me new equipment and stuff. So I went back for a while.

I used to come to the States for the Sigraph conference every year. I met some people from PDI, who then persuaded me to come over here.

I arrived in the States really expecting a bigger market, bigger budgets, more creative kinds of things—but found that it was largely the same. I mean working in advertisement in TV is pretty much the same anywhere, especially in the days of the beginning of this industry.

However, at the time, PDI was just starting to get into feature film effects, as were a lot of computer graphic companies. I worked on a Barry Levinson film called *Toys* which really gave me the interest of working on a longer format; storytelling that didn't just necessarily come on the air while people were on their way to the bathroom.

SL: *Toys* was a real breakthrough in 3-D storytelling—

AA: *Toys* was actually the first animated film that used motion capture. It's interesting, because for every film using this technique that came out over the next few years, they claimed, "This is the first film that uses motion capture." But in 1992, we were using a very crude technique with this sort of exoskeleton with pentiometers on every joint—it was all hand-built. There were also a bunch of technical breakthroughs in the use of photo mapping—of using photographic imagery mapped back onto computer generated objects, so that they looked completely real. The film didn't succeed particularly well, but the effects were pretty innovative, though I know that at ILM at the time, they were doing things with films like *The Abyss* that were equally innovative. I think *The Abyss*, also *The Terminator*, were breakthrough films. I don't think *Toys* ever had that appeal—the effects were less featured.

One of the things I found very interesting at that stage was that because of the small market, in New Zealand I had been kind of a jack-of-all-trades so to speak. I had to do everything from my own producing, to systems administration, to animation, to design.

So fairly quickly, I was sort of able to climb through the company, because of all that exposure I had as a sort of one-man-band back in New Zealand. In the US, people tended to specialize a lot more in any one of those tasks.

SL: You were only 25 when you were technical director on *Toys*.

AA: That's right. You know you never feel that you are so young at the time. For me it was largely that it was just challenging. You do something for too long you get bored, you look for the next challenge, and you sort of keep moving. *I think in a field that's so based on technology and that changes so quickly, you always have to be in a position of fear. You operate at a level where maybe you will not be able to achieve what you need to achieve. In order to move forward, you just keep yourself somewhat in that stage of anxiety.*

SL: So fear is a creative motor?

AA: You definitely have to be willing to go into a place where you're trying to do something that has never been done before. You don't know if you're going to succeed, so you have to be willing to fail in order to keep moving forward. And this is true for filmmaking in general.

SL: Were you ever tempted to leave the risky track for a more secure one?

AA: I never really did opt for it and I don't know where it would have put me. I guess just kind of doing what everyone else had done before. I think that if you're not doing something new, ultimately you'd be left behind, particularly in computer animation. An audience tires of something, and I think you have to keep giving them new ideas and taking them to new places in order to keep them interested.

SL: Then in the 90s, you worked with a number of great directors on various different productions. How did you experience that time yourself?

AA: It was an exciting time. It was the time where computer animation and computer effects in film were really being embraced. It changed to some degree the way films were being made. So to me, it was a chance to learn a lot more about filmmaking and at the same time keep myself gainfully employed [chuckling]. So it actually turned out to be good in many ways. Yeah, I worked with many great people, not just directors—also John Dykstra, the effects supervisor from *Star Wars*—some really wonderful people from which I learned so much.

SL: When working for directors like Joel Schumacher or Tim Burton on the two *Batman*s, were you actually involved in the creative storytelling process, or were you rather just the technical guy supposed to figure out the ambitious special effects?

AA: I worked on Joel's *Batman*s and I was absolutely involved. That got me more and more into the filmmaking process. As a visual effects supervisor, you tend to generally just handle a portion of the film, not necessarily knowing what's going on with the whole film. But often, you're an essential part of the storytelling. Joel is somebody who is not particularly interested in visual effects. He is interested in the results much more than the technique. Very often I found that this was actually quite freeing, because he would say, "Just go off and do it and show it to me when you're done." He would then like it or not. This also then meant that I had a chance to really direct things because that was all part of achieving the feeling of the larger visual effects scope.

On *Batman Forever* and *Batman and Robin*, I started to direct the second unit for the effects shots. That was a chance for me to get some experience there as well.

SL: Directing the visual effects unit, were you directly drawn to this new aspect and dimension of your work?

AA: To some degree, but it was not so much a new dimension, as I had done that with commercials and so on. What I found myself doing was developing a thick skin.

You know, usually effects shots get left until the last minute: after they've done all the drama, they hand the crew over to the effects people. It usually means that after an all-night shoot, at three in the morning, you're trying to get an incredibly difficult technical shot, at which point everyone's just dying for you to say it's good enough and "let's move on" [*laughing*]. And you have to be a perfectionist and just stick there and just ignore all the hassle.

SL: And nobody understands what you're doing anyway—

AA: Exactly. That's an important thing to learn for directing as well, because *you have to kind of stick to your vision and adhere to the fact that sometimes it's going to piss people off.*

SL: Do you feel that while you were doing all these fascinating jobs in the 90s, you actually also learned how to tell a story?

AA: I don't. At a certain point, I realized I didn't know enough about how to tell a story. By this time, I started to do some writing on my own. I was really just playing around with it for myself, because I realized that this was the big important gap in my knowledge base. By that time I felt, "OK, I am going to keep going until a certain point, then I want to start to direct.' So one of the main reasons why I did *Batman and Robin* was actually with the intention of saving enough money that I could then spend a year writing.

SL: At what point exactly did you realize that what you really wanted was to direct?

AA: That was right around when I finished *Batman Forever*. I went to New Zealand on holiday for a while and ended up helping out on Peter Jackson's film *The Frighteners*. He'd asked Universal for someone who could go down there to help out with visual effects. I met a guy down there by the name John Garbett, who was sort of an executive producer. At some point he asked me what I wanted to do. I said, "You know I haven't really told many people this cause it sounds like such a cliché, but I think I want to try my hand at directing." We sort of talked about that for a bit, and then I went off and did *Batman and Robin*. I planned to spend a year on the beach in Portugal, just writing. Instead, John Garbett actually came back to me—*by this time he was involved a movie called* Shrek. *He said: "Look, I've got something that uses a lot of your existing skills and that is also a directing job. Are you interested?" When I found out that it was animation, I said, "No, I am not really."* I referred everybody I knew—because my plan was to direct some small independent film.

However, they kept coming back to me. Eventually I met with Jeffrey Katzenberg who kind of talked me into giving it a try. I said, "Let's try for three months and see how we both feel." And you know the same thing as before: you get into it, there's problems, you solve the problems—and four and a half years later you've got a film.

SL: Did you feel pigeonholed or why did you initially lose interest when you heard it was animation?

AA: Not so much that, more the duration, and I wasn't particularly interested in animation as an art form anyway. Also by this time, my computer animation had taken me much more into the field of visual effects, which had taken me into live action. And I liked the whole idea of getting further into that.

I already knew that animation was a very iterative process and I just didn't know whether I had the stamina for it, although at that time, I thought about it being a three-year project. It ended up being a nearly five-year project.

And also the idea of spending a year in Portugal writing seemed really appealing.

SL: Portugal it had to be—

AA: [*Chuckling*] You know just it's this place I wanted to visit. It's relatively unspoiled and untouristed. So I thought that's a nice place to go.

SL: So when you signed on to *Shrek*, the idea was there but the story was not?

AA: Correct. I very actively cowrote the story. Animation is a very collaborative process. There are any number of people—storyboard artists, and writers—that contribute to the storytelling. But as director, you really help to shape all those efforts. And that was when I was starting to get involved in the writing. It was really more as a means of communicating ideas, which I guess is what writing is. But more specifically in this case, sometimes you get pages that you like but that are not quite right. So the easiest thing is to sit down and work with them: to work your ideas out in script form. And on top of that, Jeffrey Katzenberg is always "story story story," that's his first priority. So he allowed the room for that and helped to nurture it. And I found that it was something that I did seem to have an aptitude for.

I think a lot about directing and storytelling is about empathy—empathy for your characters, empathy for your actors, in this case the animators and the vocal actors. So you have to understand the character and try to communicate that understanding.

So I guess by being a relatively empathetic person, I found that I very quickly gravitated towards working with actors and storytelling.

SL: So storytelling came rather naturally to you—did you also try to read some of the literature around scriptwriting?

AA: A combination of both. I think I found somewhat of a natural aptitude for it. There are still like these three stages of storytelling: there's incubation, then getting the ideas out and on paper, and then there is the editing process, the making sense of a lot of those ideas. And you go through that cycle repeatedly. You take time to just bounce the ideas around in your head. Then when they are good, you write them down, and then you reread them and edit them. And again, it's a combination of the creative and the technical.

Definitely, there is theory that you apply to your writing. There is an analysis level, where you look at something and say, "instinctively this scene doesn't work," but you have to approach it from a more analytical point of view and figure out why it doesn't work. Some of what I was doing at that time was learning the analysis process; reading books on storytelling, talking to other people, and so on.

SL: What were you reading?

AA: Interestingly enough, there is a much-maligned person called Robert McKee, who I'm sure you've heard of. Who some people think is the devil—

SL: And others think he is God—

AA: Exactly. I found if you follow any of those analysis tools to the word, you'll develop something that's very formulaic and it will be bad. *But if you look at those books for what they are intended for—as a tool to figure out what's wrong—they are very useful. So I found Robert McKee's book very useful.*

But there is no way that I would ever follow it to the letter, nor do I think that it is his intention that people do. So that's probably the one that springs most to my head, but I read others as well. I spent more time actually analyzing films from the storytelling point of view—figuring out, "Yeah I like this film, now let me look at it from a more analytical point of view and figure out why I like it: what structurally works about it."

SL: Being more or less thrown into the waters of storytelling, did you ever feel pressure of having to prove yourself in the face of experienced producers, writers, and directors?

AA: Definitely. I didn't know whether I had storytelling skills or not, but there was definitely a point in proving that. I don't think it was a barrier, though. And I remember some distinct moments throughout the process where it changed. You know where I had done something and it was well accepted and I did something else and it was also well accepted and all of a sudden, people start listening. It becomes easier and easier. That's I think true of any relationship that you go through with any film company; somewhat of a proving period before you really have control.

SL: Do you remember people being surprised to hear good storytelling from you, the visual effects guy?

AA: You now there is definitely a period in any filmmaking process where you flounder for a while. And we went through a period of that on *Shrek*, where we just couldn't find the story. And I think as I started to find my voice and started to find the tone of that movie, there was acceptance and relief, because everybody was hoping for that.

It was very much a process of showing pieces of the movie to the studio, and very often the pieces would be very well accepted; but sometimes it would be like, "We don't get what you're doing here."

In animation, you present the entire movie in storyboard far before you start working on the actual images that will end up in the film. So I remember that point in the process, where I showed the whole film to the studio. Jeffrey called me very excited later on and said, "Look, I don't know what happened because I saw a lot of what went into this and didn't know if it was working. But now that I watched the film, I think it's on a great path." I guess it's that sort of Gestalt thing, that really the whole is bigger than the sum of the parts. That was sort of the breakthrough point for me and the movie.

From then on, it became much easier to do what we needed to do in order to kind of massage the story out.

SL: I am interested in how the creative process works for you. Once you have an idea, how do you translate it into your scene and how does the cooperative process with others work in order to make it happen?

AA: Well for me, particularly with comedy, it's largely about creating situations that allow humor. Very rarely does the humor emerge fully in the first draft, though. So what I often do is to work from treatment form first of all. Then I figure out the flow of the story. It's a continuously evolving document. Then I go into a scene and somewhat detail the scene out. Now in some cases, I'd write the scene out, in other cases, I would give this scene to a storyboard artist and say, "OK, here's what I basically want to achieve." For instance, the scene in the first *Shrek*, where the gingerbread man gets tortured. Basically, I had sort of given the idea of wanting to have a small cute creature tortured by Lord Farquaad. While I wanted to show him as a villain, I also wanted to create an opportunity of humor.

We played with a couple of alternatives. I thought about maybe dipping a gingerbread man in a cup of tea or something. I gave that brief to Conrad Vernon, the storyboard artist, who then developed the whole sequence, coming up with the version you saw. Of course he also substituted the New Zealand "cup of tea" for the more American milk.

In other cases, I would sit down and know exactly what I wanted to accomplish in that scene. I write it out for the storyboard artist, look at it, edit all together, and see how it works. Then make changes, rewrite it, and kind of go through that process again. The storyboarding process to me is really part of the writing process. You now some people consider it part of the visualization process; I consider it part of the storytelling.

SL: I imagine this to be especially true in animation, where you can't just go out on the set and see what will happen.

AA: I have gone through the same storyboarding process in *The Chronicles of Narnia*. I really consider it an extension of writing. I tend to overwrite. When you write a scene, you tend to put stuff in there that ultimately you won't need. You're right, in live action you just kind of go out there and block out the scene when you're rehearsing; storyboarding is a way of advancing that process. You're basically rewriting the script with the same information. It's an expensive writing tool but ultimately a very inexpensive production tool, as you don't tend to waste so much footage.

SL: How many people are you actually communicating with when creating a scene for animation? Can you sometimes just go check out yourself whether the scene works by putting the animated storyboard into the computer?

AA: Well, my editor Sim and I edit the boards together. So we just tend to do the voices ourselves initially. Sometimes, the storyboard artist and all of us do the voices—sometimes we hire temporary scratch actors to do it. Then you edit it with the sound effects, music, etc and watch the scene. Quite often by that stage, you've involved ten people in the writing process.

SL: Did you ever feel that it stifled your creativity by making you less flexible?

AA: *In animation, it's actually very flexible because you get many chances. With all the stages involved—you know you go through the writing, the boarding, the recording, editing, and the voices, starting the animation, the layout, the blocking—you get so many iterations, that you get a lot of chances to perfect things.* And even right near the end, you can have an idea and still integrate it.

In live action, it's to some degree the opposite, because once you've shot the scene it's over. If you happen to have an idea like a week later, you won't have a chance to integrate it if you've broken down the set. So, you know it's a very different process.

Emotionally it's a similar process though—the same frustrations and insecurities about scenes working or not. You have the same difficulties in making scenes work. It's just that the timing of the process is very different.

SL: On your first *Shrek*, you codirected with Vicky Jenson—how did that concretely work out?

AA: It varies from scene to scene. In some cases we split up scenes—she would take one and I would take the other and go through the whole process. In other cases, we traded backwards and forwards. You know one of us who got burned out and said, "Hey, you take this for a while." It was a pretty fluid process.

SL: At what stage do you make the decisions for actors and how much do they influence the process?

AA: They have a huge influence. For instance with Mike Myers, we developed the character with him in mind. So they can have a big influence both in the design of the character and then ultimately they bring in the comedy. You know when you're working with comedians; they bring so much to it. You tend to actually record and then rewrite after recording, because the process makes you find new elements.

In animation, it's a lot like the rehearsal process in live action: very often, the actor will bring something to the scene and that will give you an idea for the character that involves rewriting any number of scenes. And on top of that, sometimes in animation they also improvise. They will do a great improv that will make you rewrite that scene to so you can use it. Then you go to rerecord the other actors in the scene.

SL: When editing animation, is it very much an assembly of already drawn scenes—using the material you've prepared—or is it rather comparable to live action, where you have a whole number of different alternatives you can play with.

AA: It's just like in live action. The only thing is that the editing process goes on much longer. You start the editing process while writing, and you carry it on through production. So what takes three to four months in traditional live action, in animation you are talking about a period of three to four years. *Animation is simply much more thought through. You do choose every tree—in live action, you get so much more for free.*

SL: I would have thought there were randomized computer programs for that—

AA: There is software to generate the variations and fillers, but I still would be shown pretty much any type of tree there is. There are no accidents in animation, everything is put there deliberately. It's as if in live action you would have to tell your actors when to blink.

SL: Did you miss that degree of control in the *Chronicles*—that you were not able to tell your actors when to blink?

AA: You know it's interesting. It's different with different actors. Tilda Swinton told me, "Tell me what to do with my face!" She sometimes likes to be given really specific direction. So I'd go, "Raise your eyebrow when you say this word," and she would incorporate it in a very natural way. Not many actors can be that technical and still be natural.

You know, instead of control, in live action you get those happy accidents—those great moments that you didn't put in. On the negative side, you have no control of the weather [*laughing*]. And sometimes that completely changed the way the scenes worked. When you're outside waiting for a break in the clouds and you have four children waiting. As director, you've got to keep their attention and have them suddenly slip into the moment when someone yells "Sunlight!". That's really hard to do. So at points like that, I longed for the control of animation. But at those other times, when you get things that just happen—when you don't have to decide on the wind blowing that flag . . .

SL: Does reality in live action sometimes kick-start and enrich your imagination, helping you as director to come up with creative visuals and new ideas?

AA: I like to have a lot of control. You try and control as much of a film as you can, but then you sometimes have things happen by accident, that are better than the moment you imagined—it's like collaboration. Ultimately collaboration brings together a product that is better than anything the individuals could have done by themselves. Nature and natural things around you can have that effect of creating something better. At other times, it gets in the way. And it's just a balancing act—it's the game that you play.

SL: After finishing your second *Shrek*, you felt that your next film had to be live action?

AA: Actually after the first *Shrek*, I decided I was then going to do my small independent film. Before getting into *Shrek 2* Jeffrey literally called me. I said, "Look, I really had enough for now." Nevertheless, he started pitching me ideas that I didn't like. I had this one idea which I then pitched him back and he said, "Great, go and work on it." The next thing I knew, I found myself emotionally involved in the film.

So I wasn't really planning to do that, but having committed, I wanted to do a very different film—I wanted to do an ensemble piece.

You know we had seen *Shrek* in one type of world. I wanted to step out of that world and explore the characters and the construct of family. You come to a different place like LA as an outsider and end up finding friends out of which you create your own family. And that's kind of what Shrek, Donkey, and Fiona did. That thought led to the idea Fiona and Shrek also had their own real family to deal with.

SL: Could you generalize that and say that telling a compelling story is somehow extending the audiences family in some way, challenging and encouraging their capacity of developing new emotional links with those characters onscreen?

AA: Exactly. It's finding something that we all can relate to. It's something we all go through. It's this saying, "You don't just marry a spouse, you marry a whole family." And the challenge also with *Shrek* is the challenge to find something that adults can relate to, but at the same time keep it entertaining from the perspective of children as well.

SL: I found this striking about much of recent animation: that they have these two very distinct levels to them. Very funny but mysterious on an innocent level, very funny but quite sexually suggestive on the other; I am thinking of scenes in the first *Shrek*, when the donkey and Shrek repeatedly comment upon the impressive height of Lord Farquaad's "tower"—

AA: *Funny thing is, in most cases the children in the audience just laugh because the adults laugh.* I don't know why exactly—they can tell by the expressions and the body language if it's meant to be funny. And in other cases, you do things like getting donkeys caught in a turnstile and it's just slapstick funny. Any time you have that, it reaches people on many levels.

SL: With the *Chronicles of Narnia*, again have again made a family movie. What attracted you to the project?

AA: Actually on this film, I also tried to turn it away for a while—largely because I still wanted to get back to that little independent film.

I had done enough visual effects to know what I was getting into. And really had to consider if I wanted to do something of this scale. But, I grew up on these books, and knew that if I was going to do it, I would want to be very faithful to the books. I didn't think the studio would allow me to do that. So when I did finally take a meeting with them, I sort of started it by saying, "Look, this probably will be a short meeting, because here is what I would do with the film." But I found that that's what they wanted to do as well. *I continued and went to talk to C. S. Lewis's estate, and everyone just kept nodding. So before I knew it, I found myself having to do it.*

SL: So how apprehensive were you of the entire process—you had literally no experience in directing live action.

AA: You know I wasn't really that apprehensive. I felt it was something that I was comfortable doing. Obviously I had worked with actors before. It's all about this instinct and building a relationship with the actors, providing for them whatever they need to be able to portray the parts.

Even though the process is different obviously, it is at the same time easier in some ways, as you've got people in an environment together where they are playing off each other. So I don't have to provide that in this case. In animation, you've got to paint the picture in the actor's mind, telling them where they are and what's going on—"You're standing on top of the hill, looking out across a field and you see in the distance . . ." In live action you put someone on a hill and you get it all for free.

But at the same time, there is a lot of other stuff going on that you have to pay attention to. In animation, you generally only have one actor to focus on at a time. So I was obviously nervous; *The Chronicles* is a huge project with a lot of complexity to it. I wanted to have very subtle performances. I wanted to kind of step out of the fantasy genre into a more dramatic family story.

SL: Did a part of you feel spoiled by animation and the complete control you had over every aspect of it?

AA: Yeah, I actually did. I said to Jeffrey at one point that I was most worried about losing my gut instincts—because in animation you get second chances. That's what I felt a bit spoiled by.

Initially I was terrified working with children. I didn't have much to do with children and I didn't know how well I relate to teenagers—I don't know a lot of teenagers. But when we got into workshopping, I just felt I really liked it. Kids are so anxious to please. They're so energizing. They give you energy while you're working, which is not always the case with older actors. I found that while working with kids, you get a lot back as well. Also, their imagination is unspoiled.

Very often when you're working with an actor that has to act off a visual effects character—we had several of those in *The Chronicles*—they cannot act off non-existent things. But with children, their minds go there much more quickly. They're simply not carrying all the baggage that we, as adults, carry and their imaginations are much more unfettered. For instance, they'd be acting to me or sometimes just a tennis ball when in a scene with one of our computer generated talking characters—like Mr. Beaver.

SL: So directing children wasn't more difficult to you?

AA: The difficult parts are different, let's put it that way. What's sort of different from working with adults—and sometimes more difficult—is that you might have to trick them into things; trick them into what they are feeling, by actually giving them completely different direction to what the scene is really about. Just to try and find something that they relate to. The other side of children having less baggage is they don't have as much experience to draw from. You can't necessarily say, you know, "It's like this" and have them relate to that.

SL: What do you feel is more director-centered—live action or animation?

AA: It's interesting that this is such a debate. People don't know about directors in animation for some reason; I don't know why. So *very often people ask, "What does a director do in animation?" And you go, "'Well, kind of the same thing that a director does in live action." You're the conductor: you're the person waving the baton, keeping everyone marching to the same beat.* It's really a very similar process. You're the person who has the overall picture and has to make sure that all the pieces are playing together to create that kind of picture.

SL: Is there any strength that an animation director needs to have that a live action director doesn't need?

AA: Patience. Things take a lot longer. I do think that's important. I am a very patient person. I have been very lucky to gain that attribute from my father. Patience and determination—in my case I would sometimes call it stubbornness. But there are more euphemistic ways of putting that. Diligence [*chuckling*] or the willingness to keep on going with something until it's just right.

SL: Confidence?

AA: Yes, though it's not really confidence. Very often you watch a scene in its early form and it will be OK, and everyone around will tell you it's OK, because there's a machine waiting to be fed. You know they're trying to get the animation into the studio and get things going. So everyone really wants it to be good, so they tell you it's good. They want to believe it's good as much as you want to believe it. But very often there will be a faint voice in you that says, "It's not good enough": and you just got to have the tenacity—I guess that is a better word than stubbornness—to make it as good as it can be; as if you had no choice. At a certain point, it's never good enough, you just run out of time. You've got to have that patience and tenacity to try to always make it as good as it can be. I've heard it called "sacred dissatisfaction."

SL: Is animation directing more cooperative, as you have to communicate to so many people and through so many different channels?

AA: You have to communicate with as many people just at a different point in time and on a different level. That's why I say that emotionally it is sort of the same, but the processes are different. In animation, you're communicating with the actor about the intention one day and then maybe three weeks later, you're communicating to the CG cameraman how you want the camera to move. And then maybe a few weeks after that, you're communicating to the animator about how you want the character to move. And then a few weeks after that, you're communicating to the lighter about where to put the lights. You still do all of those things. But on set, you go in and tell them how you want it lit. Then you look at the lighting, discuss camera placement with the cameraman; then you talk to the actor about the performance and how you want him or her to move. You've still done all the same things but not divided up in the same way.

SL: Does live directing take up more of your energy to keep going on set, as you have to be aware of so many things simultaneously—on a creative, technical, and human level?

AA: *It's the difference between a sprint and a marathon, animation being the marathon.* You're working at a lower level for a longer period of time. It's still very arduous because of the duration. In live action, you're operating at a much higher energy level in a shorter period of time. Although, in the case of *The Chronicles*, with any of those big visual effects, it is both. You start with a sprint and then have to do a marathon afterwards.

SL: And so preparation and working style are very similar.

AA: The steps are different, but preparation is very similar.

SL: Any new elements or skills that weren't part of your work as animation director and had to learn how to do for live action?

AA: Definitely. I had to develop, or redevelop, the quick decision-making skills. And this is a big difference. When there is a whole crew waiting for a decision to be made, you have to make those decisions very quickly—you can't postpone them. And sometimes that means that you get in rehearsing a scene at the beginning of the day, blocking it out, but then it's not working for some reason. Maybe the performance didn't come out the way you expected it—you then have to reconfigure it. You have very little time to do that. I definitely had to redevelop that.

The other thing that was interesting for me and that I had to learn how to do much more quickly was the blocking. In animation you get many possibilities to try things out; thinking, "Should I do this or that with the camera?" Then you get to look at the whole sequence before you make the final decisions. In live action, you have to either block beforehand to know exactly what you're doing or block very quickly on set—obviously you would have the cameraman and the script supervisor to help you do that. But I found that this was probably my biggest weakness at the start. I was lucky to work with very experienced people. Donald McAlpine as DP, who of course has done any number of films. That was a huge help—as was the script supervisor Alexa Alden. I said to them early on, "Look, I think this is one of the things that I'm gonna be weak at and I need you help with it in the beginning."

SL: Did you feel that investors or producers were ever apprehensive of you first-time directing a live feature of such a scale?

AA: I'm sure there was that, but at the same time they gave me the money to do it, so I am very grateful. But there was definitely a feeling that there was something to be proven here. You know going into it, there was that, "Ok you directed these two blockbusters, but how are you gonna be now?" But there was obviously enough trust to let me go. And I never felt that they got in the way of it.

SL: So what would you recommend a young director interested in animation directing?

AA: You know, the most important thing is learning how to tell a story. It's knowing how to create characters. I mean I think the creation of characters is really important. I think that is one of the reasons why *Shrek* succeeded—just the love of the characters. The plot and everything aside, people come out of the theater loving the characters.

It's not about the medium that you use. You can cut out paper characters or cut out a multimillion-dollar visual effects extravaganza. It still comes down to the same basic thing as to what people walk away with and whether it was a good story. I would advocate spending time writing—spending time looking at films; kind of the process I went through in the beginning. Not just saying, "I like a film"; figuring out why you liked is important. What did the director and the writers do to make you like it.

SL: And practically? Would you recommend formal instruction?

AA: *I never did film school, so it's hard for me to say. Obviously there is huge value in education, but education comes in many different ways. I've always felt for myself that the best way of learning something is just by doing it.* Being in that position of fear, stepping over the line and forcing yourself to do stuff. One of the reasons—the trick—why it worked so well for me is that although I'd used writing exercises as a tool to push my storytelling abilities I never pushed far enough. You know whenever I'd be writing something, I'd get to a wall. I put it aside and I might never get back to it. When started directing I was employed to do this, I couldn't just put it aside. So you get to the wall and you just keep on banging your head against it until you break through. Sometimes, I found the pressure of the situation—where things were beyond my control and I was beyond my abilities—helped me to push my abilities

SL: Is 3-D simply the next step from traditional animation, or are we genuinely entering a new era of filmmaking? Will film be able to create the perfect illusion and confusion of what's animated and what is not?

AA: Personally, I think all of the above. In animation, CG is somewhat the flavor of the moment. I think traditional animation will have its day again, once the interest in CG as a new form has sort of died down. As well as that, I believe that the integration of CG in live action is more and more transparent.

For instance, one of the principle characters in *The Chronicles of Narnia*, the Lion, is a CG character. He doesn't look CG—the lion is photo real. If you saw him walking along, you'd think he was a real lion. He talks, which kind of gives the game away [*chuckling*], but the idea is that you accept him as a completely real character in the film.

SL: So here we are at the next step which wasn't yet possible two or three years ago—

AA: Correct. We saw it I think with Gollum in *Lord of the Rings*, who was sort of the first character that you completely believed. And I think ours is an extension of that.

SL: How far will that lead? Will there be a film that is entirely CG? Can there be maybe even CG movie stars one day, or is that maybe not the goal?

AA: No, I think it is a goal, to even just expand what we're doing. *One day you will be able to create a human actor in CG. You got to think though why you need to do it.* There is no point in putting a CG human in if you can do it with a real one. But if there is something particular that you need to achieve—I mean it is already used for dangerous stunts. People have talked about it in the context of bringing an actor back from the dead. I think you have to question the ethics of that to some degree. They say, "We can do a movie with Humphrey Bogart and Marilyn Monroe," but how would they feel about that? Is that a movie they'd be wanting to do? But yes, I do think it's possible.

SL: What do you personally perceive as a challenge for your future as a filmmaker?

AA: You know for me it's all about getting to be a better and better storyteller. The films I've done so far have been popular; they have been films that appealed to masses of people and I feel very fortunate for that. But I would love to do something quite dark, something that's more of a vulnerable, emotional journey for me as a director. I think that's a really big challenge for me as far as storytelling goes: doing films that take me into new place emotionally, as opposed to visual exploration or humor.

SL: Do you feel that your past three films have transformed you as a person?

AA: That's a good question because it's hard to separate that from your general life journey. I can't say that there is noticeable overall change, like, "Yes, this has completely changed my life in one way or the other." I've probably become a better communicator, because I had to. So it has probably helped in that way.

   You know *I had a child two years ago. That has probably had more of an effect to me than all the other experiences—the biggest sort of life change.* The filmmaking experience is somewhat of a slower thing, and you're growing older at the time. You're maturing anyway, so you're going through changes constantly. But I've met a lot of great people and that had an effect on me. It's those interactions that enrich your life, so I guess that I would say that these films have added to my life.

# PART II—A GENERATION OF DIRECTOR-DIRECTORS

## Section One: Self-Made Directors

# Singer, Bryan

**DIRECTOR'S CUT:**
"It's the same principle I apply to everything I do . . . is that it's a project and I am very obsessed with that project going well and being done to the best of my abilities."

**BORN:**
1965, New York

**BACKGROUND:**
"37 Jobs"

**FILMS:**
Public Access—1993
The Usual Suspects—1995
Apt Pupil—1998
X-Men—2000
X2—2002
Superman Returns—2006
Logan's Run—2007

**MAIN GENRES:**
Drama, Thriller, Mystery, Fantasy, Sci-Fi

BRYAN SINGER: I grew up in the suburbs of New Jersey, in a place called Princeton Junction. It was near Princeton University, but in a more rural area, which is now developed and has grown a lot since then. But at the time it was farm country. I lived very close to Grover's Mill, where the original aliens were meant to have landed and the *War of the World* radio broadcast came from. That's where we used to get our lawnmower fixed. This was always kind of interesting to me as a kid because it was this famous place from this famous radio broadcast, but it was a real place right by our house.

My father was a corporate credit manager for the Maidenform Company which made women's apparel. And my mother took ten years of doing nothing—just to raise me. Afterwards, she got involved in local politics and became an environmental activist, then eventually a bureau chief at the department of environmental protection of New Jersey.

We grew up on a cul-de-sac in a very tight neighborhood; there were only a few houses and everyone knew each other. I was a Jewish kid but never particularly religious—I was never Bar-Mizvaed or anything like that. However, we were the only Jews in the neighborhood, as most people were Catholic.

I was an only child and I was adopted, of which I was always aware. In fact, at the time I thought that being adopted was normal because we happened to know this other family that had two children, one of which was adopted. So I thought most families had that.

SL: So early on, you had a perception of being different from other people in some respects?

BS: Yeah, being an only child and being Jewish in a predominantly Catholic neighborhood and being adopted. So it was always kind of different. I thought of that, but then I had great friendships, some of whom are my friends to this very day. In fact my best friend from childhood is staying with me right now here in Sydney (location for *Superman Returns*).

SL: You were also part of some sort of Secret Society as a kid—

BS: You mean the Nazi Club that I did with a few friends? Yeah, when I was little, my neighbor that lived in Jason Street—its funny, we were just talking about this moments ago at dinner tonight, I didn't think you'd ask. We always loved the war books—*I have always been very fascinated by the Second World War and its iconography; so we thought it would be cool to have this little Nazi Club among the three of us. So we wore crayon Swastika armbands that we made.* One day I came home in the kitchen and proudly showed this to my mother. She freaked out. I mean, we are no super-Jewish people or heavily practicing Jews, but that was not acceptable on a human level to be wearing that. So she explained to me very definitively and in a very loud voice why. I got one of many Holocaust lectures. I didn't wear the armband again. We *disbanded* the Nazi Club [*chuckling*].

SL: Do you remember what made it appear seductive to you?

BS: I think it's the Nazi aesthetics. When you're a kid, you look at that kind of stuff. It was designed very much as a method of propaganda before propaganda was a dirty word. It was sort of designed as a method of showing power—the strong formality of the Reich's architecture, the colors, the reds and the blacks; things like that are very enticing and fascinating to a kid. Everything is presented to you. So you think it's just kind of cool and you don't realize what war and what human suffering is until you start to truly examine it and read about it and see it and think about it. When you're ignorant, the terrors of war and genocide become more statistical.

That's why I think a lot of kids today think it's cool to be nihilistic or to be in a gang or to have a weapon. . . . I used to have a gun—I used to have a rifle and it was so cool: I bought it without my parents' permission and my father ended up buying it from me. We ceremoniously took a hammer and smashed it in the garage.

My Father actually fought in the Korean War and saw combat first hand. So to him, there was nothing cool about it: it was terrible and displacing and weapons were unnecessary.

SL: Do you see any positive or human aspect about all these instruments and institutions of terror?

BS: Well, I personally made a lot of war films in 8mm—you know I would go to the Army/Navy store and we would re-enact these huge battle sequences, using these fireworks. This was in my mid-teens. It was interesting: the good guys would always lose. That was something very consistent: they would always be killed or executed or blown up. I think I made about four war films.

SL: Out of how many?

BS: Oh God, maybe 20 or 30 films, ranging in size from two to 45 minutes. I have been making films probably non-stop since I was thirteen. I have never stopped either developing, producing, or finishing a film since then.

SL: When did the idea of becoming a film director first come into your mind?

BS: One night very specifically. I was at a friend's house down the street and we were watching this popular news magazine show "20/20." They were profiling the life of Steven Spielberg; the movie *ET* had just come out. I saw this guy who was a nerdy Jewish kid who'd lived in New Jersey for a short period. He did not get good grades in school and he had a drawer full of 8mm movies. Suddenly, I saw myself in that kid that had just made this amazing movie *ET* and that everybody was blown away by. I remember thinking: "*I have a drawer, I make these movies already for fun.*"

And then I remember. It was a certain spot on the sidewalk. It was the walk home that night from my friends house to my own—a very short walk of like two blocks. *And all of a sudden it hit me that now I know what I want to do with the rest of my life: "I wanna be a film director!" I felt so good because I was thinking "now that's one thing I don't have to worry about anymore."* You could still find out the exact night if we did the maths.

SL: So rather than you choosing, directing chose you?

BS: Exactly. I felt a huge relief—like a huge weight lifted off my head. I said "this is one thing that everyone worries about: What are they gonna be when they grow up." It felt so good. I had a complete skip in my step—suddenly I was running in the night air. I was so excited.

SL: Did anything change in you life after that?

BS: Oh, I didn't do anything different. I was already making short films. So I was just making them more aggressively and I made bigger ones. *My neighbor was Ethan Hawke so I would make two films coincidentally with Ethan.*

SL: But he didn't start acting thanks to you?

BS: No. His parents, I think, were already taking him to auditions for professional productions. After our two 8mm films, he made this movie *Explorer* and suddenly there was another tangible element for me. Grover's Mill kind of had a connection to media history in a way—well now suddenly I had made films with this young actor that Joe Dante and River Phoenix had made a film with in Hollywood. Suddenly I was in some tangible way connected to Hollywood and it made it seem more possible to me. Years later and after Ethan had done *Dead Poets' Society*, he acted in a 16mm short which started my career.

SL: Did that connection prove crucial to you in gaining access to some Hollywood network, or was it more of a psychological access?

BS: There was no network. None of these things helped me specifically, though ultimately the film made with Ethan was very helpful. But also my cousin—really my third cousin: my father's cousin's children—are Lory and Mark Singer. Lory was in the movie *Footloose* and Marc Singer was in the TV shows "V" and "Bees Master." So both were successful actors.

Although I didn't really know them at the time—though Lory and I are friendly now—they were *real* and had the last name "Singer." They showed me that it is possible.

So the combination of these things—that I was somehow related or attached to the movie business and to people that had "made it" so to speak—made everything tangible in a way. *When I said to my mother and father, "I wanna be Steven Spielberg" they would say: "Well, that is a one in a million chance" and I would say "as long as it is a one in a million and not a zero in a million chance, then it's worth the effort."*

SL: After high school, what concretely lead up to your first feature project?

BS: I applied and was not accepted at several film schools—NYU and USC for example. I did get accepted to SUNY in Purchase and at the New York School of Visual Arts [SVA]. I decided that it was better to be in New York City—but my grades were terrible. You have to understand that I graduated from high school with a cumulative grade point average of 1.9. I was at the very bottom of my class: a terrible student. So to get accepted anywhere was a miracle. And to go to SVA in New York was the most ambitious way I could throw myself out of suburbia and into a major city—out of the trappings of community college and things like that.

SL: But you clearly wanted to go to school rather than directly make films on your own?

BS: Yes. I wanted to go to film school. Hey, for some reason, in my mind that was very important. So I went to school there for two years.

At the same time, I worked as production assistant on an exploitation film called *Street Trash*, which was a really cool experience, even though I was fired when I was late picking up the producer. You're not supposed to be late in the movie business: if you're late they're late and if they are, the movie is late. But the producer was my professor and friend who also hired me—he's still a friend today; it's kind of interesting. I got rehired when they did sound-recording work and stuff like that. So I got a credit on that. If you rent it you can still see it today.

SL: So tell me about the various puzzle pieces that came together.

BS: There was just me constantly making projects. When I was at SVA, I developed a project that I never finished because I didn't think it would be any good and worth the money, but I had the experience shooting. It was a 16mm project called *Plain Paper*.

After two years in New York, I took a semester off and I worked and earned money driving a bus. I worked in about 37 jobs of all different kinds in my life that I have either quit or been fired from. Restaurants, gas stations, a flower store, a hardware shop, landscaping, a swimming pool sales company—I mean I've done everything. And that's been very helpful because now I know a lot of businesses. I worked for AT&T in the mailroom, I was foot messenger in New York City, I was a wedding videographer. Everything!

SL: Were you ever afraid that you might lose focus of what you really wanted to do?

BS: Yes, there was one moment. I was working all day for the father of my girlfriend at the time: a trade-show organization company. In the early mornings, I would drive a bus for disabled kids. There came a moment when I started to fear lack of money. And I had a discussion with a friend at the time of going into the trucking business. A friend's father said—oh I don't even want to talk about it, because it is bothersome to me. One: the friend was killed in a car accident and two: *it was a period of my life where I was so afraid that I would be poor or broke—my family did not have an enormous amount of money. I was going to divert the dream and maybe start a business.* But I knew in my gut that if I started the business, I would never go back to film—it would be impossible.

I remember having a conversation with my girlfriend's father, whom I told about what I was thinking of doing. He said: "When you're in school you're a student, when you're out of school you're just poor. And if you give up on film school, you're never going to get back into it." So I decided to transfer.

Over three semesters I applied again and again to the production school at USC, so eventually I applied to the Critical Studies division. So I got accepted to USC, but not into film school. I went there anyways. I finished and got my undergrad Bachelor of Arts in Critical Studies. That was a different experience, because suddenly I wasn't like the super-kid geek filmmaker from New Jersey at SVA; I was not even accepted but sort of flowing around USC film school.

So I made it a point not just to keep making films, but to work on other people's student projects. And that's where I met John Ottman, who's my editor/composer now. He was working on a graduate thesis film called *Summer Rain*. I was Production Assistant on it and he ended up being the editor on it. Now we are friends and he edits and composes my music.

USC was also about seeing lots of great films and hearing great speakers. USC has great relations with filmmakers.

Since I was a Critical Studies major, it was never part of my curriculum to make a film per se. So I decided I'd have to make one on my own. Ethan Hawke had just shot *Dead Poets' Society* but it hadn't come out yet. So I thought, "Why don't I ask Ethan?" Ethan and Brandon Boyce—who ended up writing my movie *Apt Pupil* and who are also writing my next movie after *Superman* called *The Mayor of Castor Street*. We three were at a diner one night and decided "Let's make a short film about us."

I wrote it very quickly and we shot it on 16mm. It was called *Lion's Den*— about a bunch of friends who left high school, went away for a semester, and came back to their favorite all-night spot, realizing they had totally grown apart. One even *did* become a famous actor—Ethan Hawke, though he didn't play that part. Instead he played Chris McQuarrie who was a security guard who wanted to be a writer—and Chris ended up writing *The Usual Suspects*. The other friend of mine played the movie actor. And I played an ambiguous sort of observer—I acted in it! I really mean it: I'm terrible in it.

What happened then in my head I remember as a huge undertaking: we got a screening at the Director's Guild. I parried up with these two other filmmakers who were looking for a venue. We sent out invitations and put up our own mailing list and had put on this huge event. And I knew Ted Raimi from friends through college. So I asked Ted to introduce me to his brother Sam Raimi, who had just made *Darkman* and was making *Army of Darkness* at the time. I asked Sam if he would host the evening. Sam agreed to host as long as I made it in coordination with some charity. I used the Sierra Club, which my mother was supportive of. So we had this evening of three short films and we filled the DGA main theater on Sunset Boulevard.

Afterwards [*sighing*], I got a manager and I lost the manager, and there were other meetings I had. I wrote an entire treatment of a movie just for Martin Short, because I had a meeting with his head of development. It's funny because he'll never know that [*laughing*]. I met him very briefly once and I didn't bring it up. But nothing came of anything really, except this one Japanese company called Tokoma. They had this guy called John Johnson and a friend dragged him out to that screening. John Johnson saw my film and basically submitted me for this program called Cinema Beam. It was to grant 250 thousand dollars to seven directors each around the world to let them try to make a 35mm feature.

And that's what happened. I called Chris McQuarrie and said, "come let's write this movie together." So he moved out to LA and we wrote this movie called *Public Access*.

We had this third writer friend called Michael Dougan. It got to become very eerie and dark and it was very much a reflection of what was going on in politics at the time: H. Ross Perrot had bought time on the airwaves—so suddenly there was a third presidential candidate who as a billionaire had paid for the TV. Our movie was kind of a reflection of this idea that somebody could come to a small town and buy time on the local public access cable station while endearing the town—but under the surface he is not the one everyone thinks he is.

SL: So your budget was the 250 thousand?

BS: Yes. And that film won the Sundance film festival in 1993. The whole experience was so interesting. There were defining moments on the film. I remember pushing people very hard. I learned to pace people, though. Even if you're paying them five dollars an hour, it is always best to pay people, rather then getting them to work for free. Though a lot of people are trying to get people to work for free on movies for lots of promises.

I made sure I'm sort of the executive producer of the film, even though I had a producing partner and USC friend Ken Kokin who got me the job on *Summer Rain* where I met John Ottman. John ended up working with me on *The Usual Suspects* as well.

But it was a very long process. Weird things occurred: I ended up having a composer and an editor and firing both of them—not firing them, but they both kind of left. And Ottman ended up having the role of both, —which is how that relationship began.

SL: How much really were you in control of the entire production process?

BS: *I was and have always been in complete control. I was very spoiled from very early on. I never did tie into television or commercials or things like that, and during my first experience directing a feature, I had absolute and total control.* It was me who had the money—they wired me the 250 thousand into an account and I signed every check myself—thousands of checks. They trusted me to act as an entity. In fact, that created weird tax implications a little later and I almost got in a little trouble because taxes hadn't been properly dealt with.

Here's what it did: it spoiled me enormously because I had final cut—I just made this movie and we won Sundance.

So when I went into making *The Usual Suspects*, even though it was for a larger company and there was a larger budget of six million, I kept my attitude. And to this very day, I go into these movies with the same attitude, even when making a $250 million movie like *Superman Returns*.

SL: Did you help raising *The Usual Suspects* budget?

BS: I worked with this executive producer Robert Jones whom Ken Kokin basically introduced me to in Cannes when we were selling *Public Access*. Robert raised the money initially through a German financing group. Then, that money fell through after we had our cast. We then went to PolyGram/Spelling and did what is called a negative pick-up deal: they ended up promising to buy a film once it's done—that gets you a bank loan to make the film. Our bridge loan was the NewMarket Group, which later did *The Passion of the Christ*, I believe. PolyGram released it through Gramercy. It wasn't a huge financial success, but for six million dollars it made about 25 million dollars domestically.

You know the real thing was that it started my career—I mean the film won two Academy Awards and all those things.

SL: Staying in control of one's movie: is that advice you would also give to new filmmakers?

BS: Absolutely. *Because if you start losing control, it starts to become somebody else's product, and it doesn't have a singular focus. And I really believe a movie is written three times: once on a page, once on the set, and a third time in the editing room.* And you must never be afraid to make changes in order to make the film better, for which there is always an opportunity. And if people, a studio, or your own material gets in your way—what you've shot or what you've written—you do your best to move it *out* of the way or to talk it out of the way, or to beg it out.

This is not to say that those very obstacles are always obstacles; sometimes they are great aides and helpers. You just have to know when to take advice and when to say "OK, this is *my* movie, and I have to do this." In the end, the movie is always the thing. The philosophy I have about directing is that I develop all my movies myself with writers. So they *are* very much me: the film comes first, but I am the film. You could call me very director-centric—that excludes my TV show "House," which was developed by other people.

SL: It seems remarkable how principled and wise you were about the whole production process from early on—

BS: Yes. And it was very funny: I remember getting into a fight with Robert Johnson once because I was shooting too much film of the interview scene between Kevin Spacey and Chazz Palminteri. I however knew I needed the footage to make the performances work, and I knew I would save the film later when we were shooting the action sequences where I would shoot less film. I was deciding myself that I could violate my 5,000-feet-a-day budget allotment and shoot 9,000 feet a day instead. I just knew I would pick it up later. But

Johnson said to me during a very dark day, "If this was a New Line film, you'd be fired by now." Meaning: if this was a studio, you'd be fired. And I said, "Well, thank God then it's not a studio, and that I own this." 'Cause I own the negative. I control the negative of *The Usual Suspects* forever until the end of the universe.

SL: You seem to be quite good at convincing others of your often quite unconventional ways—

BS: *Yeah, it's called "brashness" and "unearned ego." That's the critic's Todd McCarthy's expression. He explained if you look in the pantheon of filmmakers—those that you know best—80 percent of them made films in their twenties.* And they did it aggressively and with those two character traits—and most of them are boys because there's just a certain kind of "I want it" and "I'm a boy and give me my toy" attitude that gives you the necessary blinders, you know?

SL: The script of *The Usual Suspects* apparently went through close to a hundred hands and everybody rejected it. They thought it was too confused and impossible to realize—

BS: Oh yeah, that script was rejected by everybody. There was a German company called Senator and they were very specific about wanting to make films with me and with another filmmaker who had made a movie called *Dead Alive*, retitled *Braindead*: Peter Jackson. Eventually, they did end up financing some of *Heavenly Creatures* but they passed on *Usual Suspects*. And even PolyGram/Spelling passed on that film. They only bought it later when it had the cast all lined up—no pun intended.

SL: Being in control is good, but would you recommend teaming up with a producer early on?

BS: *I think my advice to filmmakers is always the same: find somebody to work with. Filmmaking is not writing books, and it is not painting pictures: it is a collaborative process that involves a larger group than yourself. If you can't convince one or two people to go along that ride with you early on for free—I mean producing partner, or writer, or something—you're never going to convince the masses later on.* And you need people to make a film. You can't do it all. You simply can't do everything. You may get credit for everything [*chuckles*]. People may assign credit to you for everything—but that's surely not what it is.

I have strong partnerships—we have a sort of family. You should come and watch at one of my sets: you'll see there are certain actors that come in and out of my career—there's the cinematographer Tom Sigel who since *The Usual Suspects* shoots all my films, including my pilot for "House."

I also do commercials where I get the opportunity to work with many other cinematographers and different people. I worked with Allen Daviau, Russell

Carpenter, and many others. But the core group that is definitely there is Chris McQuarrie, Dan Harris, and Mike Dougherty as writers, my Production Designer Guy Dyas, Louise Mingenbach my Costume Designer, even my focus puller Jimmy Jensen—very important!

Then there's other people that I look for. You know, having shot in Australia now and when I come back, I have certain people here that are really talented.

SL: Is that what film school might be most helpful for: gaining friends to work with?

BS: Absolutely. First they are friends, *then* business partners. There is a group from film school—many of whom I am working with—but they began as friends. We talked film and we would see movies—ten, fifteen, or more movies a week. That was all we would do. With these friends I am close to this very day; both from New York and film school in LA.

SL: Would you say that this is why film school makes things a lot easier?

BS: Oh, yeah, yeah. In the old industry you used to be able to come to Hollywood and you'd get a job working on the lot at a studio. But now it's a different world and to know the business—unless you're raised into a family that's in it or something—film school is one of the few ways to actually get saturated in filmmaking and also build those partnerships early on that will serve you later.

SL: Some directors today say that thanks to the digital revolution, directing a first movie has become easier than ever before. Do you agree?

BS: You can do that, but ultimately that's not enough. You might even have a good story, but "Do you have actors?" Who is holding the camera: is that you? Well fine, so you're operating, and you're the editor, but somebody's gotta act in it. Chances are that that actor will be talking to another actor—so now that's two actors. Now then you have to decide whether you want the film to be lit nicely or whether you just want to shoot the way nature lights it. So if you want to change the lighting, is that *you* changing it, or is that maybe a cinematographer: an artist who's better at it? And now suddenly you have got a crew.

You know you can always eliminate people from the process and yes: a single person can shoot a movie. But to make narrative movies, it takes more than just you. It's a very poetic thing for filmmakers to say. I guarantee you that none of the filmmakers you've spoken to do that.

SL: They sometimes started before the 90s—

BS: Oh yeah, I did that with 8mm cameras, too. I didn't have a crew, I did all my own everything—my own lighting, my own editing, my own shooting, but ultimately I still had actors, I still had people that I had to drag along, it wasn't just bees and flowers—*sometimes* it was. One time one film I did was New York City cut to music. I ran around and it was just me. But if you're making narrative stories—making full-length feature movies to be shown in theaters—*I don't know many filmmakers who can genuinely say that they did everything themselves. In fact, there are none. If they tell you they are, they are lying.*

SL: I am interested in the creative processes you are going through. Let's talk about *The Usual Suspects*—

BS: Well, my way of working has not changed since the days I have made my little films—I have surely become more relaxed but . . .

SL: So your ways of working are not influenced by the budget you have or possible expectations that might be out the?

BS: No . . . well my thought process is always affected by those things. Particularly when talking about expectations and you're making movies like *X-Men* or *Superman Returns*. I have to be very aware because you're dealing with entities and characters and universes that have existed longer than I have.

So in that context I think about them, but in terms of my ways of working I don't. It is actually very strange to people that my style of working is so unorthodox. Whenever I am with a new crew, they are bewildered that the movies actually work out. It has taken me years to actually build the trust in the industry that I have now, because people, studios, crews, and sometimes actors get completely confused and don't know what the hell I'm doing.

SL: So what *is* your style?

BS: I couldn't explain it; you'd have to come and see it. I, for example, don't watch dailies.

SL: You don't check your material?

BS: I do occasionally if it's technical things I need to see, but I know photography, I understand lenses and cameras—I forgot to mention I had a dark room when I was eleven years old. Instead of toys and junk, I got a Pentax K1000 and eventually, for my holidays, I got a zoom lens: that was my big gift. So I've been shooting and printing 35mm photographs ever since then.

So I know what I am shooting. Also, I have a pretty photographic memory of everything I shoot. *I couldn't tell you who I had dinner with last night or what I did, but there is one thing that I have: a good visual memory.*

I also shoot very freely. Even when I am dealing with big visual effects elements, I still try to allow the moment to happen—let the actor try something.

You know I look at the location or the set and I step back from it and say, "Alright, how can I maximize this location and this set." I get very frustrated when people shoot in amazing locations, where they have beautiful sets and they don't take full advantage of them. I try to take as much advantage of the range of the actors and the sets as humanly possible. Then I key off those things as inspirational mechanisms on the day. Half the movie I got kind of planned in my head; the other half I let kind of happen.

SL: So when arriving on set, you don't yet know the shots you're going to do?

BS: No—well it depends. It's literally 50/50. If it involves a lot of visual effects or if it's a shot I know I always wanted to do, and I had that shot in my head since the beginning of the show, then yes, I know what I want to do. Oh, and I storyboard. I work with storyboard artists. But I often use those as a spin-off for ideas. In terms of where I put the camera: I decide on the day. I show up on set and get inspired there.

SL: Do producers ever have problems with that style?

BS: Yeah, well I'm usually the producer on my movies—whether I get the credit or not: I'm the producer. *People in general get a little freaked out about my ways. Like suddenly they rehearsed a scene and it'll look like I had no plan.* In reality I will find exactly where I am going to put the camera. I am very confident—and if I am not, I I'll stop for a moment and I just say, "Let's rehearse that again!".

SL: Why might others get the idea that you don't know what you're doing?

BS: I don't know. Maybe it's because I look young or something—I have no idea. So that's been an issue: I look and I have always looked a little younger or if not more than a little younger than I am. So that's always been a funny and weird thing for people to wrap their minds around. I don't know—at least it's hard to explain.

For me a movie is pieces. So actors are like, "Why are you asking me to do that?", or the crew is like, "Why are we just pointing the camera at that one thing?," and I'm like, "Because I'm gonna use it later." And there are times when I don't even look at the screen—sometimes I just listen to the dialogue, because I know that I'm going to put that dialogue over the mouth of another take. And by the way, that's been done on Academy Award–winning performances.

SL: OK, now you can look back and say, "People didn't know and I did know"—but around the time of *The Usual Suspects* or even earlier, being a young director around an established cast, you surely perceived it differently.

BS: Well, one: they weren't that famous. They were actually kind of—believe me, they weren't really that famous. At that time, Kevin Spacey was that guy from a TV show called "Wise Guy" and Gabriel Burn bragged and warned me that he had never been in a movie that had made over five million dollars; and Steven Baldwin had just done *Threesome*. Chazz Palminteri was the biggest of those.

*You know I walk on with the notion that nobody knows the film better than I do and nobody is more eligible to direct it than I am. Therefore, even if somebody has an argument or a problem with what I am doing, with my methodology it means: they are wrong!* Not that they are necessarily wrong, but it doesn't matter, because they can't direct *Usual Suspects* better than me. I developed the script with the writer and I am the one directing it. You know, I couldn't play Keyser Soze or Verbal Kint or whoever it was better than Kevin Spacey. I would not suppose that I can act better than Chazz or Stephen, or Gabriel, nor would I expect them to suppose they could direct the film better than me.

I'll give you an example: There was one moment when I wasn't watching dailies and Gabriel got a hold of them somehow. He came to me, telling me that he was very nervous about what he has been seeing—and I'm like, "Whoa!", and I got very nervous and panicked for a moment. Then I said, "Wait a minute, just don't watch them." I said, "It feels right to me, and that is as good as we've got."

SL: How did you actually work out and develop the characters on *The Usual Suspects*?

BS: With each actor I have a conversation, a meeting, and we just talk about the characters. With Kevin I think I had a couple of conversations, and then when they show up on the day, it's a little slow starting, but we then find the character in the shooting. So I don't do rehearsals or things like that. We just find it on the day.

SL: But did you have Kevin Spacey's character in your head?

BS: I had a version of it and I always had Kevin in mind when Chris and I were developing the script. But on the first morning of shooting we had no choice. By the end of the day, the character had started to take shape—also the way he spoke. I remember that at one point, Kevin was speaking with a voice that was a little too high, so I would bring him down.

And it's always tricky. Kevin and I also had it on *Superman*. He showed up for what was the first scene he had to do as Lex Luther the villain. The scene takes place in the middle of the movie in the middle of a conversation of a scene we haven't shot yet. And we had to figure out the character of Lex Luther right there—and we did. After about three or four takes it started to have the right rhythm and I got more takes. By the time we moved on I had what I needed. And two, three, four days into shooting it was a blast.

SL: So character development typically happens on set?

BS: Yeah, yeah—I am always afraid to overwork it ahead of time. If I was to analyze myself, I think I have this deep fear. I am afraid that in the rehearsal, the actor will nail a moment; he'll hit it and will never be able to reclaim it once I start shooting and that it'll kill me.

SL: Or both of you?

BS: Well it'll kill me and then I will kill them. Because then we will do 50 takes to try to get that moment again. So instead I do a quick rehearsal for camera, and then I start rolling film. And then we make our mistakes.

SL: Do you do improvs with your actors?

BS: Sometimes I ask them, sometimes I'll make up a line and yell it at them and then have them say it. Sometimes *they* improvise. I remember Ian McKellen on *Apt Pupil* saying to me, "I wanna try a line" and I go, "OK, surprise me"—it is the scene with the cat that he is about to shove into an oven. He is staring at the cat from his back porch and just says, "It is getting cold out here, Kitty." I loved it, so it was in.

SL: Do you feel that as a director, you yourself have to transform into the actors' characters to a certain degree?

BS: Very interesting question as I definitely do to some degree. *I find myself very often acting out the characters, acting out the script, walking around saying the lines when I am by myself or in front of my writers.* And in my head I imagine how they could be said. Sometimes I fight and push the actors into places until they say it the way I hear it in my head. And sometimes I let them just say it. In *Usual Suspects*, Benicio Del Toro's role was written for a Harry Dean Stanton type. Suddenly Benicio decided to do this weird voice, and I thought, "Wow, that's different, that's cool: let's do that."

So you see it depends. Once I told Patrick Stewart, "I hear it a certain way in my head and I'm not getting it from you," and he goes, "I don't understand, explain!" So I asked him, "Patrick, would you mind if I spoke it, like I want you to say it?" So I spoke the line with his English accent at him. And I tell you I thought he was going to walk off the set. You know, I am not an actor and here I am trying to imitate Patrick the way I want him to say something. It is funny, because when my awful performance was over, he looked at me and said, "You see that is how I think I sound, let's do it again."

Then, I learn something from each actor. I learn that sometimes it is OK to say faster: sometimes it is OK to say 10 percent faster, 20 percent faster—other actors don't need anything.

One of my favorite directions is "try something different—do it differently." See, I don't know what that means, but it will be different and I'll have the material. Remember: A film is written three times—and the last time is in the editing room.

I would also say sometimes, "Make a funny face," or "Do a little funny thing," or I demonstrate it. Or I say, "Do the opposite of what you just did." You see it is so hard to explain.

SL: So you get the performances you want only in the editing room?

BS: Oh yes—the performance comes from the editing room. This is because it's pieces. To me, unless I do it all in one take, which I sometimes do, it's all about gathering pieces.

Now, sometimes they are long pieces—even one long take. Sometimes they are audio pieces, sometimes they are visual. Hopefully they are audio-visual pieces and I don't have to do much repair. But to me it is gathering material for the editing room.

Now I don't shoot ten different movies simultaneously. I try to stay on focus and try to not waste a lot of film . . . or excuse me—"time"—because time is where the money goes.

But I definitely am aware that I am gathering pieces and that no one is doing a stage performance. It confuses actors. Parker Posey is an actress I am working with now and who is very confused by it. She's mostly done independent movies with Christopher Guest, where they do two takes that are very long and very fluid. Suddenly I'm here and ask her, "Look right, look left, give me a line." And she's saying to me, "This is so different, I've never done that before." And I reply, "Yes, isn't that exciting."

And lately what I have done—I used to not do it because I was afraid of this—I bring the actors in the cutting room once in a while and I show them some scenes. Suddenly it's clear: they understand.

But the crew is almost always baffled. I don't know why. It looks normal to me, but I just always seem to get these looks that I'm crazy.

SL: When writing, shooting, or editing your movies, do you analyze a lot or rather trust your instincts?

BS: It is more of a feeling—it *feels* right. There are certain themes and moments I want to exist in the movie. In any given moment there is a kind of feeling I want the audience to have, but beyond that I don't try to overanalyze scene. They just have to feel right, and fun and scary or whatever is needed. It should always be varying in a movie—you know, hills and valleys.

All I care about in the scene is how it serves the story—story is everything. *Symbolism, or the nature or the reference or the meaning of a scene, is irrelevant if it doesn't serve the story. That's just a fact.*

SL: Would you say there are two kinds of directors: some are analytically, others are atmospherically driven directors.

BS: Yes, and I think I am more atmosphere driven. My biggest influences are Steven Spielberg, Peter Weir, and David Cronenberg. I mean they are among my favorite directors—there's also Martin Scorsese.

In terms of influence, it feels right. If you enjoy a scene, it should serve the story, otherwise it's a waste. If it distracts from the core of the story—the thing you're obsessed with—then it's just indulgent.

SL: Do you see yourself becoming a better storyteller with each film, or is it more of a circular process—each story is a new start?

BS: I think each story is different. The question is, "Why am I making the movie?" and you have to have a reason why, because it takes such a commitment. It doesn't have to be a big reason. Like my medical drama—my TV series "House"—I'm making it because I'm fascinated with medicine, I am a hypochondriac and I love this character.

*Superman* is different: I'm adopted—and you know he is the ultimate immigrant. *X-Men* is about identity—I have issues regarding some personal things you might have heard about and which fascinate me. *Apt Pupil* and the *Usual Suspects* also deal with issues of identity. There are personal topics that interest me about the movie. So once I have the tiny reason to make that movie, then it doesn't matter how big it is. Then it can be *Superman*; you go into it and start examining: What is *Superman*? What do people expect from it?

SL: So out of the core idea arises enough inspiration and material to carry an entire movie?

BS: Yeah. *Superman* for instance is a movie about what happens when old boyfriends come home and back into your life. And then it may have 1,600 visual effects and villains, and plans of global destruction or what not—but that doesn't change its core. *Usual Suspects* is about a guy who has to kill two hours. He is supposed to be released but he isn't—so what is he going to do? He's going to perpetuate his myth. He's going to tell a story and he's going to get all the information off a blackboard. It's very simple. I remember in film school, my professor was saying how *Road Warrior* is all about montage and deconstructionalism. And I giggled and laughed and she asked, "What's so funny?", and I said, "I don't know, I thought it was about a guy, who was trying to get gas for his car." And she said, "You're right, it's about that as well." To me, you can never lose that. And *then*, all the other stuff emerges— and some of it on the day.

In *Usual Suspects* for example, you can talk about how it relates to mythology and villains—you can analyze as you will: some of those things occur to me on the day. But the key thing is: it is the story of that guy while there is this other guy trying to hunt him down—and both are in a room together. Now, how does one get away from the other and stomp him and the rest of the audience? If you lose sight of that, you're fucked.

SL: How important is it to give your own insecurities a key role in the creative process of storytelling?

BS: I think actors do this very often when they need to generate certain emotions. I do it as well in terms of forming my story. Right now I am in the *Superman* world—there is a scene where something is taken from Superman and he is very upset. For this upsetness, I draw from my personal experience.

Anyways, these things are the reasons why you make the movie. Some people will make *My Beautiful Launderette*; some people will make *X-Men*. Those are two completely different films but the issues are the same. This is not to say anything specific about Stephen Frears—I don't know why he made that movie, but I know why I loved it. Maybe that's the same reason I made *X-Men*— without me talking about personal things and certain levels that I don't usually talk about in public.

SL: While a story may touch you deeply, how do you at the same time manage to keep the necessary distance in order to tell a coherent and interesting story to an uninstructed audience?

BS: Part of it is that I don't watch dailies. But also not a lot of people can do it, especially on films that are large—they get lost and forget the focus of what the film is about: they run off on tangents. It's a very hard thing to do and completely intangible. You must be willing to step back and sacrifice. I was in the editing room the other day and I just cut a whole section; but a gag: a moment of the movie that I very much liked. It was something an actor did— really sweet and funny and I loved the moment and you know what? It's got to go. And I don't need a test audience to tell me, I don't need the studio to tell me, I don't need my mother to tell me. I look at it and I say: "You know what? At this point we just need to get from point A to point F a little quicker and by moving this precious little moment out, it will make other moments more precious."

You just have to stay on the message. It all goes back to what I said earlier which is my philosophy: a film is written three times. And when I go back, I step back from the movie and say: "OK I have a script, I have an intention, I remember what I did on the day, but what have I got to work with? What's the best movie I can cut together with the material that I shot?"

SL: So is it then that on the day you shot the funny scene from above, you lacked that particular distance for a while, getting carried away on a tangent?

BS: It took me a month, because we shot it several months ago. On the day it was great, and I cut it together and I actually showed it to people in the editing room. I brought them in and was like, "Ha, this is so funny, look what he's doing—isn't it so funny?"—and now it's gone.

SL: Were there people that told you it would need to go?

BS: Oh yeah, that's why you try to have a great relation with your editor. I have John Ottman and I have Elliot Graham—two editors that I trust and dear friends. *Oh; very important advice: surround yourself with people with good taste and who are not afraid to tell you when they think you're wrong.*

SL: How do you share the editing work among you three?

BS: When I am working with John and Elliot it's nice, because they both know what I'm going for. And you know something else: very often I talk before the take, and I say things to the actors. And right after the take before I say cut, I say "that's very nice," or "oh, excellent"—and the first important thing they do in the editing room: they listen to me direct and key off that. So sometimes I let the camera role and I start talking to the actors. But what I am really doing is talking to the editors. Sometimes I don't say anything. They also know my taste and what I like and we have a similar sense of humor. And sometimes I say: "Why did you do that? I don't understand, I shot a better one. Why didn't you use it? Now go back." And then John will be like, "I don't know" and he'll go back and then maybe I'll be right.

SL: Do you like looking at several alternative cuts of one scene?

BS: No, I prefer one cut. Elliot likes that—he gives me maybe four versions. John says, "This is it!" And then I see it and change it—or I don't. Or I change it a little. But I love when someone says, "Look at it, this is it." I hate somebody going, "Look, here are twenty alternatives." I say, "Show me the best you have to offer!" because I have a photographic memory of all the things I shot. "So if this is your best, we can go make it better" or "We can fix it." So I tell that to Elliot—he is very young, and he is getting to a place where he is becoming more confident to just cut it the way he wants in the beginning. But we're all friends and we can all have these conversations.

SL: Working with two editors, does that mean you always have two alternatives of the same sequence?

BS: The way the work is that each works on a scene and then, via computer, they'll send that scene to the other's editing machine. And then that person will work on the scene—and then they'll send it back again, keeping on swapping scenes. So both editors have influence on each scene.

I very rarely look at multiple versions. I go by my gut feeling on that. In terms of function of the scene, sometimes I say: "The audience doesn't need to see this, we need a moment right here where the camera is on the character for a longer period of time. So can you please add ten frames?" Even though the scene may seem to be slowing down, in the scope of the movie it may be helpful. Or we want to hold on that clue, because if you hold on it long enough, it won't be in the audience's memory and that clue won't work later on. Or we might want to have the characters say something a couple of times to make sure the audience understands. It is very gut driven, really.

SL: Would you say that in the end, it is all about getting better at manipulating the audience towards your perception of the universe?

BS: Yes, it's all about manipulating the audience. I always found it fascinating that they would criticize Steven Spielberg by calling him a manipulator. And I'm like: Isn't that why he's a genius? Isn't that the whole point? *Whether it's Breathless, or Antonioni, or The High and the Low, or Close Encounters, you're affected: you're manipulated. Any kind of art is like that: you look at a painting and you suddenly feel sad, or stared at, or entertained, or confused, or upset, or funny.*

You want to feel the audience. And sometimes that manipulation can be intellectual, meaning it's a kind of movie which is meant to cause you to think throughout and then open discussion. It could be certain documentaries, or a Tarkovski film which creates imageries. Obviously it is an emotional thing you are getting from that as well.

SL: Aren't the emotional and the intellectual rather complementary aspects of manipulation?

BS: Exactly. Everybody does something because it feels right. I never hyper-analyze things, but your gut tells you things. I am constantly thinking about the audience. I'm not sure, though, that I get off on the mass influence and power that movies allow you to have—I like the idea that they bring people together. That it's like, you know, the "cheap date." That you can be in Saudi Arabia or in Alabama and can go to a movie and have a collective experience. I like that. But what's most important to me about filmmaking—and I know it's important to me because it's the same principle I apply to everything I do, whether I am throwing a party, preparing a dinner, or I'm making arrangement for a birthday present: it's a project and I am very obsessed with that project going well and being done to the best of my abilities. I get very frustrated when people are sloppy about things like that. I had a party in my apartment when we first came here to Sydney. I don't think I had much fun during the party—in fact not much at all—but I felt a great sense of satisfaction because it was a success. Everybody had a great time and everybody enjoyed themselves. We didn't run out of food, or alcohol, and everybody left feeling good. People met people; it was bigger than people thought it would be.

So the same I apply to my film projects—I am very project oriented. It's like in high school: I was terrible in tests, but I was very good in projects, for example when it came to building my Egyptian mummy.

SL: If the director is unsuccessful in his manipulation attempts and disappoints people's expectations, the audience will often turn against him—

BS: Yeah and then that's a problem. That's something that filmmakers absolutely have to be aware of when they're making a movie: who are you making a movie for. I am thinking about the audience. And when I think about the audience for *Superman*, I think eight to 80 years. I think about every bit. It's all quadrants, as they would say in the studio.

It helps to have experience with genres and to understand how far you can take a character and what you can do. And of course the knowledge of the technical aspects of filmmaking obviously, because we employ some of the most sophisticated, so I am happy about that.

But to me, if you do it right and it's done well—whether the film makes a lot of money or not—it will exist for many, many years. And that's the goal: to make sure your film is as good as you can make it. Cause once it's done, it lives longer than you do. To me, this is the most important thing. So it's not necessarily the manipulation of the masses. There is some social commentary but most important to me is the entertainment factor.

I always wait and see whether the audience laughs at certain significant moments. We know whether we have the audience with us, if there is laughter—otherwise they'd maybe yawn or cry. For *Usual Suspects*, I remember I wasn't sure whether it would work. We had a test screening. There were all these complicated plot bits. At one point, Mr. Hackney says, "There is still a truck loaded with gun powder"—the audience giggled and I knew they got it. Otherwise the other plot bits wouldn't have made any sense.

By the way, all this was done in editing. We also had the idea of Verbal straightening out his foot only at the very end. All those little bits that make the movie entertaining were not planned.

SL: Any piece of advice you would like to give that we haven't mentioned yet?

BS: *There is a favorite book of mine by Carl Gottlieb, the writer of Jaws. It was literally a movie where all that could go wrong, did go wrong.* This is really a tale for you if you're a struggling filmmaker with a budget going wild. The town was sick of the crew being there, the shark didn't work—that's why he had so many point of view shots which later became legendary. The book is written by somebody who was there. It is a fun read, not analytical. This book expresses my message to you if you're a young film-maker: just keep pushing through, anything can happen.

By the way, everyone in Hollywood at the time thought Spielberg would be destroying his career—yet without *Jaws*, filmmaking would be completely different today. Shark and *Star Wars*, in my opinion, changed the movie world forever.

SL: And *Superman Returns*?

BS: To be honest, in my fortress of solitude as a director on the set of *Superman*, I still find myself sometimes thinking that I must be dreaming.

# Fincher, David

**DIRECTOR'S CUT:**
"I just thought, 'This is fantastic, what a great gig: you get to build stuff and blow it up and hang out with Catherine Ross and travel around.'"

**BORN:**
1962, Denver, Colorado

**BACKGROUND:**
Commercials, Music Video

**FILMS:**
Alien³—1992
Se7en—1995
The Game—1997
Fight Club—1999
Panic Room—2002
Zodiac—2006
Benjamin Button—2007

**MAIN GENRES:**
Crime, Drama, Mystery, Thriller

DAVID FINCHER: I grew up in a sort of middle class, very bedroom community in the San Francisco Bay Area in Marine County. I lived there from age three to fourteen, from the late 60s to the 70s. It wasn't as affluent as it is today, but it was a nice sort of suburb and part of a relatively liberal collection of small towns. I would describe it as more hippie-ish than more conservative places like San Raphael and Terra Linda.

Because of the time, the art of making movies was sort of everywhere and classes in middle school, high schools, and grade schools had access to Super 8 movie equipment. It was cheap and readily available and there were a lot of filmmaking courses available to very young kids. I remember taking my first Super 8 filmmaking class when I was in third grade. By the time I was eight years old, I had pretty much decided that I wanted to be a director—that was that for me.

My mother worked in mental health and substance abuse. My dad was a writer and journalist who wrote for *Life* magazine for a few years and then freelance for magazines and stories—he was sort of a science writer. He was a big movie buff and used to take me to films every weekend—it was sort of our time together. And he would take me to see his favorite movies. So from the time I was six or seven years old, I was watching, you know, *Singing in the Rain*, and *2001: A Space Odyssey*. It was an eclectic smattering of influences.

SL: Did you tell your father you wanted to be a director?

DF: Yeah, yeah—he probably thought kind of the same thing I'm thinking now when my daughter says to me that she wants to be an actress—or that she wants to be a doctor and I say, "That's great!". So he was trying to be encouraging.

But I remember watching that making-of documentary that was on network television that had the director George Roy Hill talking about the process of making *Butch Cassidy*. I remember watching this documentary and thinking . . . because *it never occurred to me that movies weren't made in real time, you know.* If a movie took two hours, it maybe took a couple of days to film because you had to go from one place to another—but it never occurred to me that it took months.

I was eight then. They showed this sort of gypsy life of going from one place in Montana to some place in Wyoming, then shooting a train sequence maybe somewhere else. And then they were building full-scale trains and blowing them up. I just thought: "This is fantastic, what a great gig. You get to build stuff and blow it up and hang out with Catherine Ross and travel around," And I kind of thought, "That's it!" Then my parents let me go see the actual movie *Butch Cassidy*. And I ended up going every weekend for probably like five weeks just to see that movie. I just loved it; also because I had sort of peaked behind the curtain—well I sort of knew more about it. And I remember appreciating it, because all of my ideas of how movies were made had been kind of dashed by this documentary.

And suddenly, I saw this whole other discipline. Also, my father had bought the screenplay which was available in this little paperback that also had a bunch of photos in it. So I read this book over and over again. I sort of started getting this idea that all that stuff was intended—like all these moments: they didn't just happen. These words were given to these people, and these people were selected because of their chemistry and their abilities and then they were sort of made part of this process that looked so much like it was happening for real. And this kind of did me in.

SL: Did you try to reshoot sequences of *Butch Cassidy* with your own Super 8 camera or what kind of films did you make?

DF: Oh, they were insane. *This was pretty violent times, you know? So I like to think my mother was often extremely disturbed by the films that I would make* [chuckling]. *They would always involve somebody getting you know . . . The Sting was a big movie and we always loved that moment in it where the hit woman Loretta gets shot in the forehead.* The movies were more of excuses really to have friends shoot at other friends.

Most of the material was based on television; detective stuff. It's funny, I remember seeing Spike Jonze's "Sabotage" video, going: "Oh my God, those are all the movies we used to make," with fake mustaches and fucking sunglasses and kids running around shooting cap guns at each other. It was very silly.

SL: Tell me a favorite story you did?

DF: I don't remember it too well. I think we did our own versions of the *Six Million Dollar Man*—anything that we could do so we could run it in slow motion and be bionic. Or there was that whole series of commercials back then in stop motion. It was all that sort of "Yay-physics" kind of stuff: "Isn't it amazing? They are here and then they're gone—"

SL: When did you realize that in order to keep on doing the "silly stuff," you would need a serious strategy to follow it through?

DF: You know I never really figured out a strategy until I was like in high school. *As luck would have it, there was a big house up the street from us—like two driveways down. It was purchased in '72 or '73 by George Lucas.* So he moved in up the street. There was a lot of stuff going in Marine County at the time. John Korty had his studios there, and Michael Ritchie was cutting in Lucas's basement, and *The Godfather* was being filmed in the Marine Art and Garden Center. I remember in second grade, kids would come to school with shaved heads, cause they were extras in Lucas's *THX-1138*.

So, there was a lot of stuff going on. It didn't seem like Hollywood, which was physically centered around a particular place. I mean, we had a very different idea what filmmaking was, because people here were *doing* it—it was extremely prevalent.

SL: So you could hardly wait to be doing it yourself?

DF: My goals initially were extremely unreasonable, because I wanted to be the guy who was in charge of everything and I didn't really know how to do that stuff.

And I do think of the director's job that you should be the guy who not only knows how it's all going to go together, but also who sort of knows how you are going to get the material for it all.

In high school, I thought I'd work at ILM for a while, then try and direct television commercials and from that I would make features. It seemed like a logical kind of progression to me. And everybody just said, "You can't just go from working at a factory like ILM to directing TV commercials". It was too big a leap it seemed. And then, "You can't go from TV commercials to directing features," which is rare that people get that opportunity. But I went sort of, "But hey, you *can* make this step."

So I sort of knew that it was going to be a long road, because I didn't want to be the guy who's loading the magazines for the guy who was shooting the scene for the guy who had the whole thing in his head. I wanted to be the guy who had the whole thing in his head.

I mean a lot of my work ethic was based on a saying that my father had: "Learn your craft: it will never stop you from being a genius." It's a valuable thing to know what everyone's doing. And from a fairly early age of making stupid little student movies, it was amazing to me how nobody really wanted to push the dolly, nobody wanted to operate the camera; no one wanted to light the scene. Everyone either wanted to act in it or they wanted to go "cut" and "action."

So I assessed my skill set and tried to set myself reasonable goals, given what I was capable of. I eventually went to the sort of bogus film school in Berkeley in the summer of '80—

SL: Why bogus?

DF: It was an extremely Northern California operation. It was very what I would call "The Resentful Indie."

SL: In reaction to the mainstream?

DF: Which is really healthy. But there are people who, I think, take it to an extreme. My experience there turned out to be very valuable, though, because I met some really good people. But ultimately, it was a very Berkeley experience.

Then John Korty was hiring. ILM wasn't hiring, and US Effects didn't exist at the time. Also, I didn't live in San Francisco and I didn't want to work there. And I didn't want to be a freelance guy, schlepping around from documentary to documentary. I simply didn't want to be that guy. I wanted to sort of find a place to perch and to watch.

I remember meeting Korty when I was eleven or twelve. My younger sister did voice-over for some of his cartoons that he was doing for "Sesame Street," and I remember coming with her when she went to do it, seeing his studio on

Miller Avenue. He had flatbed editing equipment in the house. He was very much invested in the local filmmaking scene. So I thought this was sort of a good place to perch for a while?

SL: What was your job there?

DF: You know, I did fucking everything. I started out as a PA, schlepping Xerox machines up and down the street, cleaning up. Then I helped the kind of technical systems guy there—I had some kind of background in electrical work and I helped with wiring stuff—just PA stuff—just fucking around. Then I did some assisting camera work there—loading cameras. And then I moved over to the dark room, where I was for about nine months, maybe a year—it seemed like five years. It was sort of fun, though.

SL: Maybe a bit dark for your taste?

DF: Very dark. I mean it was good. I learned about printing and things—on a big scale. You are making trans-lights that are four feet across every time you make an exposure, burning a couple of thousand dollars worth of film sheet. So you got to be good at it and know what you're doing. And dealing with the different artists; different animators—among them Henry Selick there and Carl Willat.

SL: Was that helpful in any way?

DF: It wasn't so much contacts that I made. I mean you know it's people that I still speak with and check in with from time to time. You know animation is its own kind of weird subset of filmmaking because the intention has to be so specific. So when you come from animation, your thing is about, "What am I trying to solve in these fourteen frames," or "these 64 frames." You're not thinking in terms of: "Well let's just see what happens"—you're thinking in terms of: "It's gotta be moving left or right in order to keep the momentum," or "The cut has to be moving at a pretty good velocity, the camera should be panning with it." There are all these things that make you think in terms of staging. Staging becomes extremely important in terms of how you get the idea across. Also, looking at performance in kind of fractal time—time *between* time. So you're dealing with: "When does this person blink—and how long is the pause before that person blinks and at what point do they say their line," and "Can I take this dialogue track and make this funnier by having a longer pause?" And to me the people who did that for a living were incredibly valuable. Although at the time, I probably wasn't thinking to myself, "Oh great, let me find a company that's doing cut-out animation and roost there for a couple of years." It was more that I knew Korty's reputation, I liked Mill Valley, I lived nearby, I could commute easily, it was a beautiful serene setting although enormously carcinogenic, given all of the dying techniques and things that they were using at the time. And it was this giant sort of clapboard house that had animation stands in it and artists and graphic designers and motion-control designers. *It was a really interesting time—and a very odd and special movie: special as in "Special Olympics" I mean!*

It was a very strange experience, but it was also valuable, because you just met all the weirdest, most interesting talented people under this one roof. And I had to sort of interface with all of them because I was in sort of the place doing all the still photography.

SL: When did you professionally find yourself behind a film camera for the first time?

DF: *The first thing I ever got to direct was when I swindled my way into a commercial for the American Cancer Society.* It was in motion-control: a puppet that was smoking a cigarette in utero: it's a very odd little thing.

I was working at ILM at the time and I was kind of fed up and tired of being the special effects lettuce picker, the itinerant laborer. There were seasons at ILM—you know like, "Oh the new *Star Wars* movie is ramping up." I was assistant camera or working in various departments or whatever I was doing?

SL: ILM hired you as what actually?

DF: As assistant cameraman, loading mags. I did this cancer thing in my spare time. There was my friend Kirk Thatcher who was in the Monster Shop, working with Phil Tippet and Tony McVey and several others. Then there was a friend of mine that I had known since I was five and that went to State with him. And we were all sitting around going: "We should just do commercials, cause at least we'd be doing our own stuff and we wouldn't be so neurotically waiting for what's going to happen at ILM next. Let's have some kind of say in our own destiny!" So we came up with this idea of contacting people who would be in a position to spend money on public service announcements. And so obviously we thought of the American Cancer Society. We came up with this idea for this commercial that had this 2001 Star Child with a cigarette in its mouth; we thought it was really amusing and funny. This guy that my friend Chris knew—his name was Joe, he was a truck driver delivering text books— and he wanted to be, I mean he fancied himself a producer. He called the Society in some state and said, "Hey, we have these guys, they all work at ILM, they are bored, they have this idea for this non-smoking commercial."

We had done some storyboarding and he pitched the idea to them. They asked how much it was going to cost. I think we did it for like 75 hundred bucks or five grand. And they said great and gave us a check for the money and we did this thing at cost.

There was a facility in Richmond at the time. It was a low-rent motion-control place. It was an ILM wannabe. We brought them this job, because ILM didn't want to let us use their facilities or stages. So we built the creature—I think it was built in the Monster Shop at ILM—and then we took it to Richmond, photographed it, and put the whole thing together. We used their optical printer and printed the whole thing. Then I had Ren Klyce—the guy who I worked with doing all the sound for all my movies. At the time he was in music school. He did this soundtrack so that we finished the thing and gave it to them. We thought they were going to laugh and think it was funny and amusing.

Of course, it got banned on all these networks, because they were so appalled by it. And that was sort of the beginning, as much of a sideways move it was, because we were not doing that interesting work or that profitable work. I think everybody worked for free. If you had the man-hours totaled up, it would have cost hundreds of thousands of dollars to make this thing, but we did it for seven grand. It kind of opened up the notion of being something like a director.

My second shot at directing was for a music video for Rick Springfield. That was a nightmare and I did that in San Francisco—and that's when I realized I had to leave that city.

SL: You had a full-blown professional crew for that?

DF: [*Laughs*] Well, there will be differing opinions about that. Yeah, the people that were working on it were paid to be there, but it was a very odd thing. Working in San Francisco, it was an odd time.

I had gotten that gig on the basis of our commercial. It had a budget of like 150 thousand dollars, which at the time was a huge amount of money. Music videos were starting to happen, and locally people were doing Huey Lewis videos for 40 thousand dollars—you know that was a pretty big band at the time.

Local people were kind of appalled by me, going: "Who is this guy?" "He is an assistant cameraman"—or at the time I was a "plate supervisor" at ILM. And all of a sudden I was there. It was a pretty big deal. You know, even commercials were costing only 200 thousand dollars at that time.

SL: How was it funded?

DF: I got on a plane with Joe the truck driver *slash* producer, and we went to LA. Somebody had seen our commercial and wanted to know if we wanted to do a music video. And so we had a meeting.

I never forget: it was one of the most hilarious experiences in my life, because it really pointed out that presentation is everything. They had given us the song that we had listened to, and we had these beautiful storyboards and these creature designs and the whole thing we were going to do. So we got into a plane with all these things, flew into Burbank, rented a car, and went to this music manager's office. We laid out all the stuff out for him, and he said: "Wow! That's amazing! How much is it gonna cost?" And we said, "Well, we think we can do it for 150 thousand dollars." He said, "Really?!" To him it was not a lot of money, but to us it was an enormous amount.

*So we stood up and the guy who posed as my producer had this giant kind of grin on his face and he said in this enthusiastic way that he had, "Thank you so much, we've never done anything like this before." And I remember watching these guys just going, "Wow, we just made the deal with these two chuckleheads,"* like "What are we doing?" And I remember walking out of this office on Ventura Boulevard—it was about 110 degrees out—and I turned to him and said,

"You're no longer . . . gonna speak at these meetings because you can't be trusted not to say something that's completely stupid."

So we went off and did this video and we kind of called together as many of our friends as we could. It was a four-day shoot and an enormous undertaking. Henry Selick was the art director, and Michael Owen shot it—you know it was good people. And then of course you have the local assisting cameramen.

And I remember the first day: We were shooting in an anodizing mill or something—it was horrible—and we had all these people in these horrible make-up and jumpsuits inside this place that was just a complete shit hole; an environmental disaster. And *I walked in and there were all these people waiting and I said, "I gotta use the bathroom, I'll be right back." And I went in and threw up, thinking, "I can't do this, I don't know what to tell them to do." I had that stage fright.*

SL: Did you feel like you were faking it?

DF: Well I thought, "Here are all those people that do this for a living and here there's me, and I don't do this for a living." Just to see their faces, and they were all sort of with their mouths open, "Where do we go, what do we do?" and it was just absolutely terrifying. And after having thrown up, I walked out and said, "OK, here's what we are going to do," and "I wanna put the camera over here, and put the track over here." And I remember the first AC looked at me said, "Really?" That's when I realized that I was not really going to be able to do what I wanted to do in San Francisco because it was just going to be too many people questioning me up there.

SL: So the reason you felt sick was—

DF: The enormous responsibility—well, you had to manage these expectations. And then of course, as soon as you assert yourself of what you want to do, everyone questions it. You see, I'm suddenly looking at a guy who does first AC for a living and whose job I was doing less than a year ago. And now he's looking at me and I'm like 23, telling him what to do. "Really?" and you just kind of go, "Eh . . . yeah!" and they were all kind of shrugging and the attitude was like, "If that's what you want to do, do it, but we don't really approve."

So I realized I had to go to LA because I think in LA, everybody's so unjaded and cynical; at least they'll do what I'll ask them to do, simply because they want to get on to their next job. The thing about LA that's so amazing is that the people are extremely skilled, extremely experienced, and they have worked for enough chuckleheads; they are no longer judgmental. If you go to them and say, "Hey now, I've been doing some thinking: everything on the left side should go to the right side of the room and I think the camera should be upside down," they'll just like, "OK, give us five minutes and we'll do that," while in San Francisco or in New York, you tend to find that you have more, let's say, collaborators [*chuckling*]—probably more so in San Francisco, though I have had that in New York, too.

SL: Moving on with your journey to feature filmmaking; you were now inside the structure, I suppose?

DF: I did music videos and commercials for seven years when I was offered *Alien³*.

SL: Did you feel well prepared to direct a feature?

DF: Well, not well prepared, but certainly enthusiastic. I certainly had an idea of what I thought a sequel should be or what I thought a movie should be. I felt that I had a body of work that people could look at and kind of go, "Well, here's what's to expect from this guy." *It wasn't that I felt ready or that the world was waiting for me to make a movie—but I was certainly waiting to make a movie.*

You know that was the only reason why I put up with making that many music videos and especially the commercials: because the commercial business is, you know, quite a rat fuck. So the only reason to put up with that was to be able to get enough experience shooting, enough days that you felt sort of accomplished and at least being able to run a set and tell a story—or string together five pictures. It was film school. In the end, it was *all* about being a film director.

It's interesting. Although I worked with some fabulously talented people, like Norman Reynold as production designer and Terry Rawlings as editor, in retrospect I probably should have made the film the way I made my commercials. The fact that I didn't was a mistake. Because then I would have had people that I had worked with before and that were invested in me—Alex McDowell or Marc Plummer—and invested in the notion of me succeeding.

And I had nothing but help from Norman, and nothing but help from Terry, but there were a lot of people on the production department, who were beholden to 20th Century Fox for their livelihood and that were just like, "God forbid we do something interesting, especially if the studio doesn't like it or feel they couldn't afford it."

And you know, I have not been on a set since that experience where I felt as hamstrung. It was probably one of the most expensive movies at the time and it seemed ludicrous to assume that some 27-year-old kid was given 56 million dollars and that you're not gonna resent his neck. But it was an ill-conceived experiment and I think that it takes somebody who was tougher than I was and more accomplished and more concise and more able to express himself.

SL: So you feel you were not really in control of what was happening to you on that set?

DF: I was in control, but let's put it this way: a hurdler is in control, but he is not in control of the hurdles. You come out of the gate and you're in control of yourself—you can control whether you're going to hit the hurdle, if you're going to slow yourself down in order to be able to make all the hurdles, or if you're going to knock over a couple of the hurdles in order to go for speed. Those are the decisions you have, but you're not in control of the surroundings.

My job is to put together a team and have an instinct about people and their behavior, and to have an instinct about what their faces look like and what they can bring to it and where they are going to be strong and where they are going to need help. And you put them into the situation and then you create this world around them, working with designers and photographers and costumers and set-dressers and you kind of try to create that thing where that person you've invested in—their face, their performance abilities, and the idea that you have about them—is going to be supported by the world around them. And then finally you try and sort of create a place where you can kind of give it over to them and just go, "Now it's for you; now this time is all about you playing and experimenting and trying this and trying that, and then we'll hone in on this thing together." And then finally the hope is, once we get there, it will serve the purpose of what I feel that moment in the movie is about!

Well, when you spend all of your time fighting about what are the themes and what is the content. What are the ideas that you're trying to get across, and are those ideas too lofty or too pretentious and do they have any place in a sequel or do they have any place in science fiction, or in a penal colony . . . ? It's not good if you end up spending all of your time arguing about what the contents should be in order for it to be the most successful movie—and by that I mean most profitable!

*So I was too stupid—I didn't have somebody that could go fight for me on my behalf. I was the only person that could fight for me on my own behalf, and I was 27 years old.* And the problem with that is that of course *you end up being total white noise.* By the time two years are up, nobody wants to hear from you anymore. Every time you call, and there's somebody saying, "Here's the problem that I'm having," they're going, "Oh god, it's that guy on the phone again, uh?" So it started in a contentious way and it became more and more contentious. And I have just never been the kind of person who—you know I'm just not that over-contentious kind of guy.

SL: How involved were you in the editing process?

DF: I mostly participated in almost everything [*chuckling*]. You get to make certain decisions and then you second guessed on other things. *A director is like a quarterback. You get way too much credit when it works and way too much blame when it doesn't.* And the fact of the matter is that the situation was completely untenable, because the people that were paying it had no confidence in the person that they had hired to execute it. So they were second guessing it via remote. And they were second guessing it from 6000 miles away and we didn't have the same taste. I had a very different idea tonally of what I wanted. They thought it was going to be a drag, instead of confronting the problem and say: "Look, here's the script that we love, and here's the star that we've already paid for, and here's the situation." It wasn't like you were working with David Selznick who say: "Here's what I'm presenting you with—

say yes or say no." It was like: "Well we don't know what it should be." And you kind of come in and say: "Well I think it should be this" and they go: "it's fantastic—why don't you go over to England and start doing that?!" And you say: "that's great"—and go: "that's all gonna be great." And you go there and look at what they've already built because they had already gone through this dance once with somebody else before who was in your position. And you go: "Well I can't really use this stuff" and they go: "Oh, we really like to see you use it as much as possible." and then you think because you're young and stupid and you go "I don't want seem like I'm not a team player, blablabla." So waters get muddied. I don't know of any circumstances where the movie director's agenda is the same as the studio's agenda.

SL: Obviously this whole experience is still very much part of you. Looking at it now, do you know what you would do differently?

DF: I had the trust of the actors. I really felt like I was supported. And I had the trust of the production designer, the cinematographer, and the editor. But from the production standpoint . . . you know, today I run my productions in a very different way than most studios do. I look at the production manager and think: "That's *my* person, he's on *my* payroll" And people go: "No, no, he's on the studio's payroll."

*Alien*³ was a situation where a pipeline had to be filled, and a title had to be made—but you still sit there and go: "On a normal movie, the reason that a director has the authority that he has is that the studio has looked at him and seen the body of work and said: 'this person's interpretation is what we want to see.'" And that was the initial thrust of *Alien*³. And that quickly faded. *And I had that conversation with Roger Birnbaum, who said to me: "I can release a 15 minutes black screen and call it Alien*³ *and do 15 million in the opening weekend."*

And to a certain extend that's true: I think six months after we were shooting, they were still running a trailer for *Alien*³ that showed aliens coming to earth. It had nothing do with the movie that we were making, and they were like: "It doesn't matter. That's what we do: we get the exhibitors all jacked up." And you just kind of go: "Aha, that's what the movie business is"—or rather: "that's what the sequel business is." And you know: I was just the wrong guy for a sequel.

SL: As you are luckily over that sequel business now, I would interested in the creative process you go through when deciding on a project that's your own. Let's discuss *Fight Club*: How did you get on that and what steps did you concretely go through during the preparation of the story?

DF: I read it as a book, and it started with as a book. Josh Donen, who was a producer at the time and my agent now, sent it to me and said: "I am sending you a book and you have to read it tonight." And I sort of said: "I can't read a book tonight, I am cutting a movie and I won't have time" And he said: "Well this is a book you have to read tonight because 20th Century Fox is going to buy this book and you need to buy this book first," and so I agreed to read it that night, but asked him to give me a reason why I should read it. "Tell me something about it that will be inspiring to me as to why I should read it." And he told me about the scene between Tyler Durden and the Asian shop owner, where he holds the guy at gunpoint and says: "I want you to go out and I want you to be a dentist and that you go back to school, and if you don't, I'm gonna kill you."

And I just thought it was such an amazing idea for a scene and said: "Yeah, that's really great." And I called him the next day and he said: "you know what, Fox already bought it." *And I had such a bad experience with Fox, I had no intention of going back there and go through that again. So I told him that that was probably it for me with* Fight Club. And then he called a little later and said: "You know, Laura Ziskin in the studio likes the idea of you for this movie. You might want to go tell her your take on it." And I just said: "No, it doesn't seem like this is for me. I can't do the studio version of it." So he said, "Well, just tell her that, and what you think you *can* do."

So I went to Laura and told her: "Well, this is the movie I would make," and she said: "Well that sounds fantastic. How much you think you can do it for?" And I said: "Until I have a script, I can't tell you. But let's pick a writer that we all agree on, I'll go off with him and we'll come back with a script. We're not going to come back with a script and ask you: 'Here's the script, what do you think?' The process will be more like: 'This is the script that we want to make—that we're dying to make; that we're going to arm-wrestle and fight for. And if you want to do it, let's do it." So that's what we did: they agreed to that and so we made. We went away for a year—14 months—and we came back with the promised script.

SL: How did you go about developing the story creatively?

DF: I never really thought about it. You know, it seemed kind of obvious to me—it wasn't much of a struggle. It seemed sort of like we needed to be able to gloss over an enormous amount of material quite quickly. We wanted to keep this density of information and we know we wanted to cut back and forth in time, because that's kind of what the narrator is constantly talking about in the movie. It was complex, but I never looked up and said: 'Oh, my God, this is impossible. Nobody will be able to turn that into a movie.'

I always feel I need to get the shape of the thing first. *I admit I have a problem with the third act—I find myself most interested in the first and second acts.* Unfortunately, by the time you get to the end of the movie, you're just exhausted, so it tends to be a little sloppier—and I am a little bit that way about scripts. Initially, I find myself more interested in the world and where the characters came from, than I am interested in getting to the end in the most compelling way.

But, you know, the process differs. In *Alien³*, we were moving backward from the idea of sacrifice. In *Se7en*, we knew that we were kind of making this police procedural that would become this horror movie at the end. And then on *The Game*, again, we were working backward from this terrible ending that was going to write itself—and I guess we were sort of moving forward too— moving forward with this sort of explainable twilight zone. In the end you can explain it pretty easily—explain it in movie terms. The only problems that we had on *Fight Club* was what we were going to throw out of the book, what are we going to kind of collapse in on itself from the book, and how are we going to end it? But other than that, it was fairly straight-forward.

*My process is different every time. You know, most of the time you're trying to identify the things that you love about the story and then bring the stuff that you don't like towards that.*

And then there's only so much you can actually plan before you shoot it. Things actually never work out exactly the way you think they would and there is always chaos involved. It's actually quite important to have that and you need to be flexible enough to change things if they come up. You hopefully work with actors that are for example talented enough to take their lines into a direction that maybe I have never thought of. Suddenly the whole thing makes sense, but from a different, richer perspective.

SL: Do you need a lot of feedback and communicate your ideas, or are you rather reclusive during the whole creative process?

DF: If a production designer says to me: "You know I really hate that scene in the script," that is somebody I am collaborating with, so I want to know. But when somebody who's doing costume says: "I wish you hadn't cast that person" you know, you kind of go "I don't know what to do about it now." So it depends: If it's early enough in the process and it's somebody whose opinion I value, then I am more than curious what people think about it. Once you've decided to do something as your next movie, I don't really like to then sit down with people and go: "Tell me why I shouldn't do this." I don't really do that. If I'm enthusiastic about a something, I just kind of go: "OK, let's get that out of my system."

SL: How would you describe the center of you creative enthusiasm that gives you direction during the storytelling process?

DF: Well, I mean I like to have done homework walking into something—the cynical or the half-joking side of me would say: 'You know, by the time you start shooting the movie, it's pretty much made'. And to a certain extend it is. Cause every moment is being weighed against this idea of what the thing should be that's in your head. So you are always sort of comparing it against the scene that you sort of previously put together.

Having said that, just comparing two things is not a very open or creative place to be in—and shooting does involve a lot of comparing of what you shoot with what you previously designed in your head.

*In fact, you now I really dislike the process of shooting, I've always hated it. I really don't enjoy it. It's getting up early, it's a lot of stress and aggravation and compromise.* I really enjoy designing films, I really enjoy working with writers, I really enjoy rehearsal.

SL: Not so much editing?

DF: No. I enjoy it more than shooting, but editing for me—I don't enjoy it as much as prep. I love prep. That for me is so much fun. You go on location, you look at stuff, you go: "Wow, what if we do this, what if we do that?" It's all this world of possibilities, and then all of a sudden it's like [*bitchy voice*]: "Yeah, but you gotta be able to do it in two hours, and then you gotta be able to make a company move, and then you gotta get everybody set, and then you gotta get that person into make-up, and than you gotta get a forced call-in because they were working late the night before." You know you have all that shit that you have to get sort of through. And that's the stuff that I really don't like. If all it is was about sitting in this chair and waiting for all these wonderfully talented photographers, and actors and costumers to kind of like show up and play dress up, that would be great, but that's like two percent of the job.

SL: So 1st AD is not on your list of dream jobs?

DF: The nice thing about being a first AD is that you're constantly brokering against reality. There is only so much you can do: It does take x amount of time to run 1300 feet of cable, you know, whether you like it or not: six guys and one hour fifteen minutes. So there's certain givens: to me that job is almost preferable to the six months of trying to seduce a studio to paying what they always consider to be too much for a property. And then you go promising the moon because that's what you really want to do. You're promising what it is you want to do. And then it becomes this inevitable erosion of compromise. An so to me, I'd much rather be the guy who's being pragmatic than the guy who's standing next to the guy who's being pragmatic dreaming [*chuckles*].

SL: It seems to me that filmmaking is always coupled with a creative dilemma: how much subjectivity does it take in order to be unique and relevant, and how much objective convention is necessary so it can still be communicated successfully to a broad audience?

DF: It's all part and parcel of the same thing. The craft of filmmaking is the craft of storytelling and you're dealing with storytelling in a very specific environment and at a specific altar. And at the altar of cinema, there are the ways that things have been done and understood for 125 years. And that's a hard thing to break out of. If it's an idea that's meant to be understood quickly, then chances are—and it depends on how much time you had in the film to introduce that idea within your narrative—that in the first five minutes of any movie, you kind of have set up who the people are. You simply have to start somewhere. So there are certain conventions of it.

On the other hand, when it comes to "Will it be understood by an audience?" *I think you have to make movies for yourself. I don't know any other audience that you can make movies for. I think you have to sit down and think: "Would I understand that?* Yeah, that would make sense to me," and then you go and you make that—and then if no one understands, that's the only way you can learn that you're being far too clever.

SL: Making movies for yourself, how would you describe your relationship to the audience: Is it identification or rather as an antagonist to their point of view?

DF: The movie-going public never ceases to amaze me. There are very high-minded ideas that you have, that you put into very simple terms in a movie and gloss over it and throw it away—and you kick yourself for months and in editing while you sit there and say: "Oh my God, why did you throw that away, I should have really underscored that. That was such a grand idea and needs to be part of this movie and now I have completely fucked up my opportunity to introduce it. What was I thinking? I'm such an asshole." And then you're walking down the street five years later and somebody goes: "Oh, you did that movie—I loved that thing about it." And then they tell you that they saw that which you believed was gone: it somehow must have survived as part of your storytelling.

And part of it is a bit like with acting: Acting is listening and thinking. And when you watch somebody who is thinking correctly, as an audience member you're walking and lock step with them as they're experiencing this thing. And you know it's not for real—it's a fake thing. The actors aren't really going through that, but they are learning a process of communicating an idea. And it's amazing of how many of those ideas get through without ever a word being spoken about it.

*The only fun of a first preview screening is watching the things that you never thought were that funny be really funny and all of the jokes that you thought would kill are falling flat;* and all of the stuff that you thought was silly becomes scary, and all of the stuff that you thought were really scary is just making people uncomfortable

SL: What do you make out of these audience reactions when you go back to the editing room?

DF: Well, you don't re-edit, you shape. Again, the experience of making a movie is—you know there are days, sometimes even months—between shooting two ideas. But when they are projecting, they are only seconds apart. So you have to adjust to the experiential nature of the chronology: I mean the chronology for you as a filmmaker. You know you may shoot the last scene of the movie on the first day—and you may not have a very good idea of who all these people are. Also, you are maybe forced to film out of context and in a way that destroys your initial concept of it—and it may not work. But then when you see something that you might have initially been struggling with for a long time, and you might discover that the thing that didn't seem right about it was because you hadn't seen the scene that precedes it. And if the scene just before had been shot chronologically, and you had the ability to move across town or time-travel or whatever in order to do these things back to back, then you could see that what you're doing is fine.

It's true that you always re-adjust things—because you experience things differently with a matinee crowd than you would with a late evening crowd; you experience a movie differently on television or in a home-theater than on a big screen. Movies have many lives. This whole obsession with the first weekend is just such bullshit, because it's not about the first weekend. If you really want to talk about whether the movie's going to make money, you talk about the third weekend. If it's still around then, then it's something. But then, everybody just sits and goes: "Oh god, my movie just did 36 million dollars domestically." But wait a minute: now it's going to be experienced in DVD form and now it's going to be experienced on network television. And now it's going to be passed by fans to other like-minded individuals that are going to become fans five to ten years from now. So now *I have kids in my daughter's school who go: "Man, I love* Fight Club," *and you go: "Why are your parents letting you watch that?"* [*laughing*] *"Don't come near my kid."*

# Iñárritu, Alejandro González

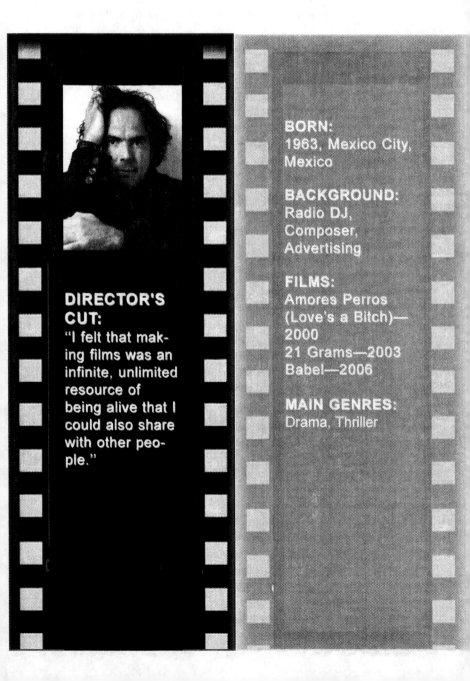

**BORN:**
1963, Mexico City, Mexico

**BACKGROUND:**
Radio DJ, Composer, Advertising

**FILMS:**
Amores Perros (Love's a Bitch)—2000
21 Grams—2003
Babel—2006

**MAIN GENRES:**
Drama, Thriller

**DIRECTOR'S CUT:**
"I felt that making films was an infinite, unlimited resource of being alive that I could also share with other people."

ALEJANDRO GONZÁLEZ IÑÁRRITU: I grew up in Mexico City as the youngest of three sisters and one brother. My father was a wealthy man until he went bankrupt when I was like four or five years old. So unfortunately, I didn't get to enjoy the wealthy part. It was a very tough and economically limiting situation. And when I am saying we ran out of money, it's completely out: we had to sell even the car. Sometimes we drank too much milk and we wouldn't have any the next week.

But the thing that I really appreciate about my parents is that they sent us to good schools. When they couldn't pay for them anymore, my father and mother were begging the school that they would let us in—my father, I think, basically got a credit. So I grew up in an environment where people have money but not me. That was hard, but at least I got the best, which was education, you know?

SL: What was the situation in Mexico at the time and where did you situate yourself in there?

AI: Well, as I guess it is everywhere around the world, the wealthy people separate from the non-wealthy people and Mexican society is, I think, ruled by those differences. In Mexico it is more about class than races, but then the Spanish-blooded people normally lead a life completely separated from the Indian and the mixed-Indian people.

And when you grow up, the social is often determining. You can feel the differences and at a young age, you are especially sensitive to them. For example, I remember being invited to the house party of a wealthy friend; or I never went on holiday with my family more than three hours outside of Mexico City maybe once a year—the first time I traveled on a plane was when I was 17. So when all the people talked to me about the great places that they had been to, I became conscious of being different from them.

SL: So you had access to this privileged world, but as an outsider—

AI: Exactly. It was that contrast I think. I mean when I was between 6 to 12 years old, I played in the streets all day and I had a great time. *I was the youngest, nobody really took care of me and I was very free. I basically lived in the streets every day: I was a street guy.*

But that changed around the ages 11 and 12, when you would maybe like to have some nice cans or you begin to like girls. That's when suddenly I realized more and more where I was at. I feel it hurt me most in my need to travel— there were these long summers where basically my friends went out and I was bored to death. And when they returned, they told me all those stories about their trips. Being able to travel became a major goal for me.

The situation made me self-conscious and it made me depressed. At one point when I was 12 years old, my father couldn't afford the rent anymore. We went to live with my grandmother for one year, with who I didn't have a great relationship. That was hard. But because it was far away from my neighborhood friends and I was suddenly completely alone—isolated. The only thing that I did all day was reading and listening to music. That was the good thing that happened to me. Now, to tell you the truth, I think it couldn't have been better. I'm so happy that I didn't get spoiled—maybe I would be a different person now.

SL: Tell me about what you discovered when reading and listening to music all day—

AI: I discovered both, sadness and that I was alive. In my grandmother's house, I spent a lot of time in my bedroom—I still remember the smell of the wood—listening to Pink Floyd and the lyrics; you know, being alone and suffering from being rejected, from limitations and so many desires . . . Not only that: I was an adolescent. I was in love with a girl, who obviously I couldn't even dream of ever being with. So I learned to be connected spiritually. I was very affected by Catholicism—my mother took me to church. I remember it was a church near my grandmother's house that has these paintings of hell and heaven that were really impressive. I began to be connected with that "be good, be bad" kind of thing and remember vividly how at that age I developed my spiritual conscience, guilt, masturbation—I discovered sex obviously. I was basically daydreaming—

And I think that shaped me a lot. I was hurt—it was not bitterness, but more of a challenge to me. *One of my dreams was that I would travel all around the world. And I did that.*

SL: So at your grandmother's, you created a universe of your own?

AI: That's it. And now I would love to return to that place in my life again, because I was in a universe of my own without being bothered by anything.

SL: So around the end of your time at school, where did you see it all going?

AI: As I said, the one thing that marked my life forever was that wish to travel. When I was 17 years old, I did not want to stay one more long summer in my house. There were these cargo boats at the port and I applied to be a worker to literally clean the floors on those. I applied with my best friend, my father gave me 500 dollars, and I spent two months working. We went to New Orleans up the Mississippi River, Alabama; then Italy and Spain. I have tremendous experiences of being at sea. I was the first one in my family to go to Europe. It felt like a triumph and it was such a powerful experience.

I did the same at 19 years. *When school was over, I just said: "Fuck it! I want to just live and Rock'n'Roll in Europe."* I took out a thousand dollars this time and lived in Europe for one year. I did everything. I'd literally live in the streets; I picked grapes in Spain; a lot of girlfriends, a lot of drinks and hashish. We also went to Morocco. I became like a fucking Bohemian. And in that year, really, I became a very wise street-man [*chuckling*]. I loved that year!

SL: Were you tempted to stay at all?

AI: I wanted to stay in Europe and find work there, but I couldn't. It was a very difficult time; I couldn't stay legally and I had to return. It was very sad, too.

I came back and didn't know what to do or to study, so I thought I would want to become a lawyer. I saw myself like defending people and the social cause like I had seen in films—I had all this left orientation in me. When I actually began to study law, I quickly realized I had nothing to do at that faculty. I went there for good reasons but it wasn't exactly what I expected. So I quit after three or four semesters.

I then went into communication, which was a more open kind of career. I thought I'd specialize in film and was actually thinking about becoming a filmmaker.

SL: Did that idea come rather out of the blue for you?

AI: No, I loved film. I had seen a couple of films that were actually the first hint that I wanted to do that. My father, who has a very good taste in film, had shown me *Midnight Cowboy* and *Once upon a Time in America*. Those kind of films made me go like: "Mmh, there is something here . . ." And I remember seeing a Turkish film call *Yol* [by Serif Gören]. It was one of the first films that really hit me hard. Twenty years later and before starting *Babel*, I saw it again and was shocked how good it is still.

*But you know, I actually consider myself more of a musician—I always loved music! I was a composer, but I was not very good at playing the guitar. So I was between film and music.*

A friend of mine used to be the girlfriend of a guy who was the director of a radio station. He was only 18 years old—a really great guy! He had a very wealthy father who had installed his son to manage that station for young people—and at that time there weren't any stations for young people.

He told me: "You now what, you have a good voice. You should come and make a test." So I went there without having any intentions and then: *Boom*, he likes it. Three, four months later, I became a DJ. That 18-year-old didn't have a clue how to manage the station and I had all the freedom. Everyday, I had three on-air hours of basically putting any music I wanted and to talk—so it was like fantastic therapy for me; like a cure: I would talk about life, I made jokes, I wrote a lot of politically provocative stuff. I could do whatever I wanted.

SL: And you felt comfortable being in the spotlight—

AI: I realized that I was doing exactly what I loved to do. Back when I lived with my grandmother, I would announce songs alone in my room, pretending to be a DJ. Now I found myself sharing the music that I loved with other people. It's like seeing a film that you like and suddenly when you see it again with a friend, it becomes even better. And I learned to entertain people for three hours.

SL: Did deejaying in that sense also teach you in many ways about filmmaking?

AI: Completely, because you have to direct audiences. You have to be telling something—sometimes I did thirty minutes of just talking. I wrote a lot of sketches for which I created a lot of characters—very political; funny and weird stuff. I could do whatever I felt like.

And you are playing with music: You have to edit the music; you have to edit yourself. You have to find a rhythm, you have to find a theme, which you have to stretch or extend at times. You know, you get to know the attention span of people. Even though it's a different medium, I would say that cinema is an audiovisual kind of art and audio is 50 percent of it.

We became the number one radio station in all of Mexico. We had success because people didn't listen to my show for the songs, but because of what happened between the songs. At 21, I became the director.

SL: Over the next years, you would try your hands at a lot of different things: you wrote and directed commercials, made short films, studied theater-directing, composed film-music and started your own company. Can you bring some meaningful order into that?

AI: Well, five years of radio was enough for me and I was really kind of, "I don't want to do that anymore—I want to become a filmmaker." I got tired of the radio and felt I had done everything there was for me. I was exhausted and depressed. I mean I was very successful, had a very comfortable economic situation and when I gave it all up, nobody could believe it. I was also very close to getting married and people were worried.

I decided I needed to go learn in other media—I wanted to go little by little. A friend of mine invited me to write for corporate TV-ads. I felt it was a great opportunity to train and start to put my conceptual skills into writing. I said I would do if the ads could be shot on film and not on video. That was my only rule. But shooting on film for Mexican TV at the time was crazy—even now: very expensive.

I ended up writing not only a lot of ideas for that channel, but also for the other four channels of that company. One day, we had a big presentation with the company's boss and he loved it. Mexican TV at the time was very stiff and I wanted to shake everything up. I remember it was like a seven-hour presentation and finally *I said: "We need two million dollars and six months." And he gave it to me.* Suddenly I exploded; it was great! I began to hire commercial directors. Several of them did a really terrible job and I said: "I will do it myself. I don't care."

So the first time I literally jumped on a set, I felt that I was really comfortable—I loved it! I wrote, produced, directed, and edited little one-minute sketches and experimented with different styles: very funny, very dramatic, very moving, or very complex. The blessing was that I was not selling products, but emotions: Father's Day, Mother's Day, Christmas . . . It became a very successful campaign.

But after five years of doing that, I got tired again. I began to get hired for some companies which I hated but which I did because it was a lot of money. So I did that for a while but was clear that I finally wanted to direct films. *I felt that I had traveled so many rivers and that it was time to go to the ocean. I didn't want to get lost in the rivers.*

But I felt like I had to learn more skills. I started studying theater-directing at a small school in Mexico City with a wonderful teacher: Ludwig Margules. And I learned so much. He could destroy anybody's careers so that people were afraid of him. He was so wise and had such an authority. But if you survived him, you can survive anything; and I survived!

I then went to America to study film for like one month in Maine—the best experience of that was to meet Judy Weston which was a very practical acting teacher. I had now learned some skills to direct: how to stage a story, how to block and analyze a scene . . . but at the same time, I think I needed to really understand the actor's point of view and how to communicate with them. And Judy taught me how I could reduce all that theory that I learned into a few words.

SL: You also composed some film-music at that time?

AI: I did some music for some terrible Mexican films. I am proud of the music that I did and how brave I was to accept those. I think I am a very good composer and I was working with a very talented musician. Together we created those things and we were having fun.

SL: What did you think film would be able to offer you that none of the other media and crafts could?

AI: *All those things were limited to me, while I think filmmaking is just an extension of yourself: you can be telling your stories until you die. And what is so beautiful about it is that you can translate everything you experience into film*—I felt that making films was an infinite, unlimited resource of being alive that I could share also with other people. So to me, filmmaking was exactly what I needed.

The other reason that I had is that film involves everything I love: the musical experience, the theater, the visual and all the other arts I really enjoy.

SL: So your first feature directing experience was for Mexican TV?

AI: I wrote, produced and directed my first 45 minute film for a TV pilot. I think it was very good and I was very proud of it. I intended to do a series of 13 episodes, for which I invited another five or six directors, but it was very expensive for TV standards at the time. They showed it as a film in its own right, but it was the old school of TV and they never went ahead with it.

I then started to develop a script by myself—a political tragedy from the peasants' point of view where the apparently communist Indians were trying to get rid of the government. It was about all the social movements that were happening in Mexico. But I felt I wanted a partner to co-write with. I got introduced to Guillermo [Arriaga] by a friend of mine. We connected very well and we shared our taste of filmmaking and filmmakers. Even if we are very different in personality, these clashes are very good and Guillermo has remained my writing partner ever since.

He immediately was a great help, because he translated all my concepts. We worked for three years. We got to write eleven interconnected, very short story.

For some reason, we reduced the stories from 11 to three, but that was the original *Amores Perros*. I think that he hated me at one point because he was writing draft after draft after draft. I get very involved and very neurotic with that kind of thing—you know, line by line, sometimes including also some blockings that help me to be clear—because really I am already directing when writing the script. So it was hard developing that project and we ended up with like 165 pages.

SL: Did you have a particular audience in mind?

AI: We didn't care. I didn't know what the film industry was about and I was just dreaming of making a great film. And I knew that I had always been more attracted to sad stories and drama—that's what I wanted to explore. *But I was a lucky motherfucker—I have always been so lucky to be at the right place at the right moment.* Because at that time, AltaVista Film just started as independent production company, and there was a small government fund to develop projects. At AltaVista, they knew me from radio and knew that I was very meticulous. They heard about me developing a script and said, "Anything that you have, we would love to see." So when we finished they saw it the next day and did the film. They simply said, "We believe in you, we trust you,"—and they did! You know, everything was against the script. It was written very factually and quite different from the way I shot it. But they wanted me to do something; I felt so responsible for that because they trusted more in my person than my work [*chuckling*].

SL: Similar to your real life memories, your films also revolve very strongly around "accidental moments"—uncontrollable events that can trigger life-changing consequences. Does that structure of your films reflect the way your mind works?

AI: As Mexican reader, I was very exposed to that structure. Not only Faulkner wrote like that, but also a lot of Latin American writers like Jorge Luis Borges, Ernesto Sàbato, or Julio Cortàzar; when I read those guys as young kid, they really influenced me in the way they structured their stories—the Latin American literature is full of that. They were always playing with time. So for me to tell the story a little bit over here and a little bit over there was like a natural process, I guess. Then my father, who is I think the best, most extra-ordinary storyteller I have ever known, always started from the middle, then he'd tell you a little bit of the ending, then you guess, but he went back to the beginning to tell you the seed of that relationship. And I guess it's the same way that you and I think—you jump back and forth in time: nobody talks chronologically.

SL: So instead of a factual chronology we let ourselves guide by some kind of emotional continuity?

AI: Completely. Every story finds its own way to be told. It's like everything else: Tequila you have to serve in a small glass, because the flavor is different if you serve it in a tall glass; or whiskey or champagne: they have their own form.

And I think sometimes form is intrinsic to the essence of the thing. And so the forms of *Amores Perros* and *21 Grams* are part of these stories' bodies themselves—it's not just a trick a flashy thing. *Babel* I think is my most chronological film so far, even if there are some elements that help to explain a little bit the timeline.

SL: But you think that felt continuity will always be prior to chronological continuity for you?

AI: I think so and I would love to do a linear story with one character all the time—I am not against that—but it so happens with me that when I want to tell a story, suddenly I find myself trapped. Suddenly I am very interested in the other points of view—and then a secondary character appears and I am more interested in *that* point of view. And I am experimenting now with even third characters' points of view: suddenly I am very curious about how other people see the situation—[*laughing*].

SL: Is the subordination of time over emotional space and perspective something where making music and making films meet for you?

AI: I have been influenced more by music than by film in my life. Music for me is the source of images. I can't create without sound or music and I find that every idea I have ever had for a story comes from music and the texture and the structure of that piece—it can be rock or jazz or a classical symphonic piece. *Babel*, for example, came from a musical experience that I had listening to a Moroccan album that reminded me of when I was 17 years old.

And when I'm developing my story or I am shooting, I always have a beat in my mind. I also give a sample of the music to the cinematographer, or the production designer, or even the actors, so they can hear the spirit or the texture of it.

SL: So while the visual idea has a musical inspiration, that musical piece has in turn distinct visual and tactile qualities to it?

AI: Completely. But I think beyond that. I am very interested in how a film smells as well. *For me, if a film doesn't smell, then it is no good. I like the skins to be shiny and sweaty and I want you to smell the walls when you enter a room—I want the people to experience that.* So with the production designer, I really work hard on the textures.

SL: What does *Amores Perros* smell like?

AI: I don't know if there is a specific smell or word. But I think *Amores Perros*—and going to Mexico City you'll smell that—has that kind of oily smell and the pollution of the streets to it; that very urban smell which is kind of a combination of cheap gas being burnt and also burnt tires.

SL: So apart from the visual, the auditory, the tactile, even the olfactory dimensions, is there maybe a space of concepts and ideas that is above and beyond these very concrete categories of human perception?

AI: I think music is the most abstract of any art—there is nothing more spiritual: The most abstract expression of human beings is music. I think films are boogers compared to music. So to me the music is like incense: A perfume of the film that is untouchable. And I love when you never consciously hear the music—I love films without music by the way. I try to avoid using it as much as possible. But when I need to, I try to use it so that people are unaware of it; that the music comes from literally inside the characters. I never put music that is like a score from the outside. Music for me is by definition not just there to justify and to pump out some emotion with which I want to manipulate people. For me, if it doesn't really represent what the character is going through—or contradicting that emotion as in "one plus one makes three"—then I don't use music.

SL: So if music is abstract and under erasure in film, what makes film such a powerful and palatable experience then?

AI: There is obviously nothing more powerful in cinema than the image—it is forty times bigger than you and it makes a statement: the reality that I present to you in one full frame, but to which you have to draw your own conclusions—the clothes, the environment, the light, the expression in the faces of the characters . . .

I think that contrary to literature or theater where the word is God, in film the image is God—that's why sometimes it is not a very friendly medium for writers. I feel that in cinema, scripts are very limited.

And it all results in film being a very physical experience. Take for example the image of "water": it can soak you; it can wet you. Or take Pinocchio: you can read about him, you imagine the sketch of the wood he is made of and he won't have that sparkle in his eyes until you give spirit to that; you create the life and give a face—a soul—to the character. A director orchestrates all that physical experience; and nothing can be more powerful than that.

SL: Do you ever worry that the audience might interpret the continuity of the structure of your films differently than you perceive it—and how do you deal with that?

AI: I trust the audience a lot. Sometimes they lose themselves during the course of the film, but I try to make sure that they won't become disconnected or lose their emotional concentration by thinking about it. I don't want that the rational process affects the emotional process. So if there is a shift in time or a shift in perspectives, I want that it is useful emotional-wise. My responsibility is that the audience understands. And I think that in the end, everybody can understand what I was trying to say.

But film and every other medium is necessarily very subjective. I obviously first select the story pieces that I want to tell and just by choosing those, I'm already directing people's attention. And I think the order of various scenes allows for different assumptions. Obviously, people don't always find that very common, but I assume that audiences that go to see my films like that.

I write my own ideas—my own things; *I don't sell hamburgers. I'm selling another kind of food and I assume that those guys really like tacos.*

SL: But do you find it surprising that your own subjective sense of continuity can be shared and universally understood by so many people around the world?

AI: You know what happens? I think that we have been exposed to so many different media now—the kids are now basically dealing with three, four, five realities at the same time: They are watching CNN and are reading the treadmill at the bottom of the screen—then a friend calls from New York while they are receiving that email from New Zealand. So the levels of realities that we are now dealing with are very virtually different. And the virtuality that we are now living in makes our minds more prepared to deal with stories that are nonlinear—you can be playing with several realities.

SL: So might a story like *21 Grams* not have been understood by an audience 50 years ago?

AI: Well, I don't agree with that. I remember seeing *Rashômon* from 1950 and there were those shifts in perspective where you go, "Oh my god"—and Faulkner was doing that in the 40s; and all those Latin American authors . . . Though the films that have been done that way are usually not very mainstream, I would say that it's nothing that's really innovative. I always laugh when people say that Tarantino discovered that: they must never have read or been to the cinema before the nineties.

SL: Do you consider your Mexican origin and identity as being at all relevant for the stories you tell?

AI: You know I make films. I hate when people want to nationalize art. It's like saying, "Are you the guy that made French paintings?" or, "So you are a dancer and Japanese. Are you a Japanese dancer?" I don't know why filmmakers are so branded by that. I think that art and expression is beyond the physical borders that we have invented: The countries, the nations, the governments, and the bureaucrats don't really apply.

SL: And you feel Hollywood or other people don't care?

AI: I fortunately feel like a global filmmaker. I have been shooting wherever I felt my stories had most relevance without ever having boundaries like, "This is not my language or my country, or I might not be welcome." Believe me, I feel so comfortable everywhere I go—and it started when I was traveling at 17. I was so comfortable even in a little house of a Japanese middle class family that I felt I could live there—also in Morocco. I suspect that the real borders—and the most dangerous ones—are within us. And I don't want to have that.

SL: Do you believe that ignoring certain established borders also allows you to introduce a certain element of chaos that is necessary for creativity to take place?

AI: Completely. I think that there is chaos whether we want it or not. We simply can't control the events. My life is very chaotic, my brain works very chaotically; I have big-time ADD since I was a kid. It's a horrible and a very chaotic mind. And I love that. I think nature is very chaotic. If you go to the woods, you won't find a Japanese kind of garden. The woods are wild and it's completely chaotic—and I love to tell stories about that chaos. In some ways I want to do films because I can become God: I can implement and control that chaos I went through myself by telling a chaotic story that happens to another character. It's my personal stories and things that have happened to me and my wife; 21 Grams in particular.

SL: For your last three films, you have closely collaborated with a core group of people—what influence do they have on the way you work as a filmmaker?

AI: I have a family, which is Rodrigo Prieto [cinematographer], Brigitte Broch [production designer], Gustavo Santaolalla [composer] and Lynn Fainchtain [music supervisor]—also Tita Lombardo, my line producer in Mexico. When I went to Mexico for *Babel* recently, it was the same people from *Amores Perros*. *There is nothing more comfortable to work with your family and people that you know. They are my accomplices; we are partners— it's not people I just hire. So the level and code of understanding is different. We are not working; we are really having an adventure together.*

And on *Babel*, there was so much adrenaline and risks that came with this project. But I love the smell of adrenaline—I am addicted to it. And I love to fail. I think it is my wildest and craziest idea so far for which I had all the trust of my family—and I trusted them—so we said, "Let's do it." It was one year of traveling around the world, with a lot of relatives of ours dying; new ones being born—we all changed as persons and it is amazing: one year together is a big thing—we are like circus people.

SL: How did the experience over that year concretely affect you as a person?

AI: *Babel* was an old idea of mine that I first began to write by myself. When Guillermo and I had finished the script, I went with Rodrigo and Brigitte and my two producers around the world to do the scouting—basically we were all partners.

Now that I am editing, I can see from the script how the process over the course of that year has shaped everything so differently . . . in a good way: it has become even more human; more accurate.

And I think as human being, I was exposed and confronted with so many realities on that project—we were shooting in four different countries and their respective languages. Working by myself a lot, I tried to subordinate myself to the realities of those languages and cultures. It was crazy and my brain was constantly working in different realities and different time zones. At those occasions, I was also really very lonely. The Japanese director Miyazaki told me: "I think directing is a very lonely craft." and I experienced it this time.

SL: Did the loneliness help you to find your way back to the roots of your creativity?

AI: Absolutely. *I feel like I am constantly projecting my own shadow——it's like I am three and I can't escape from it.* I think I make films in order to learn to make films. It's funny, but every time I start on a new project it's like I forgot everything. I always forget about the process and I'm like an early Alzheimer patient.

I met Werner Herzog the other day and we were joking about that. He told me how humiliating it is to be a director and if more people knew how humiliating it is, there would be fewer directors. So I learned that in order to survive and to keep going, you have to forget the many sacrifices you are making each time. It seems that it is a mechanism that all directors I know have because if you keep those memories, you will be traumatized and you would never want to make another film again.

I am not victimizing myself—it's the best work in the world and exactly what I want to do—but it requires a lot of personal and emotionally stressful moments, surrounded by people who are not all really loyal and nice. You find a lot of jealousy and envy.

Then I was struggling with non-actors, casting people in the middle of nowhere—almost all the people in the film apart from Brad Pitt and Kate Blanchett are people that saw a camera for the first time in their lives. So to be working with non-actors was a big experience for me: it put my patience to the limits, but it was one of the big lessons on that project—and I will continue to do that until the rest of my life.

And then when you have finished the film and can see it up there, I start to say things like: "Oh, it was so great" even though it was not great but terrible and horrible. I realize now that I romanticize really, really bad moments that we had on *Babel* and look at them as something beautiful. But then, the sum of all things makes it worth it. And I feel I am making films to be a better human being because the process makes me forget about myself as well—

SL: So films help you explore your own person?

AI: Yeah, and I hate to be thinking about myself. I hate to be struggling with my stupidity because it is always about very superficial and stupid things. When you are alone, you think about whether you might be sick; that you might be this or that. So suddenly I forget about myself and I have to worry about other things that are more fun—and I *have* to be worried about other people: I became a better person thinking about other people than me; I am not selfish anymore. The center of attention has become other things than me and that's what I love: *I escaped reality, I escaped from myself: I escaped from this fucking world——*

SL: But at the same time you get to know yourself by exploring the world around you—

AI: Yeah, it's a way to really decentralize your attention. And I think that particularly this last *Babel* experience made me a better person because it gave me so much hope in human beings. I found that the most humble and poor people I met are the best ones. In all those countries we went to, we found the most wonderful people just being interested in making others and themselves happy.

SL: If a car crash had changed *your* life, what turn might your personality have taken?

AI: I had in fact a big car crash when I was like 18 years old and completely drunk. I was doing a U-turn and some guy crashed into me. The car was completely destroyed and I couldn't move for three minutes—I was terrified to death. Little by little I began to move my finger; my left hand. And I remember that that moment changed me. It's not that I changed radically but it was one of the biggest events in my life. *Like that fear that I felt in those three minutes was something I had never experienced in my life.*

SL: So it's *without* the crash that you might be living a different life now?

AI: I think so. I think that the experience of danger and that you can really be killed—that your life can *disappear* in a second made me have a different perspective on life and maybe changed it forever.

# Gondry, Michel

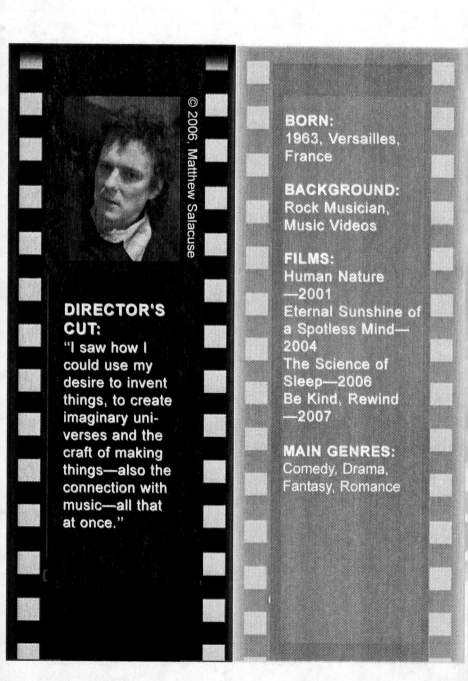

© 2006, Matthew Salacuse

**DIRECTOR'S CUT:**
"I saw how I could use my desire to invent things, to create imaginary universes and the craft of making things—also the connection with music—all that at once."

**BORN:**
1963, Versailles, France

**BACKGROUND:**
Rock Musician, Music Videos

**FILMS:**
Human Nature —2001
Eternal Sunshine of a Spotless Mind—2004
The Science of Sleep—2006
Be Kind, Rewind —2007

**MAIN GENRES:**
Comedy, Drama, Fantasy, Romance

MICHEL GONDRY: I grew up in Versailles, but not in a particularly bourgeois or rightwing way—*we all had long hair in my family and we were more like hippies,* I think. We were very 70s-consumption and going to the mall all the time. We were a very unified and close family with my parents and my two brothers. I was very close with my little brother. My other brother, we were friends, too, but with my little one, we were more like twins. We would speak in our own language: I'd start a sentence sometimes and he would finish it . . .

Our house was very small, actually, and we just had the ground floor to ourselves. Across was the house of my grandparents.

It was an artistic environment. We all played a little bit the piano and there was always music somewhere. My dad was a big fan of Jazz music. He was obsessed with the sound of the Hammond B3 organ. Laurens Hammond was a clockmaker, who had the idea to use the vibrations caused by the gear wheels of a clock to create a sound: the signature sound of the Hammond organ.

My father tried to recreate the sound with digital technology in the mid-70s, when programming was at a very early age still; so there was electronic stuff everywhere in the house. He taught my brother how to program, but me, I could never get into it. I mean I like electronics and the physical aspect it, but the programming was too theoretical for me. My brother became a very skilled programmer. He went into special effects and now he is a director as well.

SL: So what fascinated you and made you get up in the morning?

MG: I never had a problem to get up in the morning. I had always a million things to do and was also very self-sufficient. I would, let's say, build a glider with my father and then we tried to fly it. This really captivated me. Other than that, I would do photography at a very early age and process the film and print the pictures.

I had anguish at night to sleep, though, because I was afraid of death. And by building a glider, my father helped me to just have a regular way of thinking. He would make me want to go out and do stuff. My son is the same way now: He wakes up and has all these projects.

The creation of something new—to try out something new—was always what kept me going: understanding and trying to figure out the physics of the world; the geometry and geography of things. My mom would explain me some basic physic of the earth and my dad, too. And I liked to walk in the streets and find short cuts through the forest to go back home. My house was directly by the forest, and I still very strongly have this limit between the forest and the city in my head. I still visit it all the time in my dreams: the walls that separate the houses from the forest. And this limit—these geographic limits—I don't know, but they got imprinted in my brain.

I remember, for example, what looked like two red boats or carrousels merging above the forest every time I jumped off the bus. I always thought they were on top of the trees. But one day I realized that they were actually the top of a watch tower and they were implanted in the ground. Or another example is the castle of Versailles: I would see it from a map and it looked like that: 'cause that's the bird's eye shape of the castle, but I always thought it was the actual panoramic view of it. So it has always been the geography of things that I was concerned with.

SL: When you say "it imprinted my brain", do you mean that there must be literal memory traces in your brain—much like in the *Eternal Sunshine of the Spotless Mind*?

MG: I think there must be, but it must also be completely abstract; because if you think of it, it would be in many places in your brain and with many connections. And those connections and immersions that are the memory recopied in different places they found and erased in *Eternal Sunshine*.

Charlie [Kaufman] and I, we looked in medical books to see how the brain is imprinted. There is a quite well-defined geometry of the brain, while its activation is detected by the flow of blood or oxygen. It's a very low-definition process and not very precise at all.

SL: Was there a time in your early life when you'd say you turned into a self-conscious being and things in your life started to have perspective?

MG: Yeah; when I turned seven. I remember thinking, "I am going to turn seven!" I know exactly where I had this thought: it was in a supermarket near my house.

SL: What did "seven" mean to you?

MG: Well, "seven" was a big number. For me, it was a certain number of maturity. I was like getting older and was reaching a certain level.

Before that, I think before I was six, I had a lot of nightmares and a lot of anguish about death. *I was really scared of being dead. But even the void before birth scared me. People always get scared about the void after death, but probably there also was a void before; you know: nowhere.* Nonexistence always scared me. So I think I am always very active in the world and always try to construct or create things—

SL: So constructing as a strategy of survival: as long as you created something, you could avoid the void?

MG: You can see it like that; or more simply: When you are dead, you won't be able to construct anything—or the idea that when you are dead, you will be dead forever and all these kinds of thoughts . . . At some point, I even had some belief that we would be reincarnated. For several years, my family and I were members of a sect or cult, which believed that all is our imagination and we would be only One. It's a religious belief that's a cross-over of Christianity and Hinduism and whatever. But this would scare me as well and not bring me any piece of mind.

SL: That was your family religion?

MG: Some spiritual teaching we used to go to over the weekends.

SL: You don't believe in that anymore?

MG: Well, I have some stuff left in me. I mean, I got exposed to it at a very young age and you will always keep some of that. For example, we all became vegetarian following this belief when I was twelve. Now, I am the only one in the family to remain vegetarian: It makes sense to me to not eat mammals. I eat fish. I cannot change my philosophy about it

SL: Were you scared of growing up at all?

MG: No, no, I was hoping to be an adult and to have a good life; a creative life. And have a nice relationship. I was scared to not have a wife or a girlfriend. I was very shy and very withdrawn. *I was always scared to never have sex in my life.*

SL: Is there a person you particularly admired or looked up to when growing up?

MG: I was very open to adults, parents; older people in general. I remember when I was with my friends and family, I was the only one to pay attention to what my grandfather would say. All my brothers and cousins found him boring. He was an inventor, inventing lots of things: he was working on stereo images and a radio with a huge antenna that could broadcast around the world. He invented speakers, electronic bells, electronic organs, also a synthesizer in '49, which you can hear in the Beatles songs: "Baby You're a Rich Man" and "Yellow Submarine."

So I was very captivated by what he was doing and I would go and see him across the garden, listening to him for a long time. I was the only kid I knew to have this curiosity about older people. They had lived a life full of experience and that really impressed me.

I had the same thing with my teachers in school. Although I was not the best pupil and didn't necessarily have the best behavior, at least I had respect for them. And I think this was good: This curiosity kept me going and in some ways didn't limit me to having to learn at school.

I would learn from many different sources. In fact, in my DVD booklet, I give the ten advices I received during my life and who gave them to me. There was for example this guy. One day I was doing quite skilled drawings out of a Lucky Luke comic book, and he said to me, "If you want to learn to draw, you have to start from something that's real—3-dimensional—not something that has already been drawn."

And I have millions of examples of things that people told me and which I absorbed; advice that resonated a lot with me and which I have used all my life.

SL: Have your fascinations stayed the same over the years?

MG: Yeah, very much so. It's interesting, because I don't know. I mean, I use those emotions and those thoughts I had at a young age as blocks to build what I am constructing now, whether it is a video or a film. It could be slightly retarded things, but then I mix it with my experience and my observations which I had over the years. But I feel my brain was imprinted strongly at a young age on my taste, on my desires, and my vision was shaped very early on when everything was just about observing things. *You know, I always felt my vision and my sensitivities were much more detailed and deep when I was at a younger age. As I grew older, it felt I was looking through layers instead of being there.*

SL: Do we unlearn how to perceive spontaneously over the years?

MG: Maybe that's a reason, but I don't think of it this way: you connect your brain strongly at a young age and I think the impressions left are very strong. When you grow older, everything then gets compared to what is already imprinted: So the first day is 100 percent of your life, the second 50 percent, the third half of that, and so on . . . Of course, it's a very simplified version of it, but I think we record the information from outside relative to what we already harbor. But even if much is already imprinted as you grow older, it doesn't limit you completely and you can still have very strong impressions and emotions. But I do think that perception changes from kid to adult.

SL: What did you do first: music or film?

MG: I was doing lots of drawings and mechanics with Lego and Mecano and cardboard. I was also into animation: I would make flipbooks and we built a zoetrope with drawings inside and slots outside.

When I was around 16, I was at this experimental art school in Sèvre. We still did some very low level normal school stuff, but mostly drawing and painting and craft and art. I always was the best at drawing in my old class and kind of the artist, and now I was in this place where everybody could draw. So it was quite a humbling experience. I didn't have that specialization anymore. But I got to meet people with the same type of creativity coming from everywhere, because it was a very unique school.

So as an adolescent, I got more into music. I was very shy, so I thought I could find a girlfriend easier if I was in a band or if I was playing the drums just to be cool. I remember watching a drummer at school and I was really impressed, thinking he would get all the girls. I thought I wish I was this guy. I tried the drums and I tried hard—I was generally persistent in my trials and I ended up being pretty OK doing it. I don't think I was particularly gifted, but at least I could express some of my gut with it.

SL: Did it work out with the girls for you?

MG: Not at all! You get older spending time to rehearse and practicing the craft of drumming and when you are ready to play a concert, the other guy, instead of practicing the craft of drumming, he was practicing the craft of chatting up a girl—so he beats you. *If you want to get something, you just have to learn the craft of that thing, not some deterred way to get there.*

SL: You started a band with your brother called *OuiOui*, with which you were beginning to have some success—where did you see it all going?

MG: We could never live off it and it was a lot of struggle for a little bit of creativity.

I was always hoping to be successful with the band; to make a record. Then the creative part kicked in; it was really important to do something original and the people in the band were really creative. We were I think so original that we couldn't find a place in France to fit in.

SL: Too original to succeed?

MG: I think so—we were very anti-cool. A lot of bands that would be Rock'n' Roll or Punk or Alternative, they always have this way of reflecting the expectations of the audience. It's that way in every style, even if people say, "Oh, we're alternative, we are different." We started just at the beginning of the New Wave, when everything was really like 60s and pure which I liked very much. But everything was in fact very dark and the bands, often just copying a style, were really strange. They were all like crows with they hair hanging and apparently always very depressed. And we wanted to show we were very kind of puppy and naïve, but much harder on the inside. But people didn't dig inside.

We didn't fit into the different boxes of what was playing in every bar. They put on the sticker of "childlike" very soon and it was very difficult to get rid of it.

Sometimes I get this feeling today in America, when people say, "Oh, I don't like studio movies, I like independent movies." *Often, independent movies are more stereotyped than studio films. You simply have to look a little deeper to find what's really original.*

SL: At one point you started to make a video for your band. Did you feel that now you had found an artistic medium that allowed you to fully immerse yourself and act out your creativity?

MG: Yeah, I remember this moment very clearly. It was during the first video, which was not exactly a music video: I would use the music of my band to illustrate this little short film I shot with the camera of my friend. I remember coming back to my room in this tiny apartment and thinking: "I'm gonna do a city with cardboard and there will be a little freeway in the middle with little egg box-shaped cars." I had a little raised platform for my mattress. I put the mattress aside, which gave me a little stage. *I thought: "It's really cool to do that. If I can make a living out of that, I could do it forever."*

The connection of music and the image has always been very important to me. I was sharing my apartment with this guy Jean-Louis Bompoint, who is my DP now. He had a collection of 60s animation films and I got to watch Norman McLaren films very early. He was one of the first ones to make a really amazing connection between the image and the sound—his movies were like mini-operas. He even created sounds with images by painting directly onto the sound stripe to create the melody. So the way he could illustrate the music— sometimes very literally, sometimes in a more abstract way—had a great influence on me and inspired me a lot.

I think I found a good crossover of my skills and my ambition. I saw how I could use my desire to invent things, to create imaginary universes and the craft of making things, mixed with painting and drawing—also the connection with music—all that at once.

And the fact that things can be invented and work for a while, then afterwards you have the perfect physical support by ending up with these little films or videos which you can accumulate.

So the idea to do this little film was very satisfying to me. I didn't have to ask permission from anyone. I was completely self-sufficient. I had my two little lights, my camera which I could load myself; I even did the negative editing myself. And I remember the moment when I panicked because the cuts ended up looking a little bumpy. And that's the look it had in the end—

SL: And the audience didn't mind?

MG: Well, there was no audience, there was me. At this time, the festivals would not play my films [*chuckles*]; they were too amateurish for them. I think animation festivals like Ancy or Clermont-Ferrand did not accept my films because they were rough. The interesting thing people like to see, I think, in animation is the difficulties and details of the painstaking stadium when it is created. I remember this film done by a woman that sat nine months in a room making it. And that is basically what counted; and I was too impatient for that. I like to experiment and then see the result. And my films were always very crude and I liked the roughness of it. I didn't mind it.

SL: Did the fact that you were self-sufficient and didn't have to ask permission from anybody help you to be creative?

MG: Yeah. I always thought that drawing was a getaway from talking. It frustrated me that in the French educational system, the specialization in art was a very tiny part of the curriculum. It was mostly French and philosophy and I didn't like expressing myself verbally. So doing animation was a good way to be creative without having to convince people that what you want to do is right—I had to learn to do that later.

*Animation is a lot like you are plugging something directly in your brain: It surfaces onto the medium you choose, without ever having to go through any other layer.* You don't have to explain it to a lector or a technician: you can really dream and imagine and still make it happen. It might not exactly be matching what you had in mind, but at least it's pure. I like this process and I think there is something very intimate to that which reflects yourself.

I also learned to appreciate the idea that you can make something small and project it bigger. Most of the people I knew that were doing films were doing the opposite process, trying to go to places where the scale was impressive and then squeeze it out on screen. To me, the magic of making films has always been to start out with something small, very secretive, and then project it on a bigger space.

SL: When you look at your earlier videos now, do you like them?

MG: To me, they are totally up to the notch. When I see them now, I honestly find them as good as anything that can be done. *The only thing I could be embarrassed about is when I started to do jobs for other people and they didn't let me be myself.* Between the time that I did videos for *OuiOui* and I started with Björk, I often despaired when I did videos with others. Because I didn't have any money coming in if I didn't work, I always had to work and sometimes do jobs for people whose creativity I wasn't impressed by.

SL: So while festivals didn't want your videos, they were apparently good enough for Björk to hire you?

MG: Yeah. At that time she was not so big, she had just released her first album. But for me it was already a real big deal: She saw a video I did for my band *OuiOui*—it was my sixth video. I had also become more sophisticated technically then.

SL: When did you first think about feature filmmaking as a possible horizon—or was it more of an accidental encounter?

MG: I had never imagined that it would be possible to make a feature film in my life. For me, it was some old guy that has been to film school and that has all that knowledge. And especially in France, films were by people who are very much into philosophy and have a very good way of expressing themselves. And I was not in film school, and I was not a writer at all.

I would say that the *Nouvelle Vague* in France had traumatic repercussions on film critics, who then had repercussions on filmmaking—because filmmakers like Truffaut or Godard were film critics initially. So when they started to do their films, sometimes they were naïve, sometimes experimental, sometimes good—but not better than surrealists for instance; not as good I would say. But they had this way of making belief that they were right and that the others were wrong. And they took over. After that, everything was always compared to them.

It became something like the turn in France and made it very difficult for somebody who comes from the graphic arts to become a director. The visual is regarded as something like a plague. People are sure that if you are visual, you are not narrative—that you don't care about the character and the story. But that is of course completely not the case.

It's funny, because a French critic recently compared me to George Méliès: the first person to make fiction film, but who was also a very visual director. So they compare me to the guy who invented fiction. He was the first one to have a set and sometimes he would recreate a mood on stage and sometimes he would invent stories. So apparently some people get it so wrong that they compare me to the guy who invented narration in order to show that I am not into narration . . .

So I did this video for Björk that we shot mostly on film and with in-camera effects. We decided to do a premiere in a London film theater. It was simply amazing to see those images projected in a cinema and the difference it made. People are coming to see them and there will be that moment of expectation and waiting; and then you see this image with so much more detail. So I thought: "Maybe if I keep doing the same thing on a bigger scale, I could do a movie. If I keep on incorporating people into the universe I create—half from my imagination and half from their imagination—and tell a story with a lot of imagination and images for 100 minutes, maybe it would be a great movie to watch"; because from my first to my most recent video, all of them have been storytelling, really. Even if the story is a bit abstract, there is always a sense of narration; there is always a beginning, middle, a climax and an end.

And later on, I started to go to festivals with my videos to show them in a two-hour, non-stop program. I would see that people would watch them and not get bored; in fact, they would get less bored than with the first film I directed.

SL: But how is it possible that a film bores more than an accumulation of videos?

MG: I think because I had more control of what I was doing. I was, I guess, more personal: I was always being myself and not trying to be this or that. When I did a compilation of most of my videos, I realized that they were always in some way a continuation of each other—we'd explore some similar ideas. There was good variety, but I think there was still a certain arc. Even if it was separate videos, you would feel you were going somewhere. So at the end of the day, when you play them together, they seem to be coming from the same person.

I remember when I did *Human Nature*, some people found it long. I still like it, but I know I got mixed reviews for it. So I realized I have to really stick to what I like to do.

SL: Where was the initiative coming from to read your first feature scripts?

MG: Well, somebody told me I should find a lawyer, *then* an agent in LA I found myself a lawyer—a very nice guy. *Then they found me an agent and I read shitty scripts for years. I finally met Spike Jonze and he let me read Charlie Kaufman's script* Being John Malkovich, *which I thought was an amazing read. Until then, I was really arriving at the conclusion that scripts are boring;* that they are just not meant to be a good read and that it's up to the director to make them interesting.

SL: So you blamed yourself as a reader—

MG: But then I bought the script of *Taxi Driver* or *Back to the Future* and they were not so boring. I was really frustrated that I couldn't find a script as good as Charlie's for myself. But Spike was already set on doing *Malkovich* himself. I was very jealous.

SL: So what did you decide to do?

MG: One day I had this concept with my friend Pierre Bismuth about memory erasing and we started *Eternal Sunshine*. The erasing the brain bit was by Pierre, and I think I came up with the rough story line. I remember even my father telling me that at the end they should be together. I met with Charlie after I started to write out like a two or three page treatment with Pierre—very rough. All we had was this concept and we met up and talked about a lot of ideas. Then I handed it to Charlie and he did the great script.

SL: You are not credited as a writer on *Eternal Sunshine*—

MG: I am not, but together with Pierre, I am credited for the storyline.

SL: I am interested in the actual ways you and Charlie worked together: what are the significant creative and development steps you went through?

MG: I think in order to convince Charlie to work on this project, I had to underline all the possibilities of what could happen now that we had the basic storyline.

We were then thinking that in order to erase your memory, they make you relive your common memories with that person. You revisit all those places in your head which they find in your brain and make disappear.

And this triggered a really interesting process of working together with Charlie. Suddenly, we could communicate our memories to one another on such a physical level: "I visit them and you erase them"; this is how the process worked. For example, *I had this habit with my girlfriend at the time that when she would come back to the apartment, I always pretended I was dead: I would take the most ridiculous position lying on the floor pretending I was dead. And she would pretend: "Oh my god, you are dead!", and try to bring me back to life.* And Charlie had this thing where they are pretending to kill each other with his girlfriend and the pillow. So we used that in the film.

It was really fun and exciting to work with that. We would then use this as a tool to explore an interesting relationship in a way that has not necessarily been done before. We created those characters Clementine and Joel and the very detailed evolution of their relationship from being very familiar, to the point where they start to hate each other—all this background.

And the interesting thing with Charlie was that when I started to talk about relationships, he became like my shrink; he is a very good listener. I would tell him all the shit I was going through with my girlfriend, my past girlfriend, and how we had been working hard on the situation—Charlie and I would speak for three weeks in a row, so we had a lot to talk about.

SL: And he would note it all down—

MG: Well, he would not take all, but some of it you can find in the movie. It's a very good way to work. It is so rich and real and a very organic process. Obviously he writes a lot from his experience and that of other people, like actors, as well. Eventually, you end up with something that really feels comfortable to everybody. It's the same with my music videos: I meet with the singer, talk for as long as possible to find what we have in common and see how we can create a story that we feel both comfortable with.

So Charlie did a first draft and I felt that he was a little bit harsh on the character. I told him to go easier on them: less dark and with more sweet moments.

SL: *The Science of Sleep* you wrote by yourself; how often did you wish Charlie was there with you?

MG: Sometimes I wished he was there. And I could always give him the script to read it, but I was too scared. The working process with Charlie is very sensitive—also very intellectual in the sense you can't just throw ideas at him. You have to always justify them. And it's very good, because of what I said earlier: I had to learn to articulate my thoughts and explain to others why you do this and that.

On the other hand, I grew up more with the sensualist attitude, like I remember reading Buñel's autobiography, where he explains that when they shot with Dalì, they wrote out any idea that came to their minds. Each time they could explain *why* the idea was there, they would destroy it. And I like this way of working as well. Not that I would destroy it if I can explain it, but sometimes, you fall into the trap of wanting to explain it first.

With Björk as well, we would work on a very sensitive level—exchanging emotional expressions—and *then* I would think about the story. It would be all this re-cutting of meaning and it would in fact make lots of sense. I always wanted to work this way. The only way to do that is to work alone.

I don't know much about scriptwriting rules. At times, I take something from my real life and it feels right, sometimes I have to create a scene around something that doesn't exist and set that in some kind of reality. *Of course, I don't want to take everything from what I lived, but I am not used to writing something from nothing and then expect people to believe it when projected. Sometimes I feel it's artificial, but it seems that eventually it gets absorbed in the context and it becomes alive.*

SL: But how do you gain structure when working by yourself?

MG: Well, I had my producer who talked to me about stuff like that; my script girl also helped me a lot. But ultimately, it was me with myself and it was a big struggle. I got into depression, believing I had no value. I would imagine some things and write a lot; then get rid of it.

SL: When did you write it?

MG: I started it before everything—like six years ago. But the final draft I did well after *Eternal Sunshine*. Since I am French, I probably took some expressions from it—maybe even some of Charlie's; it's hard to tell. Some probably also came from my relationships with English or American girlfriends.

The script ended up being quite different from what I initially had in mind—a lot of things that I experienced; things I dreamed. There were so many elements I wanted to try to put into it and it's going into a lot of different directions. With Charlie on the other hand, it is always very linear. *I'm like a band that after ten years of making music has its first chance to record its first album—it tries to put everything in it.* Then with its second album, it can be more specific. So to some, *The Science of Sleep* can appear like a first film.

SL: But nevertheless, you went through a process in which you had to learn to limit yourself in order to say more?

MG: I always have to take out things. I always come up with a story too complex and too big for the project and the time I have. Having to let go can be very hard and sometimes it's even the idea that initially made you want to do the video or the film. But this eliminating part of the process is very creative as well: It's not just deleting.

I remember this conversation I had with my editor, by saying to her, "But that's why I wanted to do the film: for *this* scene." and she said: "It doesn't matter!" So it was out.

SL: Can that be depressing as well?

MG: No, that's not what makes you depressed. DVD is good for that, because you always think: "Oh maybe I put this on the DVD-version" It allows me to let go more easily. But in any case, you should be able to let go. You know, there is that rule: "If you can tell the story without the scene, take it out." But I have my problems with that as well and can't really agree with it, either. Basically I would then say: "You do one thing and the story is told", or: "You do nothing and then you have the story."

SL: So it's your intuition and taste that have the last word?

MG: It's the taste of my editor as well. The relationship with you editor is very important. I have worked with three editors; one for each film. They are all different. Valdis Oskarsdottir, who did *Eternal Sunshine*, is very strong minded. With her, we used to fight a lot: She would get very protective of her work and very rude to me. But at the end of the day, she did a great job, so I have good memories—but we were like a couple: We nearly physically fought.

SL: Do you think that a film like *Eternal Sunshine* could have been appreciated by an audience 50 years ago?

MG: In some silent movies, you already had some pretty sophisticated narration. I don't know if I am in a position where I can feel I am pushing boundaries. I think I try to use what I know and what I learned in my own experience, telling stories that reflect me without boring people. Even though "without boring people" is the big drama of editing: It's very easy to shoot a movie and do what you want, but then when you put it together it's painful to watch. And then you have to work so hard to make it enjoyable—

SL: Was the first cut of *Eternal Sunshine* painful?

MG: Every first cut is painful. The first test screening then went OK but reactions were a little cold.

SL: So you had to change a lot?

MG: Well, we wanted people to get lost at some point, but get them back on track afterwards. We were trying to control how long they would get lost and that it would be enjoyable, not something that made it boring. So with Valdis and Charlie, we worked on that a lot. We didn't want to make non-creative concisions. It's interesting with these screenings, because they are hardly done in France but always in America. You don't want to make your decisions based on audience reactions, but still use them to confirm the feeling you have about your film—if you feel it's a little so-and-so and everybody says: "Oh, I hated this part," then you cut it. But if you feel great about something and people say: "I didn't understand—who do you think you are?" you simply ignore all that stuff. You need to have a good producer with you to protect you.

SL: So sometimes the test audience simply doesn't know what's good for them?

MG: Yes exactly. And sometimes, once you have finished your effects—with the music and the mix—it will push the tolerance of people a little further and then they can accept the story to be a little bit more complex. So I'd say you need to give yourself a chance—if you just want to have the best screening, then maybe you won't get to the limits of what you could achieve.

SL: How did you approach the general look of *Eternal Sunshine*?

MG: I don't think about the look. I never had any aesthetic taste and if any, I would be a little bit tacky. During my upbringing, my house was full stuff and carpet with long hair and crappy wallpaper with big flowers—so it wasn't a clean and aesthetical surrounding. I never had elegance—it has to come from the idea: from the restrictions that are inherent to achieving the idea.

SL: So the rough look of *Eternal Sunshine* was something rather inherent to the story?

MG: Basically, I wanted to feel some physicality in my memories; to really feel that they are crumbling down. And if there is no changing of rooms, the floor would literally collapse and be gone. Especially for movies that happen in your head, you want to get a sense of constant physical jeopardy. We wanted the people to feel disconnected emotionally as in the movie the memory was getting erased.

I had prepared all these transitional moments—there was a lot of CGI and mechanics but couldn't afford them with the 30 million or so we had. But also, it felt that they were overwhelming in terms of the story. Three weeks before the shooting, I was panicking.

I had to reduce the effects to the mere minimum. At one point I wanted to change the speed of the camera, and Jim had this idea to speak faster and faster which we would then shoot faster and faster, so that the speed of speaking would remain the same. We couldn't achieve that, but what we did achieve was to synchronize the sound with the image. It was very eerie and detached and that was one of the easy effects we used for the erased memory. There were many in-camera effects and I think that those work very well.

Another look that was strong was due to the handheld camera, though for the dream sequences, the camera work is more established. During the first week of shooting, we started by doing close-ups, then medium and long shots, as we do generally. Because Jim was demanding many takes on himself, it was very difficult to do lots of takes of Kate as well. So I decided I won't do singles, but instead back-and-forth shots. Apart from saving time, it has the advantage that both stay involved in the shooting, not knowing who's going to be on camera—it's a lot more stage-like.

I am not crazy about the handheld camera, but I do it a lot, because it is so much faster when you have to finish your day. Instead of having to drop one idea after another because you don't have the time, you just do your shots; and sometimes it looks even better.

SL: How do you instruct your cameramen when you work handheld and without established angles?

MG: Basically, I like my cameramen to think when they are shooting. When I did the documentary on Dave Chapelle's *Block Party*, I asked each camera to be like a unique unit onto itself. That means that I wanted them to always shoot in context and as if they were the only camera shooting. I told them: "When you shoot somebody, you don't want to stay on one person all the time, but you want to see who is next to him; like a normal person would do." So they have to open their eye, see what's next to it, and then catch it and then come back.

Obviously, you don't want all the cameras to be on the lead singer. But if two cameras were on the lead singer, that was OK. Or if nobody was shooting the lead singer, that was OK, too. Then during editing, we could recreate the feeling of the concert. And I wanted to take this chance because it was a way to make it real—

SL: And give also personality to the camera—

MG: Yeah exactly. And it worked out. We did that for *Science of Sleep* and *Eternal Sunshine* as well; we followed organically what was going on.

SL: Does that liberal way of working with the camera also help you to maintain spontaneity and a creative attitude on set?

MG: It was a learning process for my first film, when I had everything story-boarded and planned out in detail. I simply decided to give much more free-dom to the actors for my next film—let them do what they want with the space. I gave up many of my preconceived ideas of where to put the camera before the actors start to act.

And for the process of directing the actor, it helped me to find a way to make them forget about the whole process.

SL: Did you feel you had to learn to direct the actor?

MG: The process of casting taught me a lot about directing, because there would be those kids, who come there with hardly any idea of what the film would be. Their auditions usually turned out to be like nothing I had in mind. So I had to find a way to communicate to them to modify what they do.

And I think auditions are the best process to learn how to do that. You have to get your actors to talk. And while I am pretty shy in general, it helped me to overcome my own shyness.

There is your actor and there is your character on paper; to exist on a real level, they have to meet half-way: so the actor has to go towards the script, but the script has to go towards the actor as well, as otherwise, the actor would just mimic the script or the character on page. *And I really don't like these movies where the actors get to gimmicky, though in general, they tend to get the Best Actor Oscars. A lot of times, for example, a beautiful actress will look ugly and she has a very good chance to get nominated, because people judge the acting on this basis of transformation.*

For me, a good actor is somebody that will bring some character on paper to life. So it has to bring what's on paper toward *his* direction. So when I cast him, I have to find what is already in him and then work with the difference. Sometimes you also cast against type, but it must not be a gimmick either.

SL: You have done it in a way with Kate and Jim, as both play characters quite different from their usual roles.

MG: Yeah, but they are like that in real life. I remember seeing Jim in-between two takes on one of his films, and he was like this lost child. Then I remember seeing him in the end credits of "In Living Color," and he was this tall white guy completely not mingling with the other people—quite a strong feeling of loneliness.

SL: So do you find that on set you mostly communicate like you would with people in your personal life?

MG: Yeah. When I started to do videos in the early nineties, I was really disgusted by pop videos: They usually put people up there—as if they are perfect or God—and I find this very condescending. It's the fashion aspect that you get on the catwalk, where people don't smile and are very arrogant. I always despised that as I don't want to feel like a piece of shit when I watch TV or go to a movie.

And I know that some actors also thrive on making their directors uncomfortable, and I don't think that's good either.

SL: You have had that experience?

MG: I have worked with some actors like that and I didn't enjoy it. I don't think their performance was good then. They would make you feel that they are the most important person—

On the other hand, I don't like movies which make the audience look down upon the characters. In some movies you can feel the director taking pleasure in humiliating his actors; his characters. I simply feel that there is enough richness in human relationships and I always try to shoot people the way I would shoot them if they were my brother, my father or my cousin—somebody I am close to and familiar with. And I think that this is how you get the best out of them. But it is not at all organized, and it doesn't feel I'm in control.

SL: But *are* you in control?

MG: No, but I feel I've got the energy to make things happen. *I feel I am always failing, but at least I give enough energy to people to keep going.*

I also learned to have this kind of humorous way where I communicate with people just to provoke them and put them at ease. I remember I had this teacher that was always cracking bad jokes—not funny at all. And he told us: "I always make jokes that are not funny, because it puts people at ease." And I realized it was a very smart way to get people relaxed. I am not saying that I do that, but I expose myself on a human level. People start to feel bad for you, but in a caring way.

SL: Do you like to give your actors a lot of direction?

MG: If actors feel they have no direction, they will feel even more insecure. But some people need a lot of preparation and others do something really touching without ever talking about it. So it depends. Generally, I try to not say anything before the first take, because I don't want to ruin it. Sometimes I find out that as soon as I start to talk, their performance suffers. So I want at least one take where they try their own stuff. *Gael [Garcia Bernal] would often ask me: "So what do you think? Is it good or is it bad?" And I would be doubtful and go: "Uhm, well I don't know . . . but don't worry, because if it was bad I would never tell you," and that freaked him out. I simply wouldn't want to additionally flatter his ego—it's neither good for him, nor for me.*

At times, I simply don't have any opinion—then I just don't know.

SL: So your communication and direction varies a lot for each actor?

MG: I had to learn that sometimes, different actors will require different explanations and ways of communication. That means that you cannot always talk to two actors at the same time. You have to discretely take them aside and say to one: "Just go for it"—to others you say: "It's very serious, it's a drama"—and when they come back together, they are on the same page. And it's interesting: some actors come with a lot of ideas and you have to learn to calm them down and say: "It's a good idea but it's exactly what you did last week. Do something else now." Or it can be that I have to find ways to say that it's not great without offending them. Sometimes I feel it is complete crap—that the performance is zero and the film will be pure shit—but I know that later during editing I might like it. So I am not as negative as I might feel at that moment.

Sometimes, if you say the scene is sad, they will do something that they believe would make people sad and it would be far from the way I want them to be sad. So I make something up—like I remember telling Patricia [Arquette]: "You are sad on the surface, but underneath you are a little happy, and underneath this happiness you are a little sad." And she would laugh at me—but in a nice way—and then she'd say it was a very good instruction.

It's not because you say "be more sad" that the person will be more sad. You have to find a way to get what you need for the story. I think I have found ways to put things into a context that helps the actors—more than telling them how they should be. Basically I help them to forget we are doing a movie, and remind them we are trying to reproduce something that's from life.

SL: Did you learn ways to increase the chemistry between actors by taking advantage of their different personalities?

MG: Oh yeah, completely. I totally use each actor to shake up the other one. With Jim and Kate, we'd do that a lot. And sometimes it would piss her off, because he would improvise and cut off one of her lines and sometimes he was pissed off, because she would not say the right line and go into another direction—but those irritations were so much in character that they were perfect. And sometimes the actors might have a very bad day but do a great scene—they can hate each other, and you say: "It's amazing how they suddenly get that chemistry."

SL: But how can you encourage that chemistry develops?

MG: Very simple; I would tell Kate: "Can you mess up your line?", or: "Can you walk to the other side of the room as he doesn't expect that"; or when she leaves the train: "Can you give him a big punch in the shoulder before you leave"; then Jim would tell her off: "What are you punching me for?"—and that's the take that actually ended up in the finished film. It was perfect, because he had to recompose himself.

I found that most actors—especially beginners—would grab on to something that they won't let go of. Even some of the more confident actors would do the same again and again. And once it becomes locked, it is impossible to work with. So the only way to unlock them is to give them a different mark or change something about the setup.

We asked Kate a lot to change what she was doing in each take to keep Jim fresh—he had to respond to that then. We did it more with her because her character is the most spontaneous, sometimes obnoxious one—

I really like the scene in the train when she is all over him and she talks to him at a one-inch distance and he has to pull back. A lot of times, actors want to be in charge in their relationship with the girl and here we realize that it's more the girl that is in charge. And that's what I wanted to create—very subtle.

SL: Carrey at one point complained that you limited him too much—

MG: Yeah, we had some conversations about it. I remember at one point, we had this big fight. He was doing this joke and I was not sure it was going to work in the context of the story. He would do it in every single shot to make sure we'd use it and I said to him: "Can we do one without you making that joke?" Jim got upset: "You don't let me be funny. It will be one of these lame movies I have done before." I said: "Well, you want me to direct you? If you don't let me direct you, how can I direct you?" So we did one take without, but in the end, we used the take he actually did with that joke.

SL: How much of a danger is it to get so caught up in the process of shooting your movie that you stop having an open mind about it?

MG: That can happen and you have to be aware of that danger. And maybe I was not as aware of it in my first film, cause I had done a very precise arc. But I realized that in life, people do unexpected things and they don't necessarily apply their personality in everything they do: sometimes they even do something contradictory to their nature—that's what makes them human, or likeable, or despicable or whatever; and I feel that it is only randomness that can give you that. I mean you can't have randomness too many times, but I like working around chaos.

Or sometimes I would give them a direction that they misunderstand because I am French—like at the beach I'd say: "She not run when you go to see him" and Kate said: "Oh, I should run" and I don't correct them, because I might realize that maybe it's even better or I could destroy the moment. *I think that sometimes, the opposite of what you initially wanted is not necessarily worse. Sometimes it can be just as good or better— often, the middle is the enemy of the opposite: if you choose the middle, you don't go anywhere.*

SL: Can you put into words how your creativity is related to the stories you want to tell and what common source of fascination they share for you?

MG: Creativity as conceptual reality is just fascinating: you imagine it's going to be real, that you will see it, but you can't quite picture it yet. Each time, it's the same feel: that it's not possible and that it's completely abstract; and this is true for everything from the story, to the actors, the art direction, the music . . . And then there is this moment when you say: "OK, tomorrow I'm gonna see that idea realized on the big screen" and that's one of the things that keep me going. And that's part of the reason why I don't like very much to start from a pre-written story. I am not crazy about getting a script already finished. I like the idea of really starting from just a concept—just something in my mind or from a conversation and then make it exist.

SL: So where does the inherent joy of creation come from?

MG: It's a lot of pain as well. The joy comes from when it's done, mostly. Say for example, you want an animation of a dancing man. You start out with let's say ____. Then you do the second image ____ an then that ____, then ____. You imagine that it's going to work, but you are not sure what it's going to look like. Then you shoot it, send it to the lab and before it comes back, you have no idea what the result is going to be like. It's like you are entering a new dimension—you put some chemicals or some elements together, and then you create something new, and that's what drives me. It's hard to explain. You combine things in little processes that allow you to tell a story. They will mean something new and you will move from one mode to another.

SL: So you create a new reality in a sense?

MG: Maybe it's a new reality. And I think it comes down to experimenting with reality. You know it's like when I had me *Legos* and a motor and the thing was supposed to move. You click it, it creates a vibration and it actually starts to move—that's the same process.

SL: Do you think that there is a danger that you could ever lose your fresh approach?

MG: Well, I had this feeling when I finished my first film, but then I went on to do two of my most creative videos I had ever done; so I regained trust and confidence in me. I know that the brain's capacity is getting a little reduced when you get older, but on the other hand, you gain in experience and I think it is very close to what instinct is. Instinct is what you do without thinking: It is really combining all your experience into making decisions without intellectualizing. And I think if I get good at that, I will counterbalance the fact that my brain will slow down.

SL: What about the possibility of losing some of your curiosity which made you want to explore reality in the first place?

MG: But there is so much to explore that I think I will always have a place to go. *I just did the* Block Party *documentary, and everybody asked me: "Why did you do that documentary? You didn't get to do any of your tricks." And I said: "Well, I hope I have more to sell than my tricks." And this documentary is a way of exploring that.*

SL: So you plan on exploring more unknown territory in the future?

MG: I take risks all the time. I mean doing a movie together with others is taking a risk in itself. You know you are going to be judged severely by everybody. When you do a video, it's good or bad and you're OK. But a movie, you are going to be judged—everybody is a film critic and they will write everything possible.

I mean I don't read everything, but I google me sometimes as I am curious about what people think of what I've done. And sometimes it's mean. Sometimes people want to bring you down—

SL: And as get older and maybe more comfortable in your lifestyle, is their a risk that your willingness to expose yourself and be vulnerable might diminish?

MG: This willingness will be there, because my motivation consists in doing something without being certain of the result. It's like experimentation. And it's funny, because I remember the first film I did with my friend and DP We hurried to cut the negative and then I rushed to see the results in the lab. Bompoint, who is like five years older than me and always acts like an older brother, said to me: "I remember when I was your age. But you will see in five years, you will have lost the drive to run to the lab," But five years later, I haven't lost it at all and I think I will always have that.

SL: Is the willingness to run into open daggers the only way to avoid mediocre results in the long term?

MG: Well, you can find mediocrity in a lot of areas—people running business, or shops—but I guess it's about the same ratio as in the creative world. I don't know, I think some people tell their children: "Well, you can't have all you want, you have to learn to accept that you are not that good." So they put a limitation on them. And I guess I got lucky to have parents who were not like that. My father was a bit like that, but he did that only to himself. He stopped himself to be more creative because he had a complex and he was bitter. Seeing my father like that, I thought: "OK, I will do not do that to myself!"

A lot of people look at individuals that changed the world because they changed life: great physicians, great artists, great painters that were actually genuine. They set their goals up there but in fact, it overwhelms them and they limit themselves. This is especially true for directors—and I think it's basically due to the fact that we shoot so little and have so much time to talk; conferences after conferences. If I just think how many times I have been talking about myself in the last two weeks because I have been doing promotion of my last two films—it's obscene. So I could totally become a preacher.

SL: Does that have an impact on you?

MG: Well, I have to be careful because I start repeating myself and I might become overly confident in what I am saying, which is dangerous. I try to enjoy the process—I try to bring the conversation to a place where I can explore; and sometimes I learn stuff about myself. It's good to listen to other directors and hear what they have to say, but it's only one point of view. I think the *Nouvelle Vague* in France was very preacher-like, and as a director, you have to learn to find you own truth, because otherwise you just become a follower—

SL: Would that also be an advice or value you try to give your own son?

MG: My son, I teach him to finish his projects. Also respect, curiosity, and creativity. I was always happy that he had a different personality from mine—I see it as nature's subjectivity that it can come from me or his mom. He is much more forthcoming than me. A lot of parents, I think, resort to religion as a tool to give their children ethics. But religion gives you ethics by fear and then it doesn't mean anything.

SL: It seems you have very strong ethical points of view. Do you feel that your aesthetic ways of perceiving the world and expressing yourself are strongly linked with your values and your ethical points of view?

MG: I hope they are completely connected. And I hope there is more ethics than aesthetics in the work I am doing. Aesthetics is not something that touches me. And aesthetics has been so much misused by directors copying other directors or photographers who by that have mistreated ethics. *Aesthetics is the first thing I would let go. On the other hand, I think if you follow your ethics, you will also have strong aesthetics.*

It's funny, because I was thinking of ethics lately and how I would define it. And it would be "don't hit somebody who is on the floor," but also "don't copy," or "be yourself."

SL: Interestingly, you say that aesthetics would be the first thing for you to let go of, while as a filmmaker you have experimented with many innovative styles and forms of expression. Is that all part of your ethics in a way?

MG: To me, if you talk about aesthetics, it's the appearance of things. Maybe you could say that any aesthetics is only valuable if it's the response to an ethics. Maybe that's the way it works. But then, think of the very well-designed Nazi uniforms by Hugo Boss: What do you call the ethics in that?

SL: You could argue that it's unethical or cynical exactly because those uniforms seduce the masses to agree on an aesthetic level with the ideology of the people that wear them—

MG: *And on an aesthetic level, the Nazi uniform, as well as the Fascist aesthetics, are very strong—it works very well because it's functional. I know it was Hugo Boss because I just got that suit for free by them [chuckles]*

SL: Not a uniform, though?

MG: No, I'm not a Nazi at all. That's the danger of basing ethics on aesthetics: that's how you become the director Leni Riefenstahl. It's terrible. And a lot of people don't care. They mention D. W. Griffith as being the inventor of cinema, but never mention that his movies were propaganda for the Ku Klux Klan. And I think you can't separate the two.

SL: A lot of directors today come out of film school—do you feel that without your life experience outside of film school you could have achieved similar things?

MG: I guess I can't be objective about that because probably I would feel a little jealous or be dismissive at times, as I did not have the chance to do it. Sometimes I would complain that people criticize directors like me who are coming from video or commercials because—and that's true—we get paid decently. But on the other hand, we only did videos and commercials because we couldn't do movies; we had to really earn a living. And I had a son and I never asked my parents for any money. A lot of directors who go to film school don't have that constraint. That way, it might filter out people that can't afford to go and favor those that had an easier upbringing—but it's a crude simplification of reality.

And there are two sides to it: I guess you learn stuff in school and I actually enjoy going to film school to give conferences—I would have liked to spend more time in school. I like to feel that energy and this idea that you are not here produce a result. I spent like one week at MIT last year and it was great to just talk about ideas; it's really enriching.

SL: How much do you feel your French origin and identity influencing the work you do as a filmmaker?

MG: *I don't have much national identity. I mean when I take the plane and I see all the people with big noses going to Paris, then I realize I am French. And there are little things and basic chauvinisms, but I have been having American girlfriends for a long time now.* Also, I feel my family has always been more about people with the same creative background. I started my band *OuiOui* with my brother, and my aesthetical ethics—to go back to that—are coming from my family, to which I have always had very strong links. And my family, that's also the art school, maybe five to ten friends. In a way, I don't want to disappoint them. I don't want them to look at my work and feel, "Now I have betrayed my roots and goals we kind of set when we were adolescents, because I get paid more money."

My son is now at this age when *he* is setting his goals—when he is talking about deep or artistic philosophy with his friends. The goals I set with friends and family were basically not to use our skills to pretend we are something we are not. And even if I get paid more money, I always have that in mind.

I want them to be proud of me. And it works: They are proud that my name is out there and we were together at school. They are not envious. A lot of times they say, "It's great that you made it, because you represent something we all believed in." And that's the best compliment for me.

You know, I recently bought a countryside house for my auntie in the mountains, and we transformed some of the rooms into an animation lab: and I always have this back-up plan that if everything goes wrong, I will go back there and do my little animation films—and it's gonna be great fun!

# Segal, Peter

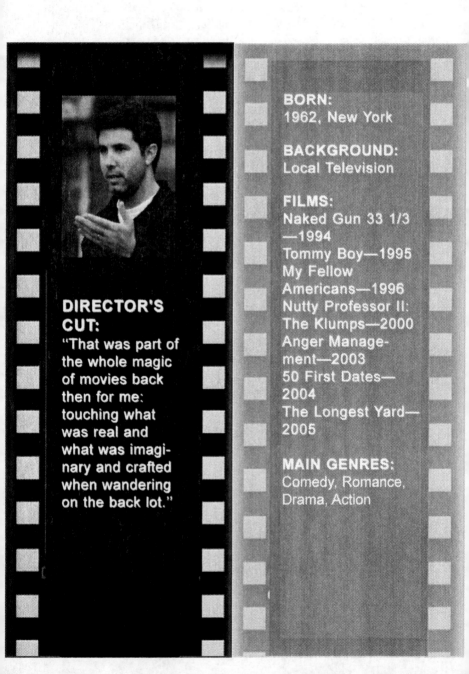

**DIRECTOR'S CUT:**
"That was part of the whole magic of movies back then for me: touching what was real and what was imagi- nary and crafted when wandering on the back lot."

**BORN:**
1962, New York

**BACKGROUND:**
Local Television

**FILMS:**
Naked Gun 33 1/3 —1994
Tommy Boy—1995
My Fellow Americans—1996
Nutty Professor II: The Klumps—2000
Anger Manage- ment—2003
50 First Dates— 2004
The Longest Yard— 2005

**MAIN GENRES:**
Comedy, Romance, Drama, Action

PETER SEGAL: I grew up in Manhattan, then later in the suburbs about 40 minutes outside. My father worked in publicity for some of the studios. Then my father had a company move and we moved to LA. I lived here until 16 when my parents got divorced; I then finished high school in Phoenix.

My introduction to film came by way of my father bringing home some of the movie reels that he was allowed to bring home at the weekends. We projected them on a big bed sheet in the basement. So when I was a kid, I saw everything from *Lawrence of Arabia* to *It's a Mad Mad World* to *Diamonds Are Forever*. I became smitten with the whole world of movie and filmmaking, but never ever dreamed that I would get involved in it.

I had no idea, even later in college. Like many people, I just really enjoyed movies.

SL: So the universe of movies and moviemaking was quite present to you as a child?

PS: Correct. And I guess some of these things subliminally fed my curiosity. For example, I would visit my father on the old MGM lot which is now Sony and my favorite thing to do was to ask permission go out wonder the back lot and to just explore. And at the time, in the early seventies, MGM had a much bigger lot than Universal Studios does now—before they sold it off and it became condominiums. But *I remember walking around the greatest back lot in history and one street would be New York, and you'd turn around and you'd be in Paris and you'd turn the corner and you'd see the famous swimming pool where Esther Williams did her movies. It was just amazing to get lost in this wonderful fantasy world.* I was about eight or nine then.

SL: How did that all fit into your world as an eight year old and how did you make sense of it?

PS: I thought it was so exciting to see the fake sets and to go up and touch them.—I found it so fascinating just to find out what was fake and what was real. I'd knock on the brick walls and by knocking, you could realize that, you know, this is made out of plastic and wood. And that was part of the whole magic of movies back then for me: This really touching what was real and what was imaginary and crafted when wondering on the back lot.

I was then also given an opportunity to visit some of the television sets. Again, just getting lost wasting time during an afternoon after school—like in a fake medical center. . . . I also thought it was fascinating seeing people walking around with make-up on, saying to myself, "Hey, he's an actor; he's in the movies," or, "He's in TV." But then again, I think there's a fascination with people all around the world—people who are construction workers or gardeners have that same fascination with the whole movie industry. And I thought that I was just one of the many that actually wanted to be a part of that.

SL: So you touched these fake objects and they touched you somehow—what did you think you'd want to do one day?

PS: At that point, I thought I might become an architect. And so looking at the sets on the back lot, I can see now how that possibly fed my interest in architecture and design; of buildings and houses. And to this day I feel that if I hadn't become a director, I would have loved to become a production designer—because I do have a taste for the design and the look of a movie. Even my wife quips now, "You're not like most men: most men wouldn't care how I decorate the living room, you actually do."

SL: So you get to be production designer at home?

PS: Yeah, exactly. But I learned to shut up and let her have the last word, of course.

SL: But you realize how your early impressions did shape your ambitions?

PS: Oh yes, and I do remember learning quite a bit from just walking around the set. And I made a little movie when I was eight years old, called 'Lost in Space'. I used grocery bags and made a space suit and went up in our attic—I had this black insulation paper against the two-by-four supporting the roof. I used that as the star field and there was a big train set control board I used as my switchboard. *And the neighbor's roof was made out of white pebbles, which I used as the surface of the moon. So I created some little Super 8mm movie that my father ended up editing together.* And still, I just did it for fun. I had no dreams like Steven Spielberg did when he was growing up in the Arizona desert that that is what I wanted to do.

But I look back now and I realize that all these little pieces that I experienced probably fed me the bits of ingredients that added to me finally figuring out what I wanted to do.

SL: When did the idea of becoming a director strike you for the first time and how did you convince yourself that you were serious about it?

PS: It all happened in one class. I did not go to film school; I was a broadcast journalism, and English double major at USC and I had no idea what I wanted to get into. It was great; the first two years were intensive writing. But in my sophomore year I wondered when we were going to be exposed to the visual aspects of news-gathering. I thought, "When does the broadcast part kick in?"

It was in this one television production class that something clicked in my head and I said, "Wait a minute, wait a minute, *this* is what I wanna do!"

I decided to go get an internship at the local news affiliate KCBS. I was basically clipping articles and working in the publicity department, still not knowing what I wanted to do, thinking maybe television production—I definitely liked the world of production. I got a job as production assistant on a children's special. *My first job was as a fog guy—spreading fog and making sure it's distributes evenly on the set. And one day the director yelled at me because the little kettle that produces the fog squirted out and made an accidental burst of steam. He yelled at me ruining the tape and I was horrified and ran off.*

But I stayed in local television after I graduated. I did some children specials and eventually worked with another producer on some sports specials. I ended up working on this informational program about things to do in Los Angeles over the weekend called "Friday at Sunset." Because no one was watching that program on Friday evening at 7:30, I asked, "Can I liven this up a little bit, rather than doing little five minute informational segments? Can I do a takeoff on something?" So the producer said, "Yes, what would you like to do?" "Well if I'm gonna do the best pizza places in LA, let me do a spin on it." And soon I started parodying famous movies that I had seen growing up and visited the sets of on the back lot. So I ended up doing a takeoff of *Citizen Kane* to find pizza, then a segment on the best pool halls in LA. I also did a take-off on *The Color of Money*. And so on . . .

I won several local Emmy awards for these pieces and I was thrilled and I thought, "OK, this is what I'll do. I'll just stay in local television—I'll be a happy camper. I'm having fun. I'm turning things into comedic segments." And I was content—well it led to an offer to do a special on HBO. The actual HBO executive said, "Are you familiar with Roseanne?" This was in her heyday and I said, "Oh yes, oh my God: working with Roseanne!" And he said, "Well, her husband, Tom Arnold," and I went, "Oh." But *Tom introduced me to a world of little known comic actors like Jim Carrey, Chris Farley, or Ben Stiller. We got them together and they did little cameos in these series of specials that I did for HBO.* Then I won another award which is now extinct: the Cable Ace Award. That got me an introduction with David Zucker, who was the comedy czar of the *Airplane* and *Naked Gun* franchise. He asked me if I wanted to come and interview for the third installment of *Naked Gun*. At that point, I was at the most nervous I've ever been in my entire life because I thought, "I am actually going to interview about directing a movie?!" So I studied the script and I studied every movie that they were parodying; from *White Heat* on. I went in with a few ideas and one thing led to another and I got the job.

The USC newspaper, which I had worked for when at USC, sent a reporter to do a story about: "Young Alum Comes Home." I was invited to homecoming that year and somebody introduced me to the Dean of USC Cinema School, Elisabeth Daily. I just looked down on the article that was written about me—it was on the back of the paper—and the headline said: "Segal Proves Film School Not Required." And I was incredibly embarrassed and quickly covered up the paper with my plate of food, because I didn't want her to see that. I also dreamed that if I had an opportunity, I'd come back as guest lecturer to these cinema students. Since then, I've been loosely associated with the film school, donating some time and money because I think it's a great school. And somehow or other, I've been adopted as alum of the cinema school, but I never actually went there.

SL: When you see a script, please try to describe the significant creative steps you go through from the first read up to the moment when the script is actually ready to be shot.

PS: Well, there is a long process. First and foremost when I take up a script, hopefully I have responded to the one-liner to what it's about. At that point, it's extremely rare that you read a script that you really respond to first-off. And when I do, I get very excited. What I like to do is to completely lose myself just as a fan of movies. I just read it from a total lay-person standpoint. I don't try to analyze it, I don't think of how I would shoot something, or how I would cast it. I just try to read it and see if I can get involved in the story.

SL: And is it easy for you to detach yourself to that degree?

PS: Absolutely; I have to! Then, if I respond well, I like to put it down and walk away from it for a day—and then go back and read it again. Because I found that *sometimes, it could be just something that I ate for lunch and that put me in a great mood and makes me respond so well, but then I took a meeting on that project and said to myself, "What was I thinking, this really isn't as good as I thought."* So I like to give it the 24-hour test and re-read it and see if I still respond the same way.

And if I do, I go through the whole process of taking meetings with studio executives, producers and so forth, to see if my ideas match their ideas of what I can bring to the story and how to tell it. That process seems to take forever and by the time I actually sit down and work on the project, it's already eaten up a lot of time.

Then you start to really analyze it and break it down. It's really not worth doing that work before the job is even yours and I don't like testing fate on that. And often I find that I have to find some fault with the script to be able to tell the executives how I can fix it. I get more nervous with scripts that are really good and that don't need any work. Because then I go in and say, "I really like it, can I do it?" And I feel I'm always at a disadvantage when I do that. I'm always more at an advantage when I can say, "Yeah, there are some problems, but here's what you need, and if you just fix this, it can really be something."

SL: But you only start to fully analyze it once you have got the job?

PS: I don't necessarily break it down into the kind of details that I would break it down into during pre-production. But absolutely, you have to analyze it and really have a great take on it before you go and meet on it. Otherwise you are going to give a half-ass meeting and will not get the job.

SL: Do you write yourself at all?

PS: Yes, I do. For everything that I've directed, I did some writing; on some movies more than on others. But, you know, I would say that at least for half of the movies I've worked on, I've written a considerable amount. I don't often like to take credit because what I do often involved more re-writing than writing, and I like the original writers to take that credit.

SL: What are essential elements—structural and narrative—that your comedy absolutely needs?

PS: Well, there are so many different kinds of comedy. And that's what I like to talk about when people ask, "So why do you find comedy your genre?" The reason is because they are all different and there is always a new way.

For example *Naked Gun,* my first movie, was a joke book: it was all about the joke. My second movie *Tommy Boy* characterizes a "dumb comedy." Then after that, I tried my hands at the political satire with *My Fellow Americans*—then I got more into fantasy and adventure with *The Nutty Professor.* Then I got to do romantic comedy. And they are all like different horses in a stable. Each one has a talent, a skill and a personality. And you need to apply different talents and skill to each kind of movie—they are absolutely not the same! And as long as I can find different kinds of stories to tell within the comedy genre, I'm completely content.

And I'm sure I'll look to direct other dramatic things as well—fantasy and adventure—but right now, it sort of feeds upon itself. If you're successful doing a comedy, you get offered more comedy. And it's easier to get those made. As I said, as long as I can find something I can sink my teeth into, I'm very happy.

So getting back to your question: The elements a comedy must have are always different. If you set out to make a joke book comedy, the number one thing is that it better damn well be funny. If you're telling a romantic comedy, the jokes are important, but not as important as the chemistry between your two leads. If you're telling a political satire, I think you have to make sure that what you're satirizing and what your message is reverent important and well told. It's a very tricky thing with what you're trivializing and turn into jokes in certain political stories. Sometimes you can really offend people with certain subjects—sometimes it's good to shake things up and sometimes you can fall into a trap and make mistakes.

SL: Did you have to make these mistakes initially in order to teach yourself about the subtle differences you just described—or how did you learn?

PS: I learned everything about the joke book comedy form David Zucker. I mean, he is one of the masters of that genre. And a lot of people have tried to do that genre and failed miserably because they think it's very easy, while in fact in think it's the hardest kind of comedies to do. Because once you establish a pattern of telling four jokes per page in a script, it's very hard to deliver that kind of success you need joke by joke in order to have a funny movie in the long run. If you set out a slower paced comedic tone so that the story is more the star, it's like taking a deep breath in a longer race. You're not sprinting anymore, but you're a middle distance runner and you can focus more on the story. Now when I started to get more into that kind of long form storytelling that wasn't about the joke, I just watched movies. *I had no one to teach me; 'cause I didn't study at the cinema school at SC, I just read or watched interviews with other directors and how they went about things. It taught me the things that I could emulate.* I was always envious of directors who were asked to visit the set of a Steven Spielberg movie or were asked to sit down with Warren Beatty for a dinner. I wanted to be one of those young directors except: I was never asked. So I watched "Inside the Actor's Studio" or attended certain guest lectures at USC and listened to directors—that's how I learned.

SL: What are the important character attributes you'd say came to assist you in applying what you had learned?

PS: Patience, perseverance, and psychology. I used to say that directing was 90 percent psychology and 10 percent photography. I've now changed that. I think it's 60 percent casting, 30 percent psychology, and 10 percent photography.

First and foremost, script is God. And then those portraying that script are the ingredients that make your story successfully told. You just need the right people in your story.

Getting the movie made takes a lot of perseverance because from getting a project going to getting all the ingredients in sync is like mounting an army. Everyone who's made a movie knows: once you've made one movie, you're a veteran of movie-making. That doesn't mean that you know everything about making movies, it just mean you're a war veteran in a way. A movie takes over a year to make. So you need a tremendous amount of perseverance to get through it—and stamina. And during that whole process—if you plan on surviving not just physically, but in the business—you have to have a lot of patience. Because actors won't do exactly what you have in mind. The weather won't behave exactly how it's supposed to. Certain shots that you've dreamt up sometimes are almost impossible to actually execute. You have to take a deep breath, rely on your instinct and gut most of all, and then use your patience to make it work.

SL: And during that process, how comfortable are you at delegating responsibilities instead of trying to control it all by yourself?

PS: When I started out, I was gripping the reigns to tightly I realized. I wanted to control every aspect and every frame of the movie had to be just so. But after making a couple of films I realized it's better to delegate and to rely on the artistic talents of the people you hire to do their job—and then to guide them. In other words, before I tell my production designer exactly what I want, I find out what *his* ideas are; before I tell an actor exactly how I want a scene read, I now let them try what *they* were thinking first. And I think that's incredibly important because if you don't, it will make the process stagnate by not allowing very talented people to do what makes them good at their jobs.

So, on my movies now, people are contributing to the overall movie more—and I think it makes a better movie.

SL: And you lost your fear that others might start taking over for you?

PS: Ron Howard said to me when we were working together, "You know, I don't care if a good idea comes from the craft service person: it's all about the movie and whatever it takes to make the movie better." My name is on it as the director at the end of the day, so I will receive the benefits and all the negativity that comes with that title. It's like being a professional athlete: you get paid a lot of money because your career is brief. *And when people ask why people can get paid so much, I often invite them into the figurative cockpit just before a movie is released. Your name is there and you're about to get either praised or bashed by the world.* Everyone is a film critic: Your next door neighbor is one, your dentist is a film critic; the guy who's cleaning up dog poop on the lawn across the street from you is a film critic. And they will tell you exactly what they think of your movie. And if you're an accountant, not everyone is going to look over your shoulder and tell you how improperly you counted John Smith's taxes, or comment on that crown that you just put in someone's mouth as a dentist. You're not going to get two thumbs up or two thumbs down on your book report, but sure enough you can't go anywhere without everyone telling you exactly what they think about the movie you just made. That's one of the tough things about moviemaking, and one of the things that's so intoxicating about it. Everyone knows what you do, that's why you spend so much time doing it: you want it to have a good effect with the masses.

SL: What is your working relationship with the following people: Writer, Producer, Editor, and Director of Photography?

PS: I adore writers. I love to have writers on the set with me, because I think—as opposed to some people—the script never stops being re-written until the final day in post. And so the more the writer is there, the more you can collaborate and make the story better. So I love having the writer around.

The Producer: It depends on what kind. There are so many different definitions and so many kinds of producers . . . I like having my producing partner, Michael Ewing, nearby because unlike a line producer or an executive producer who may have greenlit the picture, he the person I can count on for an opinion—about tone, about story, about what's important. Because the movie making process is so big, we can often forget what's at the heart of it: it is telling a story. And a good producer can be a great mind to bounce ideas off.

An editor is ultimately the person you will spend the most amount of time on a movie with. And like I said, the final re-write is in the editing room. That's where you take everything you have done over the past nine months and sort it out. You can reconnect the dots and you can re-write a scene to have a completely different tone or meaning. It's fascinating. Perhaps that's why my editors are usually my best friends.

SL: How much of a movie can be re-written while editing.

PS: You can't re-write it completely, but you can re-write it enough to significantly change a direction that the story was taking—an intended line or an intended scene: It's fascinating and it's limitless how you can re-shape a story in the edit room. That's why to me it's so challenging.

SL: And your relationship with your DP?

PS: I have been blessed to work with some of the best DPs in the business, in my opinion. It's so fascinating working with and learning from them. I think there is a misconception, though, that the DPs come up with the ideas for the shots. At least for me, that's not true. I come up with my own ideas for what the shots are because I storyboard the entire movie. But I like to bounce those off them and have them add to it and discuss, you know, how for example lighting can affect the mood of a scene. So working with the DP is one of the most creative relationships I have with anyone in the moviemaking process. The look of a movie is incredibly important to me.

SL: The fear of losing control over your movie—have you ever had that fear while working with a DP?

PS: I never felt that way at all because I don't think a DP wants to direct the movie. I think they want to be in control of helping the director visualize what he has in his mind. I felt it's always best to come in with an idea of what I want and I've never known any other way of how to do it. As I've gotten older and wiser, I realized you can stray from that idea as long as you come to the set with a plan so that those 150 people looking at you at least know that you have a direction. Then everyone will relax. I've never wanted to come to the set and clap my hands, take a deep breath and say, "OK, where do we start?" and then have the DP tell me, "Well, maybe what you want to do is start here—" I always wanted to come to the set with a game plan and have them offer suggestions. And that's how I have created some very good relationships.

SL: What's your favorite part of the production—where you feel at your most creative, or freest to express yourself?

PS: Editing—by far. I think is my favorite part of the process—or it has been up till now. *I think the shoot is so grueling that by the time you get into the edit room, editing is like the eye of the hurricane.* I like to vent to the editor about my daily frustrations of each scene we're cutting—what went into that day and how difficult it was. And then, once that's out of the way, I feel like that therapy session is over, and now it's fun to just put together the pieces of the puzzle.

SL: Every director faces the challenge of creating a feeling of emotional authenticity that translates truthfulness into the final scene. How are you familiar with that problem and how did you learn to overcome it?

PS: First of all, the first movie I made wasn't much about a story; it was about telling jokes. But as I got more experienced in comedies that were more story-centered, there's something that hits your gut when you've created a scene that you know works on whatever emotional level you're trying to convey. Whether it's dramatic, romantic, or comedic: the scenes that work best often tap into something that's real. It's either from your own experience or someone else's experience and you can always tell genuineness in that kind of scene. And you can tell when something is fake because it always rings like clanging tin—there's something just off about it and I think any sensitive audience could feel it. *I think audiences are a lot smarter than filmmakers originally think. I think there can be an arrogance among filmmakers that an audience will swallow anything they dish out—and that's not true. They can smell crap very easily, so you better not be serving crap; they'll be able to detect it.* It's great when we screen a movie for the first time to a test audience because then we realize what we've made well and what we've not made well—and you can re-edit a film on that. But there's no greater challenge than to find the truth in a scene—it's a moment that connects with an audience. And if you can achieve the kind of response from an audience that you're going after—whether it's a tear or a laugh or a shock—there's no better adrenalin rush for a director than being able to manipulate a group of 500 people in the theater. It's the closest thing I can think of to performing as an actor.

SL: Let's imagine an inexperienced but confident director starting production. What's your advice of what he should invest all his energies into and which aspects he should rather try to delegate?

PS: Billy Wilder once said, "As a director, you are maybe asked 100 questions a day. So don't spend too much time thinking about any one of those because at least half of the time you'll be right." So at least, answer something. *Buy a pair of new tennis shoes and stay off your feet as much as possible as a director. These are things that seem insignificant, but which aren't.* The road; the journey is long on any movie as a director. And a first time person who gets an opportunity to direct will perhaps grip the reigns too tightly and tire out. What that does unfortunately: It clouds your senses of what the whole movie is about—and that's to tell a story. While wanting to be in control of every detail is very important, you've got to keep your eye on the ball and the big picture—and that is the story. And the more you can relax and breathe and stay rested, the better your brain works and the better you can focus on what's important.

SL: In how far do you feel that there is a danger in Hollywood to get pigeon-holed into a particular genre as a director?

PS: Well, it depends. If you're content in your genre, I don't think anyone would feel pinned. But I've known directors, who've been very interested in breaking out of their genre and were unable to—either a studio was unwilling to give them a chance or they just didn't know how to do it. So I decided to relax about that and let my career take its own course. And as the stories unfold—whether I have a story that I'd like to tell or whether I come across a story that appeals to me—I'm just going to take it one step at a time. I think it would be wrong for me to say that it's time for me to direct a drama, so I'm going to look for a drama. If I found a drama that would appeal to me, then I would do everything I could to try to get that story made. But like I said: It's great when it works, but it's nice to know that people can come back to something that they're good at and where their strength lies.

And that's the advice I would give: if you have a great story to tell, tell it! Don't just want to change genres to prove something. That's where I think people will find it harder and start to make mistakes. In the end, it's all about the story—and it's nice to see good movies, no matter what genre.

# Section Two: Via Film School

# Sommers, Stephen

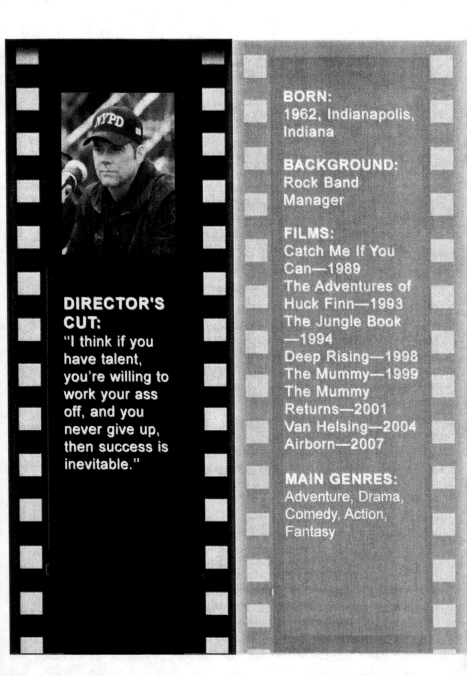

**DIRECTOR'S CUT:**
"I think if you have talent, you're willing to work your ass off, and you never give up, then success is inevitable."

**BORN:**
1962, Indianapolis, Indiana

**BACKGROUND:**
Rock Band Manager

**FILMS:**
Catch Me If You Can—1989
The Adventures of Huck Finn—1993
The Jungle Book —1994
Deep Rising—1998
The Mummy—1999
The Mummy Returns—2001
Van Helsing—2004
Airborn—2007

**MAIN GENRES:**
Adventure, Drama, Comedy, Action, Fantasy

STEPHEN SOMMERS: I grew up in Saint Cloud, Minnesota, a small town in the Midwest. My father was a pediatrician, and my mother was a homemaker. We were five kids. I always loved going to movies, but never thought it was ever possible that I could do it myself. Nobody within a radius 500 miles from there had probably ever directed a movie.

SL: What things fascinated and mesmerized you as a child; made it special to you?

SS: Girls. Beyond that, I'll have to think. I wasn't technical at all. In fact, the first time in my life that I ever picked up a camera was the first day at film school.

*I have always loved history and geography—that's why all of my movies take place in foreign countries.* They are all period pieces. I have shot now in India, Egypt, Jordan, Morocco, Britain, Canada, also Czech Republic. So what happened is that I love movies and love traveling.

Also, one thing I always loved to do was to write—I always had an imagination. That was the main thing. I simply had this vivid imagination but I just never knew what to do with it, except writing. I thought, "Well, coming from Minnesota, I'm never going to be a filmmaker; but writers, they come from everywhere."

SL: You studied in Europe for some time. Why did you go and what impact did it have on you?

SS: The funny thing about me is that when I was 19, I absolutely thought I had to get out. No matter how good it is where you are, I think at that age you just want to leave. And I ended up going to school in Europe. I studied in Spain for one year and a half.

My freshman year I went to the university of St. John's in Minnesota. Then I left for University of Seville. Even through time here on college, I didn't know what I wanted to do with my life. This is how I talked my parents into letting me go over to Europe. A buddy of mine and me, we wanted to get out, we wanted to be exchange students. At that time if anybody ever asked anybody what they wanted to do and you didn't know, you'd say "lawyer." So we both said to our parents, "You know we want to be lawyers, but international lawyers, and so want to have a leg up by learning another language." And that sounded good to both of our parents. So that is how we both ended up going over there.

SL: You ever actually studied seriously over there?

SS: Oh yeah—for a year and a half, we went to the university of Seville. But traveling to a foreign country, your eyes open up. I guess the problem right now with America, and the elections proved that, is that most people don't care about what the rest of the world thinks. Most people in this country haven't even left their own town, leave alone the country. They don't know anything. I don't think most people in this country could tell you that Britain is an island.

So it opened my eyes, and within a week of arriving in Spain, I knew I wasn't going to be a lawyer. It opened up possibilities.

SL: But you were supposed to come back to the states after a while?

SS: We, we weren't sure. We were going to come back after a semester initially, and then we stayed up the whole year. Then we both returned for a year, and then I went back for the first half of my senior year.

And it was during that time, that at one point I ended up going to Paris. I remember it was right before Christmas and I was flat broke. I went to a party and I met all these buskers at a party. I was going to go home the next day, but all these guys just went, "Oh, no, you gotta stick around. We'll show you how you can make money." And they introduced me to the life of busking in the streets of Paris. And that changed my life.

I guess the first time I discovered I like theater was during my senior year in high school. I got talked into auditioning for a play. And I had no interest in acting, but I got talked into it by all these girls. And really I did it because of the girls. And it turned out to be the most fun thing I had ever done.

I just thought, "Oh, this is fantastic. Working with actors in theater, I just love it." And of course, during my first day at St. John's I went to the theater department. I walked around and basically it was filled with all these master-thespians, who are wildly arrogant for themselves and thought that they knew something. I never went back.

But then when I went to Europe, I met all these actors who were trying to make a living at it. And they knew what life was really about. Instead of trying to be master-thespians, they were trying to make a living at being good actors. And that's really where I got to play with actors.

SL: So you thought you might become a writer?

SS: So when I started working in these street theater groups, I started working with actors and I really enjoyed it. *When I finally got to USC film school, I found that 95 percent of the people who arrived wanted to be directors. Within a year, it drops down to about 5 percent.* Mainly what happens is that everybody thinks that directing is what they want to do—they think that that's all there *is* to do. But there, they suddenly realize, "Oh no wait, I'd be a much better editor, or a soundman, or they like the music aspects, or the lighting, or cinematography or whatever." The vast majority realizes, "I don't like actors," or, "I don't want to talk to actors, I can't deal with them." I like working actors and dealing with. You just have to know where they are coming from.

SL: You also got to act yourself in Europe?

SS: Well [*laughing*], not really. It was mainly directing and writing. And I managed three different rock bands; in Paris, London, and Dublin. The way I got into it was that I knew all these people over in Europe and I knew I could make a living. The day I graduated from college, I flew to Europe with a one-way ticket and three hundred dollars in my pocket and stayed there for a couple of years, working there in street theater groups.

It also depended on the season. Like one day, these British guys in Paris, they came up to me and said, "You're American, you must know about money, you want to manage us?" And so I'm like, "Oh yeah, sure." And the next week, I flew to Dublin not knowing anybody, and I just went around in a Taxi from club to club, booking these guys. That's how I started. I booked the bands and managed as well—then I went to London for a bit. You know, it was a good couple of years of great experience of working with actors and musicians—

SL: and waking up to life—

SS: Yeah exactly: learning about life and all the possibilities.

SL: So how did you find your way into film eventually?

SS: Well, at one point—I guess I was 24 or 25—it suddenly hit me one day. I thought, "Oh my god, what am I going to do with my life? I mean I am having a good time, but I'm always flat broke and I can't just manage street theater groups and Rock'n'Roll bands. I have got to do something with my life." *So I thought of the two things I enjoyed doing, "I like to write, and I like to work with actors." It was literally, "Should I head to New York and Broadway, or California and Hollywood."* But then it was easy, "I know I've always loved movies; that's where my heart is. I'm gonna go to Hollywood."

When I was at St. John's I actually took one credit of film classes—you know, Italian film, Spanish film—and my teacher had mentioned a university that actually taught how to make movies. I contacted him, "Oh yeah, University of Southern California." That's how I got the application.

The thing about USC is that half of the people they take in are techno buffs—they've been making movies since you know they came out of the womb. And they know every thing about camera and stuff. And for the other half, they want to find people with eclectic, creative backgrounds. At hindsight, I laugh and go, "How did I ever get into USC?" But it's clear: I had to write this essay, and I had this strange background of going to university in Europe and spending all that time over there working with actors, street theater groups and bands. That's why I got in.

In your first semester, you did 8mm films. I remember borrowing my dad's pocket 8mm camera, because they said you have to show up with one. And at my first day in class, I looked around and all the guys had these things what looked like bazookas. Of course they were cameras with had every possible invention on them. And I had this little pocket 8mm that instead of f-stops had a picture of a sun and clouds.

And I thought, "I'm never gonna make it through this—all these guys have these fantastic cameras." But then, you have to make a movie every other week—like a 5-to-7 minute short film. It's funny, but what happens is that you can learn the techniques and technologies pretty quickly. But it's very hard to teach people how to be creative—and some people could never figure out narrative. And so really quickly, I figured out how to work a camera and how to play with the lighting a bit, but a lot of guys that were really good at the camera had no idea how to tell a story.

So the first month at film school I thought they were going to throw me out; but then after that, I was pretty confident. I think a lot of the extremely confident guys from the first month never made it through the first year.

SL: So where did your ability to tell stories come from—is it something you learned while traveling?

SS: Maybe innate [*laughing*]. I really don't know and have no idea where it comes from—it somehow channeled through me somehow.

I took a couple of screenwriting classes, and they were really good. They don't try to teach you to be creative, they just teach you where to put the slug lines.

Actually the best thing was: I arrived a semester early, and I took a playwriting class with a wonderful teacher, Herb Shoar, at the USC drama school. He was the best!

I always liked to write, but nobody ever kicked my butt. Herb said, "By next Friday, you are going to have ten pages written; by the end of this month, you're going to have the first act written." He really forced me to write and he has given me the best advice anybody has ever given me as a writer, *"You have to approach writing like its ditch-digging. Monday through Friday, or on weekends if you can, you have to do it every single day. If you wait to be creative, you'll never finish anything."* And he is so right: I sit here all week, from basically 9:30 or 10 in the morning to about 6 or 7 at night. Sometimes I'm creative in the morning, sometimes I'm creative in the afternoon; sometimes I'm creative for an hour a day, sometimes it's for seven minutes a day. But you have to sit and keep writing, and looking, and starring, and pacing. A lot of times, I'm not getting anything done. I'm writing a line here, go back, and re-writing a scene there, and suddenly at six o'clock, right when I am about to head out the door, I get this idea and 'Boom', I write like five pages in 20 minutes.

SL: So for you, good writing is about patience—

SS: Oh yeah, you can't be taught creativity. Either you are or you're not. Bill Goldman, a friend of mine, says in his book, "Sometimes your best screenplay is your first." Thankfully for myself, I'm constantly learning. I was always creative, but I wasn't always good. Every script of mine, I get more experienced and more knowledge. And I guess I am getting more creative, in the sense that my creative muscle gets stronger and stronger. So that is a good thing. You can improve and you can train yourself to be better. But unless you've got the creative juices going on, I think it's pretty hard.

So when I got to USC, I just wrote; then directed all that stuff. It's funny because everybody went in thinking they want to be a director. I was the opposite in just wanting to learn something technical so that when I get out, I could earn a living in it and pay off some of my bills. But somehow three years later, all I could do was write *and* direct.

In your final year, they used to do this thing called "Four/Eighties"—everybody from Sam Peckinpah, Robert Zemeckis, George Lukas, John Turtletaub, or Jay Roach—a lot of the directors who came out of USC over the last 50 years did that: Every year, over one hundred 20 minute scripts are turned in, of which they pick five. And then all of the final year students who are eligible will read the scripts and pick the ones they want to direct. There will be five to ten directors attached to each script. Then you'll go in front of a panel of professors and they grill you like rabbit dogs. One person gets picked to direct each film. And that year, I wrote a script and it got picked to be one of the five out of 120. They usually don't like writer/directors, but somehow I won the gig.

In fact I know exactly how I won it: they attacked me really viciously—when I left, I was sure I didn't get it. You know there was one specific point in my script that was unexplained, which in my opinion was supposed to always remain unexplained. It was just this one little blank and I thought people should fill that on their own. But they hammered me, and came up with all kinds of things how one could fill that blank, "Oh, what if that fairy-godmother showed up", or "What if he flips the coin into a wishing well and he wishes this blank to be filled in?" I just said, "Look, I don't know if you're right or you're wrong, but let me think about it. I am not going to make a decision right here while you're grilling me." That's why I got the gig. I asked one of the professors and he said, "We do that to most of the students. Most of them will quickly buckle and say: 'Ok, I'll do this.' And they'll sit there and grab on to one of our many lame ideas that we are throwing out, simply because they want to please us."

But that's the recipe for failure. When you're on a movie set as a director, every day problems come up that haven't been figured out in the script yet—every day! Then, everybody's got an idea of how to fix it. *As director, you have to sit back, listen to everybody, and then say, "OK, everybody shut up and go away. I have to think about it."* You have to be decisive and figure it out quickly, but if you just latch on to something and say, "Oh, OK, I'll go with that", inevitably you are going to get run over. You can't just willy-nilly grab people's ideas because they are throwing ideas at you all the time—some are great and some are bad. Making feature films is very collaborative, but at the same time, the director has to have the ultimate vision. All the best films have one clear vision. A film can't be a series of 15 different people's personal opinions. That doesn't mean there are not a lot of actors and crew people that have a lot of great ideas that will help you along the way—

SL: Did your graduation short directly lead towards your first feature?

SS: When I was finishing film school, I ended up writing and directing this student film—it won some awards and did pretty well. It screened around town and at the academy for about 1200 industry people. Back then, these Four/ Eighty things were really the thing. Strangely enough, after forty years of being this really big event deal, my semester in 1988 was kind of the last hurrah for this thing.

The morning after the screening I had my cast and crew and family over for breakfast. I couldn't even sit down because I got 38 phone calls from everybody in town. *My parents were all excited, "You're actually going to get a job working in Hollywood!"*

So I went around the next couple of months to these meetings and at the end of it, all anybody wanted was, "Do you have a script?" When you direct a 20 minute student film, there's so many people above you that have directed feature films. At the end of the day, all they cared about was "Do I have a script" that either I had written, that a friend had written, or a script that anybody had written, and that I could be attached to.

So I went home for Christmas and my parents asked, "Who are you working for?" and I said, "Nobody."

Then I went back, and I remember sitting around, trying to write some stuff. I got this call from this low budget company that I almost didn't go to. It was like a two o'clock meeting, right after lunch and I had never heard of these people. They told me, "You know we're a management and production company, and we're trying to make low budget films." This time I had leaned from my past experiences and I told them, "Oh, I am writing a script *right now* as a matter of fact." They asked me what it was about: For once I shut my mouth, "You know, I don't want to tell you right now, but I'll be done in about five or six weeks, and then I'll give it to you." Now they got excited and I had to ask them, "What are you guys looking for?" "Well, right now we're looking for a teen-action-romance comedy," and I said, "You know, that's what I am writing." And of course, I wasn't—I was writing some space opera.

*I remember pacing around this coffee shop, "Think Stephen! It's gotta be teen-action-romance comedy." And in matter of like half an hour, I came up with this idea.* I went home, wrote it in about 6 weeks, brought it back to them and they said, "Hey, we love your script, come on in." On the way, I remember reading this article about the making of *Risky Business* that got made for seven million dollars. I knew they're going to ask me about budget. So I thought, "My script is bigger than *Risky Business*—it's got a football game, a pep-rally, it's got a lot of these car races in it." So I told them, "You know I think I can do this movie for about seven million dollars." And they looked at each other and said, "Well, we've got 800,000." So I took a beat and said, "I can do it for that." And they all laughed at me and said, "OK."

The only way we could do it was to go back to my home town, Saint Cloud, Minnesota, with a bunch of friends. The mayor shut down streets, the principal of the high school shut down his school for the pep really. Half the town showed up for our staged football game. That's how I made my first low budget film—they paid me 5,000 dollars for the script, and 25,000 dollars to direct it. And that's how I started.

SL: You and Bob Ducsay your editor have been working together since then. How important are such long-term relationships for you?

SS: On the set, your allies are usually your 1st AD, your line producer and hopefully the cinematographer. But all the way through pre-production, production and post, the editor is your guy. He's the one to watch your ass and help you out. Because I have such a good relationship with my editor, we're making and editing that movie together. Although I have to say I hate Bob during all of production. He is constantly making me go back, saying, "Grab this or that shot." He's got a list of things that he thinks I missed.

But then when we finished the principal photography, we never shot a single frame after that. Both *Mummy* movies are very big and complicated movies. I directed six movies, without doing any pick-ups, re-shoots, inserts, nothing. In fact, *Van Helsing* broke my record. We needed four small shots and one line of dialogue. That took about two thirds of a day.

*You hear about those movies that have to do one, two, or seven weeks of re-shoots—and that's just incompetence and laziness on the part of the director and/or editor.* A lot of times you can't help it. Sometimes when an audience doesn't understand, you go: "How can they not understand, it's so clear." But sometimes they just don't, or they want more or something different.

A lot of times, it's also the studio's fault. When the director, crew and AD say they need 80 days, the studio might shout at them, saying, "You got 60!" And that's when they come back after 65 days without having finished the movie. Then re-shoot costs twice as much. Suddenly you're flying people in from all over and you're rebuilding stuff that you already had.

SL: Did you get to know Bob for your first project, or were you already friends before that?

SS: I knew him in film school, but we didn't hang out or anything like that—we were never on any crews together. I had edited the 45 minute film of a friend of mine and I figured he would probably be able edit my 90 minute film *Catch Me If You Can*. My second editor, Kelly Matsumoto, was Bob's assistant at first. She had actually never cut two pieces of film together back then. Now Bob and she are a team.

SL: I would like to learn more about your working style. How do you approach the general look and atmosphere of your movies?

SS: So far, I have written everything I directed. As I am writing, I visualize. I never really visualize the actors, though, because I don't like to put faces on them. You never know whether you will get an actor, if they want to do it, or whether you can afford them. As I am writing draft after draft, my writing style is incredibly visual. You can see exactly how it's going to be. Then obviously, I hope my cinematographer and production designer will take it to the next level, but they have a pretty good idea what they are looking for when looking at the script. We frequently turn to movies where I tend to think that this is what I would like my movies to look like.

But each movie is different and depends on the color pad—on *Huck Finn*, I wanted it to be very gold and very blue and I had many discussions with my production designer Janusz Kaminski.

On *Van Helsing*, I had Allan Cameron and Allen Daviau and we sat down and watched all the old horror classics together. One thing we all love about those is the production design and atmosphere. They are incredibly smoky and dusty and dark and they have this fantastic feel to them. I've always been in love with German expressionist filmmaking; you know *The Cabinet of Doctor Caligary*.

I very much tend to work with the same people and there's a lot of people I have been with forever. My second unit director has been with me since film school, where he was my camera operator. Also my script supervisor has been with me since my first film.

SL: So you start out by trying to figure out the general tone and atmosphere as a team—

SS: Yeah, and I try to precisely describe things, depending on where I am in the movie. Just looking at *Huckleberry Finn*, the *Mummy* and *Van Helsing*, they are all very different. *I tend to do a lot of research. For the* Mummy, *I was reading every book on Egypt; watched every documentary.* That gives me all kinds of ideas and visuals. I have those three by five cards where I write little sentences like, "In this documentary I loved this shot, in this documentary I loved the way this tomb was shot in the twilight." And I would go to the Rembrandt Museum in Amsterdam—those things inspire me tremendously; it's a lot of looking at art, going, "Oh, it's gotta be those black mummies."

SL: What about your approach to music?

SS: It's funny, cause most directors in Hollywood would consider music their weakness. We don't know anything about composing music. But basically you know what you like and you know what you think the movie needs. And Bob is very instrumental and together with Kelly, they would always edit it to music. It just helps dramatically. And while you might not use the same music, you get an idea of different things by playing around. Sometimes I'd think, "Oh, this scene should just have a pounding beat." And then you realize, "Oh no, it works much better if it's really soft and quiet." So you play with it a lot.

Mainly I go through this kind of vamp with my composer Alan Silvestri. He watches the movie by himself to get a feel of it, then we watch it together to spot it. Deciding where the music should start, and where it should end—it's just really a very collaborative process. I just throw out ideas and feelings,

"Alan, I was thinking about this, or this." And then he'll do his first or second draft and call me up. Then I'd go, "Oh, I love this," or "I think this is a little weird Alan." So it's just discussing and, you know, "being creative."

SL: On the *Mummies* and *Van Helsing*, you have made vast use of special effects. How do you go about working with those?

SS: Special effects, I just write them. They are in the script. And if it's written but we don't do them, people go, "Oh, but the big special effects were there—"
*But the effects that really work and make the money are the ones where people really like the story and the character*—for me, it's always about that.

Now people like *The Mummy*, but when we were making it, we were like, "People have been making fun of mummies for 50 years, are they even going to want to see this movie?" At the end of the day, somehow people loved the script, and loved the characters, and thought the story was really interesting.

So my point is: special effects have to help telling the story. If you start the movie in order to have special effects sequences in it, the audience gets bored— they want to know what's going to happen with the characters. For me it's all in the script: I try to describe it as clearly as possible.

On *Van Helsing*, I probably spend at least a thousand hours working on the coach sequence alone. Without cutting, every shot had Hugh Jackman in it. But suddenly, it turns into a stuntman—and then it turns into a computer generated Hugh Jackman. You know, every department needs to know what they will need to do for that shot.

Then with ILM, I spend hundreds of hours in all three production stages again. Because one a lot of the special effects you do, it's a frame by frame deal. Especially with all these creatures, *I literally have conversations where I go, "OK, the werewolf starts to raise his arm on frame 32 and the arm should start to swipe on frame 112."*

The guys and gals from ILM are incredibly creative and visual, but sometimes they can't see what's in the frame, so I have to guide them through. Bob will show me a cut sequence and tell me, "Oh, you can't believe how great this is, this is fantastic." So I'll sit down with him and go, "What is this shit?" Here's what it is: we push in on a wall, then pull back on a couple of pillars, then the camera dollies around over a bridge, then dolly into a blue screen: It's just these empty plates. Even though I shot it with story board, I have all the effects drawn in. So I am thinking about them when I shoot it.

When it's edited, it's never exactly the same. A lot of times, it's really like doing an animated movie more than anything else. I'll spend two to three hours a day, five to six days a week for 12 months of post-production.

SL: Is there any part of the production process where you feel at your most creative or that you simply enjoy most?

SS: It's always different. Right now, I am writing on a movie called *Flash Gordon* and I love the writing of it—it's so much fun! It's just me in my room. There is no pressure, no hundreds of crew people, and no tens of millions of dollars.

I mean, pre-production is kind of nerve-wracking, because you try to get it all together; so that's probably my least favorite. Then production—*you know there are only a couple of directors who like production. Most directors hate the shooting process of a movie. And you go, "Wait a minute, isn't that the filmmaking?"* But the pressure is on, and the money is being spent. And if you're a good director and you care it's pre-dawn till post-dusk. You have to go go go, have to be decisive, and have to be completely prepared. You know, there are hundreds of people whom you're directing and giving answers to: you just have to be on the ball. I mean there are odd directors who just float through it but for me, it is really an intense five or six months. But at the same time, the juices are flowing and it is really exciting. So production is like a love-hate relationship.

Then I used to just love post-production. Post is just a love-fest, it's so nice. It's just me sitting in a room with a couple of editors. Now, it's not that I love it less, but it's just that it is harder because of all the special effects. That adds a whole new element—it's there where ILM and all the special effects people go into production. And then it's like making a whole new movie again.

So, I like it all, and I hate it all.

SL: What are you looking for in a story in your stories to really grab you?

SS: Only two things: great characters and great story. It's like when I was writing *Van Helsing*: I didn't want to write it about a guy who takes on the three most famous monsters in film history. I thought people would kill me for that and it wasn't until I saw that poster of *Dracula and his Brides* one day and realized, "What would a guy do with three gorgeous women for 400 years? He'd have babies." But then I thought, "Wait a minute, they'd be born dead. Everybody would be like: we need to bring our children to life." But that's what Dr. Frankenstein thought of—he's the key to life: he's trying to invent life. "So Dracula would need Frankenstein," and so on. So I used all the mythology and created my own mythology. And that's how the story emerged. Suddenly I thought, "Now, this is a story." I started off with three of the greatest characters in film history; then I created and embellished a bunch as well.

SL: What about some important attributes that you feel are most important for you as a director to make these stories come to life?

SS: I think most important are two things: I am always very prepared—completely prepared—and very decisive.

I have that theory: *I think when a director arrives on a new set with a cast and crew that don't know him, they all expect to hate him because so many directors are nut balls, indecisive and underprepared.* But if you can show up and you're prepared and decisive, you'll win over every cast and crew.

Also, you have to know how to be collaborative without letting the whole thing go off the rail. I've written the scripts and I will storyboard and shot-list every single scene. I have a good idea of how I think each line should be delivered. But then when we get on the set, I always tell my actors in my sort of speech before we start shooting, "The first couple of takes, it's all yours, because I want you to surprise me. I am not going to give you any direction, unless you really ask me to." Actors just love that. It tells them that you trust them and they are free to play around. They quickly figure out that we're working together. You know I think the best performance come when actors feel like they can embarrass themselves and you're free to make an ass of yourself. Because if they feel that way, they can sit there and go: "You know what, I'm gonna burst into tears in this line. Maybe it's inappropriate, but I'll risk it." Sometimes it doesn't work, but boy if it works, that's what makes great performances: When they give you a performance that no one is expecting. So after a couple of shots, it may be perfect and then we'll move on. But I may want try a couple of takes of my version. I may think that an actor should maybe yell a particular line. And then they may whisper it and it may be twice as good.

SL: A young director faces the alternative of either going to film school or investing that time and money into a first feature film—what would you recommend?

SS: I don't think there is any correct answer. I think film schools can be great. They are invaluable because they teach you the nuts and bolts. You get to spend three years with a bunch of other guys and girls who love exactly what you love doing. All you want to do is talk movies all day long. And so it's really fun and educational. It's not like going to college. When I was going to St. John's College, I had no interest really in studying. And I didn't know what I wanted to do.

Of course, if you can afford it, just do your own film. Also, if you can get a job working on a film crew, hey, you get a lot of experience there. I wouldn't be surprised if 90 percent of the people of USC graduate film school never worked in the entertainment industry. People think, "Oh, you go to USC film school, you will get a job." No! Ten percent get a job, one percent maybe get a job directing.

SL: But when you think about what film school actually costs, that's already a small feature budget.

SS: Yeah, but at the same time it's not just a matter of the money. Do you know *how* to make a movie? See at film school, you start of learning how to make a five minute movie, with no sync sound. You learn every crew position. It's not just about directing. Not that you want to be a cinematographer or an editor, but you learn to understand how to do everybody's job, so you can communicate properly as you go through life. You will be able to communicate with all the different crew people in their own language and in their own terms.

And also, during those three years, you are meeting a lot of other people who help you along the way and who you can help—so you're networking. It's not just spending the money. If you took that money and made a film: what if that film didn't work? It's over, you're done. You spent the money, you're shot; you'll be selling real estate in Utah. So you got three years to slowly learn a craft.

SL: So let's say somebody is working on their first feature with an obviously limited budget—800,000 dollars like yours. What aspects would you recommend to go ahead and spend money on, what aspects should you have rather neglected to save time and energy?

SS: You're right; it really depends on how much money there is. When I was in film school, every movie was different. As a first time director, simply focus all your time on getting great performances with the best actors you can get and telling a clean, clear story.

I think so many newcomer directors are getting blown out of the water. Studio producers tend to go off and grab these guys who have just done a couple of television commercials or rock videos, giving them a 100 million dollar feature. And they're dying, because it's like going from kindergarten to graduate school; you can't make that leap. And it's not just a matter of being creative. You can be the most creative guy in the world, you know there is a difference from playing on the PV football league to going to the NFL.

*Go watch* Something about Mary: *the ugliest-looking movie I have ever seen. And nobody cared; including me. I just noticed it, because I thought, "Even the sequence in Miami with these white ugly skies couldn't get a break."*

Because at the end of the day—it doesn't matter if you have the most fantastic score or beautiful cinematography: if the characters are uninteresting and the story is boring, nobody cares. People don't care if it looks like crap. All movies that really work have great character and story. People might go the first night, because they like the trailer or they hear that the special effects are good, but then it will drop off if no one likes it.

But if you're first time director trying to get out there, just do something small that won't overwhelm you. If you have no money, and you have no equipment, don't do a story that got action and special effects in it. Forget it!

And even a bad crew can't kill you. What you will have to concentrate on is: *you* have to be good, and you have to get performances out of actors that probably aren't the most experienced actors.

SL: How important is it to be able to sell yourself?

SS: I know a lot of directors nowadays, especially at my age, who have publicists and whatever. I don't do any of that, I have no interest. I don't have time, I'm busy writing. I think if you're a director that doesn't write, you have to get out there. You have to go to parties and dinners, but I am no expert for that.

I am going for my story and if I pitch something, I really have it figured it out tight. I pitch it or I write a speck script. And so far I've been 10 for 12: I've written 12 scripts and 10 have been made.

SL: Is it a coincidence or does it rather feel like a logical outcome of your past experience that you have become a film maker?

SS: Yeah, I think it was a logical outcome. I had no other choice. *My wife will tell you, "Thank god this whole directing/writing thing worked out because you really don't have anything else."* And that's the whole thing.

The worst six months of my life was right before I got into film school and I was working in a credit department. I had no car, I was living in a bad area in china town, working in a terrible credit department with no window and a cubicle, being yelled at by housewives all day long about their credit. I thought my life is over; this is the worst thing.

And in hindsight, these months so motivated me for the next three years. I worked my ass off and I didn't mind working 15, 16 hours a day, seven days a week for the next three years at film school, because I was passionate every hour I was doing it.

Also Europe: most of it was fantastic—such fun and educational and life-altering. But then there was a lot of times where I was flat broke, where I was really hungry, where I didn't know what I was doing with my life; But all kind of lead somewhere—even bad things. *I would tell people: it's good to flounder sometimes, 'cause floundering makes you think more and makes you try to figure things out.* If everything is going so smoothly, going from high school to college to grad school, then family perhaps, it's not so ideal. I think a lot of people coming out of USC graduate school still don't know what the hell to do with their lives. They'd never gone anywhere or done anything except movies. The best directors have life experiences, I think.

SL: What is the downside of being a director?

SS: Unfortunately, you can never give up. People always say: "Well I'm gonna go to Hollywood and give it three years." But that simply doesn't work! It's the people that give it three years and then they get to the end of those three years and say, "OK, I'm going to give it another three years." And it's just a matter of gutting it out. I think if you have talent, you're willing to work your ass off, and you never give up, then success is inevitable.

# Ratner, Brett

**DIRECTOR'S CUT:**
"'Dean, my whole life I dreamed of being a director. If you don't let me in, I'm going to be living on my mom's couch for the rest of my life.'"

**BORN:**
1969, Miami Beach, Florida

**BACKGROUND:**
Rock Band Manager

**FILMS:**
Money Talks—1997
Rush Hour—1998
The Family Man—2000
Rush Hour 2—2001
Red Dragon—2002
After the Sunset—2004
X-Men: The Last Stand—2006
Rush Hour 3—2007

**MAIN GENRES:**
Action, Comedy, Thriller, Fantasy

BRETT RATNER: I grew up in Miami Beach in one house with my mom, her brother, my grandparents, and my great-grandmother. So we were a very close family. Where some kids are shy and don't talk to strangers, I was a very curious and inquisitive kid. I would always ask questions: "How did you do this, how did you do that?" If I took a plane ride with my mom, I would walk up and down the aisle and ask people where they were from or what they did; then I remember asking my grandparents to tell me stories.

*I had no discipline whatsoever, but a tremendous amount of love and support from my mother. I never had to go to school if I didn't want to. My mom even preferred me to stay at home and hang out with her.* At some point, I remember, I wanted to travel around Europe with my friends and my mom let me miss three months of school because she said: "You are going to learn more from traveling than you are from going to school. Just make sure that when you are in Paris to go to the Louvre; in Milan go to La Scala . . ."

At school, I was very badly behaved—according to the teachers, I had ADD. And I wasn't paying attention in class and I didn't get good grades. It's when I wasn't interested and it was just textbook kind of stuff, like mathematics, without a beginning, middle and an end to it. My mother would go see the teachers and defend me and tell them, "Why don't you teach him in a more interesting way, maybe he'll pay attention then and be more disciplined." So she always blamed them, you know?

SL: Do you agree with her?

BR: I was bored. That's why I couldn't pay attention and maybe my ADD would kick in. I mean they told my mom, "You should medicate him" and my mom was like, "I'm never gonna medicate him!" But when I loved the subject, I focused and did very well—was fantastic at it.

SL: You say you were a very curious kid—

BR: Just in general. I was interested in people and remember that I was always asking questions . . . *I mean by the time I got to high school, I had convinced my teacher that I shouldn't do my homework or take any tests.* Or if it was my US-history class, I would instead make a film with the kids acting as Abraham Lincoln or whatever—with some teachers I got away with it. It wasn't really about grades to me—I just never cared about those because I had no pressure. My mom was like: "The kids who are unhappy are the ones who have to perform." My mom never said you got to get straight As or you'll get in trouble. She said: "If you want to be an idiot and not do your homework, then it's your problem."

I just loved making my little movies. I had gotten a Super 8 camera as a gift from a friend when I was eight and kind of taught myself how to work it.

When my mom turned 20 or something—she had me at a very young age—we ended up moving out of the house. We got an apartment in a building with predominantly old residents—you know mostly retirees living in Miami

Beach. But I lived in this building, so the building was like my set, and all the people living in it were my actors [*laughing*].

SL: What was cool about making films?

BR: I think it was the storytelling thing. I loved telling stories and I was fascinated by movies from a very young age. My grandfather would take me to this movie theater. A lot of the movies that I saw I think influenced the movies that I ended up doing—especially my first two. You know my grandfather was a foreigner and I took him mostly to see action movies, because you don't really have to understand much to enjoy them—*Beverly Hills Cop* and *48 Hours* and *Midnight Run*. So that's why I ended up making a movie like *Rush Hour*.

But I think very early on, I really understood what it meant to be a director. The first movie set I was ever on was *Scarface* with Al Pacino. I literally ended up skipping school every day and hanging out on the set. My mom would pick me up there and drop me off because she didn't really care.

I actually am an extra in *Scarface* 'cause *I hung around so much at the set that De Palma said: "Hey kid, get in the shot!"—so that's my claim to fame.* And I finally met Al Pacino some time ago and said: "You know, you are the reason I became a director." He is like: "Why is that?" I said: "Because I was watching you act and you were so amazing and I thought: 'Oh, I could never do that, I could never be as good as him.' But then I saw De Palma directing you and thought, 'I don't want to be him, I want to be the guy telling him what to do.'"

'Cause I'd make myself invisible and I would literally—literally—stand right next to them when they had these conversations. It's then that I understood what the director did: he was really controlling the set. I mean I saw him collaborating with the DP, telling him how to move the camera, or telling the actors what to do . . .

I remember later, I was driving with my mom and I saw them shooting something on the side of the road: "Pull over, pull over!" I said, and it was the set of "Miami Vice." I would go regularly and watch Michael Mann and Abel Ferrara and a lot of other directors. I just remember watching. And then, when it really clicked for me, was when I ended up seeing the movie. I was *there* and I watched it happen and then I got to see the end result on TV. I mean, when you are a kid and you watch something, you don't always understand how it's done. And I even remember in film school: a director would come and speak. Until they came, I would watch their films and go: "Oh my God, how the fuck did they do that?" So I prepared to ask my questions to them and they would offer their often very simple answers, like: "Oh, this happened by accident." *It all seemed like brain surgery to me when I was a kid. I was like "Jesus, how am I ever going to get to do that?"* Even now I have to pinch myself because I am making this huge movie *X-Men,* which is loads of visual effects.

SL: How old were you on the set of *Scarface*?

BR: That was '82, so I was 13. I said: "This is what I want to do," and that's all I thought about every day of my life. I understood what these directors were doing and maybe I started to mimic them. I see people I haven't seen in 20 years now and they go: "When you were a little boy, you told me you wanted to be a director."

But I remember even earlier, in 1980, I saw *Raging Bull* and I fell in love with it: I became obsessed with it. I watched it over and over and over again.

I mean imagine, I was 11! And most 11-year-olds weren't even allowed to see it: it was an R-rated movie. But my house was the house that kids could come over to and watch a movie.

SL: What made you obsess about *Raging Bull*?

BR: I don't know the specifics—the photography, the execution of it, the performances. Come on, it's like the perfect movie! But I had enough taste at that age to know: "Wow, this is something good." I mean now I can intellectualize it and try to tell you everything that's great about the movie. But the truth is, at 11, I don't know why I thought it was good, but I thank God that I did.

My inquisitiveness was like: "Who made this movie?" Someone told me: "Well, it's Martin Scorsese." "Well, how did he become a director?" And they told me he went to NYU film school. I said: "I'm gonna go to NYU film school" So from the time I was 11, I was like imgonnagoimgonnagoimgonnagoimgonnago! But that was like *seven years* away! When you are 11 years old, seven years is a fucking lifetime [*laughing*].

I realized, I got to figure out a way how to get there quicker. So I told my mom—I don't know if I was acting or pretending: "Ma, I'm really not happy with my class. These kids are too stupid for me and I'm not learning anything. I want to get out!" So she went to the principal of the school and complained and got me to skip two grades! And that's how I ended up being the shortest kid in my high school.

So instead of seven long years, film school was five long years away. I ended up graduating at 16. In my last year, I went to my school councilor who said: "Well, your grades are not that good," but I was adamant and said: "But I *got* to go to NYU."

I scheduled an interview at NYU and thanked God that I got a woman: I thought I could be really charming and she'd let me in. So I put my little suit on, took my briefcase full of my best little films with me and also my little projector to show them. *The lady at NYU asked me a bunch of questions and then after looking over my application she said: "How dare you apply to this school?" and I said: WHAT?" This lady was so rude!* They are not even supposed to tell you this, but she said: "You know, you have probably the worst grades of any student that has ever applied to this school. What makes you think that you can get—" I said: "No: but here are my films, let me show you—" And she went: "No, we don't look at your films."

You see, back then, film schools weren't really connected to Hollywood. Nowadays of course—you know, I'm on the board of NYU now—you have to have a short film, a short story, some poetry, a video. Now they look for that stuff. Back then, it was your application, your SAT score and maybe an essay.

So basically that lady said: "You know what? Go to day community college for two years, get straight As and then maybe we'll consider letting you in." I said: "You don't understand" she goes: "No, *you* don't understand: you are not getting in here!"

I remember walking down the street and I was devastated. I was in tears, and I said to myself: "I can't let this woman decide my future. I have to do something about this!"

And I remember making that decision at that moment—and not every choice will affect your whole life—but this choice that I made right there was to go to the Dean's office. I walked up to somebody in the street: "Where is the Dean's office?" I walked in and I saw the secretary: "I need to see the Dean!" they said: *"Well, you need an appointment—three months from now, on the third day of the month—,"* I said: *"This is life or death"* and *literally I believed this:* Life or Death! She said: "Well, he is coming out of his meeting; you have two minutes with him." I went in there and said: "Dean, my whole life I dreamed of being a director. If you don't let me in, I'm going to be living on my mom's couch for the rest of my life." His name was Dean David Oppenheim. He said: "Get this young man's docket on my desk by tomorrow morning!" I didn't even know what the word "docket" meant.

So I went to back to Miami Beach and three weeks later, I opened the mail and it said: "You've been accepted to NYU film school" And that was a defining moment for me because if it would have said no, I would have accepted it. Probably I would have been making films in my backyard with my friends to this day. Maybe I would have persevered, but it would have been a whole different path. It was that choice I made asking that person in the street for the Dean's office . . .

SL: You think you might not have become a professional director?

BR: Mhh, well . . . I think it would have taken much longer. And I had a brilliant professor that Scorsese already had; Haig Manoogian. He totally inspired me and became like my mentor. He didn't teach you from a book, he taught you from his own personal life experience. He said: "Technically, you can learn everything about filmmaking in a book in three days. But what you can't learn, really, and you have to have it in you, is storytelling."

So that became something that I focused on: Using the tools of my craft to tell a story in the simplest way. And the equipment at school was very limiting. It wasn't until I graduated and I started doing music videos that every time I got a bigger budget I could figure out: "Ok, when would I use a dolly versus a steady cam, when a crane, and what would be the reason. . ."

In film school, you have forty kids in a class and you break them down into little five-guy groups. And one film you direct, one you shoot, one you edit, one you produce and one you production-design. And I was like: "I give you like 200 bucks if you let me just direct your film." I just felt that I could hire the kid who was known as the best editor at NYU. There were kids that had passion and talent for these things, and I was talented in finding those people. I didn't want to waste my time.

And I missed out on learning a lot. So later when I got to music videos, I decided to learn every single person's job on set, so I can articulate what I am looking to accomplish. So doing music videos was another film school for me. I was getting paid to learn.

But I learned great lessons at NYU. There was this one kid in my class that literally made me want to quit. He did a film where we were supposed to tell a story in one shot. He had a three-minute roll of film and everything was happening as the story was unfolding. It was about getting high. I didn't even understand it but loved it and thought it was fucking ingenious. I thought: "Never in my life am I going to make a film as good as this" And I wish I could find this guy—maybe he'll read this conversation because literally it was one of the most brilliantly executed short films ever—this kid was like Stanley Kubrick to me. He probably works like in a video store now, right? The professor stood up and asked: "Why is this film so bad?" And the fucking kids at NYU—they are very vocal—they started cursing at the professor. "You're a communist!" He just said: "The greatest story ever told is the Bible. Why? Because the Bible can be understood by everybody." And then I realized that there were only three people in class that really got this film. I didn't get it because I never smoked pod.

And that became the most valuable lesson I ever learned: "Don't make films for just you and your friends, cause it's the film *business*. Make films that many people can watch and enjoy and understand and interpret, otherwise you are never going to make it."

SL: But aren't there examples of successful movies where directors did just that—maybe *Clerks* by Kevin Smith?

BR: My professor wasn't saying: "Don't make personal films," that's different. "Don't make a film that only you and your friends are going to *get!*"; and by the way: you either have it or you don't. Your taste level either is the same as millions of people or it isn't. It's not like: OK, why does Spielberg make commercial films? It's just who he is: it's personal. And that stayed with me all the way to Hollywood. You know, you can say: "Brett makes commercial films," but I can go through each film and tell you why it was personal to *me*."

And I also think it was an interesting message to get from an art school professor, saying: "Make films that people understand and can identify with. *If you want to go make experimental films, then go and do that. But don't make an experimental film that's supposed to be narrative.*" So I was inspired by him and I was able to apply that.

My final project in film school was this film *Whatever Happened to Mason Reese* with former child star Mason Reese. But he broke his leg in the middle of shooting and refused to continue. The professor told me to throw it out and start a new film. "No!" I said, "this is what the film is about: Mason Reese!" *He would verbally abuse me in class, but afterwards he'd say: "Let's get a cup of coffee." He knew I could take it.*

And finally, I ended up winning a film festival with this film for Best Producer; not Best Director. Why? The actor wouldn't finish the film: I basically took a film that made no sense and saved it by using stock footage, animation and a score to try to help the audience understand. I made a film that worked; that was emotional and funny. The guy said it wasn't the best film in the festival, but he knew that I had to work from nothing. I was able to make a film that had a beginning, middle, and an end.

SL: Even Spielberg chipped in 5,000 dollars for you to finish that film—

BR: When my professor told me to throw it away, I thought: "Oh, I'm fucked." Because when you graduate from film school, the only thing you've got that can possibly help you get a job is a short movie—unless you want to be a PA. But my professor specifically told me that I'm not meant to work for anybody as I would immediately get fired.

So I went into this shop and saw this magazine called 'Forbes' that had the 40 most powerful people in entertainment on the cover. I went back to my room, called 411 in California, and I got the names and addresses of every single person on that list. I sent a letter with one scene of the movie to all 40 people. *And I was so happy every day, because I was getting 39 rejection letters. I was asking for money, but I didn't need the money: I just wanted the relationship. But imagine this: every fucking one replied!*

SL: Everybody accepted your offer for a relationship—

BR: Yeah—the people on top, that's why they are on top: 'cause they answer calls. Finally, the Dean of NYU calls me. "Steven Spielberg's office called here looking for you." I'm like: "My mom definitely called one of my friends who pretended to be him." So I went back home with the number he gave me and called: "Is Steven Spielberg in?" "Who's calling?" "Brett Ratner" "Hold on, he's waiting for your call." I literally freaked out. "Oh my God, Steven Spielberg is gonna come to the phone . . ." My heart started palpitating. She says: "Can he call you back?" I fell asleep on the phone and I got a call in the morning from this woman Kathleen Kennedy: "Steven saw your film; he's tied up in a meeting, but he was so impressed. We want to tell you that we don't finance any short films, but send us the film in the future." So I went back to the self I was in the Dean's office several years back: "You don't understand, I'm gonna be a big director like Steven Spielberg!" I kept her on the phone for like 10 more minutes. A month goes by and there is a check in the mail from Spielberg. I was showing the cheque to all the girls, thinking it would impress them.

Obviously Kathleen went to Steven and said something. And now Kathleen and Steven and I are friends; I mean the irony is crazy . . .

SL: So did your short film allow you to get a job as you hoped?

BR: I knew Russell Simmons from film school. He started the hip-hop label Def Jam Records with Rick Rubin—and he became my best friend, but he never took me seriously. He was like my big brother.

When I finished my short movie, he said: "I've got a screening for you." But of course, he didn't know anybody in Hollywood. So he invites all the rappers to my screening. We then went to Miami to see a concert which Public Enemy was opening U2.

Out of the blue, Chuck D said to Russell: "Maybe we want Brett to do our next video." And Russell went: "Brat who?" "Brett Ratner; right there next to you!" And Russell was so proud of me. I never wanted to be a video director. Back then, there weren't guys like Bay or Fincher who had crossed over into feature. Music videos were bad and I had no desire to do that. But it was an opportunity. They gave me a 30,000 dollar budget and we followed Public Enemy around the states with U2.

The first day the video aired on MTV, was like a defining moment: It was the first time in the history of MTV that they put the director's name on the video. All of sudden, Brett Ratner's name is on MTV every half hour. So all the other rappers who knew me from Russell started calling and beg him: "Oh, can Brett do my video?" That's how I started to be a music video director, which I did from age 22 to 26.

SL: During those four years, did you know that eventually you wanted to do feature films?

BR: Well, if you look at my music videos, they are very narrative. I was trying to tell stories. I would copy for instance a scene form the *Untouchables* or from *Scarface* shot by shot—seeing if I could do it, but telling the story with rappers instead of actors; they loved it. Most videos by other directors were kind of flat, there was no coverage—it wasn't very cinematic.

But it wasn't only the visual. I learned how to deal with people. *The most difficult people you could ever work with are the recording artists.* And then I started working with Madonna and Mariah Carey. Very early on— from when I got the agent at William Morris after winning that award for my short—she'd say: "I'm gonna send your film to Jeffrey Katzenberg—" And I said: 'No! Don't do it. I am not ready. If you convince them to hire me to do a movie, I couldn't do it." I was smart about that. You know people who have delusions of grandeur—I was not delusional at all. I was very aware of my capabilities. So I told myself: "I'm not going to do a movie until I do a hundred music videos."

SL: Why did you feel incapable of directing a feature?

BR: I didn't know the job; I knew how to be a director: how to tell a story. But I didn't know how each tool and each piece of equipment helped me tell my story in the best way. It was a great way for me to experiment and it taught me the craft of filmmaking.

I also didn't understand what all the jobs were. *Now, if my DP got sick on my movie, I could tell the gaffer what I want. I could do the job of every person on my crew—and that's why I think I'm a good leader.* I'm always very clear of how I want to translate the script onto the screen and I am very articulate on what I'm trying to accomplish. And at the end of the day, they all want to work with me again because what I told them I was going to do, I did. But I did it in little three-minute stories, for which I had to figure out a way to tell them in the easiest way.

I also had the rule that I wouldn't collaborate with my DP more than once. I would go: "who is the best camera operator in the world?" So every other week, I would work with a different person. Now for my features, I get to hire the best people in the world.

SL: Did you actually make your a hundred videos?

BR: Yes.

SL: Was there any point where you were afraid to get stuck in the music video world?

BR: *You know what? I have transcended every wall that has been put in front of me.* Yes it's true: People in the industry can kind of put you in a box, and then most people get stuck. I don't mean to boast, but I'm one of the only guys out there that have done as many different genres as I have. I did rap videos. All of a sudden Madonna wants me to do her video. I made those transitions.

SL: So how did you make the actual transition to film?

BR: I was desperate to do a movie, but I didn't want to take it if the script wasn't good. I started to get offered these little urban films cause I was doing mostly black music videos. But in the last minute, my instinct just told me not to do it. I walked away from a few opportunities. And I still didn't think I was ready: I hadn't done my hundred videos that I set as a goal for myself.

It then so happened that again Russell Simmons started this show on HBO called the Def Comedy Jam. I was watching them picking from hundreds and hundreds of black comedians. The one guy who stood out was Chris Tucker. I put him in a Heavy D music video and it was a huge hit. It was the first thing he had ever done. He went on to do this Gary Gray cult movie about smoking called *Friday*. It cost like a million and made like 20 million. It made Tucker a star.

Chris Tucker then signed on to *Money Talks* with this director that got fired because he couldn't handle Chris. "Tucker won't listen to me, he keeps improvising," he complained. Now, the director's job is to get the actors to listen to him. If he's not gonna listen to you [*laughing*] it's a disaster. He suggested that Tucker be fired, but at the end of the meeting, the studio exec Michael De Luca said to the director: "Well, *you*'re fired." So less than a week before shooting started, they had no director. Tucker says: "Oh, I remember that cool white boy, Brett Ratner." De Luca says: "Oh, I've heard of him, he's great!" Michael de Luca was the youngest exec at New Line and he was very familiar with all the music video and commercial directors—again a guy with taste; he just new what was good out there.

Mike brought me to the meeting, showed me the script and said: "You can change anything in the script, but you can't change the set pieces." They had already put the deposits down on all the locations and they didn't want to lose the money.

And that's how I got to direct *Money Talks*. It was a hit, made good money and the studio said: "What do you want to do next?"

SL: So for *Money Talks*, the bed was already made for you: everything from the script to the crew was there—

BR: Yeah, and now I'm the go-to guy in a crisis. *X-Men* I took on with six weeks prep. I don't know one director who would have done it. But I loved the script and for me, the script is the Bible.

SL: Did you feel that coming from music videos, people initially questioned your storytelling capacities?

BR: I think there was some judgment, but then when you look at my music videos, they look really more like little movies. And if you look at my movies—people always say: "Oh, your movies are so fast-paced"—but they are not. I am not doing quick cuts and music video-type flashy stuff. I haven't used a lot of songs but only traditional score. I had a composer in my mind that I wanted to use before I even did *Rush Hour*. In fact, I came up with the idea of *Rush Hour*, so I could work with Lalo Shifrin.

SL: *Rush Hour* originated from your idea but you didn't write the script?

SL: I can probably write something, but not as good as Jeff Nathanson, who only writes for me and Spielberg.

Before I had a script, I had this idea to put a black guy and a Chinese guy together, as nobody had ever done that before. You have to understand, I grew up working with black musicians and Kung Fu and martial arts was a big part of the hip-hop world. I was a black belt myself. I started looking for buddy movie scripts that were out there that allowed me to match up Chris Tucker with Jackie Chan. I thought that Chris's verbal comedy and Jackie's physical comedy were going to be brilliant together; I found about four or five other scripts where you could put a black and a Chinese together—but they weren't buddy cop. *Rush Hour* was the best one, because it wasn't written as a comedy, but as a thriller. I hired Jeff, who re-wrote the entire script for then. He didn't get any credit, but you know, it's the Writer's Guild that decides.

You might have noticed the title *Rush Hour* has nothing to do with the movie—I added a line where he goes: "Officer is there a problem?" and he says,

"Yeah, Rush Hour." Because the original script was about two white cops that get caught up in rush hour traffic—

SL: How does your cooperation with the writer concretely work?

BR: I basically just come up with like five or six set pieces I definitely want in the film, then the writer writes the scene. *For the third* Rush Hour *I was like: "Where do I want to be when I shoot a fun movie where the studio just gives me 120 million dollars and says, 'Do what you want to do.'"* And with Jeff, we have talks that go like: "What is the Magoffin, what is the plot, what are we gonna talk about, who are the villains gonna be?" That's how we came up with the French. They can't be Arab and we don't want to have drug stuff. "Oh France—everyone hates the French." And it offers great opportunities for comedy. The French are assholes—the waiters in the restaurant, the hotel staff; there is also the cabaret and the beautiful girls. So I make a list: "The benefits of shooting here, the benefits of shooting there."

SL: Rarely the same person directs two sequels to his original movie—was it as easy to motivate yourself for the third *Rush Hour*?

BR: First of all, I had the best time of my life making those movies—also the hardest. But I have Jackie and Chris who stay on top of me—these guys really care. We all created the franchise and they love it. And when you create something, it's like your baby. So when people watch the movie, I hope they can see that the characters have grown. You know, I like friendship and people and enjoy the fact that people want to work with me again. *Unless all my friends can come to my premiere, why have one?*

The greatest compliment ever was when I showed Nicholas Cage *Family Man* for the first time and he had tears in his eyes. I said: "But you were *there*, you did it!" and he said: "Yeah, but you totally moved me. There is not one frame I would change in it" If no one else liked the movie, Nicholas was there with me making it and he felt I made the right decisions—and that made me feel good. The fact that he cried meant a lot me.

SL: A good script needs character and story—that's the standard idea. But how are they concretely related and how do they build upon each other?

BR: Look, here's the thing: the most important thing that made *Rush Hour* work was the chemistry between the two guys. If they didn't have chemistry—no matter how good the story was or how great the characters were, you wouldn't have cared about them.

I love a movie like *Harold and Maude* and now you'll go: "What the fuck is Brett talking about? There is no relationship between *Harold and Maude* and *Rush Hour!*"—but I love films with humanity and heart; about relationships and people. If I asked you the plot of *Rush Hour* right now, you wouldn't even be able to tell me because it's about the relationship between Jackie and Chris the audience cares for: People liked that and came back to see them.

But the structure of *Rush Hour* is a thriller—take out the comedy and you watch a thriller unfold. That's the *choice* I had to make—that's the *tone.* Then while I'm shooting, I go: "How far do you go with the comedy?" If I make it too funny or too goofy, then people walk out not caring, not believing that Chris is really scared of these villains and that they are a real threat. So I better made sure that the villains—like Zhang Ziyi from *Crouching Tiger*, and John Lone from the *Last Emperor*—were great and charismatic as well.

There have been many buddy comedies that didn't work. But I looked at the ones that did and figured out why: Why did *48 Hours* work? Because the villain was great. It wasn't written as a comedy, it was written as a thriller. And Eddie Murphy was a fish out of water which was dropped into the middle of that world. The comedy came from the situations this guy was put into and his character, not from his one-liners. So I cast my writer Jeff Nathanson to do the same with *Rush Hour*—Chris Tucker and Jackie Chan were total fish-out-of-water characters; first when Jackie was in LA, and then Chris when they went to Hong Kong.

SL: Do you believe that *Rush Hour* could have worked as thriller, if you had made that choice?

BR: My point is: the story and the plot *have* to work as a thriller; as a film that you believe and the comedy then comes from the situations. So it's not that it couldn't have worked—it wouldn't have been as successful; and I wouldn't have hired Chris Tucker.

SL: After *Rush Hour II*, you left comedy for different genres for a while. Was that a conscious decision?

BR: There was never a strategy like when I did, you know, film school first and then my hundred videos after that. I just started to get the respect from film-makers, cause they are the first people to appreciate a good film, whatever the genre is. They know how hard it is to make a film that works. Then Roman Polanski becomes my fan and I'm like: "Oh my God"—I just made a contemporary version of *Beverly Hills Cop*.

*The truth is that when I did* Rush Hour, *I was always envious of Paul Thomas Anderson, because Paul was friends with Kubrick and he was hanging out with the important people. So I said: "Wow, one day I got to do an important film to have the big directors respect me or be my friends.* But then, all of a sudden after *Rush Hour*, Academy Award Winner Warren Beatty calls me and says it's his favorite movie of the year and that he wants to work with me. And Jonathan Demme literally calls me out of the blue and just becomes my friend."

SL: Did you know what story you wanted to tell next?

BR: I was offered every big movie you can think of because of the *Rush Hour* success. And all of a sudden, my agent says: "Read that script. It's called the *Family Man*," and I go: "I don't want to read a script called the *Family Man*. I want to read . . . [*imitating tough guy*] *Fight Club*, I want to read like cool movies, you know?"

*So finally after three months, I read the script and I cry. I go: "Oh my God, maybe I'm having a bad day." I read it again, and I cry. I read the last pages, I cry. I read the last 5 pages, I cry. I'm like: "Jesus, this movie moved me!"* So I call my agent and she says: "It's too late. Curtis Hanson is directing it." "Oh, at least I have good taste." I told myself. So I went to see the head of the studio and said. "Look, even though Hanson is directing it, I love this movie. I don't want to jinx it, but things happen in Hollywood—so if something happens, I want to direct this." And they go "Sure, we'll let you know" or whatever; obviously a waste of time . . .

Three months go by and I read in the trades that Curtis is off the movie. I call my agent: "What the fuck, I want to do this!" They go: "We asked them to hire you and they said that you were too young—you don't have a family on your own." "What are you talking about? I'm a family man! I'm just not the father in the family, I'm the child." And I literally begged and begged and begged and finally, the hired me. And I think *Family Man* is the movie I'm most proud of today—it has the most heart and I love that movie. Something in me had to do it.

SL: So the shift to a romantic movie didn't frighten you?

BR: Oh, I was scared. I never dreamed I'd do a romantic fantasy like that. And when I did it and people loved the film, then all of a sudden I got offered movies that I never *dreamed* of being offered: I got offered *Memoirs of a Geisha* for example.

SL: Did your exploration into new genres allow you to discover any new aspects of making films that comedy couldn't offer you?

BR: Oh, totally. I had to use another side of my brain. It was a completely different approach. You get away with a little bit of surrealism in *Rush Hour,* but in, for example, *Red Dragon*, it was FBI and criminal investigation and forensics—you had to be so real and so specific.

SL: What did "using a different side of your brain" concretely mean for your work as a director?

BR: It's a different kind of directing, I guess. You have to make the audience feel that this guy is a killer and that they are close to getting him. It's more about the composition and the camera work and the *approach* to telling the story, than it is having the actual story unfolding. It's a very complex story and every piece and every dot has to connect. I think during *Red Dragon*, I really grew up as far as the camera work and the design of the movie are concerned because Ted Tally wrote such a great script that I was really able to concentrate on these aspects. It's a whole different way of making movies for which you also have to hire the best actors. The attention goes in a different direction. In *Rush Hour*, the characters and the chemistry are really carrying the film. If there are holes in the plot, it's not going to really kill anybody, because they are being entertained—they are laughing and enjoying it. In *Red Dragon*, you have to really concentrate as the clues and the subtlety unfold and reveal themselves. If I had bad taste, I would have made a really bad version of it. In my opinion, the most important thing you need as director—apart from big balls—is taste.

SL: What's taste?

BR: Taste: you need it for aesthetics, for visuals, for wardrobe, for materials, for actors, for the crew, for the people you work with—there is good taste, there is bad taste, and there is no taste. And that's the truth. If you don't have taste and you don't know better, you hire somebody who will make the bad choice and you don't know if it's good enough.

SL: But how do you know if your taste is tasteful?

BR: I don't think about it. I mean, each person is different. Taste kind of leads into tone a little bit, when you look at a movie and you don't even have to see the credits to know Scorsese directed it. He has a control over the look of the film, the performances—you see that that's been *directed*. There are choices that have been made—decisiveness and thoughtfulness have gone into it. And it's not random. To be a confident director, you have to be able to control the tone of the film.

And after that, it's important that a director has a point of view which is closely related to the question of style. Even Hale Ashby: watch his movies, and they have humanity—they have his persona in their film. You can see how those directors' personality and humanity and their point of view connects to the style of their films. I feel if you know me and then you see *Rush Hour*, you will say: "That's Brett: he is in that movie." And that was the greatest compliment I got when I was begging Nicholas Cage to do *Family Man*: I showed him *Rush Hour* and he said: "I'm so happy you showed it to me, because *you are* in this film. That means you have a control over your medium."

SL: What exactly do you mean when you say "I'm in it"?

BR: It's not a particular camera angle or shot; it's not like Spike Lee with the shot floating down the street. *And it's also not like: "Oh, Brett loves ice-cream, so there is ice-cream in every scene." And it's not trying to make it my own, either. It's not as simple as that. It's a tonal thing. It's my personality, my persona, my character that's in here. Brett's heart is in this movie. Brett's spirit is in the scene.*

SL: So it's something you don't have to think about consciously but which is always already in you?

BR: It's automatic, and that's because I have control over the medium. When I did *Red Dragon*, Jonathan Demme gave me the best advice ever. Before we started shooting, I called him and was freaking out: "Jonathan, what do I do—oh my God, Anthony Hopkins is in it." He said: "Brett, I'm your fan. Don't think about what *I* did. Make *your* version of this movie. Do what you feel is right. There are no rules."

And it was helpful that there were three movies that existed: *Manhunter* by Michael Mann, *Silence of the Lambs* by Demme, and *Hannibal* by Ridley Scott: Three brilliant directors making three different films in exactly the same genre and they came out completely different from each other. It was the best film school ever: It helped me decide what I wanted to do with my film and what tone I wanted. Do I want to make a slick, stylized and kind of thriller-esque version of the story like Mann's? Do I want to make a psychological film that will scare you by what you don't see rather by what you see, as Demme did? Or do I want to do a complete horror film version of it as did Ridley Scott? So these three together communicated to me the kind of movie I wanted to make.

SL: But how did these three films concretely help you to eventually find your own movie?

BR: Because they defined for me what the story was. I saw what Mann did with the original book and I didn't like it. I'm not saying I didn't like the movie, but I didn't like it for me—

SL: So you excluded choices the others had taken?

BR: Since the book gets into the mind of a killer, I wanted to make a version that explores the damaging psychological effects of abuse, showing that inside a monster there is still humanity which I think Michael Mann purposefully chose not to. In my opinion, the greatest scene in the book is when he goes to the museum and physically eats the painting that tells him to kill these people. He had fallen in love with this blind woman and he doesn't want to kill her. Even though he does horrible things, he is still a human being and he has a heart—and love can maybe save him. It's a brilliant scene in the book and in my movie, and it wasn't in Mann's because he wasn't interested in the psychological aspects and the relationship with that blind girl. He was more interested in the FBI agent stalking that woman. So it was just another approach.

SL: You said that you heart is in your movies. Can you put into words how you believe your personality concretely influences your filmmaking?

BR: I think no matter what the tone or the type of film, I bring a lot of energy and enthusiasm. You know, my very short attention span doesn't cause me to cut the scenes very choppy, but just makes the overall pace of my movies very good—it simply corresponds to the person I am. So if I was a different kind of guy, I would probably sit there and hold on longer; though I do hold on stuff when it's important for the narrative. I just think my energy is in it: in the comedies, in the dramas: my films have a certain life on their own to them. I always identify very much with the identity and heart and the relationships in my movies.

Also, I'm very happy to be there, which makes me very positive—you know I try to keep that enthusiasm and energy going. 'Cause it's a long grueling process. People get bored, people get tired, and I try to keep the focus on what we're trying to accomplish. I treat every scene like it's a short film. That's my trick: every scene has to have a beginning, middle and an end. It helps me with transitions, how I'm going to start the scene and how I am going to end it—visually, esthetically, with the dialogue, with everything.

SL: When being deeply involved in the process of shooting your movie, how easy is it for you to stay in touch with the story's big picture and to keep your creative storytelling-sensors open?

BR: The big picture is very important. Cause from doing fifty or so mini-movies that is one big movie, I'm always thinking how one thing connects to another.

I like to do a lot of takes and don't mind trying out many different things. It sometimes helps me discover stuff that I wouldn't normally have thought of—you only find it when you are working/playing.

If the scene is great, then I know it comes to life as you film it. If it's not working, I'm fearless and improvise it right there. *I try to live in the moment, so I can have pure choices, pure instincts—I try not to think about what's right what's wrong then.* I tell myself that whatever choice I am going to make that day is going to be the best version, meaning; I'm not afraid to change something because it's written or because it works on the page.

Also, I'm very communicative and open to people's opinions. I collaborate closely with my crew which has worked with from the beginning—all the same people. If somebody has an idea and we can come up with something better, that's great. I think every person on the team is a filmmaker in their own right. And I am very open to the actor's suggestions as well. It doesn't mean that I always listen to it, but I like their input and it helps me get a different point of view. They are intelligent; they have a point of view. *Sometimes I wish I could could call myself, 'cause then I could collaborate with myself.*

SL: What about you collaboration with the producers—are they rather a limitation or an encouragement to creative results?

BR: Producers are there to fight for the cause of making the best film possible and to keep the studio kind of away. He gets me the actors and the crew that I need. I worked with very collaborative producers and also those in the background who are the muscles.

A producer is a filmmaker as well and if he wants to be my partner and be there in every script meeting, I'm open to that, too. So I don't shut up producers—I need them, I love them.

SL: Do you feel you have to be in complete control creatively?

BR: I don't feel I have to be: I *am* in complete control. It's my film. When the lights go down and it says: "A Film by Brett Ratner" there is no ego there, because I'm very confident that it's my film: Every single choice on that screen—every single piece of wardrobe, the color of the pain on the walls, the shoes and the hair of the actress—every detail is something that I had a say in.

SL: What do you think are the greatest misconceptions about the profession of a filmmaker?

BR: *You know, I think some directors have to pretend like they know what they want. I'm not afraid to say: "I really don't know what I want here; let's try something. I'm fearless when it comes to that." I mean either you know or you don't know.* 'Cause when I do know, I'm very specific and clear about it.

So I think the biggest misconception is—also addressing this to a young filmmaker: you don't have to pretend like you know what you want. It's OK and important to collaborate and figure things out. Find a DP that you work with, find an actor that you trust: That's why you only want to work with the best.

And sometimes, I have to see it. Some DPs know what it's supposed to look like before they put the light up, and some directors cut the scenes in their head before they shoot it.

You know, I was the kid in class who had to listen to the teacher, take notes, study, study them again. Then there was a kid who didn't even have to take notes. He'd just listen, come back and get an A. I would still get the same A, but I just had to work harder for it.

SL: You had a different style—

BR: And you have to know your limitations and your strengths and apply that to your job. In order to win—to be the best at something—you have to know what you need to do in order to succeed. You have to know the script, you have to storyboard: certain rules and parameters. And as I get more experience, I get better—it's like training.

SL: But do you feel that you get better every time, or is it rather that every new project is a completely start in terms of possible success and failure?

BR: Every project is a new experience. There is different actors, different characters, different parameters; there is nothing I can take with me that helps me tell a better story. Like I said, it's about choices and taste. I think the best directors have a total control over the tone of the film. 'Cause it's all personal—

And believe it or not, *I get more scared every time. I was the most secure and confident on my first movie. I had no idea what was going on and I was so sure that I was gonna do a good job.* It was something I had been thinking about since I was a little kid. Once I realized what can go wrong, the fear started setting in: failure and all those things that you get scared of. When there is nothing to lose, it's somehow easier. When I had all this success, how do I top that?

SL: Could that be a reason why many of the great directors whose taste we admire have gone back to making one or two mediocre films at some point in their lives?

BR: I guess it is a phenomenon—something that happens—but it makes sense to me. I think bad luck comes from bad ideas. There are about 100,000 different reasons why that might happen: they go lazy, lose focus, a personal problems— who knows what makes them fail or not do a good job.

But who's to say that a movie is bad? What makes a movie good? That's what's so beautiful about the movie business: it communicates on such a broad level; on so many different degrees of likes and dislikes. Some people love and some people hate exactly the same movie.

You know, I think talent lasts and if directors have it, they can do it again— some people lose passion or perseverance, but I don't think talent is something that you can lose.

I think I have high hopes and low expectations; and what I learned from Demme was try not to compare myself to anybody. "I'm gonna do what I think is right, I'm not gonna analyze what's been done in the past."

SL: But how can you prevent failure for yourself?

BR: I don't think I can. I think it's gonna happen one day. I think the truth is: I'm not the kind of guy who is going to live on a ranch in the middle of nowhere. *I'm a guy who likes to socialize and talk to people and find out what's cool and what's changing about the world and what life is like. I haven't lost touch with reality yet.*

SL: So staying in touch with reality prevents you from becoming irrelevant?

BR: I think so. As director, speak to young people and follow what's changing about the world and what people are thinking. 'Cause what might have been brilliant a few years ago might suck now; might be dated and old and boring.

SL: Is there a kind of project that tempts you now but you might not yet feel ready for yet?

BR: I respond to story and script. I mean I would love to do a musical, but I never ever thought I could do one. But then if I read one and it moves me and I feel I can apply my style and experiences or my knowledge, then I am not afraid of anything. I have done four different genres in seven films. But I read brilliant scripts that I turned down because I said, "I don't know how to do this."

When you look at the great directors from fifty years ago, they went from comedy, to drama, to western, to musical—if you're a director, that's your job: you tell stories. It's only now that people go: "Ok, this guy does comedy, this one drama, he does . . ." And there are only a few of guys left that do that. I want to be one of them.

SL: How has filmmaking allowed you to explore yourself and the way you see yourself?

BR: Well, I mean I've grown up and learned a lot. Each movie is such an emotional rollercoaster: it starts off with enthusiasm, then at one point disillusionment sets in, then the oh-my-God and panic stage—then you see the footage and you get past it.

*Rush Hour* is not necessarily a deep film, but I had to really think what I believe in, what I like, what I don't like, what I love. And I still haven't made the film that has said everything I want to say. I think it's my whole body of work that is more likely to do it.

But I'm still discovering who I am and what I want to say and what I believe in. I did my first movie at 26 and I'm still very young; time will tell and I'm not in a rush.

I'm just happy to be doing this—I can't believe they pay me for it. I eat, sleep and breathe it. I can never stop. I have been very lucky in my life, but Bob Evans told me: "Luck is when opportunity meets preparation," so I was smart enough not to take the opportunities without being prepared, 'cause otherwise I would have fallen flat on my face.

SL: You are the director of that Brett Ratner biopic and have the opportunity to pitch it to me, the potential producer. What do you tell me?

BR: That would be so fucking hard, let's see. "The kid grows up with his entire family and he—" No! "Brett Ratner gets in all the doors and gets to all the right people and hustles his way to the top and finally gets the opportunity of a lifetime to have his dream come through. And everyone in the theater is on the edge of their seats: "What the fuck is he going to do now? He's gonna land flat on his face, he's gonna fail!" and he turns down the opportunity, hoping that by working hard he will learn everything he should learn—and finally gets the opportunity again and succeeds" [*laughing*].

The Human Drama: "That he gets to all the right people and they all like him, but just being liked by somebody who can help is not enough. At the end of the day you have to deliver!"

SL: Might be a hit. What should we call it?

BR: Jesus! It's called *The Good Life*.

SL: The director has got the last word.

BR: *You can't be afraid to fail. I know if I fail, my mom is still gonna love me. Maybe not everyone had the love I had, but know that your true friends will still be your friends.* You can apply that to anything else. Find something that you love. When you love it and you're good at it, the money is gonna come. But don't think about it. There is nothing wrong with being a chef, but if you want to build buildings, why should you work as a chef?

# Waters, Mark

**DIRECTOR'S CUT:**
"It is that thing just when you're watching some-thing and you're kind taken by surprise by an inspired moment —in either art or just in life."

**BORN:**
1964, Wyandotte, Michigan

**BACKGROUND:**
Theater Director

**FILMS:**
The House of Yes—1997
Head over Heals —2001
Freaky Friday —2003
Mean Girls—2004
Just Like Heaven —2005
The Spiderwick Chronicles—2007

**MAIN GENRES:**
Comedy, Drama, Fantasy

MARK WATERS: I grew up in the Midwest—first in Ohio, then we moved to South Bend, Indiana. It is basically the heartland—I like to call it Cornset and Inbread—where I come from. My mother's family was mostly farmers in Indiana and my dad's family was from the Bronx in New York. They kind of controlled the Irish funeral business in New York. My dad went to school in Notre Dame 'cause he was a catholic boy and met my mom there.

The thing about Indiana is that the rest of the world seemed extraordinarily interesting after you've spent your childhood there. You have to learn to amuse yourself because you don't have the distractions. You can't just go out to a nightclub or go see an art exhibition. You pretty much have to just play in your own imagination to amuse yourself because you are not going to find amusement *there*, which is a good thing as well because it makes the rest of the world seem special. My brother and I we had enormous ways of entertaining ourselves by playing elaborate games or putting on shows and running haunted mansions for the kids in the block—just to amuse ourselves because of the artistic vacuum around us. The world of the imagination in our family was very elaborate but unlike my brother, I never thought I would actually do something like that as a vocation.

My brother Daniel is actually a filmmaker as well—he is really more a screenwriter than a director; he wrote the movie *Heathers* and *Batman Returns.* He was somebody who was obsessed with films. He wrote his first screenplay in like sixth grade about him being a secret agent in his elementary school . . .

I on the other hand was never involved and had no interest in theater or making movies or anything of that kind. I can shamefully admit that I never even saw *Star Wars* when it came out—I saw it when it got re-released a few years ago. *I was actually the classic all-American over achieving kind of guy. I was Valedictorian. A total math geek*—I was actually on the math team and the debate team. At the same time I was on the Varsity Basketball and Tennis teams and I played football and did track. I was always doing sports. In Indiana you either work on your car or you play basketball—and I played basketball. So I was very focused on the classic high school stuff while trying to get laid. And my brother was home watching reruns of the *Rockford Files* and writing screenplays . . .

And now it's actually our little sister, Kathleen, who is the black sheep of the family because she is a litigation attorney and doesn't work in the business—

SL: So growing up in this small minded environment, you did have a notion that there is a world out there for you to be discovered?

MW: When it came the time of the end of high school, there was never any question that the three of us would get the hell out of there. We left Indiana and never returned back. We come for Christmas to visit the family, but that's it.

The one thing that helped was that my dad blew off his marriage after 13 years and with three kids. It was actually the best thing that ever happened to us. *Even though it was stressful for the two of them as parents, we really had no idea why my father and mother had ever even met—they seemed so completely different from each other. When they separated—I was about six then—we were actually happy.* My father became like a young man and moved to Montreal and later to Toronto. We would actually get to travel quite a bit visiting him and take trips over the summer. So unlike other people in Indiana who were stuck there all the time, we were always kind of escaping to go and hang out in different places in the country and around the world. So we got a little bit of a taste how the other half lived; a taste that there is a big world out there outside of Indiana.

Also, when my dad was with his—what became our step-mother—would take us go see movies in the drive-in. The three of us would get in the front and then the two of them would sit in the back and make out. And we'd see all kinds of weird movies: like all the Woody Allen movies we have seen in the drive-in [*chuckling*]. I loved it, but it was purely recreational to me. My brother and I were also Bond movie obsessed and liked the big popcorn moves like *Jaws*. But the fact is that my interest didn't extend beyond that.

SL: So what was your horizon at the time you graduated from high school?

MW: I was extremely motivated, but I was pretty locked and loaded on this middle class price; you know, I was kind of like the "Good Son." My brother was the crazy one and I was the one who would support him when he works at the post office—these were our assigned roles in the family.

I got a full scholarship to go to Penn in Philadelphia as a pre-med. So when I went there, I was like, "Great, I'm going to just excel and do well at the Ivy League School." But once I got there I started to have a sea change in philosophy . . .

Because Philadelphia is really close to New York, I found myself going into New York City quite a bit and I got taken to see some really interesting avant-garde theater there. And suddenly I had this thing where I realized, "OK, theater isn't about doing revivals of *Pippin* and *The Music Man*—theater can be this thing where you can have a really world-rocking, earth-shattering, mind-blowing experience that is intellectual and visceral at the same time and that is actually about something meaningful." It was that exposure of being able to see that there is a whole world out there—a world of which I already got a little bit of a taste via my father—of artists and writers and everything that is going on in New York and even in Philadelphia on a smaller level.

SL: So theater made you realize that an alternative lifestyle might exist beyond that empty middle class world of status?

MW: Oh yeah. And also it comes down to who you are attracted to as people. The fact is that suddenly you look around your classroom and see, "Ok there is all these guys in my organic chemistry class who are sabotaging each other's experiment," and you are like, "Oh my *God*, am I really gonna spend the next ten years of my life with these people or am I going to be hanging out with this cool group of people that are doing these bizarre theater shows on campus." And also: never underestimate the power of women [*laughing*]—you are not going to meet any women in your pre-med classes and suddenly, during theater, you are meeting these really fascinating, gorgeous cool women and it seems like the place to hang out. *And being a heterosexual male working in theater is a good thing too—you're considered to be gold in that community. So as a young man, I was like, "This seems like a pretty obvious decision!"*

But in the meantime, it still took me a while to admit that what I found attractive and interesting was something that I wanted to devote my time to. But then I proved to myself that I *could* have succeeded by getting straight As in all my classes. After a while I said, "You know what, I'm done!"—and then totally kind of started to move on. I stopped taking pre-med classes and started to take theater arts classes and English and philosophy. Meanwhile, I didn't bother informing my parents of this and when they got my report card, they were like, "What does this stand for?" "You know, Art!" [*Laughing*] So I had to kind of reveal to them that in their eyes, I sort of had gone off the deep end. Suddenly, the golden boy was off doing these crazy things and theater.

SL: Why didn't you tell your parents?

MW: First, I knew that they would disapprove so strongly. Their goals for me were much more along those middle class lines to then go off have a nice boring career as, you know, a doctor, or a lawyer, or an investment banker.

By the time I graduated from college in 1986, I had no more interest in that. One of my friends from college was the recruiter for an investment banking company and I got offered a job there that I blew off by saying, "I'm not gonna do that, I'm going to travel to Europe and study theater in Germany instead." That suddenly confirmed for them that I was starting to take a different path. The good thing was that I got a big scholarship to go to college so my parents weren't paying for me.

SL: So you made up on your plan to go study theater in Europe?

MW: The year right after graduation, I actually just worked in theaters in Philadelphia. My focus was still not on filmmaking—I was much more heavily embedded in theater and my brother was the person who was carving out the film thing. Dan graduated from college in 1985, traveled out to LA almost immediately, and I think he sold *Heathers* in 1987. He has that classic thing where he worked in the video store during the day and wrote the script at night—so he was having a film career, while I was doing what I like to call my "wandering poet's menstrual phase" where I literally did go and traveled around Europe.

I basically made a lot of money as a bartender while I was doing plays on the side. For the most part, I was actually acting and directing at the same time but I never thought I was actually that good as an actor. I always felt like I was surreptitiously spying on the acting profession so I could learn to be a better director. And then I took acting classes—I always had this attitude that I had no interest in getting a headshot or an agent but, "I'm just here to learn the game so that when I'm dealing with actors, I will be more knowledgeable."

I stationed myself in Berlin for a short time and thought, "I'm just gonna work in theater in Berlin"—it was kind of a romantic notion. And when I got to Berlin I realized that I didn't need to actually be there—but I did need it in order to justify for myself that it was OK to just make a life trying to work in theater.

So when I came back to the US, I saved up some more money and moved to San Francisco. When I was seeing all these plays in New York, I found that whenever I saw a really great show, it was oftentimes from different groups in San Francisco. While Chicago is a hotbed of more straight plays, in San Francisco there is a little bit more of an expressive scene—a place where you find more of a visual-, avant-garde musical dance theater. I lived there for the next five years after college directing and acting for theater.

SL: So how did you suddenly start to feel attracted to working in film?

MW: I went down to LA to visit my brother who was working on movie sets. During this time it was mainly on the sets of *Heathers* and some other movies he did some work on. Watching these directors in action, I said to myself, "Wow, these guys really have no idea how to talk to actors. They know how to play with the crane and cameras and all that stuff, but when they come up to talk to an actor . . ." Also, I would read my brother's screenplays and think, "These are brilliant screenplays!" I was blown away by his writing, but then I would see the scene acted out and go, "Oh my god, that's not right!" There is that classical joke: How many directors does it take to screw in a light bulb? One hundred: One to screw it in and 99 to step back and go, "I could do that better!" I was like that!

I suddenly told myself, "You know what? If I could learn all this camera and crane crap—I know how to talk to actors better and I know good writing when I see it." My idea of writing wasn't studying screenwriters—it was studying Shakespeare, Sam Shepard and David Mamet—cause on the stage you can't use cinematic trickery to cover up the fact that the writing is no good. So I had different criteria of judgment.

But I realized that maybe that could be interesting for me to work on. And so basically, back in San Francisco, I got a Super 8 camera, took a film class at the community college and made some black and white silent films.

SL: What did you expect or hope to find in film directing that theater couldn't give you?

MW: I found that I really loved it because of this compulsory part in me that hated directing theater knowing that I had to eventually kind of extricate myself in the process. I used to joke that in theater as a director, you have to use a broom to walk off the stage covering your footstep and let the play exist just with the actors. If you are a good theater director, that's what you do but I had immense trouble with this. I was the guy who was still backstage five weeks into the run and handed the actors notes. And I realized that this isn't the right way to do it. In film on the other hand, you get to stay in contact with your baby. You shoot the movie, but after you have shot it, you edit the movie; and then you go and mix the movie. You keep playing with it until it's done and that was immensely appealing to me.

And as I had a great time doing these Super 8 films, I sent them to the American Film Institute (AFI) on a lark and got in—which I wasn't expecting. But once I was in, it seemed kind of crazy for me not to take advantage of it and give it a shot.

I knew that if you want to work in the American film industry, you do have to pretty much come down to Los Angeles eventually in order to find other people who are interested in making movies and in order to get the money. So if nothing else, going to AFI was an excuse for me to get down here and get serious about it. I started that in the fall of 1992.

SL: You say you "didn't expect to get in"—in retrospect, do you think that your short films made an impact or was it more your life experience before that?

MW: *I think the head of the center, this intense Hungarian guy Dezsö Magyar, found my films appealing. They were really dark weird movies—one of them involved a guy performing autoerotic asphyxia while his wife binged on chocolate in the other room.* So they were kind of hiding their obsessions from each other. It was kind of comedic and also pretty intense.

And on top of that, I wasn't a guy who did his undergraduate degree in filmmaking, but who came at it from a very different perspective, having done a number of things and actually been working in theater for a few years. So just in terms of having diversity in class, they found that very appealing as well.

SL: And once at AFI, you quickly found you had made the right choice?

MW: Let me tell you my crucial AFI story. The first day of my first film shoot at AFI was the first day I actually worked with a real film crew. I would just walk on the set and we did like 28 setups during one night of shooting—and I remember feeling completely satisfied at the end of that day and saying to myself, "You know what—for most of the work I do and most of the work everybody does, it feels like you are operating on only four cylinders and you are not doing things at your full capacity." But when I shot that first day on the set, I felt like I was actually working on all cylinders at all times. When I left that set, I was like, "This is great! This is something I can see myself doing because I love it!" And it was extremely addictive as well.

Interestingly enough, Darren Aronofski and Rob Schmidt were also in my class and none of us were actually asked back into the second year program, while the bulk of people who were asked back don't actually make movies anymore. Our second year program was basically just writing screenplays for films we wanted to direct.

So once I graduated I was trying to set up one of the screenplays I had written but I couldn't quite get anyone to pay for it—it was quite an ambitious movie for a first time filmmaker and the budget was about five million dollars—we really couldn't figure out any way to make it cheaper than that.

SL: And then you decided to instead go with an adaptation of *The House of Yes*—

MW: I had seen Wendy MacLeod's play back in San Francisco and thought it was fantastic. The play didn't actually have good productions like in New York, London, or even Los Angeles—so basically, nobody had seen the play in the normal places where people option and buy plays, while in SF it was a huge hit.

I remember when I was still in San Francisco and not even a filmmaker, I called the agent and got a copy of it. I told them, "I would love to make a movie of this some day"—and then I just kind of put it away and forgot about it.

But a year after being out of school and struggling to get more expensive things set up, I realized that if I could make an adaptation of *The House of Yes*, that would be a movie which is all in one location, with only five main actors; and I could shoot it really quickly and really cheaply. So I revisited it, contacted the playwright and convinced her that I wouldn't screw up her play.

SL: How did you convince her that you could be trusted to not mess it up?

MW: Well, I told her that I had gone to film school and presented her with a resume of theater things that I had directed. The short films that I made at AFI were only small video projects and none of them I felt were like great calling cards—so basically I wouldn't let anybody see my films.

I said to Wendy, "You just have to trust that I know how to direct that movie!" On top of that, I completely storyboarded the entire movie and I made shot diagrams for every scene. So when I talked to my future DP, people could see that it was pretty mapped out.

And only by kind of offering her script approval and cast approval did Wendy eventually allow me to get an option on the play for a very cheap price. She ended up really loving my adaptation and loving Parker Posey when I attached her to play the lead. So Wendy was kind of on board and very supportive and miraculously that movie came together.

You know, your first feature is always a thing where it feels like it's just going to fall apart at every given minute. And there were several times where we felt like we had financing and it fell through and, you know, we had a certain cast member attached and then that member would drop out. We had three financing entities attached to it that dropped out after we had attached Tori Spelling to play a supporting part in the movie—and *Tori Spelling's dad came in and basically offered to buy the movie for more money than the financers before. And the good thing was that he wanted nothing to do with the creative part of the movie. He basically said, "Here is the money; you go off make the movie."* It was in fact the only time where I was able to make a movie without any creative involvement besides my own filmmaking team. The movie came out pretty good and we got into Sundance.

SL: Tell me about the writing process of the script and how confident you felt in writing it—

MW: There are a few things: first of all, I felt that reading my brother's screenplays was a great education. Because he is a terrific writer, I could see when his scripts were working and working well—like getting a really good sense about when something is going to be clicking. Also the fact that my background was more theatrical than cinematic gave me a feeling that in some ways it was actually more about making a play work than to make a film work. You have less gimmickry to hide behind and you can't overwhelm people with your pure technique the way you can in film. I found that that helped a lot. And there was also the fact that this is a play which had gone through a lot of developments over the years before it was ready. So even though we ended up changing things structurally—there were a few big shifts in the structure and we also gave it some sort of book ends—I knew I had a sort of backbone of her play to fall back upon at any time. It was a guiding point I could use and I knew that it was essentially going to work. So in other words, doing an adaptation is very different than writing an original screenplay. Also the writing process on this was really fast—I think I wrote it in five weeks.

There is one thing that Stuart Rosenberg liked to say and that I always kept in the back of my head during the process. He was a very pragmatic teacher that laid down the heavy truths about things and didn't like to sugarcoat anything. He said that if you tried to do something in a movie that didn't make sense and you go, "Oh no, it's because of this and this and this", it's your fault for not communicating better. And I always told myself that I need to communicate to an audience in a way that they can understand it, because if they don't there is no one to blame but myself. You can't blame the audience and go, "They are too dense, they can't figure it out."

SL: You just mentioned that you got to screen *The House of Yes* at Sundance. What was its reception and where did you feel you were standing as a filmmaker at that point?

MW: The good thing was that when it premiered at Sundance, it was one of the first films to actually sell to a distributor. It got a lot of critical acclaim and it was really gratifying for me to watch it with huge audiences who really were responding to the movie. That was such an exciting thing. By the time the film festival was over, more people had seen my movie than any of my plays. So it was another aspect to the film that was incredible.

SL: Was that an important motivational aspect for you?

MW: Well, it was exciting to know that it could travel—and also nerve-wracking.

It's interesting because at that point I felt, "Now I'm in the system, I should be able to make whatever movie I want." And I actually spent a great deal of time trying to make the movie that I already worked on before the *House of Yes* just called *Strike*—a kind of modern adaptation of the Lysistrata by Aristophanes. *But I found that it's just as hard to get a second movie set up; anytime you can actually get a movie made it's a minor miracle.* And to get people to put millions of dollars up to get a movie on screen is a special thing. So I couldn't get my second movie off the ground, which was very frustrating to me . . .

SL: . . . and which, I imagine, surprised you—

MW: Yeah, because you think, "I'm in now", but you're not really in. It's like, "Didn't you read the reviews for the *The House of Yes*? Give me the money!" So I went through sort of this dark period—I got offered this movie *Head Over Heels* and I said, "OK, I think I could make something funny out of this—make a modern day Billy Wilder kind of movie." But unfortunately I was working with a producer who was this kind of philistine and just had a completely different vision of the movie that I thought we were making. So I ended up just having this terrible experience of making a movie where I spent the entire time fighting with this producer who had more power than me over what movie we were making. And when we were over and done, it was a movie that I was completely not proud of and didn't even want my name on it. But I was told it was bad to take your name off a movie because it would hurt it at the box office and you should just be a team player and not say anything—but it ended up being a real death nail for my career at the time. The expression "Movie Jail" is definitely true: where basically nobody wants to hire you. The studio executives may like you, they may like your ideas about the script, they might even love *The House of Yes*; but if they are the people hiring a guy whose last movie was a bomb, then they feel they look stupid around town to hire you. So nobody wanted me and I said to myself, "You know what, I just need to try get back to writing on my own. Also, I need to not be too picky and only accept a perfect project." I also felt that I just needed to keep learning to actually direct better. I ended up doing a TV cable movie for VH1. I shot the movie in 20 days, had a great time shooting and kind of got excited about the filmmaking process again.

When I came back to LA after making that movie, I took a meeting with Disney about the *Freaky Friday* project. It was interesting because I had nothing to lose and I was in a position where my career couldn't be any lower. I took the attitude that I would just go in and tell them what I thought about the screenplay, which I thought was terrible. I went, "Ok, you got a good idea for a screenplay here, but you really got to throw this thing out. If I was going to do *Freaky Friday*, I would do this and this and make it big and exciting and musical and make it modern." I thought I was just going in there kind of tacking the meeting, but when I left, it turned out that it was exactly what they wanted to hear. They were willing to take a chance on me.

But once again, that movie also was fraught with peril and looked like it was going to fall apart every step of the way. We had for example Annette Bening attached up until ten days before shooting when she dropped out. We got Jaime Lee Curtis in the last minute—of course she ended up being the best thing for it.

*And* Freaky Friday *suddenly changed again completely the way people in town perceived me. And then in LA, it goes from, "We can't trust you," to, "Whatever you say is gold"—which is also dangerous. Once you have a hit movie they unfortunately feel like they don't have to be critical anymore,* "OK, we just trust you to make it good, because we don't necessarily know how to make it good ourselves."

SL: The first movies you made were comedies. It seems to me that comedy is an increasingly popular way for young directors to get into the studio system—

MW: I disagree because I feel it's just as easy in some ways to break in doing like an action thriller vain thing—but then usually people that approach the comedy angle in terms of breaking into the 'Hollywood system' are genuinely people who are either writers; or in my case it's theater director. I would say the "shooters"—the guys who direct videos and commercials—are the guys who get hired by like Jerry Bruckheimer to direct *Gone in Sixty Seconds*. So big action movies that are mostly about shooting effects and stunts are often first time filmmakers as well, but they are first time filmmakers that come from an alternative pathway. Because it's certainly not like in the old days when Stuart Rosenberg—he directed *Cool Hand Luke* and was one of my professors at AFI—was coming up, where there was an apprenticeship system in which you would basically do TV shows, then move up to do TV movies; then get to do actual movies. You can't do that anymore. You are pretty much on your own in terms of starting your career now.

SL: Now that you have made these immensely successful comedies over the course of just a couple of years, are you goals shifting in any way in terms of the kinds of films you want to make in the future?

MW: It's interesting: I would say when it comes to the question "Do you want to do comedy or not comedy," *I find that any script that I like—any material that I respond to—has to be a little bit funny. If it's not remotely funny, to me, it's kind of like with people you hang out with at a dinner party: you want to be able to have serious conversations about religion and politics—but if you aren't having some good laughs and sharing a sense of humor with your friends, then the party is a bore.* And so I feel like all the great movies that I love have a sense of humor to them. Without a sense of humor, it's just pure solemnity.

Like Stanley Kubrick—still probably one of my favorite filmmakers—has a great sense of humor to his work as well as it often being emotionally and violently intense. *Lolita* is kind of a comedies . . .

SL: But there is a difference between films that have comedy in them and films that are comedies—

MW: I would say that there is a wide range of stuff that interests me but that everything has an element of humor to it. One director I really admire is Robert Zemeckis who does a wide range of material but always makes it really accessible and exciting to a wider audience. There are certain few million dollar movies that I have in my back burner that are kind of dark weird movies that will probably play in art house cinemas—and I hope I will get to make these movies at some point in my career. But if you want to make a movie with the studio system, you want to make a movie that a lot of people will want to go see.

I think because of the fact that I am from Indiana, there is this part of me that asks, "Would my little cousins and my mother *and* my aunt wanna go see this movie?" And if the answer is "no", then it is probably not going to be a commercial film. And just having this kind of Indiana perspective about what's really truly accessible and entertaining is something that's a good thing to hold on to.

SL: What are some of your own personality traits that you feel are a firm part of the way you make movies?

MW: I would say one thing is hyperactivity. My energy level is very high and I hit the ground running every day not only during the shooting phases, but also when I'm casting or when I'm working on a script with a writer. My ideas pop into my brain very quickly and I don't necessarily have a filter between what I'm thinking and what I'm saying. I basically go straight into talking about what's on my mind—my mind jumps around in an almost schizophrenic fashion; and not quite as I barely keep it in control when I'm able to think in seven places at once and be thinking ahead of what I'm doing on the next set; and also be talking to my actors in front of me, and working with my DP, and answering the costume designer's question. I am the person who all the decisions basically have to come through. It brings me back to my first student film experience I told you about: the place where I can be operating on all cylinders is the place where I like to be. And if I don't bring my whole self to bear, then I am probably not going to make a good movie. But that is the challenge and the fun of it—*I don't get stressed out by it and I get energized when the world is moving as fast as my brain is. So instead of having to take Ritalin for my ADD, I get to make movies with it.*

One of the things that bugs me most is that people want to "be a director": they actually don't want to direct movies—they just like the idea of being a "director." I think it's true for a lot of artists: they actually don't like the process of making their art or doing the work that they are associated with, but they like calling themselves that name—like "writers" that don't like to write.

The other thing is that I think I have an egalitarian kind of brain about ideas—and this, I feel, is really crucial and different from when I see other directors work. While I have real confidence in my own opinion and I feel I know when something is working or not working—and I am really not shy about expressing that to people—I am also somebody who's willing to admit that I'm wrong. I also don't feel that my idea is the best idea just because it is mine. I think as a director my real job is to be the person who recognizes the best idea in the room and to then be able to execute it. Be it whether it comes from the craft service person, my assistant, the DP, the actor, or my producer: I feel like I'm the person who has to soak through everything that's being offered up and say, "OK, this is the best thing to do"—and there is no ego involved in doing that. Because when the movie is done, everyone looks at it and says, "That's a Mark Waters movie." So why not take advantage of everybody's good ideas? Not only am I able to take a bit of my imagination and mobilize enormous amounts of resources to make that kind of vision happen, but also am I the person who gets to interact with all these other really talented people who all have to work through me to get something on screen. So I get to be the focal point of all that creative interaction.

And the good number three to all this—the obvious one, and I hope I'm not speaking out of term—but I feel I have a humanity to the way I look at making movies. *Even when the characters are villainous, I'm always looking for ways I can really relate to them as human beings.* Like for instance, going back to Parker and *The House of Yes*, I think the biggest thing that we brought into that movie and which didn't really exist in the theatrical form, is the way you cared for, and emotionally related to this truly reprehensible character.

And I think that's just partly my worldview—call it being from Indiana, call it from just being a middle child, or catholic, or just being a nice guy—I feel like I'm always trying to give a balanced approach to my characters; always looking for the gentle hand that's next to the mean hand so that you're able to keep your characters relatable. And that's what I think makes a movie like *Mean Girls* work better. Suddenly is not just a parade of bitchiness: People are not being kind to each other but there is a reason for everything.

SL: What about your own humanity? What is it about the stories you tell that touches you deeply and makes you want to put all your energy into?

MW: It's that thing when you're watching something and you're just taken by surprise by an inspired moment—in either art or just in life. It could be a moment in an actor's face: when his face changes and an emotion happens. Or it could be a dazzling montage or cut or a great shot: It's like an unexpected moment in the universe. It's the exciting part of what's working in your film that's like the little mini jolt of crack.

That's the thing that got me into theater, too. It's capturing those moments and being present for when something special and something inspired was happening that you weren't planning on. And the big kind of thematic thing that I always try and tie into all my work is that my characters are going on a ride they never intended to take and it ends up taking them into a direction that's illuminating—where they are put in situations and do something they weren't expecting to do.

While I think that's my macro-level idea, that's what I try to kind of keep alive even on the micro level when I'm making the movie: that each moment is a ride you never intended to take—something surprising is going to happen that will give you a jolt of energy.

SL: Would you be able to put into words how the experience of making films has shaped you as a person?

MW: You know, it feeds back and forth between the movies and my life. My life changes, but then my life changing affects my movies. The fact that I was married and had a child on the way—and then had a little girl being born right around the time I started to work on *Freaky Friday*—was a factor in even taking that job. I was like, "OK, now I have a wife and a daughter," and making a movie about a mother and a daughter suddenly seemed like something more interesting than when I was the young man who made *The House of Yes*. It's a two way street how things affect you. But I am definitely a different guy after all this than the guy who went to Penn pre-med.

# Section Three: Straight Out of Film School

# Forster, Marc

**DIRECTOR'S CUT:**
"Growing up, my foundations were pretty much in my imagination and the little world I created in my games."

**BORN:**
1969, Ulm, Germany

**BACKGROUND:**
Film School

**FILMS:**
Everything Put Together—2000
Monster's Ball—2001
Finding Neverland—2004
Stay—2005
Stranger Than Fiction—2006
The Kite Runner—2007

**MAIN GENRES:**
Drama, Romance, Fantasy

Marc Forster: Though I was born in Ulm, Germany, we moved to the Swiss ski resort of Davos shortly after, where I also grew up. We moved for several reasons. At the time, my father had a sort of lab that he turned into a pretty big pharmaceutical company. He sold it to Pfizer in the early 70s for which he received a lot of money and made him a huge shareholder. At the same time in Germany, there were a lot of Baader-Meinhof [German terrorist cell] kidnappings going on. We got threats from them and were on their list. We had a cottage in Davos and my parents thought this to be an appropriate, safe place to go.

My father traveled constantly. So I never really got to see him. My mother was traveling quite a bit, too, so I sort of was a little bit of my own . . .

SL: This must have been somewhat of an unusual childhood, growing up relatively isolated in the midst of all these mountains and lots of tourists coming and going—

MF: It was strange and also difficult in the beginning. Everybody I knew came from wealthy families, while most of the people there were from rather farming or other rural backgrounds. Also, we spoke High German at home and I could not understand the other kids' Swiss German.

But once I adjusted to my new environment, it was fine. It was a beautiful upbringing because my parents were not really into TV—we actually had no television at all for the longest time. What it helped me to do: Our house was on a hill and I played a lot outside. There was a forest in the back and I just played.

While I think a lot of children are used to just consuming, I always had to invent my own games. It definitely stimulated my creativity.

SL: Did you spend a lot of time alone?

MF: Yes—with my sort of invented, invisible characters [*chuckles*]. I played cowboys and Indians or pirate games in the archetypical structure of the good, the bad, and so on. Later, when I actually had some friends, some of them participated. Before I just played it on my own and imagined the rest.

SL: Did you grow up with the notion of being somewhat of an observing outsider and of not belonging?

MF: Yes, always—absolutely! I mean I *was* an outsider. Basically, I never really got to set roots in Germany because I was too young. Then, when I came to Davos, I went to primary school and was an outsider because I spoke a different language.

SL: What did you feel were your foundations?

MF: Growing up, I didn't really feel I had any—they were pretty much in my imagination and the little world I created for myself in my head or in my games. That was sort of my fall-back and love and security in that sense.

SL: You have two older brothers—did you feel free and encouraged to explore, being the youngest in your family?

MF: This could play a role. *In a sense, I was allowed to be playful. I didn't have any responsibility and nobody really expected anything from me. Also, my parents didn't really want to have another child—I sort of happened by mistake.* My oldest brother was deaf and both brothers were only a year apart from each other while I was four years apart from the younger one. I think that might be why I never really had any expectations or pressures on me.

SL: Did you have a sense of wanting to do something different or unconventional in your life—maybe also as part of your quest for the meaning to life?

MF: Well, I always just felt like, you know I somehow always loved playing these characters. My mother was sometimes even slightly concerned by me playing and portraying them. I wasn't a great student—I always barely passed. When I was around ten, the school teacher said to my mother, "Look, there are two students in my class that are just sort of slightly retarded and they can't stay in this class. Your son is one of them." My mother got very aggressive and really fought for me and said, "Look, my son is not a retard, he is brilliant"— and so I had to go to Zurich and do six weeks of psychological testing. They are sitting in front of you and say, "Marc, so let's draw a tree [*chuckles*]" and then you draw the tree and they evaluate whether the tree has roots or no roots. And then you do mathematics, and other testing. When the results came back, they were really, really good. The teacher then basically said, "Look, I don't have room for retards or geniuses—if you don't fit in you don't fit in and your son doesn't fit in." My mother and I decided we had to do something. So I went to boarding school.

SL: In what way does being Marc today feel the same it did when you were a child—where has it changed?

MF: I think that I became more aware of things as I grew up. My mother meditates a lot; also spends a lot of time in the Amazon region and Tibet and Nepal. From when I was very young, she gave me these spiritual books to read; Krishna and stuff. My parents both were not religious and always had issues with it. They told me I should try and study any kind of religion to really form my own opinion and perception of who I wanted to be. Ultimately, I think it did have its impact on me—I never thought about death or mortality so much as a child. As a late teenager, the concept of reincarnation, of different dimensions, of life and death became more present—it was a subject that fascinated me: our time on this planet is limited and we are part of the cycle of life.

SL: Do you see this as a recurring theme in your life and the stories you tell?

MF: In the beginning I didn't even realize that most of my stories, *Everything Put Together, Monster's Ball, Finding Neverland, Stay,* or *Stranger than Fiction,* they all have as central themes either exploring mortality to a degree or exploring different realities. They are all stories of becoming more aware or more conscious with your own identity and with yourself as a person. *Monster's Ball* is for example about breaking the circle of violence. In the end, Halle [Berry] can either shoot Billy Bob [Thornton] or forgive him. *Forgiveness has been a very strong element on my mother's side. She would say, "You know, you cannot expect to be forgiven, but you have to forgive."*

SL: After high school, what options did you consider?

MF: At 14 or so, a friend of our family took me along to see *Apocalypse Now* in the cinema—as my parents never went, it was my first time. Seeing the movie, it left me in such a dream state, that I really got sort of hooked to see more and more movies. When I was 16 or 17, I pretty much knew that I wanted to tell stories. First, I was interested in writing maybe novels and fiction, but then I realized I really wanted to tell visual stories. So I tried to figure out what's the best way to do this. So I looked for different schools in Europe—Fémis in Paris, Filmhochschule in Munich, also schools in London—and one day I read an article in our local newspaper about NYU. They mentioned all the directors that had been there—Oliver Stone, Martin Scorsese, Jim Jarmusch, Spike Lee, and so on. I liked their movies and I heard that the program is really one of the best in the States. So I applied.

In the same year of 1989 however, my father lost all his money. Our entire wealth, accounts and houses: everything we had was confiscated. There was betrayal and wrong investments, some of it illegal—one person escaped to South America, one committed suicide, another went to prison. It was a huge disaster.

So when we had lost everything, I was suddenly accepted at NYU: the only school I applied to because I really wanted to go to New York. But now we couldn't afford it anymore. So I wrote 30 letters to all the wealthy people I knew: growing up wealthy, you know a lot of wealthy people. The first person I called after writing all these letters was Robert Louis Dreyfuss. He was an old friend who had a house in Davos and whom we knew from skiing. He went to the war, he didn't have any kids but plenty of money. He said, "Look, I pay for the first year and if you have any talent, I will pay for the second, third and fourth years." So I made sure I had a lot of talent. I shot a lot of shorts and professors wrote me recommendations.

SL: You never considered going to film school in LA?

MF: No, I always had this fascination about New York and the art scene there—I thought it would be a more inspiring city than LA.

SL: How was your NYU experience?

MF: It was a very good experience—very tough for someone like me who hadn't lived in a city before. I grew up pretty spoiled and suddenly I was on my own and I simply had to survive. The main thing, though, was that I just intended to make movies.

You know people ask me, "Do I need to go to film school or not" and I say, "If you have a story to tell, you should obviously tell your story, no matter what"—because it's a passion: passion is the life force. And if you have the passion to tell a story you will succeed no matter what you will do in life. I personally never make a decision for money. I only make any decision in life for passion, because if you do it for passion, the money will follow.

SL: Though sometimes decisions can't be taken because of lack of money—

MF: True, but making a decision for money reasons is something else. And I have been confronted with that temptation several times on projects on which they offer you so much of it. You know I could live for plenty of years that I don't need to work anymore, but it would be dull.

SL: So, for example, you believe that if you hadn't found anyone to finance your NYU course, you would have found a different way to make movies?

MF: Yes, absolutely; because there was never an alternative. *You know, after NYU, there were so often moments of desperation, moments of no money, moments of no way out, moments where you think, "I'm not going to survive and I need a job." But unfortunately I can't do anything else.* All I can do on this path is to make movies. If I could be a chef, there might be a different path—but I have that passion to tell stories.

SL: A cook tells his story by choosing and arranging his ingredients—

MF: Absolutely, that's why a cook is an artist—I wish I could do it.

SL: So you think your passion for storytelling is non-transferable to alternative crafts?

MF: It started with me loving to play those childhood games. You know there are certain junctures in your life that will change it forever—like me moving to Davos instead of growing up in Ulm; or me going to boarding school, or me first being accepted to NYU, then Dreyfuss paying for tuition. Then making this decision at one point to move to LA: you know, there are certain crucial decisions that I or certain people took for myself that amounted up to what happened.

Today, even getting *Monster's Ball* or *Stranger than Fiction* offered, or being able to make *Everything Put Together* and getting the financing of that—you know every piece was sort of a decision where people either helped me or others were responsible for it.

SL: What made the experience at NYU important to you?

MF: There were three or four teachers who were really influential and really taught me a lot. One of them taught me the importance of detail; expressions encased in faces: a face telling a story without saying anything. You just look at one and it tells a story by itself—the eyes, the muscle tension, and so on.

Someone else taught me the structure of writing and storytelling. There was Christin Joy who truly gave me the intellectual understanding of filmmaking and the true intelligence behind it.

Another important element is the fact that when I came to New York, I couldn't speak English very well. At NYU, you start making these films called

'Sight and Sound': You shoot black and white 16mm and after cutting your film, you put a voice-over together. You don't have synch sound, and as I couldn't speak proper English, I couldn't write my voice-over. So I had to tell my first short in silence, which was a fascinating experience. I suddenly realized that I don't need too much dialogue and that I can tell stories in very little words. It truly helped me later, trying to cut dialogue. By the way, this Tarkovski book *Sculpting in Time* was also a great inspiration on that.

SL: Going to film school with filmmaking buffs all around you, did you ever feel intimidated?

MF: Yes, I truly thought when I arrived that the competition will be so hard and all those people would have so much more experience than me. *Apart from a photo camera, I literally never had a camera in my hand. And I set myself a rule that whatever happened, I had to watch one film a day. I started alphabetically by director and watched their most important works; if I loved them, I watched a lot, for others it was just their main work.*

SL: How useful was film school as a meeting and networking place to you?

MF: As I mentioned before, I was always a bit of a loner. While I'm still friends with two or three people from there, I never creatively collaborated with any of them.

Roberto my cinematographer and Matt the editor, both of which I have been working with for several films, I met when I moved to LA. Roberto I met when I was looking for a DP and someone recommended him.

SL: After NYU, did you feel prepared?

MF: Yes and no. With a friend, I wrote a script which I still like but which we never made. My basic idea was, "I need to make a feature and it needs to be simple"—also one location. The whole film would be one 85-minute shot from the back of a cab. One shot, but different people and different, suddenly changing environments—except once, where they switched the cab and would take the camera into a new car [*chuckles*]. I tried to raise money and nothing actually worked.

In '94 and '95, I worked on two documentaries just to make some money. I felt I needed to get out of New York to not get stuck in documentaries and never be able to raise money for my movies. So in '95, I moved to LA and made this little experimental film called *Loungers*, based on the play of a friend of mine. We shot it all in one house. It was never really released because there was a lot of music in it and people singing—the music rights were never available. It was experimental and had no real feature.

SL: So you it didn't make the festivals because of rights, etc?

MF: You know, to be honest, it was late '95 and I just got to LA. When we shot it, I was just happy to do something. Through the film I got an agent from a very small agency. I met a lot of people and took a lot of meetings, but nothing came of it: nothing happened! And then there came a long dry desperation from '96 to '99—for three and a half years, literally nothing. I had no money, I hated LA, I didn't feel like moving to another city . . .

SL: What did you do to survive—substantially and creatively?

MF: *I basically just tried to survive, you know? I borrowed money from a lot of friends, because I was very stubborn and said: "The only thing I am going to do is to direct! I am not gonna wait tables, I'm not gonna work on other film sets: I'm here to direct, that's what I want to do."*

Eventually, my mother got very concerned because I borrowed so much money. I was in such debt that she said: "Look, you need to come back, you need to get a job, you can't go on like this."

At the same, I kept on writing for several scripts: I thought I just need to create the material myself. That's when I wrote *Everything Put Together*, which a friend of mine—the producer—raised a hundred thousand dollars for. Radha Mitchell, the main actress, was a friend and said, "OK, we can do it for a hundred thousand."

SL: What drew you to the story of *Everything Put Together*?

MF: Radha Mitchell plays the woman who is pregnant and is about to have a Baby and she's very happy and all her friends have Babies in suburban America—it is Babyland. Shortly after she has that baby, it dies of Sudden Infant Death Syndrome; for no reason. So it is sort of a psychological horror and in the vein of Polanski's *Repulsion*—the downspiralling of how she slowly goes mad.

SL: Remember the first cut of it?

MF: I really liked the first cut and it was the one getting us into Sundance. But when I showed the movie to the producers—the producers were my co-writers—they didn't love it. They found little things wrong with it and I was a little icky about changing it. I then showed it to Stuart Beard who became a mentor of mine. He is British and a legendary editor who cut *The Omen*: a really special guy!

He was just so smart and I learned so much from him in one session after he watched my movie—it was one of those changing moments in my life. He later also had some great ideas with *Monster's Ball*.

I re-cut the movie and made it tighter—I cut like 15 minutes out of 108. The producers liked it but still weren't so sure. The film got a tiny theatrical release here in LA as well as a DVD release. And then everything started growing.

Sundance 2000 really changed my life. The critics responded positively and I got a very good agent. Also, the writers of *Monster's Ball* saw it there and sent me their script.

SL: So you say Sundance changed your life—how did it change your self-perception as a director?

MF: My self-perception didn't really change much. I just thought, "OK, I've got another chance here to make another movie." I think that ultimately when you make a film, you're just always happy to get the opportunity to make your next movie. For example, you just finished your own short film now and all that matters is that this film isn't too much of a disaster so you can go make your next movie [*chuckles*]. Yeah, that's really all it is about. As long as it breaks even, it is not too much of a disaster. *Ultimately, it is not about one movie; it is about a body of work—who cares about one film? We all sometimes make shit movies and sometimes great movies. There's not a single artist or director or painter who always made great stuff—it just doesn't happen.* The main thing is to keep going.

SL: There are quite a few young directors that get recognition and awards at festivals but whom we hardly hear from again. Were you ever anxious that you might not break into that next level of filmmaking after Sundance?

MF: Of course, there was always that fear that I can't make more movies. You always have the concern, I think, at every stage of your career. It doesn't matter when—one has to understand that it is as hard for you as it is for me as it is for Ridley Scott to make movie—because everybody has different needs and expectations and different deal-making positions. But I knew after *Everything Put Together* that I just needed to find the right next script.

We put the deal together which was pretty hard and difficult and finally when Billy Bob said yes, we got a green light. They had tried to make *Monster's Ball* for six years prior with any conceivable incarnation of director and actor and I just tried to make this film work for me. They said we give you three million dollars, 25 days to shoot and then we shot the film in May 2001. I just knew I could make that film happen.

SL: Did you know immediately how you would go about?

MF: I was very naïve. I didn't realize until later how lucky I was in being left completely alone in doing that film. I never had any interference of producers or the studio or anything. I mean the studio had a very low risk and not very high expectations. But, at the same time, there was never a preview, there was never a test screening—I just gave them my cut, they said 'great' and released the movie. The film then somehow, out of the blue, became a commercial movie. And with Halle winning the Academy Award; all this changed the fate of the film and my life again.

SL: What was your first impression of *Monster's Ball* when you first read the script?

MF: My agent at the time called me and said, "read the script!"—I remember I read it in one sitting and I just loved it: it was beautiful and I thought I need to make this movie.

SL: What attracted you to it?

MF: The atmosphere: the way the writers created the atmosphere. I felt it was about interrupted silences—and it was just very well written.

SL: Though initially, not sure whose story we are watching: there is no clear protagonist. What, if not the protagonist, hooks people to the story and makes us care?

MF: Yes, we follow several people for a while and actually, all the characters are equally dislikeable [*chuckles*].

I think it is mostly the curiosity that leads you along. She is abusive to her child, he sort of lives in the shadow of his racist father which doesn't make him very sympathetic either, and the other character, Sunny, is sort of the victim. But there is no one that you truly want to identify with. And having three people die in the first half of the movie, you would think that nobody wants to stay in the theater.

But this is the way I wanted to tell the story: from an observational point of view, being an observer of these people's life and be more intrigued and curious about them rather than to actually identify. I actually thought that I would never achieve that anyways because nobody wants to identify with them.

SL: But how can you take the audience's curiosity and carry it to the next level, bringing a certain insight and depth to the story and its characters?

MF: I think the humanity of the characters and that they are not necessarily good or bad people is redemptive in a sense. The characters ultimately try to become better people, and I think you can start to connect with that. Once they start trying to actually change, you can follow that.

SL: Did you instantly have particular characters or cast members in mind?

MF: No. But I was just so *involved* with the characters—it was all about them. *In fact, I never wanted to cast Halle Barry. I only cast her in the end when she surprised me with her passion. In the beginning, I thought she was too glamorous and too beautiful.* I simply thought she wouldn't work for that character. And then when I went to the south, I saw all these beautiful women in this really poor neighborhood. I remember thinking to myself how limited I had been in thinking her too beautiful for this part— there are a lot of beautiful poor women down there.

And if I hadn't cast her, the film wouldn't have become what it is because she really made that sort of commercial bridge in a way. It would have been that small independent film and very few people would have seen it.

SL: Do you watch a lot of movies for aesthetic reference when thinking about how to shoot your own?

MF: Oh yeah! On *Monster's Ball*, I watched especially Terence Malick's movie *Badland*—it had sort of the scope and feel of what I was looking for, so I looked at it very closely; and also *Five Easy Pieces* by Bob Ruffalson with Jack Nicholson,

Aesthetics is a key element. For instance, I never liked blue lighting for night shots. So for *Monster's Ball*, I discussed it with my cinematographer Roberto and said that we shouldn't go into this whole blue lighting. We should stick with the whole sort of yellow-ish tobacco kind of cigarette look of the south—also she's smoking.

Visuals are very, very important to me. A lot of directors, I think, were mainly writers—like David Mamet or John Sayles—who are phenomenal writers, but whose films are, I don't think, *visually* that interesting. As they come from a very strong writing background, often they could care less what it looks like. And I disagree with that in the sense that film is about both. *Ultimately, film is a visual language, which I am conveying with every image—the saying goes, "An image says more than 1,000 words." That allows me to usually cut a lot of dialogue as it is no longer necessary.*

SL: So how do you concretely approach a story visually?

MF: It' all about thinking what would have the best emotional impact and what would be the most interesting visual approach for the story we are telling in the film.

Roberto and I, we both are growing with each film. The good thing is that we have the same taste in cinema. We both have a similar understanding and try to approach each film from the beginning with no ego or prejudice. The few of the very established DPs I worked with, I always had to fight with them to have them shoot *my* film. But I felt like Roberto understood me, had sensitivity and that he understands filmmaking and character. I think a lot of DPs understand beautiful images but some of them don't understand character when they read a script. Roberto would never put a camera anywhere just because of the shot, but only because it makes sense.

SL: You two seem to be amazingly in tune when working on a scene together—

MF: We discuss every shot together. Usually, I do 90 percent of blocking and the way I imagine it on paper before. I like to follow my instincts and don't analyze too much.

I will then discuss it with him on paper as well, telling him, "These are the angles I like and if you have anything to add, let me know." Then he might come with an alternative angle—I might like that idea or parts of it, and we start our dialogue. We discuss it back and forth and figure out the most interesting ways. On the day of shooting and on location, we discuss it again and ask ourselves whether we should stick to the original plan or whether to look at some other angles.

You know, location is such a strong visual statement and huge part of the storytelling because the surroundings often tell you how the character is feeling. When I select them—usually on my own, sometimes with the production designer—I ask myself how they feel and what visual approach I should use them for. Then shots come to my mind already.

SL: What significance do creative partnerships have for the way you work?

MF: A tremendous influence. In fact, apart from Roberto, I try to encourage all my keys to participate with creative ideas. I like to leave things open to suggestion; costume designer, production designer, first AD and so on—we are a family. I tell them, "Hey, once you have an idea, just tell me." For instance, on *Neverland*, there's a shot when Johnny Depp throws a stamp up to the ceiling of a country house; that stamp sticks and later when they leave the country house, it just flutters down to the floor. That shot of the stamp falling down, was the first AD's idea. He pulled me aside and said, "I suddenly thought of this beautiful shot of the stamp falling down", and I said, "I love it, let's shoot it."

*My goal is to create a film that has not just all grown on my ego. I think that ultimately it is the ego that kills creativity.* I set the foundation of the vision. Everything is very clear as I tell them what I like— locations, colors, etc—but at the same time, let the others have a certain creative freedom within that space. If I don't like their ideas, I can always kill them.

There was a scene in *Stranger than Fiction* for instance, for which we did the rehearsal between Emma Thompson and Will Ferrell. At one point I said, "I'm bored, I can't look at you guys; I'm sorry, but I think this scene is long, it is dragging, we should cut half out of this." Emma, who's a writer herself and a highly intelligent woman, she looked at the scene and said, "You're right." So we found a space where we thought it was overwritten. They tried it again and it suddenly worked. It was perfect. Emotionally, it just worked and fell into place.

SL: I would like to discuss an impressive scene, where the emotional and the visual fall into place, even though it must have been a very complex journey to get there: the extraordinary sex scene in *Monster's Ball*. How did you work it out yourself, also with Roberto and the actors?

MF: With the sex scene what happened: I read it on the page and when I met with Billy Bob and Halle, the first thing we said was, "Look, we all need to talk right now about the sex scene." As we can't avoid it, I want to talk about it early on. Also before I cast Halle, I wanted to bring it up because it's a crucial scene; a turning point in the film. I didn't want to be told where to put the camera. So I said, "You both have to trust me so I can shoot the scene in whatever way I want. In exchange, I will give you both final cut over that scene—so basically I go in the editing room and I cut it and then show it to you and if anything is too exploitive, the two of you basically can tell me to cut it out." And they agreed to that.

I start the scene when she tells him that she needs him. Obviously, he grabs her from behind as he does during his sex with hookers. Suddenly, there is a moment when she looks at him and where they have eye contact: he realizes it's not the hooker, but somebody he cares for; so they turn on to have sex on the sofa. *Before we did it, I walked myself through in front of them——I showed them, "I'm on the knees, then I'm on the sofa; then they have heavy sex, they fuck each other and they fall down onto the floor.* Then it becomes more tender, until it's like actual love-making and caring for each other." And that is sort of how the scene ends.

SL: Were you surprised of both actors' open-mindedness?

MF: Billy Bob understood it from the beginning and Halle I told, "Look, you want to do this role, you have to go all the way, because otherwise I can't give it to you." It was my prerequisite. Otherwise, I wouldn't have cast her.

SL: And that also helped overcome your own insecurities of how to handle it?

MF: Yes; and the first thing I did there was obviously, "No-one in the room!" The whole room was miked and they were by themselves—and the first shot is from down the hallway: We basically let the camera run the whole magazine until the end.

SL: You just described how you walked yourself through the scene before shooting it. To what degree do you have to identify with your characters as a director in order to breathe life and a sense of truth into a scene?

MF: I mean, I live the characters emotionally at night while I am directing—when I'm sleeping I am the character in thinking what would I do. I live those characters inside me. I feel them and it's slightly insane and it's very hard but I need to live them because otherwise I can't direct them.

SL: Is identifying with your actors emotionally also key in communicating your ideas to them?

MF: Communicating with every actor is different because every actor comes from a different background, is a different human, and has a different way of approach or school. You have actors as different as Billy Bob and Johnny Depp. They are very similar in a sense—highly sensitive, coming from this very instinctual sort of place, being just very much in synch with me—you know you don't have to talk much with them and they just get it. There is not much conversation taking place. I tell them how I see the characters and they say, "Yes yes," and they do their thing; there is very little exchange. And there are some other actors whom you basically have much more interaction with.

SL: In your experience, is communication with experienced actors easier?

MF: Absolutely. I mean working with somebody like Emma Thompson, who I think is one of the best actresses working today; she is so skilled and gets it so much and simply does it. And she can give you 15 different reads in 10 minutes if you want. A brilliant actress, she invents a character, but then gives you reads within that character.

It gets tricky if you're working with people that are not great actors. Say like Puff Daddy, who is an entertainer and a performer and singer and a rapper or whatever, but he is not a trained theatrical actor like Emma Thompson from the Royal Shakespeare Company. And it takes a very different approach how you work with that—or if you work with somebody like Dustin Hoffman who is very analytical and comes from method and has a very different approach altogether again. Then there is Billy Bob Thornton, who changes very much depending on whether he does comedy or drama.

And there is Johnny Depp, who re-invents his character, but once he does his character, he pretty much sticks to one way; he doesn't give you many different reads to your left or your right once he has found the bases of that character.

SL: While actors vary greatly in style, so do directors. Have you ever been interested in the way other directors work?

MF: I have no clue how other directors work as I have never really been on other people's sets. I think everybody has to find their own style. *My mother used to always ask me, "Can't you be an assistant director or go to other people's set in order to learn how to direct?" and I said, "No, I am not interested in it."* It is like painting: you go to school, you learn the technique and understand it, but then you have to make it your own, you have to find your own style. Any innovator, any interesting artist in this world always tried to think outside their box and do it according to their own approach, their own way. You can't copy someone else or how they do it; and that's the interesting thing about it.

SL: What your mother said is probably an advice many people get, as it certainly goes against our common notion of apprenticeship that we learn and grow up with.

MF: Picasso said that for him the hardest was to learn to paint like a child again. Technically, he could paint perfectly—a house, a tree—but then to re-learn and unlearn in order to paint like a child again was the biggest obstacle and challenge of his life. I think it's the same with filmmaking. You learn the technique, you learn the language, you understand the 180 degree rule, you understand how to block and shoot a scene. But once you do that, either you expand and find your own way of storytelling—understanding the rules so you can break the rules. Just try to find your own style—that's what makes it all so fascinating. When you look at people like Michael Mann or David Lynch, you know what having a style means.

Copying wouldn't work, as a big part of the filmmaking I do happens in pre-production—choice of script and how you approach it, casting, locations, the decisions of the key collaborators you hire, the color scheme you want to have: There are so many decisions you make constantly and there's nobody to copy from.

SL: Are you surprised at your own capacity to gain such strong command of the different characters and universes you have created and dealt with in your films?

MF: Maybe it comes from the fact that I might be living slightly different universes all the time in my own life . . .

SL: It sounds like finding your own style has also been a lot about exploring your childhood universe, attempting to reconstruct a world in which you hadn't yet incorporated conventionally structured and prefabricated conceptions of space and time—

MF: Absolutely. Especially today in cinema, we have arrived at a point where everybody always looks back at the 70s—the "Golden Age" of cinema—or maybe also the French New Wave. Everything now is so predictable, cookie-cutter made—especially in American cinema. There are very few voices out there that are really original and stand behind their work, because the studios mainly have to feed the consumer. Though the situation seems to be shifting right now . . .

What studios often don't understand is that the consumers have become very smart. People know so much more about movies than ever before, everybody can make their own movies if they want to with their own home video camera—through the internet there is so much more information out there about film. On DVDs, you can learn about how everything gets made. So people have a real deep understanding of filmmaking. And I personally think that yes, there might be a large amount of people out there who just want to be entertained, but there is also a large amount of people out there who want to be surprised.

Look at a director like Lars von Trier, who with *Breaking the Waves* started something really interesting in filmmaking again, comparable to what Fassbinder did in the 70s: that kind of hand-held shooting. I think it was such a groundbreaking film for so many other people to start a new way of visual conception. Take a film like Soderbergh's all handheld *Traffic* or even a big commercial film like the *Bourne Supremacy* which I thought was an excellently crafted movie—and it was all hand-held.

SL: How hard do you still have to fight in order to get your vision of a film produced without having to compromise on key artistic elements?

MF: I was lucky, even with *Neverland*, that they always left me alone and I never had interference or problems with producers. The thing is: it always depends in what kind of situation you work. *We made the whole* Neverland *movie for 22 million. With that little money and that kind of cast there is no risk for the producers—they are going to make their money back, no matter what.*

If suddenly I have made the movie for 120 mil, I'm sure Harvey Weinstein would have been breathing down my neck—because it wasn't like with *Gangs of New York* or *Cold Mountain* where he is afraid because he had to make his money back.

SL: So how could you make the decision to shoot it for 22?

MF: At Miramax at the time, for up to 20 mil Harvey could greenlight his own movies—he didn't have to ask Disney. So we were told, "You have to make it for that amount—you just have to figure it out. And if you need more money you can ask later for it and we can give some then."

As my prior film was three million, I said sure. So we started shooting and then we just figured out we need a few million more somehow. Like once you get a greenlight and get some money, I come from the school of, "Oh, let's just do it—and we can work it out later," somehow if you work with those people, you will find money to finish it.

SL: And then came along the story behind David Benioff's script of *Stay* [movie not yet released at the time of interview]—it triggered a new era of script auctioning in 2003, with New Regency eventually acquiring the rights for well over a million. Did you feel a certain pressure to deliver?

MF: No, because Arnon [Milchan, Executive Producer] just said to me, "Look, I want to go back to the good old days, when I made *Once upon a Time in America* when I made *Brazil* and *King of Comedy*. Give me something I haven't seen. This is an auteur's theme. You cast whoever you want, you do whatever you want, I give you a certain amount of money—don't come back and ask me for more." So we agreed on a price and I delivered it to him. He was willing to take chances on this movie and this is what we did.

SL: Do you realize that your creative ideas are received more readily now that you have acquired a certain reputation?

MF: Maybe . . . yes. I think there is definitely something to that. I nevertheless think it is still as hard as it always has been to get a certain movie made. Also, it is not necessarily easier to get it my way. The thing is that it is still always a battle. You know you're always fighting, negotiating and not about creative things but just to get the movie greenlit. It is always complicated. The key thing to me is to choose and work with people that are not completely ego driven. *I truly try to find people I enjoy working with—I think this is really one of the most important things. Because life is too short to spend it with people that basically make you miserable or have huge egos that you will not enjoy your time with.*

Ultimately, a film has its own life; its own character. On the one hand, you have to learn as a director that you can't control it all. If you believe that, eventually it will bite you in the ass. Maybe you can make one film like that, but ultimately it has its own organism and it lives and it breathes and it has its own blood pumping through its veins. If you try still, you will suck the life out of it and it will become a ghost of what it could be.

SL: How have you concretely grown as a storyteller over the years?

MF: I think when you start out to make a movie, you think you can do anything and everything is possible; but the more you do, sometimes the more cautious you become. But I still try to break it down and keep my creativity open to let anything happen so that magic can occur. At the end of the day, when you direct movies, that's what you're hoping to do: create some magic. You can only control as many things as that, and ultimately you have to let go in order to let that magic happen.

SL: Do you feel that experience has made you more playful in you approach?

MF: Yes—absolutely.

SL: What do you hope of having achieved in the two projects you just completed and that you hadn't yet achieved artistically before?

MF: Every time I make a film a try to do something else. I also choose my projects very differently. That is what brings me joy—always trying to find a different path.

Though my recent two films were much harder and more complex to shoot, that obviously doesn't necessarily mean that they are better films. You know, often simplicity is more interesting. But I think that artistically, they were much harder than my previous films; I feel there is an artistic achievement there. Unfortunately, that doesn't mean that people necessarily like them better.

SL: Do you think if you had stayed in Europe, you could have gone down a similar path you're on now?

MF: *Back then, every time I tried to do anything in Europe or when I asked for information about film school, everyone would just say, "Oh, it is so hard, you can't do it, we can't give you any money; no!" I always heard no no no!—so I thought, "OK, I'll try it in America" and I never heard no here.*

SL: Would you say a young director with a great story should be confident that he will eventually succeed?

MF: If someone has a story they want to tell, they should just get out and shoot it: there are *always* ways to shoot it. Just never take no for an answer.

# Story, Tim

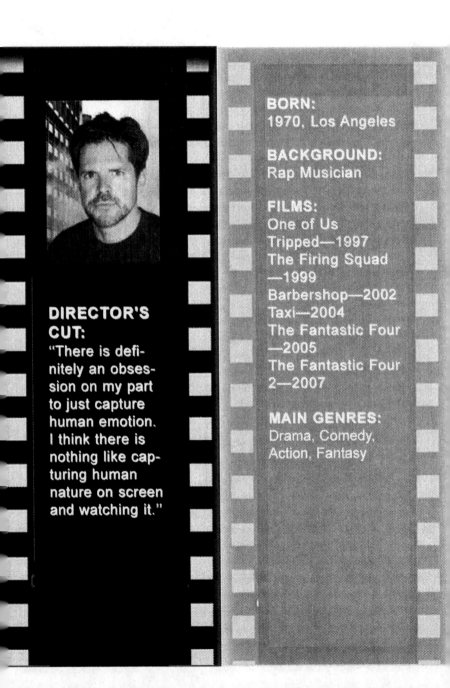

**DIRECTOR'S CUT:**
"There is definitely an obsession on my part to just capture human emotion. I think there is nothing like capturing human nature on screen and watching it."

**BORN:**
1970, Los Angeles

**BACKGROUND:**
Rap Musician

**FILMS:**
One of Us
Tripped—1997
The Firing Squad
—1999
Barbershop—2002
Taxi—2004
The Fantastic Four
—2005
The Fantastic Four
2—2007

**MAIN GENRES:**
Drama, Comedy,
Action, Fantasy

TIM STORY: I was born and raised close to Los Angeles in Inglewood, in a middle class home, growing up with twin sisters and a five year older brother. My parents both worked at the department of water and powers—about as far away from the entertainment industry as you could think.

The interesting thing about my neighborhood was that if you went six blocks to the east, you were in the gangster-hood; the rolling-sixties-hood. And if you went six blocks to the west, you were in Ladera Heights, which is considered the black Beverly Hills. *So it was an interesting way to grow up because one minute you are out with your boys and a shootout happens and the next minute, you're eating dinner at one of the finest restaurants with such and such.* A lot of the friends I grew up with, their fathers and mothers were doctors and lawyers. So I grew up in the middle of several worlds.

And that always was an interesting thing to me. It kind of comes into a lot of the films that I like to do. I take advantage of having the education and knowing both, the streets as well as "the higher class"—if that's what it is.

My mom made sure we traveled a lot—and she was the kind of person who would buy whatever I needed to try something out as soon as I showed an interest in something. My mom and dad were simply extremely supportive of every creative or other talent they could bring out in us: my sister was a basketball athlete, my brother was a musician, pretty much playing any instrument there was.

And then there was me, who loved music and films. We had studio equipment in my house, which got me into rapping at one point. My brother had a film camera and always made little movies with me and my friends. I was always the star. But at one point when I was twelve, he got too old and gave me the camera. I started making movies and coupled that with learning music as well. So during my time in high school, I was inside this rap-group, but going in-between film and music.

SL: Did you feel that your future was completely open?

TS: *The message my mom sent me was, "You can do anything—you can be anything you want."* She always talked about options and kind of taught us three to just be and venture and see everything and then figure out what it is you want to do. She always was that way.

So with all of the stuff going on in my life, I just always found myself being that "anointed leader" of a situation, no matter what it was. I just found that I ended up running the show. And running the show was I think just my producer's head, which always goes, "Let me get it done!" I remember doing a talent show in high school, and I was the director, the producer and all that stuff. it was just because I knew I had the support of the students. So I grew up with all this support. Later on, when we get to some other stuff, it will show you where my head kind of comes from.

SL: At one point, you were about to become a professional rapper—

TS: You have to understand: In my neighborhood in high school, you did one of two things. Either you danced or you rapped. And so I was a rapper. I was with a group called TDF—the part of what was considered Ice-T's rhyme syndicate of rappers, DJs, and friends. Ice-T at the time was huge in the rap world, and really we were like buddies. So basically, I had always considered myself a very cool nerd—I held a 3.7 grade point average. I really had the weirdest upbringing in the world.

*We were about to close a record deal at Warner Brothers for my group. And literally the day we were supposed to sign the contract, one of the group members in my rap group was shot and killed.* And this comes back to the whole thing of us being in the midst of being at times upper-class, but also dealing with the hood.

SL: So you shared that experience of different worlds with your friends as well?

TS: Exactly. At the point when he was shot and killed, I decided to do film. I asked myself, "What is the one thing that I wanted to do with the rest of my life, regardless of success or not." And film was it. So I applied to film school at USC and got in directly after high school. That's when I started my pacific film education. And after getting out of film school, I figured out that the only way I was ever going to become a director was if I directed a movie. So I started writing a script, and trying to figure out a job that I could do that had the least amount of brain power—so I became a messenger.

SL: Why doing a job without brain-power?

TS: While I was being a messenger, it allowed me to basically write my script and get paid at the same time. A movie that I loved back then was *Chinatown*—so I said: "You know, I am just going to make my own version of *Chinatown*."

SL: With your parents working for the Los Angeles department of water, you were pretty much at the source . . .

TS: That's it [*laughing*]. It took me about six months to write the script, and basically I just picked up every book there was. A lot of Sid Field books and others that dealt with how to write a script blablabla—and I read them until they became monotonous. I also dissected *Chinatown* pretty much.

I then start writing my script to this movie called *One of Us Tripped*. At some point I went, "Hey, now it's time to film this thing." At the time, *Clerks* had just come out and there was a newspaper article where Kevin Smith wrote the recipe for doing a movie for 27,000 dollars. I literally cut that article out and told myself, "Well, if he made it for 27,000, I am going to make it for that amount."

I used all my friends to be in it, which meant I didn't have to pay anybody. I sold music equipment I had in the studio at my house, Ice-T gave me money, my mom gave me money, I had a little credit card that had maybe a 2,000 dollar limit on it and I basically just put everything into this movie. I did it for 30 grand.

Originally, it was only supposed to be an expensive resume. It was important to me that I'd be doing a feature film: I didn't want to do a short, because I wanted to figure out whether I could tell a story over an hour and a half.

It actually didn't take me that long to do, but I found out that in doing films like this, you didn't need 30,000 dollars when you started—you only needed 9,000 dollars for shooting it—and then you needed the other two thirds to get the film out and so forth.

SL: What did you shoot it on?

TS: I shot it on 16mm color. I knew I couldn't afford the Avid so I ended up cutting it on a flatbed. The flatbed only cost 500 bucks for a month, so I could rent it for three months and it hardly cost me anything.

I showed the movie first to my friends, who were all in it. At some point, I showed it at the Baldwin Theater, which was pretty much the only black-owned theater in the country at the time. There were about 400 of my friends and family showing up. Then, there was a person in that audience who knew somebody working for a distribution company. So because of that screening, I could now sell my movie which wasn't my plan. The cool thing about it is that I ended up making about as much as I paid for the film—and I was able to pay off all my debts: my mom, my friends . . .

SL: How was the reaction of your friends to that movie?

TS: It was really cool. I mean I do want to say that for the most part, everybody either knew me, or knew the people in the movie. So the reaction was great and people had a ball. I think they were just supportive of the fact that, "Wow! Tim said he was going to do a movie and he did a movie!" And I think that everybody kind of applauded the fact that I set a date. You know I always think of this as one of the main things that I tell young filmmakers: set a date and tell five people about it, so that if you don't do what you are saying you'd do, you are going to be completely embarrassed. And next thing is me being in that theater, making my money back.

At that point, I started writing another script. I felt encouraged and figured that if I could just double my budget for so long, I would end up making a film costing millions of dollars or whatever. So I did the next movie, which I figured would cost me around 60 grand—it ended up costing me 200. Because this time I shot it on 35mm and I had a DP—on the first movie I did everything myself. So suddenly, I was 200,000 dollars in debt for this movie called *The Firing Squad*. In the midst of doing that, I pretty much ran into an old friend of mine from USC who was doing music videos. If you are looking for a way to pay off your bills and if you get good at it, man, they will pay you big! So I started doing music videos in '98 as well.

SL: What important lessons did you learn on your first movie that helped you on your second?

TS: There were many lessons that I learned. On my first film, I was going to have a DP shoot it for me and at the last minute, he pulled out. And I just went to the camera place and basically said, "Look, my DP pulled out on me; could you teach me how to shoot this movie." *I grabbed one of my good friends that I knew I could depend on and said, "Look, you have to go over to that shop and let them teach you how to load this camera"—and he became my camera assistant.*

I just learned that at that level, you can't depend on anybody. There are a bunch of friends in your life that you know will be there one hundred percent—and they are smart enough: They can learn how to turn on a sound recorder, they can learn how to load a camera. Basically, that's what I did: I surrounded myself with people who I could trust. And really, one of the biggest lessons at that was that you really can't depend on anybody except your family members and your friends. At that level, it is all about you.

SL: How did you improve as a storyteller from your first to your second film?

TS: You know, with the second film, I basically had a chance to actually design my shots, because now I had a DP. On the first one, I was just shooting. I would try to do things and I would try to figure out what's the best way to tell that story. Really, the cool thing about the first one was that I didn't have any restraints—maybe a location I needed to be out of before a certain time because I was stealing it, but I basically shot like run-and-done. I didn't worry too much about, "Was the lighting perfect?" As long as you could see what was going on, who cared? It was just about me shooting some stuff and just go.

The second one, I finally got into actually composing shots. Working with a DP, now I was able to actually storyboard. So things looked good.

SL: So the fact that you didn't have to hold the camera anymore to frame each individual shot paradoxically allowed you to actually better master what was in the shot?

TS: You know what: You give up a little bit of creative control by not holding the camera. It is interesting you ask that question, because my one thing that I might want to go back to is to actually hold the camera.

What was great about not holding the camera is that you could totally get into your actors. You suddenly don't worry about technical stuff anymore, as you are more concerned about your actors. Because at the end of the day, filmmaking is about story and characters. You know the technical side of it all—yes, you want this to be great, too—but finally I was able to pull myself out of the technical and just deal with the storytelling and the characters. And that was the best thing for me: to step back and not worry about whether the camera is working, or whether it is in focus.

SL: Did it also allow you to discover a whole new dimension of being a director on set—a dimension you couldn't discover as long as you were organically linked to that camera?

TS: Absolutely. My second movie was also the first time that I dealt with actors that weren't my friends and that I found through a casting process. While your friends are going to do what you say and it doesn't matter, this time I had to figure out how to talk to them—I didn't know how to do that. This was the first time I had to become clear: "OK, this is what I get out of that person, this is what I want."

SL: They didn't teach you any of that at USC?

TS: You know what? At USC, you had these small films you were doing, but for all of them I used my friends. Then in the second semester, I did these smaller films and yes, I used a couple of people, but it wasn't a lot of people—maybe two or three. So I didn't really learn how to talk to actors.

It was interesting: *I had a teacher at USC who was the first teacher who looked at my stuff and went: "What the fuck are you doing? What the hell is this? This is shit!"*

So I started to go and just hang out in acting classes. While I was writing my script, I would find a theme out of famous movies that I wanted to try my hands at and go film it. Because I was going to so many of those classes, I knew some actors and could actually ask them if they wanted to do a scene with me—that would also allow them to put more stuff on their own reel.

SL: So how do you learn to work and communicate with your actors?

TS: Well, one of my biggest things I like to do is to really *learn* the person. So I make it a point if anybody is going to be in one of my movies, we spend time together so I can get to know them as a person. And that can be as simple as just going to dinner and talk about whatever; what they do and so on. At some point, maybe ten percent of that conversation will be about the actual movie we are doing, but it's more about just trying to figure *them* out.

And I must admit, I try to put a lot of it in the script. Because if you're able to really work on the script and get your script where you want it, you can direct a lot of your movie through the script. Judging that you're a confident director, actors are not dumb. They are very intelligent people and they don't want to look bad. So if you can put most of your information in your script, you'd be surprised of how it comes through.

So I sit down and try to get a shorthand with the actor before stepping on set. Because once we step on set, everything becomes: "Hurry up, hurry up, we gotta go." I try to do as much rehearsal as possible, but since *Barbershop*, I haven't really been in the position to do as many rehearsals as I would like to do.

You know, I really like to go through most of the movie more than once if I can. Not every scene, because there is some things that you just can't rehearse.

SL: How do you rehearse with your actors concretely?

TS: I think I have kind of developed my own little method. I once heard Spielberg talking about him type-casting, which is not a negative thing at all: it is a positive thing because in certain roles, if you cast somebody that is essentially that character, then you don't have to go into a whole bunch of trying to get them to do certain things. They are going to respond as that character would respond. All you have to do is to get them acquainted with how fast you want a thing to go or this and that.

*I think the best directing is when you don't say too much. I keep it really vague.* I usually don't give my them much more than: "Hey, I want to start here and end up here," or "I think it would actually retain more power if you continued sitting." I think actors have a natural move they want to go. They *naturally* want to walk over there on this line, and if I find that they are moving too much, then I walk in and find out what they think, making it more of a discussion and conversation.

I learned that if actors really don't believe and agree with what they are doing, their performance is going to be bogus. I want them to be 100 percent comfortable. Here's what I would say: if you cast correctly, just get out of the fucking way!

SL: Would you say that in order to really be able to direct an actor, you yourself have to become their character to a certain extend?

TS: You know what: yes and no. It depends. I found that normally in the movies that I have done, at least one of the characters is a part of me. For example in *Barbershop*, I must admit that I'm a part of every one of those characters. I probably identify more with one or two of them, but for everybody else, I understand where they are coming from. And I think I pick projects where I actually naturally understand the characters for the most part—or at least the heroine or the hero. Although, you got to love your villains: to literally be in love with your villain. The best villains are the ones where you can say:, "Hey, that makes sense!" Maybe the way he is going about doing it is a little messed up, but he believes in what he is doing. Take Darth Vader: he feels that everybody will be just better off by taking certain radical steps. And when you look at that, you go, "I get that—I get his point." But at the same time you can't go around just killing people [*laughing*].

So I have always found a little part of me in there. None of them can be bastards or people you simply don't like. And I think every good actor pretty much knows that in advance as well. But I don't want to say that I always identify with a character through and through.

SL: Are you a director that likes to be surprised by the outcome of what you planned for your film?

TS: Oh yeah! You learn quickly that the movie starts off as one thing when you have a script, then you shoot something else, and then you edit something else. Once I get to the editing room, one thing I like to pride myself on, is that I am able to step back and go, "OK, I know I started off with a script and I know I shot a bunch of stuff, but what movie did I actually end up with?"

I think, as a director, you better learn to be willing to let go of what you 100 percent envisioned in the beginning—because sometimes you didn't get it. Sometimes an actor's performance wasn't quite exactly where you were trying to go. But what's great is when it's better. And you got to be able to loosen up when putting the film together, without however overlooking the fact that you maybe wanted to do a, b, and c. *You simply have to learn to embrace the unfamiliar and what has really happened, rather than what you wanted to happen but couldn't get.*

SL: So how does that work concretely? You look at the different takes very openly and then only in the editing room do you decide which one actually tells the story best?

TS: Yes. For the most part, you want to get the takes that *feel* more real. Normally, I look at all the takes, but I must admit that when I am actually shooting, I kind of know when I think they've hit it. But when I get into the editing room, I can always kind of go back and say, "Hey, there was this take where the guy did this and this and get that!"

SL: Have you stored all those previous takes in your head or do you have to note them down?

TS: Yeah, it's weird that it works that way, but I can remember it all in my head. And I can sit there and tell my editor, "I know it's there."

SL: How much do you rely on your editor?

TS: You know, I rely on him quite a bit. I need him as a founding board, but at the same time, I've already got the movie in my head by the time we finish shooting. So it's just hoping that what I've got in my head will come across the way I see it. So I depend on them, but in the end I depend on myself more.

SL: You just mentioned the distance you need to have once you are in the editing room. How do you establish and maintain that distance to your own material, especially in a comedy, where you see the same jokes over and over and it's just not funny anymore?

TS: You know, that's a really good question, because when it comes to comedy, one thing I've learned is that if a joke is genuinely funny you don't get sick of it. It's kind of odd but that's the way it is. One thing you also got to understand is that when I test movies, normally you are able to test it two or three times— and I test it with small groups of friends and this and that—if you're not sure about something, leave it in and try it with an audience. What's odd about films—even with *Fantastic Four*—there's stuff in there that I thought wasn't funny, but where people laugh. It's like, "I didn't know that was funny!" But I have to remember that sometimes you get too close to a movie and you have to step back and let it be what it is?

SL: Music has always been an important part of you. What experience have you made with sound in your movies?

TS: I mean sound is so important: When they say it's 50 percent of the experience, I 100 percent believe that. You *see* the visual—but once you add the music and the little things that are in the back here and there, it's *everything*.

In my first independent movies, I didn't really have the whole thing of sound and couldn't do very much—and you find that good sound elevates the material so much. As soon as you put that music behind and the atmosphere—those people yelling outside the window—it adds another world and it puts these layers and textures to it that simply weren't there before.

And I really learned a lot about sound. When we mixed *Barbershop*, we had this idea that while they are inside the shop, it feels and sounds like home. So we took a lot of advantage of sound design and mixing: there is always a TV set, there is always this general atmosphere, and you just find that it works. In *Fantastic Four*, once Ben Grimm has his suit on, he is kind of there; but once you add the sound of rocks and the way of him walking, all of a sudden he comes to life.

SL: Do you feel that your first two films might have lacked impact and appeared like weaker storytelling because of limited sound design?

TS: You know what? The sound didn't sound great, I didn't really know so much about it; also I didn't have the money to put all the stuff in the back. But what is cool about that is that you learn to just work with what you got. I think, one reason why independent film is so great to do is because you learn how to just deal with the actors and the environment: it teaches you to concentrate on character and story. All these other tools that come to your hand—like visual effects, sound, etc—they just elevate what you're doing.

SL: Pure storytelling—

TS: Exactly: Pure Storytelling. And that's why independent films are like the best school.

SL: But at one point, you made the successful transition from being an independent director to filming for a studio. After your second film, how did the transition that resulted in *Barbershop* actually come about?

TS: I had number of people that were looking out for me. Once again, that's where that support team comes in. A friend of mine at USC told me about the script. I had an agent at William Morris who I met at USC—and who is actually my agent to this day—that also knew about the script. And I also had a manager that I was going after, who was the executive producer on the project. So to this day, I don't know who gave me the script in the first place.

It was the second script I read in Hollywood. It needed a lot of work, and I basically just took the gamble and stopped doing music videos to concentrate completely on *Barbershop*. It took me about a year to get the script in order. We had a few actors to come to the project, and once Ice Cube got on, we basically got a green light and went ahead. I remember my first meeting with the producers . . . You know, music video directors didn't have the best reputation at that time. I basically let them know that I come from film, and I was able to prove my point.

SL: As a director, you have worked with three very different budgets in a very short time. You self-produced for a low/no budget, then you did a small-sized 12 million studio movie with *Barbershop*, then in the summer of 2005 you finished the *Fantastic Four* Blockbuster with a budget in excess of 100 million dollars. In what significant ways does the budget have an impact on your work—both in positive and negative ways?

TS: You really find that directing is management more than anything else. It's managing actors, managing money, managing time, managing people—and you find that in something small like *Barbershop*, it's simply more contained. I actually feel more comfortable that way. And as you get films like *Fantastic Four*, what you have to learn is that your whole management style has to be readjusted. You know you have to really all of a sudden teach yourself how to manage more people, more time, but at the same time, as they always say, you never have enough time or money. So you are managing on a bigger and bigger scale, and it's just that.

The negatives are that the bigger ones are not as intimate as I actually thought or what I am used to. But here's what interesting about that: *if I can now learn the management of making the bigger films intimate, that's where I think I can succeed.* So it can be less personable, because you are dealing with more people, more departments, and a bigger sculpt you don't always have the control over. But if you can figure that out, that will be the whole trick.

And of course, one of the biggest positives, too, of doing big things like *Fantastic Four*, is that they are throwing everything at me they can: explosions, special effects, prosthetics, everything! Now I have the courage, the experience and knowledge to walk into *any* situation and make it what I need it to be.

SL: Taken the money and pressure involved for the movie to do well commercially, did you still do pretty much what you wanted, or were there any constraints that made your work more difficult in the end?

TS: I . . . I'll be perfectly honest when I say I wasn't able to make it fully mine. I am proud of the product, but there is a percentage of it that isn't me. And I must admit: It is a fair amount that is not me.

But if you look at the scenes that are just actors and where I didn't have a lot of stuff to deal with, those are the ones I could control and that I own more. But when it comes to the big stuff, at the end of the day, I never dealt with the action in big special effects. So I was learning. But in the future, I think now I have been given this education where I can now walk into bigger films and make them a 100 percent me.

SL: Tell me three character traits that you consider crucial to you as a director.

TS: I don't know if this is the right word, but I think 'thick skin', cause you're gonna get 'No!' back to you a lot. I was about to say 'tenacity', but this is very much into direction of thick skin. You know you can't give up: you got to keep going.

*What kept me going? I guess confidence:* you got to be confident in what you are doing. And that confidence interestingly enough comes from at least knowing what you are doing and what you want to see in a movie. Confident people are not afraid of telling you, "That's not the way to do things."

The other thing you need is instinct. And all of that is really based in me learning story and learning character and having the right people around me to help with these things.

SL: Working at a "thick skin" "tenacity" "confidence" and "instinct" will equip a young filmmaker to get his ideas onto film?

TS: I think the main thing once you have found a script is that you have to figure out: How much can you make the movie for, and how much can you get? And if you think you can get 100 grand, then you need to make a movie that you can at least take to post-production for 100 grand. You have to make your script match your budget. Often people would write a great script that would simply cost too much to do for the amount they can get.

You can tell that if I've got a scene in my movie that takes place at a ballpark, there is no way in the world that I am going to be able to have 100 extras. It's too big.

SL: But in the beginning, you don't know your budget yet—

TS: Well, but to a certain degree, it depends how you are going about to get the money. If you think that you'll get it from another production company—from investors and all the other stuff like that—then you just say OK and write the stuff you want to write. But I have to tell you: I've got a lot of friends that have been talking to a bunch of people who have planned that they will get them money—and they are still sitting around, waiting for those people to call them.

My personal way of doing movies, especially at the independent level: write a script that you can do and produce on your own. That means: if you've written a script that's going to cost too much, then put it aside and write another one that you can actually film; about two friends that live in a freaking apartment that is yours, they work at a warehouse shop that your father owns, that happens in the daytime because you can't afford light. And that's my thing: write a script with few characters.

When you start getting into a situations where you got to depend on a lot of people for money and so on, then you are going to find that everybody out there will tell you, "Yeah, we'll do it," but really they are bullshitting you. Don't get me wrong: There are exceptions to the rule, but if you're concerned about making your first movie, make it simple.

SL: Does that involve not giving away too much control and responsibility to other people?

TS: Yeah, not on that first level of getting into directing. Your first level, especially if you don't have all the contacts in Hollywood, write something you can actually do. In my experience, it's just that when you depend on yourself and people you know you can get stuff from; it just makes you life easier at that level. 'Cause the biggest thing at that level is just completing the project. So many people do movies, and it's sitting in the closet right now—

SL: Rather shoot on film than DV?

TS: Well, I grew up on film, but I must admit: the fact that we have DV now, my gosh; you can pretty much do a film with the camcorder in your house. It's all about the story and the characters. Most people are not going to care, as long as they see what's going on.

SL: Your film school experience seems to have been mixed—was it worth investing all that time and money in it?

TS: *What I love about film school is that there is a community. There are so many people I met there that have helped me with my career;* also many teachers that have helped me beyond film school. So it is great to be part of that community; that is: if you can afford it. If you can't afford, then take the money you might have used on school and go shoot a movie.

SL: So you think without film school you might have run into problems getting together your actors and crew the way you did?

TS: No, because that's not me personally. Because I am a people person, so I meet people that can help me. I like to say that I met them on my failures: If you do things wrong, you'd be surprised of who you meet, just by going through the process of doing shorts and little things here and there. You meet people. And those people know people that introduce you to people. And before you know it, you've got a whole community of people waiting to help you. And that's why one of the biggest pieces of advise I give to directors is: just keep shooting! Take out a scene from a movie and shoot it.

SL: You seem very confident that if you keep on working, a network will build around you that will listen and eventually help and finance your project—

TS: You said it better than I could. I'm a complete believer. Keep working and the community and the contacts around you will get bigger and bigger and get you all you need. You'd be surprised at how few people you need who say: "I'm gonna help you."

I've got really good friends that I knew when I was in college and that I met right after, who are now executives at companies in the industry. And you look up and all of a sudden your community of people that are in the industry that can help you is huge and tremendous.

And the other thing that happens by continuing to just work is that you get better at what you do. If you do enough things wrong, at least now you know what not to do. Cause a lot of times it's not knowing what to do, but knowing what *not to*—then at least you know that *that* didn't work last time, so I can do it this time. *If you keep working in this industry, you will find that survival is sometimes the best way to be creative and become talented. At some point, this leaves only a few things to do that are correct.*

You know, there is one interesting quote I remember which is one of the biggest things when becoming a director. It was James Cameron in a book, "If I got to tell you how to become a director, you will probably never be one." Get out there and learn for yourself: don't be afraid to land flat on your face.

SL: Did you ever feel that you being black mattered or influenced your career in any significant way?

TS: You know what? To answer your question: no. I always knew—and this is where my upbringing comes in—how to talk in every community. And the cool thing about that is: *I really found out early on that for the most part, especially in Hollywood, it's about entertainment. It's a people-community, and emotions have no racial content.* You know, when I think about filmmaking, it is all about creating a certain emotion from a setting or an actor's performance—and if you learn how to tell a story and to make characters vibrant and to get emotions into your audience, nobody cares.

You know, I don't say that there is no racism in the world, as that is not true. But at the end of the day—I hate to say it—the entertainment business in Hollywood is about money. And if you can learn how to tell great stories and character, sometimes that can equal business for certain people. And you can never forget that this is a business. If my films weren't making enough money, I wouldn't be here long. Or let's put it this way: Hollywood wouldn't continue to give me money to make more films. And of course my independent take on it is the thing that keeps me trying to make good films.

SL: If you met an alien that has no concept of what a movie is, how would explain your fascination with it?

TS: I probably would explain it . . . wow good question! I think there is nothing like capturing human nature on screen and watching it. There is definitely an obsession on my part to just capture human emotion and human nature, and I think all the films that work are just that: When you see something familiar, when you see people and situations that make you wonder, "What would *you* do?" A lot of films are a lot of what ifs.

SL: And how have the constant what if questions influenced you personally over the years?

TS: I watch more. When I'm at that Thanksgiving dinner, I simply tend to observe more. Sometimes you would catch me in a trance—like my mom talking to my father, or my sister talking to her children—just starring. And in other cases I start to kind of egg situations on simply because I want to see how a person is going to respond to a certain set-up. I ask questions that I sometimes already know the answer to, because you want to know if that person will bs you, or whether they will look at you and admit, "You know, I don't know?"

So that's the biggest thing: I just tend to watch people way more than I used to.

SL: And you understand more—

TS: Yeah, I understand more. And what's even more interesting: When I don't understand, I'm quick to ask questions, "Why is that like that, why did he just do that, why didn't she get mad at you when you asked that?" You find that why becomes the question you ask most. I think it's a kind of a refreshing question.

# Mangold, James

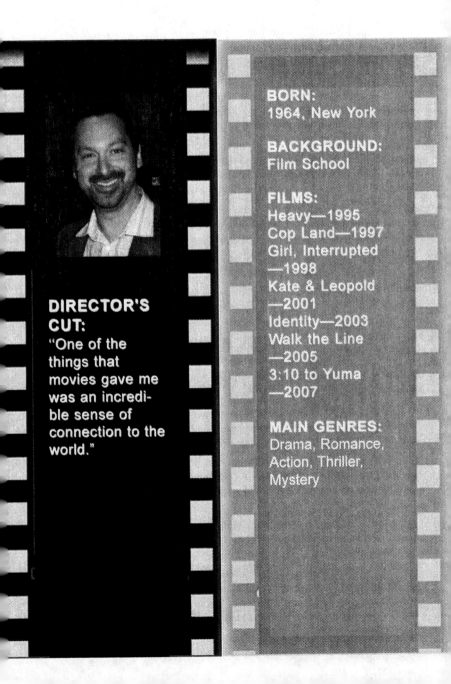

**DIRECTOR'S CUT:**
"One of the things that movies gave me was an incredible sense of connection to the world."

**BORN:**
1964, New York

**BACKGROUND:**
Film School

**FILMS:**
Heavy—1995
Cop Land—1997
Girl, Interrupted
—1998
Kate & Leopold
—2001
Identity—2003
Walk the Line
—2005
3:10 to Yuma
—2007

**MAIN GENRES:**
Drama, Romance,
Action, Thriller,
Mystery

JAMES MANGOLD: I was born in New York City in 1963 as the son of two painters. My parents met in Yale.

Until third grade, we lived in the Lower East Side of Manhattan of which I have vivid memories. My Dad then got a Guggenheim grant and my family bought a fixer-upper house about three hours upstate.

When we moved, we also began traveling to shows around the world that my dad was having. That's when my first movie experiences really took place. We went for example for a summer to Italy. He bought a Kodak Super 8 camera, which became quite a focal point of family life. He was making family movies of myself and then my new-born little brother. I was in fourth or fifth grade—and that would be when I made my first film with my dad's help.

*We made a movie about a monster, called* The UGH, *which was made out of all the world's depression. When anyone saw it and said the word "Ugh," the energy collected at the North Pole and formed this creature, which came down and started attacking everyone.* And I built models of New York City and buildings, and then literally made this creature out of the word "Ugh" a 100 million times—its fur was just the word "Ugh" written on paper over and over again and sown together. I shot this movie with neighbor kids and was really proud of it.

In the same year, I also worked with another kid in my class on an adaptation of Roald Dahl's *James and the Giant Peach*—I was also incredibly fascinated by magic. I was learning magic tricks and reading sleight-of-hand books. All these things continued, and then I started to collect comic books and was very involved in and fascinated by puppetry. So all of these theatrical derivations were really interesting to me.

SL: And film gave you an opportunity to combine it all into a coherent universe?

JM: Certainly, though obviously that didn't occur to me when I was in fifth grade. But towards the end of my high school career—before we had moved a little further south into another town in the Hudson Valley—I kept getting more and more proficient. I was making pretty complicated double system movies with lighting, special effects, double system sound, scores, dream sequences and flashbacks, and I built a cutting room for myself in the attic of our house. I was fairly proficient at all levels as a kind of one-man-band moviemaker.

And movies had given me at that point an incredible sense of stability, self esteem, identity, and power. As the son of two liberal painters—my dad, who as a minimalist paints color fields with a pencil line drawn on them—*I was a fairly strange bird in a fairly conservative town full of kids who are mostly children of commuting cops and firemen from New York City.*

The point is that I was kind of estranged and was not an incredibly networked kid—I moved there in junior high and I was a little at a loss for making connections. And one of the things that movies gave me was an incredible sense of connection to the world—they kind of put me in charge of the world.

To give you one example: As my last film in high school, I was making a pretty Walter Mitty-esque film about a guy who lives this fantasy life of being a football hero and a stud, and kind of getting retribution on the people that pick on him. Starring in the movie opposite the guy who was playing the dreamer was this girl I had a crush on. The guys who actually had picked on me only the year or two before were playing the bullies in the film. So I suddenly had being able to control and orchestrate the very forces in my life that I had actually felt most powerless against. Somehow, in the way I could enlist people in the community with their excitement for making a movie, I could in a way eclipse my own boundaries as a person in that school and become something more and more interesting to everybody.

SL: And suddenly everybody respected you—

JM: And I respected their world. It's like *I was suddenly in the world, interacting in the world and accomplishing things.* All the time I had spent developing skills in my attic. Working on these things was like a social entrée into the world for me—and it was a way of connecting with people that I didn't know before.

SL: Did you have an audience for your films—did you show them anywhere?

JM: We just premiered *Walk the Line* in the Beacon Theatre. The last time I had been in the Beacon Theatre was as a sophomore in high school, when I showed my Super 8 film called *Barn*. It was a kind of horror film about a haunted barn that's alive and is trying to save itself by kidnapping a child and trying to swallow it.

SL: You should have shown it preceding *Walk the Line*—

JM: [*laughing*] Yes I should have. Unfortunately they showed it at the wrong speed back then. I shot it at 24 and they were playing it at 18 frames per second. We were about to get an award and they were showing my movie to a packed house of like 2000 people. Then I went running upstairs to try and tell the projectionist. I ran into a pole and got an incredible smash on my head—I almost passed out. When I finally made it to the projectionist, who flicked it to 24, I said, "You have to go back, nobody understood the first five minutes"; and he said, "Sorry kid, can't do that." So that was the first out of many lessons on what can catastrophically happen in a screening in front of thousands of people.

You know, I was only 14 or 15 years old and competing with kids in college and 16mm films. What it was for me was a huge thing in the sense that it made me feel that I could gain access to other parts of the world and travel and experience things through making movies.

SL: Did you ever feel any sort of pressure or expectations weighing on you that because your parents were artists, you somehow had to match their example and find your own artistic vocation?

JM: Well, in a way I felt oddly that I was rebelling against my parents; certainly not completely in that I was finding a career in the arts. But my parents were like poets—I mean they go to their barn where they paint quietly. Then they'd come back, make dinner, and then they do the same thing. I was working in a medium that required collaboration, cooperation, leadership and politicking, and money. I mean in a sense, the difference between making a movie and making a painting couldn't be bigger.

I felt that the art making I was learning was definitely something wonderful and exciting to take part in. And I learned that from my parents. But I also learned that—and for no other reason than finding my own way—I wanted something more active. This was the moment of, you know, real white suburban anger in the United States—the moment that begat Ronald Reagan a little later on. It was kind of a low point in American self-esteem in terms of the Jimmy Carter era and gas lines et al.

*I quite frankly felt the irrelevance of my mum and dad's art-world to the world I was living in. I found it deeply frustrating that they painted for an incredibly rarified community of people who lived in a bubble—even if a kind of culturally educated bubble—while the vast majority of my world did not know, or care or ever touch this world.* Growing up in suburbia and feeling the power of movies to reach people and to make them think and evaluate certain questions, and the complete inability of the "fine arts" to ever reach these parts of the world made me frustrated with the idea of it. And I often had to defend my parents' work to friends or peers or kids from school who didn't understand how my parents could make money making these abstract images.

I am really proud of my parent's work. I think it's magnificent. But while it's not that you inherit your friends' skepticism, you do inherit the sense of disconnect and an awareness and a dissatisfaction that the purity of your parents' efforts is not reaching people. I wonder whether if I had stayed in the city, I would have felt that way . . .

SL: So your peers' suburban skepticism allowed you to put your parents and their work into perspective—

JM: And in some way it makes you ask the question whether it's an archaic form. I mean, in real terms, the society and the culture—for bad or for good—has moved on. My dad would often say that he felt he is a poet. But how many people actually think or read about poetry anymore? It's a very small world.

It's an interesting point for me, because at the same time I would go with my dad and see *Jaws, Apocalypse Now,* or *Taxi Driver.* I would see such powerful, huge artistic and strongly dramatic films in my local upstate movie theaters. Those films were also pressing and pushing the boundaries of what movies had been and what people were willing to see. And I was much more attracted to the kind of power contained in that kind of canvas—I mean frankly: what young man wouldn't be?

SL: So when you graduated from high school, the movie world was your horizon—

JM: Absolutely. I knew early in high school I wanted to be a movie director. I just know I liked it and I knew it was fun. Whenever there was a story about George Lucas or Steven Spielberg or Martin Scorsese, it seemed like their life was a dream—the idea of doing that seemed like a fantasy.

SL: On imdB, an old high school mate claims that you wrote underneath your yearbook picture something along the lines: "I want to become a world famous motion picture director"?

JM: Is that what I wrote? But I mean, trust me, I have seen a lot of things on imdB. But I am sure I said something about wanting to be . . . I just wonder— it's curious . . .

SL: Well you did go to Cal Arts to study film right after high school—

JM: That's correct. Literally, I'd come out to California the previous year to look at film schools with my Dad. I was accepted into the other major film school in Los Angeles, like USC and UCLA, but what is weird for me is that I never even got out of the car when driving up to USC. I was so unimpressed with the world of that school—

SL: You could see that from inside the car?

JM: Yeah, it isn't as if I was unimpressed with the scale—obviously they are huge compared to Cal Arts. In fact, I was unimpressed with the scale—it was too much and I didn't want to go to such a big, huge campus. When I went to Cal Arts, it felt like my high school—something I could understand; and I remember even in my gut instinct, it felt like a place where I could be unique.

SL: Were you afraid about not being special anymore, once you'd leave suburbia and enter a place full of teenage filmmakers like you?

JM: Well, probably. *You know, I don't know completely how I made the decision, but I am really grateful I went to Cal Arts. The other schools are much more teaming with young directors-slash business people, angling on becoming great filmmakers.* Cal Arts was such a wonderful experience for two reasons: one is that 90 percent of the students in the film school weren't interested in making particularly narrative movies. They wanted to make film art. In a way, you really were in a very special and rarified place, wanting to make story films that worked in a narrative way—like classical Hollywood or European movies. And the second reason was that one of the greatest film teachers of all time was there, who became both, one of the great friends of my life and a great teacher: Alexander "Sandy" Mackendrick.

When I arrived, I had no idea who he was or that he would be my teacher. At Cal Arts, they have a mentoring program, where you get a faculty member as a mentor. And immediately upon meeting Sandy, I wanted him to be my mentor. And he was like, "I don't work with undergraduate students in their first or second year." I then showed him my *Barn* movie. He remembered it from my admission's pack and he actually agreed to work with me right away. And I actually ended up being his teaching assistant in my second year.

For my third year at Cal Arts, he told me he wasn't going to speak to me anymore unless I joined the theater school. He felt that I drained him of everything he could possibly teach me—I mean, this overly dramatic way was his way of speaking.

So I auditioned for the theater school and got in. My third year, I spent almost entirely as member of that theater school.

SL: So Sandy was overly content with your progress?

JM: Sandy wasn't the guy who'd say, "I'm really happy with the way you've learned." Sandy was an incredibly tough and unsatisfied teacher, but with an extremely warm heart. He was an impressive presence—a very tall, 6-foot 4-inch, strapping Scottish man, with an incredible brain. I mean if I wrote a bad three page script, he would write me seven pages of notes on it in the most perfect longhand, with pictures and charts and diagrams. He was an extraordinary teacher and the effort I got from him and the amount of time he put into teaching me was phenomenal.

SL: It is almost unheard of for a successful Hollywood director to change careers. Was he bitter in any way?

JM: I wouldn't put it that way. If there has been a period of any of that, I think he was long past it.

Sandy was a very inspiring presence. But I did sense—and the thing that he made me aware of was—that the world out there was one in which a movie director better be armed and ready. And you better understand how hard you have to work to defend your vision and also to shepherd you vision. Not only do you have to protect it from attackers and compromises that could diminish the work's power, but you also—even more alarmingly—have to protect it from your own sloth and laziness from demanding more of yourself. And he taught both of those things very profoundly. He was brilliant about dramatic structure, about film structure, about film grammar. I mean it wasn't literally only philosophical—he was an incredible teacher.

But at the end of two years, I went into the theater school to train as an actor and really had a very life-changing year. I was just fully immersed, working in an actor's studio every day, taking movement class, voice training, and so on. I also acted in five or six plays.

SL: So the idea of acting school was for you to become a better director?

JM: It was to be a better director. For Sandy, the idea of film school was a lie in the sense that when they were trying to teach you how to make dramatic films with actors, invariably the most integral and important component of a movie coming alive is the relationship between director and actor. And it was the one that was most neglected in most film schools; that while the students would spend a huge amount of time trying to raise money to rent a steady-cam for their short, or to bate whether they should use a 10, 23 or 55mm lens, or trying to shoot it on Super 16 or 35, he felt that all this effort on the technical side was often blown because the acting was so atrocious in student film. And that eventually you would watch these overblown or overproduced efforts that at their core were just completely bad performances and therefore looked, for example, like very bad lighting—it was hard sometimes to separate which it was.

It is as if there was no core to the apple; just endless dressing. That frustrated him and I understand why—now even more so. It's a giant distraction in film schools that in a way, by avoiding the world of the actor, young filmmakers are avoiding the most central relationship of their lives in the workplace.

So drama school was incredibly freeing for me. What was great for my experience was that I didn't take some acting class for directors. I just became and *was* an actor, learning and studying and feeling what I felt and having my own observations. I assembled in a way my own curriculum from just being an actor; and not getting some kind of quickie class on "how to talk to an actor," which still promotes the idea of the actor as some kind of space alien that you have to speak to in some special language. That is I think one of the great mistakes of actor-training for directors: It tends to build up a sense that the actor is some kind of unique and strange being, which must be approached like a fawn in the woods with special language and apparatus. And all it does is to make the director more and more alienated from the process, and more and more out of their body, unable to be themselves with an actor. I was lucky that I didn't have any of that kind of training.

SL: Upon finishing Cal Arts after four years, you got instantly hired by Disney to direct a TV movie—

JM: I got hired right out of Cal Arts because of a short film that I made as a writer/director—well director, really, for them. Michael Eisner and Jeffrey Katzenberg, who had just taken over the studio, saw my film and gave me a deal. *Two months after graduation, I found myself writing in my office at Disney. And from then on, everything just sort of went south.*

Essentially, it's that I ultimately didn't feel like they had any plan at all for me, and I was kind of a 21-year-old with a deal by a studio which barely understood how the business worked. Ultimately, I was fired from directing a TV show after less than a week into shooting. They told me it was too dark. But I still believe it was because they wanted my deal to be over and to get me off the lot.

SL: How were your feelings about all that at the time?

JM: Oh, I would have stayed. I mean I wanted a place to belong. It was the most depressing thing in my life when I got flushed out of Disney. I wrote this animated feature for them, but that's just a job they threw at me to work off my guarantee and money.

Ultimately, when I came out of Disney, I was broken. I mean, I wondered whether I wanted to make films any longer. It was a very harrowing political experience. I wouldn't know where to begin explaining—suffice it to say that I wasn't prepared at all to deal with this universe of people and politics. I was not ready for the cynical world I had entered.

So I learned through making mistakes. In a way, life had been too easy for me. With so little struggle, I had fallen into a studio job directing a TV movie. It was literally like a film school fantasy that I would get a deal immediately upon graduation.

*My problem was that when I faced mediocrity or an executive telling me how I needed to water something down, I sneered at them. I felt I was on a mission to make movies better.* I had attitude when I heard people talking in a way that to me sounded over-commercialized, over-sentimentalized, unoriginal, or trying to make things like other things, as opposed to unique onto themselves. I felt like that was my job: making movies better. What I didn't understand is: you're not supposed to have attitude until you've done enough work to deserve having an attitude.

Let me put it this way: I overheard a conversation where one of the greatest directors in the world got basically just pushed around about film stock he could shoot his movie with. Suddenly it dawned on me that I was being more difficult with the studio than this huge esteemed filmmaker. And I realized at that moment that I must be doing something wrong. If people like him are willing to bend over and compromise their vision to the studio and I am not, I must really have a misplaced sense of my own power and potency.

SL: So you started to feel that maybe you had the wrong attitude?

JM: Well, after I was fired and starving, yes I felt that [*laughing*]. I mean I was kicked out!

SL: So you decided to go back to film school—this time New York's Columbia University.

JM: After struggling for two and a half years and getting incredibly depressed, I just decided that I had to do something with my life—because I was really depressed. I almost decided to be a novelist and started to send short stories and poems into quarterlies.

Then, I made a very simple solution: to go back to the last time I had been happy in my life and inspired about film; and that was at school.

So I enrolled at Columbia University. I was the ultimate student at that point. I had seen the darkness of the world out there and I was not interested in going back to a studio. I was interested in doing something as great as I could in the wonderful comfy confines and protection of a film school. I wasn't one of the restless people who rolled their eyes. Instead, I was so happy to be there.

And I was very fortunate in that I met a couple of great professors—one of whom was Milos Foreman. I took a directing class with him where I would just send him 30 or 40 pages every week. It was really just having an audience again. I was being encouraged to write by someone who cared about film and whom I was able to freely send script pages to. I was so inspired to be working and getting read by somebody like him that I just became a writer. I had to fulfill the promise of this opportunity that had been handed to me.

And, I mean, Milos is a filmmaker. I had always had problems in screenwriting classes where I was being taught screenwriting by screenwriters, because I felt that somehow they didn't get what I was trying to do. Milos, I felt, really understood.

At Columbia, everything I learned about screenwriting I learned from him; it wasn't in the screenwriting classes. Milos didn't speak in the world of act-structure or outlines—he understood it like almost doing scene-work in a theater. What I was doing initially was writing a storm to *find* my movie. I was writing much too much in order to find the film I wanted to make inside all this work, as opposed to designing it in an outline form.

And then I had what I thought was a good idea for a film that I really felt strongly about. It was as his student that I wrote my first feature film *Heavy*, which eventually won Sundance in 1996. Milos was incredible help in getting that script written.

SL: How many years did you go to Columbia for?

JM: Three really. After that I was busy writing my script *Heavy*, the first draft of which I wrote with Milos.

SL: Could Milos' involvement help you in any way to attract potential financiers and production resources for that film?

JM: No! His involvement didn't mean anything to a financier—it's hard enough for Milos to get a movie made. It was impossible. But I cobbled together from just twisting arms of family and friends and any dentist I could meet. Then there was the producer Richard Miller twisting his family's arms—and together we put up 350,000 dollars. And that's what we made the movie with.

I mean we tried to get finances everywhere and we were rejected everywhere. We tried everything! *The references mean nothing in this world. In this world, it's all about stars and a concept that is innately sellable.* Other than that, particular for a first-time filmmaker, they have no expectations that you're going to do a good job. So they need guarantees for sales—and that's actors of note, or a storyline that somehow has an instant audience base.

Making a movie about a lonely fat pizza chef is not a movie storyline with an instant audience base. On top of that, making a movie with hardly any dialogue and with no guns in an age when everything is about *Reservoir Dogs* and people just ripping it off left and right, where every movie is about somehow being a pseudo-noir, rock'n'roll fest with kind of postmodern characters running around with very large guns. My films seemed almost antithetical to that.

SL: So you also did not have a production company with you onboard?

JM: *We* made it. I mean Richard was also a producing student at Columbia and we just made it.

SL: How did you find your crew?

JM: We hired them one by one, interviewing other film school students or local people. For instance, our sound recordist was a boom operator who was making a conversion to sound. Our DP was mainly a gaffer in movies who was making a conversion to being a DP. You get it. One by one we assembled a crew. I mean I like to believe that the script was good and we could move crew and creative people in New York. And there was a great environment for making independent films at that time. But there wasn't a financing environment. Nobody wanted to finance these movies per se—certainly not a near silent film.

The one thing I had made at Columbia was this 35mm silent film, and I was really fascinated in many ways. I was hell-bent on returning to what I had always loved about making movies since the age of 12.

*The truth is that I had always felt completely empowered on my sets and that it was only at Disney that it was like suddenly I was confused by how much I was allowed to use my own voice and whom I was speaking for.* So *that* was the alien situation—and now I was back to what I knew and what I loved.

In many ways, I had designed *Heavy* to be a movie where if I was never going to make another film after that, that would have been OK.

SL: And you have often said that this has been your approach to all your films so far. But when you find a story that you feel attracted to, what gives you that inner energy and direction to invest yourself to such a degree in that story for such a long period of time?

JM: I am living in the world of my films. I've either written or cowritten all of the films I've made up to this point: I am not showing up thinking only about a lens, or a shot, or a point of view, but it's like a world that I know forwards and backwards.

And I always remember something that Sandy told me years ago. Though he didn't write his scripts, the first thing he would do when he came aboard a movie, was to write the entire script out in longhand into a notebook. That allowed him in a way to digest the material so he could start to own it. He would become one with the material—by re-writing it all down, it would move through him. It was his own way of becoming completely connected to it.

*When I'm directing a film, I feel like I'm enacting or dramatizing all these fractals of my own personality, my life, my mind, my heart.* I feel like I'm in a world of just that. That's why I think writer/directors have less of a need sometimes to put a kind of obvious visual signature over and over again on their movies. We feel like there is already such an obvious psychological signature there. I think that I've kept a lot of my themes alive while moving from one genre to another.

And, I mean if anyone looked or noticed, there's things I do in every movie in ways I shoot them all. But I don't think of it as my signature. I don't need to go through this kind of conscious effort to become the director who only uses 500mm lenses. Instead, I think of the heart of the movie and the feelings of the film and the characters as kind of a signature. And I am not anymore concerned with it than that. I really do feel, at least as a writer/director, that so much of what I do—who I am and what I feel—is in the work without me trying to put it there.

SL: Directors obviously always say that story and character are the two substantial elements of a script. How do you feel about it: does story rather form and condition character, or does character essentially shape and structure the story?

JM: *Story comes last for me in a weird way. I have to know the characters. And until I find them, all story seems like falsity to me— just imposing plot on algebraic people.* For me, it is all about the characters and their environment: the most important thing that helps me understand character and story is geography. You know that diner in *Heavy*, that town in *Cop Land*, the apartment in *Kate and Leopold*, that motel in *Identity,* that theater or the recording studio in *Walk the Line*. There are places—and I sit in those places, thinking about the pizza food slot or the window between the engineer and Sam Phillips and the recording artists at Sun; I think of these relationships through windows, and portals, and doorways, and life starts to come out if I inhabit these spaces.

So it is always critical to me to have an idea of physical space. That's why I hate rehearsing films in a blank, quote-unquote, "rehearsal" stage. I love to be somewhere where there is sensual activity going on with the real world—where you get a splinter if you run your finger along the wall; where an actor doesn't device things that actually couldn't work in the real place.

SL: So I assume that this translates directly into your writing style: you start out writing a scene feeling the places and character, not yet knowing where it will carry you?

JM: Yes, absolutely.

SL: This seems very much contrary to the advice often given—

JM: I mean I have done it a little bit in both ways, but it's always in order to eventually get to the character. I knew *Cop Land* was going to end with a showdown between my local sheriff and the NYPD cops that populate the town he lives in. So I was moving the narrative towards that, but I didn't ever chart it out. I just hate and reject my own material when I see it in that form—you know: "Scene 7: Freddy gets angry when he discovers that they have been lying to him. Scene 8 . . ." If I can't be living through the feeling of the movie, I in some way reject the whole thing, because it sounds atrociously bad and simply seems like a cliché to me.

In *Walk the Line* for instance, I asked myself, "How do I find that energy that was Johnny Cash and how do I make it out of images and sounds?" I sat down and said, "What is this place, how do I dramatize this feeling of the outlaw, how do I make this beat of this music feel forbidden and dangerous like it should feel, as opposed to somehow quaint and nostalgic and friendly"— the way people often think of country music. *The first thing I wrote was: "Wind blows a razor wire fence; A crow pecks at a Bud can; from somewhere we hear a beat emanating from this large dark fortress, the sign swings 'Folsom State Prison.'"* But I didn't sit down, going, "I'm writing the beginning of the movie." In fact, I didn't know whether it was the beginning or the middle or whatever—I just wrote the beginning of the movie without knowing it. But then I didn't stop and go, "But where does this scene go? How does this fit into my three act structure?" I didn't; I just wrote what I thought would be a great movie scene.

I always remember what I think John Huston said: that basically you always know you're OK if you have got three or four great scenes—those components of a movie that truly move people. Every movie has weak scenes; the question is: do you have those really *great* scenes?

Both, in *Citizen Kane* and *It's a Wonderful Life*, we can each find a badly acted scene or a clunker of a line. But the fact is: there are moments that are hugely transcended for us. We all can think of a moment we get bored watching the *Wizard of Oz*, but we can think of moments where tears are running down our faces.

And so sometimes, banging your head about structure is very useful, but sometimes you can have a great structure that is like a meal you never remember: It flows fine, but there is nothing to stop you and make you go: "Holy shit! That, I'll never forget."

SL: For your past six films, you have used original scripts that were either your own or that you co-wrote. You also did a novel-adaptation and a biopic and next you'll do a western. Do you feel naturally most drawn to any of the above forms?

JM: I don't know that yet and I try to stay open about it. And if I did know, I wouldn't want to say it yet. I am very aware of the unique opportunity that I have been afforded, which is a chance to really explore and learn, while having my career.

*Billy Wilder's 16th movie was his first comedy. I don't know where I'm going to settle down, or if I'm ever going to settle down.* But I'm having such great fun, and I feel I'm learning so much. I feel I learned so much making *Kate and Leopold* and *Identity* that helped me on *Walk the Line*—help relax, help me run a better movie, help me find more of what I wanted. I was having more fun telling the story and not feeling tight like I had to make something important because I was making a movie about important people. But I keep learning and bring the lessons from the previous films into the new one.

I sometimes feel a kind of disappointment when I see filmmakers working so hard to actually brand themselves so that the press writes about them as a voice of this or that region or culture—or a kind of noir or horror voice—when there may be so much more in them. And I think it has been carried to some kind of undue level in the kind of post-Kubrickian music video age in which directors have almost become these sort of advertising commercial directors who take a narrative and try to make it look incredibly slick. But at the same time, I feel like we've almost gotten embarrassed about feeling things in our movies—and I think it's really important that we never get embarrassed about that. I don't know why I go to the movies if they don't move me.

SL: Does your scriptwriting style change depending on the sources you adapt your script from?

JM: My scriptwriting style is always exactly the same. I mean obviously you write a horror film different from how you write a comedy—the tone is different, but I sit at the same desk, I work the same hours. It's not a process difference; it's just a tone difference. From the inside, it's always more similar than you'd think.

You know in *Walk the Line* we didn't know how it was going to end, and in *Girl, Interrupted* I also didn't know exactly how it was going to end. The ending was more of an adaptation of *Girl, Interrupted* meets *Black Narcissus* by Michael Powell and *The Wizard of Oz*. It was kind of combining real life stories with very artificial elements that I felt helped give it a kind of frame.

SL: How concrete are the characters in you script when you write them and how much do you stay open for the actors' own input?

JM: Oh, they are completely alive for me. But do the actors bring entirely new things, and am I incredibly receptive to how everything changes with them? Yes. But they are alive for me. I am alone at night, feeling like I am seeing the movie and living with them.

SL: So would you say that as a director, you have to be able to transcend your identity to a certain degree in order to get fully imbued with the story universe and to fully identify with the actors you are directing?

JM: Sandy always said something very simply, "Sometimes you need to just walk in their shoes." Also he'd tell you, "Walk through the blocking you are telling them to do: how would you do it?" Meaning: sometimes you'll find that what you're asking them to do is so awkward and an odd feeling to your physical, sensual self.

But yes, what you say is true in every way. The truth is: one of the things that I think is wrong in practice—although right-headed—and that's often taught to directors, "Don't dare ever speak a line or act out a role in front of the actor you're collaborating with." The good part of that is that you should never think of an actor as a kind of mimic that you're trying to get to do what you do. That would be very disrespectful. But I think that's common fucking sense.

But on the other hand, you should never feel as though the idea of acting and inhabiting the challenges of, "How would I hold this gun," or "How would

I stand there with this guitar," or "What does it feel like when I stand here with this microphone" is something a director should stay clear of. For instance, when I was directing my last film, of course I pick up the guitar and I stand there with the mike, and I feel that spotlight on me: I am trying to understand what my actor is going through at this moment. What is he feeling, what is distracting him? How is the place that I have set up? Is the crew in his eye line? Is there something the way the DP is positioned that makes it hard for the actor to keep his eyes open because there is a light blazing right in his eyeballs? There's a million things you could learn. Beyond that, there are also the sensual things you can learn just by standing on that stage or on that set—or in that window—and feeling the physical space that they are feeling. And that is what I think many are sometimes denied.

SL: But how does knowing how it feels to walk in the actor's shoes concretely help you to communicate your idea of the scene to the actors themselves?

JM: I just feel like I completely relate with them and I am unashamed and uninhibited. Great actors have an incredible sense of truth and an incredible bullshit detector—and given that, you then have the supposition that you can't bullshit them. I think that is the most important thing for me about my relationship with actors. You can't talk a special language, you can't speak in some kind of politically correct, ying-yangy kind of surreptitious, elliptical speech; they'll just be resentful of you for not being direct with them about what you're feeling. Because what you're asking of them is to be incredibly direct with what they are feeling.

Now at the same time, you can't be insulting, you can't label and you can't ask for results—results meaning: "I want you happier now," or "you're not good enough, dear," or "Make me cry with the scene"—those are terrible terrible things to say to an actor. But they are also terrible abusive things to say to your girlfriend or wife. You wouldn't speak to your child in results, saying, "Go upstairs and write me a good paper *now*—better! make it better!" *It should be common sense that you shouldn't speak to people in results. It's not the way you respectfully talk to anyone struggling with a challenge.*

Having said that, the thing is that I try to have a completely uninhibited, enthusiastic, and uncensored relationship with them—actually with everyone I work—without processing it too much. And that my relationship should be as close, yet as authoritative, as it is with my crew. I feel as though they recognize that the more I feel like a free spirit to them, the more they connect with me, follow me, and feel free in telling me what they are frightened of. I then feel as though we're truly united.

I remember a day on the set on *Walk the Line*, when I was asking Reese to do something. She didn't understand it. "Why don't you just do it for me?" she asked me—not in a challenging way. And I did it. "That was good!" she said. Then *she* did it. And she did it better [*laughing*]. But the thing is: Reese is not frightened that a six foot male with chest hair is going to do a better job at being June Carter than her. She is just interested in what I need, because she is a professional and an artist. And because I feel to her—and this is speaking about all my actors—like someone who is deeply in love and thrilled by the work I do, they never have a sense that I'm thinking that I could be as good as them. I don't begin to think I'm any good. I just begin to think that sometimes I could communicate as succinctly with my body and my voice and my mannerisms and my gesture and a gut kind of sense of things; that I might be able to show it without doing some outlandishly long analytical chat. Of course, this is a generalization because life and cooking time and technique are a little different with each actor—your relationship is different.

SL: Did you learn methods and theories at drama school that you now find helpful in your work with the actors?

JM: I would say that I understand the Method and that I understand all the other methods. But very much like modern religion, everything is a blend at this point. Other than Shelley Winters, I have not met and worked with an orthodox method actor.

At this point in my career, I do get to work with some really fine actors—actually from my first feature I feel like I've gotten the opportunity to work with truly great actors. Many of them would be called method by the press, but it's not quite as elaborately methodical as that. The word method is used in a lot of ways now and really tends to be used to describe actors who try to really inhabit the kind of life force and energy of their character. But they all should be doing that. *How* they do it is their own journey and something that they bring to the table to me. One actor's process is different than another. But they are all bringing their unique life experience and also their unique DNA of personality to the role. There is no way to subjugate that. And frankly, even the most extraordinary external actors, like Laurence Olivier, brought huge amounts of who they were to the roles.

SL: Do experienced actors maybe also have a greater capacity to empathize and identify with a broader range of different personas?

JM: No, I completely disagree with that, because I would say that the premise of your question is wrong: *a great actor is not necessarily an experienced actor. My own feeling is that we all know how to act and perform. We all know how to fully connect and fully pretend we're somebody else and fully play.*

We do depth scenes, we play bad guys and good guys: we play hard, and we commit completely. Many of us learn how to be embarrassed and grow up and not to play anymore. Actors tend to be people, who are channeling that imaginative energy and have retained the power of that play as opposed to having lost it. They have harnessed and bridled it and can steer and control it.

Having set the table that way, I feel more confidence sometimes that I can get a great performance from a non-actor, which only means someone doesn't *call* himself an actor. It doesn't mean that they don't innately have the ability to act, which, as I said, comes from childhood. This means that I could cast a musician or a person I met on the street in a role, if I feel that they have that innate ability to play. Whereas I could cast someone who calls himself an actor, has been on television for eight years, and really doesn't know how to act. They might look good in a suit or a bathing suit, know how to present a personality that is attractive, and know how to hit a mark and say a word. But there is no ability to truly inhabit a character. While I don't think it means that the person has necessarily lost empathy or feeling for the world, I believe they have lost a skill from childhood that they have never acquired or re-investigated. And they now probably lost that muscle forever.

SL: So a lot of acting is a direct translation from the playful, flexible beings we were as a child?

JM: I believe so. *I believe it's a kind of play—a primeval mask play. It's something very primal that we do. Whenever I see great actors snap in and do this, I have seen something deeply biological happening—it seem like the most raw state of their being.* It's not some kind of pretzel they are twisting themselves into, but something that you could believe to be occurring in Africa or Asia, or in a culture 200 or 300 years ago, where dances and rites and theatrical pageants are performed and people become other people for a moment.

SL: So how would you describe the difference between working with experienced and non-experienced actors? How does that change your concrete directorial work with them?

JM: It's not that different. The essential difference is that you can have for example a very experienced actor who is very nervous and has very low self-esteem, even though they've accomplished so much in their lives as actors. It might be startling to you that they could be so frightened. But the fear and the sense of panic is a part of their process. Whereas you could find a non-actor who is the opposite of that—and remember this is about what people call themselves. You must meet people all the time that tell you, "I'm a writer; I'm an actor; I'm a filmmaker." There are no requirements; there is no driver's license test you have to take to call yourself that.

I have found that one of the most exciting combinations are different kinds of combinations of acting techniques in the same scene—a clash, you know? Vanessa Redgrave versus Winona Ryder: they are just completely different actresses. Winona is kind of finding her way in, doesn't have much of a plan in advance; has never been on stage. She is a modern film actress of behavior and naturalism. Vanessa Redgrave is a renowned stage actress from a family of world famous thespians, who has been on the stage for years, and who has an incredible control of language and accent and physicality; also an incredible discipline.

But for me, there is a unique tension that comes into the scene when having two different kinds of actors at work. In *Walk the Line*—I mean Joaq is a very naturalized, less organized or predetermined actor. He walks into a scene and finds his ways essentially through the material and through the text. Reese is a brilliant actress who does a lot of mental work before she shows up—she has an idea of what she wants to do.

SL: Do you believe the different approaches of actors will somehow show in their performances and can be traced in the finished picture?

JM: Yeah, but you hope that it doesn't show in the sense of someone solely thinking about that. Everyone has a different approach and you sense that in rehearsals and in their work in advance; you sense all sort of things. But you could never also generalize completely. *It's not like Joaquin is not doing his homework and not like Reese isn't alive and awake at the moment. Is just that people bring different kinds of work philosophies to the set and they shape the kind of movie you are making.*

SL: Is it essential for you that the director comes to understand and appreciate each actor's approach?

JM: You come to understand each actor's cooking time and their way of being. Then you make adjustments. One of the great things about watching Reese and Joaquin work together, is that they each address the other's flank, meaning Joaquin is more amorphous and sensual, and less shaping of the scene. He is not aware of the scene; he's just living in the moment. Reese is a much more disciplined actress who is trying to kind of carry the show as well as play her role. There is a very interesting thing that happens: for Joaquin, the scenes have suddenly more shape as he's getting such concrete stimulus from his scene partner. From Reese's point of view, she is never quite sure whether the scene is going to work the way she planned it. So she has to be ready and alive in the scene in a way that she might not have to with another actor, who's exactly playing the ball the way she expected it to be hit. So what you have is suddenly two actors slightly off balance, but in a way that makes things more interesting, not dull. The moment is alive. Does that make sense?

You know, here's the thing that's most important for me: when I make a movie, I want it to be a movie. I don't want it to be a film version of what could have happened on stage, or in a novel. It has to be a movie and it could have only been a movie. The answer to that is sometimes easy if you're doing some kind of special effects movie; obviously you can't make a stage show about living dinosaurs.

But when I am making a dramatic film, I want it to be about human thought, about human feelings that are so intimate and fragile and indescribable that you couldn't have done it on stage. That what you're seeing on screen, only film is uniquely able to communicate. And part of that requires that the performances happen as though you don't know how the hell they did that.

How did they get to that stage, how did they create that kind of intimacy, how do they do that with a lens so close to their faces?

SL: You regularly get very layered, award-winning performances off your actors. How much would you say is actually due to the actors' on-set performance, and how much of it is created and controlled by you and the editor in the cutting room?

JM: I think in the end, it's always about the actor. There are really connections that an actor can make with a director and I believe I can help on a percentage basis to make the role more interesting, make the portrayal more layered, help guide the actor. But I can't help make an actor out of somebody who can't act. And obviously rendering a good actor's performance worse by the selection I make would be insane.

Though there is something self-congratulatory in your question, it's true that I have come upon actors who really do act in pieces. You think that their performance on set seems flawed. But when you begin to cut it together, it seems quite brilliant. One could argue that we are "saving" their performance. But one could also argue—I think even more persuasively—that they're just true film actors and their work is only meant to be perceived in the context of an assembled scene. They are so skilled in what they are doing that they are giving you the pieces that you need in order to edit the scene, instead of giving you live-theater. And you could further argue that therefore I'm not saving anything, I'm just doing my job.

It's similar to the fact that some of the best music for movies doesn't sound that great without the movie. Some of the best work is actually tailored to the work. It is such an integral part of it that when you try and strip it out and examine and scrutinize it, you may get nowhere, because it's suddenly been unmoored from the thing it must belong to in order to function.

SL: When you go to the editing room, how much of the movie is already fully completed in your head, and how much is still flexible and open to changes—also thanks to those magical film moments that sometimes happen in actors' performances and that you can't plan ahead of time?

JM: When I get into the editing room, I know the movie a lot. I'd say it will change five or ten percent in terms of what's in and what's out and things that will surprise me. But I think that at least at this point for me, I know on the day we're shooting how the material should be cut. It's not to say that there are not discoveries to be made, but it's part of just being experienced.

For instance: what is the thing I always know—or try to know? It's my first and last shot of the scene. There may be a bit of a mishmash in the middle—there might be so many characters talking and acting and things happening that I am not sure where I am going to be at every moment of the scene when I cut it. But I like to know: what is my transitional image—my incoming image from the outgoing scene—so I can make sure that dramatically and in power and in terms of a sense of composition, I am both, completing a thought properly and strongly and not just trying to find an end beat in the cutting room.

SL: When you edit, do you have to be there for all of the editing, or do you have your editor present you with a rough or first cut of the scene?

JM: I have an editor and I trust his cut. I mean it is not even about trust. I'd be the editor if I was there for every cut and it would be silly if I didn't even give the editor time to process the material. That's one of those moments that I feel like I am getting an interface with someone.

But what I *do* do, is to explain and let my editor know the architecture of the scene that I imagine. My natural inclination is that I'm going to reject anything he does, until I've seen implemented the architecture I shot it in. If there are problems with that, we can then address it as opposed to him deliberately trying to be so "original" that he actually never tried to cut it the way the material was actually shot. Most importantly, I will communicate the sense of what I thought was the first shot of the scene and how I saw the transition working from the last scene.

The cut from one scene to another—from one physical reality to another—is by the way the most abstract cut in movies. It's not something we can do with our eyes, you know? When we look at the world with our eyes, we make rapid eye movements called "saccades" that take your eyes from one object to another, while our brain deletes the whip-pan. We just see something pop, and then we see something else. The cut is therefore something very natural to our brain and our eye, as long it's in the same space: as long as it is a part of the same physical space that we were watching. *The part of movies that is completely abstract to our living- and seeing experience is when within a blink of an eye, we are carried to an entirely new place, with perhaps new characters in it and a jump in continuous time as well. That's a huge abstraction that only movies can do.*

So therefore, that cut from one scene to another is the most creative cut in narrative movies, because it is rife with so many possibilities and you get all that abstraction of the outgoing scene pressing against the incoming one.

SL: As each movie and each story makes the audience create a unique story-universe, cutting in space and time opens up creative opportunities for the director to sculpt his story individually—

JM: It presents a huge opportunity for the director for greater meaning. When a movie cuts within the geography of a single scene, our cuts are enslaved to continuity and reality and performance. They need to somehow match in order to feel like real-time cuts. But the cut from one place to another is abstract, which allows to actually create meaning in that transition—to allow the film transcend its humdrum realistic-ness, and to try and say something in the details or the way one image is placed against another. You can compare that jump from one scene to another with the way the written word can create meaning with headings or transitions from one paragraph or chapter to another: while it's not more difficult for the audience to follow, that's usually the places where the greatest metaphors or allegories and meaning occur.

SL: Do you test-screen a lot?

JM: No; I mean the whole process in Hollywood involves screenings for test audiences. But I find that you learn most of what you need to learn just from the vibe and feeling in the room. Of course, you have to test it—it seems to me kind of foolish not to screen the movie to people, if ultimately the goal is to have people enjoy it.

SL: What about your test screenings for *Walk the Line*—did you have to change elements?

JM: It didn't change much at all, actually. In fact, it was interesting in that it was a very high scoring movie and the audience loved the movie—so it was an easy screening.

But for the few things that the people complained or remarked about, when we tried to address them even modestly, it was a house of cards: while people pointed out certain moments that they wish were different, if you made them how they wanted them, they liked the movie less. So it was an interesting conundrum. And the danger of test screenings is that sometimes an audience is a little like babies in highchairs hitting an apple away they don't want to eat. But then if you don't give them the apple, they complain that you didn't give it to them.

*The whole process of listening to opinions from a test audience is very complicated, because* a) *it's subjective, and* b) *sometimes people aren't in touch with the elements that a story needs to have in order to deliver the other elements they desperately want it to have.*

SL: Could you say that you have achieved relative independence from the Hollywood studio system in the ways you make and finance your films today?

JM: Well, the word independent is very tricky and a weird word these days. When I made my first film *Heavy*, I wasn't independent, even though it was an independent film. When we appeared at Sundance, I was advised that if I wanted to see my film distributed, I would have to cut it by ten or twelve minutes. We received no American distribution.

*The whole actual trip to Sundance is like a media elite test screening,* in which buyers come and watch the movie with other media elites, critics and kind of tastemakers. And the movies that seem to catch fire are bought and distributed. That's a very savage thing; in and of itself a very corporate endeavor, in which movies are kind of pitted against one another. That's not necessarily a way to encourage the most daring art.

So my point is that for me, I've never really felt the difference. The forces of compromise don't only exist behind the gates of Paramount, Sony, or 20th Century Fox. They also exist behind the gates of independent distributors like

Miramax or Lion's Gate. Everyone's doing test screenings; everyone needs an audience: the forces of marketing have become so powerful that very few people are immune from someone whispering in their ear what they think should be done to their film.

Having said that, I always wanted to make movies for a wide audience. As I said in the beginning, I wanted to make movies that might change, or at least open people's minds. And in order to do that, I felt like I had to preach to the unconverted and not the converted. I had seen and I knew the very real reward of my parents' life of making art for a kind of very distinct world—an educated, cultural world onto itself, but one that wasn't part of the rank and file of the nation's life if you will. I wanted to make movies that challenged or reached people that others might give up on. In order to reach those people, you need to work or at least try to work within the system to some degree.

SL: Do you now have a pool of investors you go to when are looking for financing a new movie, or is it as complicated as ever?

JM: It's always hard, because movies cost a lot of money and there is so much risk. And if you're trying to make interesting films—which I am—then every movie is a movie that makes the investors nervous, because it's essentially designed to be slightly eccentric or a round peg in a square hole. In the business world, that's not how you make money. If people are looking for square pegs, you make square pegs.

*I am planning to make a western next and that might seem like a very commercial thing to do. But on another level, there hasn't been a successful western for many years.*

SL: So there is no core group of investors that you have gradually built and kept throughout your various productions?

JM: You see, I am a Hollywood filmmaker. I mean, I have relationships with the studios that we make movies for—as does my partner Cathy Conrad. I know the people who run Sony Pictures, I know the people who run 20th Century Fox.

But I don't have what Woody Allen has put together for six or seven movies: a kind of run of financing for himself. I would love that—I mean I would have a lot of interest in something like that, but that's not easily come by right now, because the business isn't so filmmaker-driven; it's project by project.

I mean when I was trying to make *Walk the Line*, we went to everybody, including independent financing sources, and they all passed.

When making my western, then I might finance it through a studio. The fact is that I wouldn't have anything against it. I have friends and I know plenty of people, who have utilized other sources, all of which are run very much like at the studio. I mean, there is all sorts of banking and investment services and there is several very wealthy people who are playing, trying their hand at investing in movies. But it's all being run and administered by film people.

SL: Also in regards to your own difficult experience at Disney, would you recommend a young filmmaker to remain in relative control early on, making sure that the picture he's working on is really *his*?

JM: Stay as personal as you can, whether it is as an independent filmmaker of for a studio. Make a movie that is yours and that you want to make. Make a movie that if you died after this movie . . . I mean I practically wrote this in the dialogue of *Walk the Line* with Sam Phillips, "If you had to sing one song before you die in five minutes, what would it be?" It's just: Don't sing me what you think I want to hear what I think makes you unique. Instead, tell me what you would leave me with that would tell me something about you, and your heart, and your mind, and your life. Think about movies and images you love—your idea of movies: what would it be?

*I know so many filmmakers that start making movies that aren't them. Sometimes, they even have a fabulous career making movies that they never feel like they even own or have anything to do with.* In a way, they started a track in which their voice isn't even their own voice; it's a kind of imitation of somebody else's voice or an imitation of somebody's film, and that's what people hired them to do.

SL: Many great directors have also made some mediocre movies throughout their careers. If there is a learning and internalization process of how to tell a story, how is this possible? And how are you trying to avoid that for yourself?

JM: First of all, making films is so complicated—each story, each set of characters, each location, each visual style—it isn't reducible to a science. It isn't like learning to ski, and then once you know how to ski really well, you're just a world-class skier and that's that. Every mountain is so different: some mountains run uphill, some mountains run downhill, some mountains are not mountains at all, but are great flatlands, meaning. The job changes so rapidly. That is one answer.

The other answer is: My mother had this saying which I think is really true. She believed that everyone really only has a few truly original ideas in their lives; just a couple of them. I think that what you'll find in those directors is that in our early work, we're applying our original ideas. And that at a certain point, even we can start to feel like, "I need to do something else, I don't want to just keep staying here, I need to keep exploring." And that exploration to keep yourself interested in your work can also be felt by your audience as a sort of abandonment of what you did and what they liked.

And I have seen that in music, in movies, in paintings: the problem is that an artist can't stay stagnant, even though an audience sometimes would like them to keep doing the same thing.

SL: So making films doesn't involve this linear learning process that we usually assume exists in some way?

JM: Right. I don't think that you become a master and then suddenly everything you touch is masterful. *I think filmmaking is a lot like architec-*

*ture: not every building by a master-architect is equally great. Each building is a new challenge.* The demands of the building, the finances of the building, the creative materials used to produce different results: some are successful, some are not. I think there are plenty of directors who go through the cycle you are talking about and then come back around again and make brilliant work of a whole new kind. I think that one of the really interesting aspects about it all is that it's up to us to keep inventing ourselves. But also not pretending that we're going to stay everybody's favorite forever. It's an impossible thing to try and please that.

SL: What do you think can be most inspiring and helpful when looking at other people's creative past?

JM: Well, I think you can learn everything about boldness. I think one of the greatest dangers, specifically for filmmakers like myself, is to be inside the system. I think when you're outside the system, there is a little more perspective. Inside the system you have the advantage that you're near all these financing sources and you're on the pulse of kind of a huge creative industry and factory. But you have negatives of the exact same sort. There is a kind of magnet and a kind of mindset to be very, very cautious of. Conventional wisdom is rarely right.

So the great inspiration you get—specifically for me when I watch old films—is that I see how bombs and perceived misfires of the moment become some of the most important landmark films of our time. And that's a very important lesson to be conscious of, whether you're making films independently or inside the system. I mean *Citizen Kane* was a bomb, *The Wizard of Oz* was a bomb; *It's a Wonderful Life* was completely unappreciated: these are movies that are a huge part of our culture.

I think it is mistaken to think that just because you have a great hit in the moment, it means you made a great film. It is important remembering that movies live for years and decades and that the real winners are determined in the long run.

Sandy Mackendrick is a great example for this. *The Sweet Smell of Success* is a genius film, but one that hardly anyone heard of until a few years ago. That film has existed in almost complete anonymity. It was a huge flop when it came out in theaters, but is one of the great films of our century.

I see a movie like Sydney Lumet's *Verdict* which is one of the great court movies of all time, written by David Mamet. It's an underappreciated movie—it only came out on DVD recently.

I think that once again, the lesson that needs to be learned over and over again, whether you're talking about fashion, or theater, or film: sometimes, being number one means nothing. I haven't focused on trying to be number one in my business. I am trying to stay solvent and dependable enough at delivering a piece of art that works as a piece of entertainment so I can continue to do what I do. But at the same time, I'm not interested in trying to play all the cards and press every button to become kind of a hit machine: because that's the very danger. *The directors and writers that we admire have been people who were really just furthering their own exploration and journey as filmmakers and have made the kind of films they wanted to see.*

Stephan Littger was born in 1979 and grew up in Cologne, Germany. After obtaining his graduate degree from Oxford University (thesis title: "Maybe Truth is a Woman"), he wrote and directed the award-winning short film *Memories of a Sick Mind*. Stephan now lives in New York and is currently working on his first feature movie.

"That—well that is my *way*—*where is yours?*" *Thus I answered those that asked me 'for the way'. For* the *way*—*it does not exist.*

*Thus Spoke Zarathustra;* Friedrich Nietzsche